JOURNAL FOR THE STUDY OF THE NEW TESTAMENT SUPPLEMENT SERIES

25

Executive Editor, Supplement Series
David Hill

Publishing Editor
David JA Clines

JSOT Press
Sheffield

The Understanding Scribe

Matthew and the Apocalyptic Ideal

David E. Orton

Journal for the Study of the New Testament
Supplement Series 25

for my parents

Edwin R. Orton
and
Dorothy L. Orton

Dan. 12.3

Copyright © 1989 Sheffield Academic Press

Published by JSOT Press
JSOT Press is an imprint of
Sheffield Academic Press Ltd
The University of Sheffield
343 Fulwood Road
Sheffield S10 3BP
England

Typeset by Sheffield Academic Press
and
printed in Great Britain
by Billing & Sons Ltd
Worcester

British Library Cataloguing in Publication Data

Orton, David E.
    The understanding scribe : Matthew and the
    apocalyptic ideal.
    1. Bible. N.T. Matthew - Critical studies
    I. Title
    226'.206

    ISSN 0143-5108
    ISBN 1-85075-181-1

CONTENTS

Chapter 7
MATTHEW AS SCRIBE   165

PREFACE

This study is a lightly revised version of my Ph.D. dissertation entitled 'The Scribes and Matthew. A Comparative Study of Perceptions of the Scribe in the First Gospel in the Light of Intertestamental and Early Jewish Literature', which was submitted to the University of Sheffield in December 1986. I owe a debt of gratitude to my two supervisors, Dr Philip R. Davies and Rev. Dr Bruce D. Chilton, for their invaluable encouragement and advice throughout the course of my research. Dr David Hill, though he had no direct influence on the course of this study, nonetheless was in many ways its inspiration; his course on Matthean Theology was an indispensable basis for the early stages of my research. I am very grateful to him for accepting this book into the JSNT Supplement series. Many friends at Sheffield gave of their time to discuss various aspects of my work, both in the Staff and Postgraduate Seminars and privately. In this regard I am especially grateful to Dr Alan Winton. Professor Graham Stanton, who examined the thesis, offered helpful criticisms and encouragement to seek publication. Professor David Clines graciously agreed to edit the manuscript for publication.

Research was made possible by the financial support of the Petrie Watson Studentship, awarded by the Faculty of Arts of the University of Sheffield, by a research grant from the Tyndale Fellowship for Biblical Research, and by an award from the Sheffield Grammar Schools Foundation Fund. I owe sincere gratitude to all the awarding committees.

My greatest debt, however, is to my family, especially to my long-suffering wife Annette, who was effectively a *Strohwitwe* while bringing up successively and concurrently our four lovely daughters from infancy.

I have dedicated this study to my parents, my first teachers.

Sheffield
Christmas, 1988

ABBREVIATIONS

AB	Anchor Bible
ANET	*Ancient Near Eastern Texts Relating to the Old Testament*
ASTI	*Annual of the Swedish Theological Institute*
BA	*Biblical Archaeologist*
Bauer	*A Greek-English Lexicon of the New Testament and Other Early Christian Literature*
BDB	*A Hebrew and English Lexicon of the Old Testament*, ed. F. Brown, S.R. Driver & C.A. Briggs
BETL	Bibliotheca Ephemeridum Theologicarum Lovaniensium
BEvThS	*Bulletin of the Evangelical Theological Society*
BJRL	*Bulletin of the John Rylands Library of Manchester*
BZ	*Biblische Zeitschrift*
BZAW	Beiheft zur Zeitschrift für die alttestamentliche Wissenschaft
BZNW	Beiheft zur Zeitschrift für die neutestamentliche Wissenschaft
CBQ	*Catholic Biblical Quarterly*
CBQMS	Catholic Biblical Quarterly, Monograph Series
DJD	*Discoveries in the Judaean Desert*
Enc.Jud.	*Encyclopaedia Judaica*, Jerusalem
ET	English Translation
ExpT	*Expository Times*
FRLANT	Forschungen zur Religion und Literatur des Alten und Neuen Testaments
HTR	*Harvard Theological Review*
HUCA	*Hebrew Union College Annual*
ICC	International Critical Commentary
IEJ	*Israel Exploration Journal*
JBL	*Journal of Biblical Literature*
JEH	*Journal of Ecclesiastical History*
JES	*Journal of Ecumenical Studies*

JEvThS	*Journal of the Evangelical Theological Society*
JJS	*Journal of Jewish Studies*
JQR	*Jewish Quarterly Review*
JR	*Journal of Religion*
JSJ	*Journal for the Study of Judaism*
JSNT	*Journal for the Study of the New Testament*
JSOT	*Journal for the Study of the Old Testament*
JSOTS	Journal for the Study of the Old Testament, Supplement Series
JSS	*Journal of Semitic Studies*
JThCh	*Journal for Theology and the Church*
JTS	*Journal of Theological Studies*
LXX	Septuagint
MT	Masoretic Text
NIDNTT	*New International Dictionary of New Testament Theology*
NovT	*Novum Testamentum*
NTS	*New Testament Studies*
OTS	*Oudtestamentische Studiën*
RB	*Revue Biblique*
RQ	*Revue de Qumran*
SBL	Society of Biblical Literature
SBLDS	Society of Biblical Literature Dissertation Series
SNTSMS	Studiorum Novi Testamenti Societas, Monograph Series
TDNT	*Theological Dictionary of the New Testament*
TLZ	*Theologische Literaturzeitung*
TS	*Theological Studies*
TZ	*Theologische Zeitschrift*
UF	*Ugarit-Forschungen*
VTS	Supplements to *Vetus Testamentum*
WMANT	Wissenschaftliche Monographien zum Alten und Neuen Testament
WTJ	*Westminster Theological Journal*
WUNT	Wissenschaftliche Untersuchungen zum Neuen Testament
ZAW	*Zeitschrift für die alttestamentliche Wissenschaft*
ZNW	*Zeitschrift für die neutestamentliche Wissenschaft*
ZThK	*Zeitschrift für Theologie und Kirche*

PART 1

INTRODUCTION: MATTHEW AND THE SOFERIM

Chapter 1

THE SCRIBES IN THE CONTEXT OF GOSPEL STUDIES

1. Preliminary Considerations

All strata of the synoptic Gospels speak of a number of apparently distinct groups or coalition parties among the religious leadership of the Jews who had contact with Jesus, either in the course of his ministry alone or also in the developments leading up to his trial and execution under Roman law. For the most part, this contact is negative. In literary terms the Jewish leaders serve as a foil to the proclamation and authority of Jesus, highlighting the latter in consequence; in historical terms, in some way they created or upheld the circumstances which inevitably entailed a confrontation with Jesus, both on religious and political grounds, whether they are to be held directly responsible for his death or not. The opposition of Jewish leaders to Jesus is one of the fundamental common denominators in the Gospel accounts of Jesus' ministry, and, at least by the criteria of multiple attestation and coherence this state of affairs belongs to the bedrock of tradition about Jesus[1] and there is no compelling reason to doubt its essential authenticity. However, this does not automatically extend in equal measure to *all* layers of tradition and redaction in the Gospels, since there is evidence that (a) some layers may have greater knowledge of, or better access to, early traditions concerning distinct parties in the time of Jesus; (b) some layers, having more pressing concerns, may have regarded accurate distinctions between the Jewish leadership groups as uninteresting or unnecessary for their purpose; (c) some layers may reflect aspects of the circumstances prevailing at the time of the tradition or the redaction rather than those of the situation they purport to describe.

In the final analysis this study is concerned with *one* of these layers at the end of the process, namely that of the composer of Matthew's Gospel, and will thus deal principally, in our investigation in this chapter and in Part III, with what is usually called the redactional level of the Gospel. We shall be investigating the nature of Matthew's understanding and picture of the scribes. However, it will be necessary to have in mind the situation which Matthew inherited, the nature of the sources he used and the thought-world to which he belonged, as far as these can reasonably be established; and the establishment of this background in some of its neglected aspects is the prime concern of Parts I and II of this study.

The Gospels and Acts give the Jewish leadership and factions the following group labels: (independently) Pharisees, Sadducees, chief priests, rulers, scribes (lawyers), scribes of the Pharisees, scribes from Jerusalem;[2] (in combination or association) scribes and Pharisees; chief priests and Pharisees; chief priests and elders; chief priests and scribes (of the people); chief priests, elders and scribes; chief priests and captains; chief priests and the whole Sanhedrin; Pharisees and Herodians; Pharisees and Sadducees.[3] The traditions witness to Jesus' contact with individual members of various groups such as the Zealots, and at least one (Simon, Lk. 6.15; cf. Acts 1.13) is numbered among his disciples; so, too, individual 'rulers of synagogues' and 'scribes', and even 'Pharisees', are portrayed as treating Jesus very seriously, seeking his company and his advice and perhaps becoming his disciples.[4]

A cursory reading of the Gospels might lead to the conclusion that many different groups voiced opposition to Jesus, occasionally joining forces to do so; though in the end this may turn out to be a true, if somewhat vague, impression, closer scrutiny shows that the data are very confusing, and it is not at all easy to see who is who.[5] Serious problems, indeed, complicate any attempt to establish the precise contours of the various groupings from a social and historical point of view. Who the Herodians (Mk 3.6; [8.15, vt] 12.13 // Mt. 22.16) were, for example, is not clear.[6] The Sadducees are known from Josephus and also from rabbinic literature, where we learn something of their social standing and of their doctrinal differences from the Pharisees; yet occasionally they are shown in collusion with the Pharisees (though only in Matthew: Mt. 3.7; 16.1, 6, 11, 12; cf.

22.34). The Pharisees, who are depicted as plotting Jesus' death (Mk 3.6) later disappear altogether when it comes to the actual arrest and trial of Jesus, while the 'chief priests and scribes' (Mk 11.18; 14.1) or 'chief priests, elders and scribes' (Mk 11.27; 14.43; 15.1) etc. actually contrive this.[7] In addition, the fuller picture offered by Matthew, particularly in ch. 23, may be rather tendentious; thus on the one hand it is suspected of admitting serious anachronism (since the anti-Pharisaic stance is taken to reflect the situation of the Jamnian period [c. 85 CE onwards] when the Tannaim were effectively barring Christian Jews from the synagogues),[8] and, on the other hand, of painting a misleadingly negative picture of the Jewish leaders.[9] Matthew is also suspected of fudging matters in his failure adequately to distinguish scribes from Pharisees,[10] whereas Mark speaks of 'scribes from Jerusalem' (e.g. Mk 3.22) and 'scribes of the Pharisees' (Mk 2.16) as if he knows of, or at least has traditions of, distinct groups;[11] indeed, Mark has been accused of beginning the confusion himself.[12] Luke maintains a distinction between scribes ('lawyers') and Pharisees in his version of the 'woes' (Lk. 11.42-52; cf. v. 53) and apparently reflects Mk 2.16 in his mention of 'scribes of the Pharisees' party' (Acts 23.9). The Fourth Gospel, in its maverick way, though it maintains the synoptic emphasis on the opposition of the Pharisees and chief priests to Jesus, mentions neither the Sadducees[13] nor the scribes[14] at all. Further, there is the curious fact that the Essenes, named by Josephus, Philo, Pliny and others as one of the major parties in the Palestine of the period, are not clearly identifiable anywhere in the Gospels (nor, it should be added, in rabbinic literature, despite a number of ingenious attempts to make them so).[15] There is a real need to account for this, since it is scarcely conceivable that both Jesus and his first- and second-generation disciples should have completely escaped the influence of a group which Josephus more or less equates in importance with the Pharisees.[16]

Access to the full picture is further complicated by the fact that Josephus, whose testimony concerning the Jewish religious parties is itself tendentious, is really not a great deal of help as a contemporary, objective control for the purpose of assessing the historical reliability of the Gospel data on the Jewish leadership. Furthermore, little of the material in the Mishnah is a thoroughly reliable fund of historical data concerning the pre-70 CE period. And in particular, though the

NT record of disputes between Pharisees and Sadducees is amply
confirmed in this material, even this seems to be stylized and
stereotyped; there is little clear information about the Pharisees
themselves, and distinctions between the *perûšîm* and the *ḥakhāmîm*,
and between the *ḥakhāmîm* and the *sôferîm*, are inconsistent,
confusing and certainly anachronistic in many cases. Jacob Neusner
has demonstrated the need for a painstaking sifting of the layers of
redaction and tradition in the rabbinic literature, before it can be
used confidently for historical reconstructions of the pre-70 period.[17]

All this adds up to the fact that in the socio-historical problem of
the identity of the scribes in distinction from and in addition to other
groups, the data are highly complex and not a little confusing. John
Bowker, who at a later date was intending to publish a full study of
the New Testament scribes (cf. his note to this effect in *Jesus and the
Pharisees* [1973], p. 23 n. 1) refers to 'the extremely complicated
problem of the relationship of the Scribes to the Pharisees'.[18] And
this is in fact but one aspect of the problem.

We have stated this issue in some little detail because it concerns
fundamentally the nature of the data we have to work with.
However, it is not the aim of this study to make firm historical
judgments on the religious parties in the time of Jesus, nor yet on
such groups from later periods as may be reflected in the redactional
(and traditional) contributions to the Gospels. It is hoped that our
study will cast some light on the issue, at least as regards the
historical circumstances of the scribes in the experience of the First
Evangelist, but our main interest lies in the Matthean perspective on
the scribes in relation to the proclamation of Jesus. Our concern is
with the meaning of the term 'scribe' in the context of the Gospel and
its thought-world.

Matthew's Gospel, as we have mentioned, is particularly noted for its
'Jewishness', seen especially in its emphasis on the interpretation of
the scriptures and the right implementation of the Law, but also in
its narrative style. It does look, *prima facie*, as if Matthew would be the
most likely Evangelist to have a sympathy and concern for the scribe.[19]

Now, how does Matthew in fact regard the scribes? Is he simply
ignorant of the Jewish parties, or naively anachronistic, or interested
only in cataloguing the representatives of Israel who have rejected
the Messiah?[20] Such views are commonly held by scholars who see

no alternative explanation for Matthew's changes to Mark's mentions of the Jewish leaders. But in fact, as we shall show in detail in Part III, Matthew has a *special* interest in the scribes which appears on the surface to be ambivalent (contrast e.g. Mt. 5.20 with 23.2, 3a; 23.23ff. with 23.34) but is actually a vital and central aspect of his whole perspective on the relevance of the gospel of Jesus and his church for Israel and the world.

In many ways this is actually a crucial issue in assessing the perspective of the Gospel as a whole. Its contrast between the scribes/Pharisees on the one hand and Jesus and the disciples on the other has implications, for instance, for our understanding not only of the debate concerning the Gospel's Gentile or Jewish origins, but also of Matthew's attitude to the Law, his interpretation of the scriptures, his concept of true righteousness and the performance of the will of God, and for our understanding of an important section of the early church in its relations with incipient Judaism. It is also a crucial issue, as we shall show, for our understanding of the nature and message of the Gospel itself—for in the same way as it is an important aid to our understanding of the book of Jeremiah to have some concept of the traditional role and function of 'prophets' (and perhaps of the deuteronomists as interpreters and legal experts), so it is likely to be a considerable gain if we are able to suggest a specific tradition of authoritative religious writing within which to set the author of the Gospel.

Though it is hoped that light from another angle may be shed by this study in the continuing debate about socio-historical reconstructions of the Jewish leadership groups as well as other debated matters upon which it touches, it should be stressed that our main concern is with concepts of the scribe rather than with such matters. The study has two main foci of investigation.

(1) It is primarily and ultimately concerned with the *First Gospel*, its attitude to the Jewish leaders and the scribes in particular, and its apparent portrayal of a scribal ideal (if we may already anticipate an aspect of our findings) in the disciples and, by extension, in their emulator, the scribe who is the author of the work. It is an attempt to understand the Matthean community better, a group itself in serious conflict with the Jewish leadership; in particular it is an attempt to gain an insight into the *concepts* with which the author has worked, which have played a significant role in his understanding of the

church in relation to Judaism and in his understanding of his own role as the author of what is apparently a self-consciously definitive and authoritative religious *book*. This study is therefore on the one hand pursued with all available historical- and especially *redaction-critical* tools; on the other hand, it is a *comparative study*, which seeks not so much to find literary sources or dependencies (though such relationships certainly are not excluded *a priori*) in the OT and intertestamental documents to which reference is made as to cast light from them on a work for which in various ways they form the conceptual background.

(2) A secondary but important concern of this study is specifically with the *intertestamental* literature itself, a rich deposit of scribal enterprise in its own right, which has, astonishingly, hardly been touched as a resource for information about scribes of the Second Temple period; here again, it is not our concern to deal in a thoroughgoing way with the socio-historical data that may be gleaned from the texts, but rather with *concepts* of the scribe. The world of religious academia in this period was no less concerned with itself than in other generations, and the perceptions of the scribe expressed in the material certainly shed light on the scribes as a literary and social force; but beyond this, insight into the self-image of the authors is bound to aid us in the understanding of that literature itself. Geographically, historically, socially, even credally, the origins of this material—especially Qumran literature and many of the apocalyptic writings—overlap to a significant extent with the sphere of the First Gospel, both of its sources and its redaction and composition, so that the comparisons we attempt to draw have, *prima facie*, every chance of usefulness for Matthean studies.

Such are the concerns and intentions of this investigation. To begin with, we shall endeavour to set the study in the context of previous studies of Matthew and of the scribes.

2. The Scribes and Matthew's Gospel

A. *Trends in Recent Study*

Gospels scholarship, which for a considerable period was primarily concerned with establishing the historical and social background to the life of Jesus, made the best sense it could of the somewhat confusing picture of the various configurations of prominent groups in the Gospels. To a large degree, the endeavours of Jewish scholars have concentrated on the data concerning the Pharisees,[21] and the Pharisaic attitude to the Law (as compared with that of Jesus),[22] to a lesser extent the Sadducees[23] and 'Herodians',[24] and some have dealt variously with the problem of the relationship between the Pharisees and the 'scribes'.[25] In most of these cases, the concern has been a historical one: in the case of Christian scholars, usually with the historical circumstances of Jesus' life; in the case of Jewish scholars, usually with the historical foundations of Judaism.

There is a trend to regard the Gospel accounts as at best tendentious sources for historical data on the Jewish leaders, at worst, ill-informed, anachronistic and simply unhistorical. It is now common, as we have mentioned, for form- and redaction-critics to claim that Matthew, writing about 50-60 years after the events he describes, is prone to some seriously anachronistic perceptions and perspectives upon the events of Jesus' lifetime. According to these scholars, the Jamnian situation of the mid- to late-80s, which was busy producing a new and desperately identity-conscious Judaism, so affected Matthew's community in its rejection of the Jewish Christians as Jews that Matthew's use of his sources (which had already known some perversion before this) is heavily coloured by his reaction to the events of his own day. This is taken to explain, for example, the heightened and quite vituperative anti-Pharisaism in ch. 23, which can scarcely be ascribed (at least in anything like such intensity) to Jesus himself. A corollary of this is that Matthew himself probably knew very little, if anything, of the circumstances of the Jewish leadership groups in Jesus' day, and that his portrayal of the scribes and Pharisees is misleading, and even arbitrary.

Some scholars, particularly Christians, painfully aware of the embarrassing anti-Pharisaism (frequently identified with anti-semitism) of Matthew have finally decided that he has both seriously misrepresented Jesus and the scribes and Pharisees on the one hand,[26] and, on the other, has become a considerable embarrassment to the present-day church in its renewed desire to heal the wounds caused by generations of unnecessary friction between Judaism and Christianity. Over against the Christian apologetic interests that colour some of this scholarship stands a related desire amongst Jewish scholars to rehabilitate the pre-70 CE Jewish leadership, particularly the Pharisees, as the honoured forefathers of the classical rabbis and modern Judaism. There is sometimes an underlying apologetic agenda here; in some cases the methodology is in consequence somewhat suspect.

The debate over the Jewish or Gentile authorship of the First Gospel shows no sign of abating. Though a significant proportion of scholars view the Gospel as Jewish rather than Gentile, the notion that it has a fundamentally Gentile, indeed anti-Jewish, perspective, is the basis for a number of influential studies, including Nepper Christensen's *Das Matthäusevangelium—ein judenchristliches Evangelium?* (Aarhus, 1958), and, more importantly for our subject, S. van Tilborg's *The Jewish Leaders in Matthew* (Leiden, 1972). Against Tilborg, the view taken here is that the Gospel reads perfectly coherently on the understanding that the whole work has a Jewish-Christian setting. The tension between Matthew's church and the Pharisee-dominated synagogues makes good sense within the context of a predominantly Jewish church, evidently in the process of accommodating increasing numbers of Gentiles but still very much aware and protective of its Jewish heritage. It is a heritage which may have been non-Pharisaic before its inheritors became Christian. This view will not be defended in detail at the outset of this study. Readers will judge for themselves whether the Gentile view is effectively countered by the mass of deep Jewish affinities with the redaction of Matthew to which attention is drawn in this study.

Van Tilborg's monograph starts with the assumption that 'Mt does not deal with the scribes as such and they had already lost something of historical importance in his eyes' (p. 3); Matthew is not interested in distinguishing between the Jewish leadership groups and we should not lay stress on the content of any one group label (pp. 3, 6). Tilborg does not, therefore, deal with the scribes in their own right, concentrating largely on a study of a selection of epithets directed against the Jewish leaders. This fact, together with his assumption of an anti-Jewish Gentile authorship, unfortunately limits the relevance of his work to our study. Tilborg does not seriously consider the possibility that Matthew may indeed have a clear concept of, or an interest in, the profession or art of the scribe, which is the focus of our investigation.

B. *Matthew's Knowledge and Treatment of the Scribes*

One of the prime recent monographs on the treatment of the Jewish leaders in the Gospels and the most convenient statement of a representative position is that of M.J. Cook, *Mark's Treatment of the Jewish Leaders* (1978), and we propose to take this as our starting point.[27] Michael Cook's work, though its main focus differs from our own, being specifically aimed at an assessment of the Markan redactor's work[28] in relation to those parts of the traditions about Jesus that concern the Jewish leaders, contains a forceful statement of the view that Matthew, whose source for the Jewish leaders is deemed to be Mark's Gospel alone, displays complete ignorance concerning the religious parties operative in the time of Jesus. This view calls for an early consideration in this study since it specifically denies that Matthew had any knowledge of the scribes.

Cook's opening salvo is directed at the apparently weak structure of Matthew's editorial work on the Jewish leaders vis-à-vis Mark. We need not at this stage consider his claim that Matthew is at a loss as to who the 'Herodians' are in Mark (of their three occurrences in Mark, Matthew appropriates only one [22.15f.]).[29] Our concern is with Cook's assessment of Matthew's understanding of scribes. In his words (p. 21): 'Matthew's comprehension of scribes is a matter of far more consequence than his problems with Herodians—for "scribes" (or "scribe") are the most frequently mentioned group in Mark, appearing 21 times. Matthew seems perplexed by "scribes"'.[30] As a consequence of his perplexity Matthew *first* brackets scribes with Pharisees where he can (in 10 cases out of his 22 mentions of scribes [Cook makes the total 23]), *because he is unable to distinguish between them*. The supposed document Q need not have provided the association of scribes and Pharisees in the woes of Matthew 23, for instance: all the specific denunciations and accusations apply to what Matthew can understand of *both* groups. *Second*, in further cases (Mt. 9.34/Mk 3.22; Mt. 22.34f./Mk 12.28; Mt. 22.41/Mk 12.35) Matthew freely replaces 'scribes', a term he does not comprehend, with 'Pharisees', 'with whom he is more familiar and hence more comfortable'. *Third*, in many other instances, Matthew omits scribes altogether (as he did with two of the Herodians references) (Mk 2.16/ Mt. 9.11; Mk 9.14/Mt. 17.14; Mk 11.27/Mt. 21.33; Mk 14.1/Mt. 26.3; Mk 14.43/Mt. 26.47; Mk 15.1/Mt. 27.1). Cook's statistical analysis of Matthew's use of Mark leads to the conclusion (p. 25) that 'only once

[Mk 2.6/Mt. 9.3] out of twenty-one times does Mt reproduce a Markan reference to scribes in a manner implying that Mt knows who they are—and such a reproduction could result from mere copying!' In non-Markan material, Matthew makes 13 mentions of scribes, 10 of which bracket scribes with other groups (chief priests in 2.4, Pharisees in 5.20; 12.38; 23.2, 13, 15, 23, 25, 27, 29); an eleventh is 23.34 (of a different type—we shall discuss this in detail in Chapter 6); and the twelfth and thirteenth mentions are of scribe in the singular, and possibly unrelated to the 'scribes' under discussion. 'There are, then', concludes Cook, 'grounds for suspecting that Matthew is not himself familiar with the identity of the "scribes" and that he relies totally on Mark in this respect' (p. 25). The rest of his argument, after a more summary treatment of Luke's Gospel, concentrates on the redactional activity of Mark and the reconstruction of his sources.

Our own concern is with the application of a less statistically governed and more contextually oriented consideration of the data on scribes in Matthew. We are open to the possibility that there may be a rationale behind Matthew's redactional procedure here that is superior to the mere fudging-over of unintelligible data which Cook suggests. One or two *a priori* considerations are in order at this point (they are not, however, intended to be logical steps in our overall argument).

(1) For a work considered almost unanimously in current scholarship as the most 'Jewish' of the Gospels, in regard to its use of Scripture and its attitude(s) to the Law, in its 'rabbinic' structure and literary techniques, to the extent that its Judaeo-Christian origin has been strongly maintained,[31] its closeness to Paul's thought emphasized,[32] and its affinities with Qumran Judaism recognized, it would be surprising to find that its author, or even a whole school of authorship,[33] was 'perplexed' by the Jewish leadership groups, as if Jewish instruction and authority were entirely outside the author's experience. Even the supposition that Matthew presents a Gentile point of view in parts of the Gospel does not alter the general impression of its overall 'Jewishness'.[34]

(2) To the extent that Matthew is accused of anti-semitism and extreme anti-Pharisaism by a number of scholars it would be very strange if he had little idea of the nature of those to whom he was so violently opposed. Many scholars indeed seem to view Matthew's

stance in terms of the dictum, 'there is none so righteous as the newly converted'; perhaps he is a now ostracised ex-scribe (see next point), maybe even an ex-Pharisee, certainly someone with an axe to grind against a group known to him. The Qumran documents offer abundant evidence that antagonism to the Pharisees can be a thoroughly Jewish phenomenon.

Matthew's 'omissions' of the term 'scribe'

To return to Cook's argument, we note that certain factors are immediately plain when we take a closer look at Matthew's mentions of scribes. To begin with, despite Cook's claim that 'Matthew omits more than half of Mark's twenty-one references to scribes', Matthew still has *twenty-two*[35] uses (there are also some dubious variants) of the word γραμματεύς—one more than Mark. But we shall deal first with Matthew's 'omissions' of Markan mentions.

The 'more than half of Mark's twenty-one references' which Matthew 'omits' turn out to total precisely eleven.[36] These consist of: three replacements of 'scribes' with 'Pharisees' (Mk 3.22/Mt. 12.24; Mk 12.28/Mt. 22.34f.; Mk 12.35/Mt. 22.41); three deletions of the clause in which 'scribes' appear (Mk 9.14/cf. Mt. 17.14; Mk 7.5/cf. Mt. 15.2; Mk 12.32/cf. Mt. 22.40f. and Lk. 20.39, which also omits): and five deletions of the term 'scribes' only (Mk 2.16 diff. Mt. 9.11; Mk 11.27 diff. Mt. 21.23; Mk 14.1 diff. Mt. 26.3; Mk 14.43 diff. Mt. 26.47; Mk 15.1 diff. Mt. 27.1). Closer examination, however, reveals that not one of these alleged omissions gives any hint that confusion is its cause. Indeed they can be adequately explained on quite other grounds, namely that they occur in the service of saving the reputation of the scribes.

The *replacements of 'scribes' with 'Pharisees'* are hardly omissions; rather, they appear to be clarifications: far from being confused, it seems Matthew presumes to specify who these (opposing) scribes are in terms of Pharisees. Thus Mt. 12.24 (//Mt. 9.34) specifies the 'scribes who came down from Jerusalem' of Mk 3.22, who outrageously accuse Jesus of working by Beelzebub, as 'Pharisees'. Mt. 22.34f. specifies Mk 12.28's 'one of the scribes' as 'one of them' (i.e. one of the Pharisees), 'a lawyer'. This change is part of the overall conversion of Mark's positive account of a particular scribe who is apparently commended by Jesus (Mk 12.34) into a typical controversy narrative. In Matthew's account the Pharisees are portrayed as typically plotting (22.34; cf. v. 15) and sending their best man ('a lawyer') to 'tempt' Jesus (v. 35). Of the positive features of Mark's account (cf. esp. Mk 12.28, 32-34), Matthew retains only the courteous address διδάσκαλε (22.36; cf. Mk 12.32). In the context Matthew has chosen for the pericope (22.15ff., 41ff. and ch. 23) an unequivocal commendation of a scribe would have been quite out of place. Instead, Matthew chooses to interpret the motives and allegiances of the scribe negatively and use the pericope as further anti-Pharisaic material. The change from scribe to Pharisee is but one aspect of this larger adaptation. Mt. 22.41 is also governed by the context of dialogue with the Pharisees (as in the reference just given), who here quite naturally are directly addressed by Jesus in preference to Mark's similarly context-bound use[37] of the term 'the scribes' as a vague, general reference in 12.35.[38]

The five *deletions of the term 'scribes' only* are best understood as clarifications of a similar nature. In the context of a controversy pericope, Mt. 9.11 simplifies the 'scribes of the Pharisees' of Mk 2.16 to 'the Pharisees'; and in the other four deletions (Mt. 21.23; 26.3; 26.47; 27.1) Matthew consistently alters Mark's 'elders and scribes' to 'elders of the people'. This may be because he feels the latter already include those scribes responsible to the governing juridical body;[39] clearly Matthew feels the 'elders' are the proper authorities here (cf. his insertion at 27.41 diff. Mk 15.31). But already it looks as if Matthew is trying to exculpate the scribes as a class from complicity. Again, Matthew may be attempting to add accuracy to the Markan picture; at least there is a degree of clarity and consistency here which casts serious doubt on the notion that he is simply obscuring matters as a result of his own confusion.

The remaining three 'omissions' are those created by *deletion of clauses in which 'scribes' are mentioned*: Mk 7.5/Mt. 15.1; Mk 9.14/ Mt. 17.14; Mk 12.32/Mt. 12.40f.

1. Mt. 15.1. The first deletion, of Mark's clause 'and the Pharisees and the scribes ask him . . . ' in 7.5, is purely a stylistic necessity, in view of the fact that precisely these two groups are already mentioned in Matthew's verse (15.1), as the subject of the very same sentence!

2. Mt. 17.14. Mk 9.14b-16 is not paralleled by Matthew or Luke, and occurs at the head of a long section of Mark to which Matthew and Luke only inconsistently adhere, although the 'omissions' they

make roughly coincide (Mk 9.14b-16, 20-27, 33-34, etc.). In the latter sections there is no mention of scribes. It hardly seems justified, then, to suggest the omission of 9.14b-16 is caused solely by the mention of scribes. It may have to do with the state of the recensions of Mark available to Matthew and Luke (since Luke also omits here). But alternative explanations are possible, and our preference will be clear from our discussion of the context.[40]

3. Mt. 22.40f. The third alleged deletion is of Mk 12.32-34a, again paralleled by neither Matthew nor Luke, and consisting of a commendation of an individual scribe by Jesus because of a wise answer. If Matthew has made a deliberate excision here, there is a more ready explanation for it: namely in order to obviate the incongruity of v. 34b, which Matthew and Luke *do* parallel, with v. 34a. It is not within the purview of Matthew to admit the wisdom of Pharisaic scribes,[41] so that there may also be a polemical reason for this omission. It is clear that Matthew sees this person whom Mark calls a scribe (unlike the person Matthew *chooses* to call scribe at 8.19—see below) in a negative light (cf. the use of the verb πειράζειν in 22.35 as well as the association with Pharisees and Sadducees there). Mt. 13.51f., as we shall see, provides *Matthew's* idea of the wise 'scribe' who is 'not far from the kingdom'; for Matthew, Pharisaic scribes cannot conceivably be credited with such insight.

In Matthew's eleven 'omissions' of the term 'scribe', therefore, which might be expected to produce the most substantial evidence for the notion that Matthew is embarrassed by the term, we find no evidence that the author is confused as to who the scribes were. This redactor indeed seems to be at pains to reduce the apparent relative neutrality of the term γραμματεύς[42] by specifying that *these* scribes are in fact Pharisees. We may go a step further and suggest Matthew indicates these are Pharisaic scribes as opposed to other kinds of scribes. This is a disputed area, as mentioned above, but scholarly answers to the question of the existence of Sadducean or scribes other than Pharisaic ones consist largely of flat contradictions, as the evidence produced on both sides is slight.[43] The problem in fact appears to be one of definition, and of the usage of the word 'scribe'; and it is hoped that this study will shed light on scribal categories by recourse to actual first-century and earlier terminology, to be found both within the Gospel of Matthew itself and elsewhere.

Matthew's use of the term 'scribe'

In Chapter 6 we shall discuss in detail the clearly *positive* uses of the term scribe in Mt. 13.52 and 23.34, but following our review of the 'omissions' it should be evident from Matthew's actual usage of the term in the rest of the Gospel that he is by no means detachedly neutral or even deficient in his understanding of it.

Of Matthew's 22 uses of the term scribe, only 9 are paralleled in Mark (a few others may be derived from Q—cf. e.g. Lk. 11.45-52 with Mt. 23). It is evident that the majority of instances associate scribes with another group (or at least with another title). In 6 of the 9 instances paralleled in Mark, Mt. 15.1 (//Mk 7.1); 16.21 (//Mk 8.31); 20.18 (//Mk 10.33); 21.15 (//Mk 11.18); 26.57 (//Mk 14.53); 27.41 (//Mk 15.31), Matthew reproduces almost exactly Mark's juxtaposition of the scribes with another leadership group.[44] Except for 15.1, where the other group is the Pharisees,[45] the scribes are linked with chief priests and/or elders. If there is a confusion here it must be attributed to Mark rather than Matthew; but it remains possible that Matthew uncharacteristically allowed himself to be governed by Mark's usage in up to four instances (16.21; 20.18; 26.57; 27.41—though in the second of these Matthew again omits the article and in the fourth he adds 'elders' to the group). It may be, however, that literary considerations (the juxtaposition of *three* groups in opposition to Jesus) are the controlling factor here. Certainly the fact that Matthew treats Mark with respect at these points is no indication at all that he is slavishly following distinctions he does not understand, and in any case here as elsewhere *the scribes per se never stand alone as opponents of Jesus*. They are tainted by the company they keep. 21.15 retains the exact title of the group in Mk 11.18 (the chief priests and the scribes) but provides them with a new context in which they are questioned about a scripture (Ps. 8.2) and are 'moved with indignation' whereas in Mark's they are bluntly reported to have 'sought how they might destroy him'. This looks like a tempering of the criticism against the scribes in Mark, consistent with the Matthean changes we have discussed above.

Among the 13 non-Markan instances of scribe in Matthew there are 10 further cases of a juxtaposition of scribes with another group. In 2.4, the 'scribes of the people' are associated with chief priests in Herod's court at the time of the birth of Jesus (here perhaps showing some sensitivity to the historical circumstances; there is no mention of the Pharisees). Otherwise, the other Jewish leadership group named in association with the scribes is always the *Pharisees*: in 5.20; 12.38;[46] 23.2 and (in the single context of the 'woes') 23.13, 15, 23, 25, 27, 29. With the exception of 23.2 (discussed below) the juxtaposition of scribes and Pharisees in these verses occurs in the formulae γραμματεῖς καὶ Φαρισαῖοι (ch. 23), τῶν γραμματέων καὶ Φαρισαίων (5.20), τινες τῶν γραμματέων καὶ Φαρισαίων (12.38), all in a clearly stylized phraseology which quite evidently for rhetorical effect conjoins the two terms into one by the omission of the definite article before Φαρισαῖοι, creating a probable hendiadys. All these instances occur in a context of acute controversy.

Cook's inference is that Matthew's scribes are linked with Pharisees and other groups because his concept of scribes is too weak for him to allow them to stand alone. But 12.38 is one indication that this is not the case—there the implication must be (by the same token) that the Pharisees are too weak to stand alone! Rather, we find that Matthew has good reason for introducing the Pharisees and others with or in place of the scribes, just as he has good reason for introducing the scribes in 12.38 (see n. 46).

Matthew in ch. 23 and 5.20 has no interest in distinguishing scribes from Pharisees, it is true. But this does not have to be because he does not know who they are: the clear implication of the passages is precisely that he *does* know who they are, or, to put it more cautiously, *he has a clear notion of their role in the story*, namely (in 23.13ff.) hypocrites and the opponents of Jesus and the disciples; (in 5.20) false teachers of a false or inadequate righteousness; (in 2.4) *so-called* scribes in a position of authority as legal experts; (in 12.38) quasi-scientific inquirers (the request for a sign is for a kind of objective proof) who are fair game for riddles composed by a higher mind (cf. also the wisdom allusion in this context, 12.42). Here there is certainly no hint of confusion. The criticized and harangued worthies are of the Pharisaic party and they like to be called 'scribe' or 'teacher' (cf. the rivalry in appropriation of title which seems to lie behind 23.8ff.) as well as *perûšîm*[47]—which epithets Jesus (and/or Matthew) uses against them with heavy irony: '"scribes and Pharisees"—hypocrites!'

Cook's suggestion (p. 25 n. 40) that these denunciations of ch. 23, as well as 5.20[48] and 23.2, are inspired by Mk 12.38ff. is rather unlikely. It may be doubted whether Matthew uses Mark at all at

23.1-5. In particular, it is difficult to see how 'Beware of the scribes, who love to walk in long robes ...' (Mk 12.38) can prompt Matthew's respectful 'The scribes and the Pharisees sit on Moses' seat, therefore do and observe everything they bid you ...' (23.2). On Cook's argument, Matthew omits mention of scribes where possible because he is confused by the term. Why, then, would Matthew *retain* such a mention where, furthermore, it appears on the surface to conflict with the whole thrust of the chapter: the drastic censure of the scribes (even if 23.3 does add a qualification of this positive view)? We shall return to this verse, but for the moment let it be observed that οἱ γραμματεῖς καὶ οἱ Φαρισαῖοι, both in form and application, appears to be a different kind of expression from γραμματεῖς καὶ Φαρισαῖοι ὑποκριταί. 'Confusion' can only be an unsatisfactory and last-resort explanation for Matthew's usage in this chapter. We shall argue that there are more than sufficient clues to aid our understanding of Matthew's consistent concept of scribes and Pharisees.

The three other non-paralleled Matthean uses of 'scribe' (8.19; 13.52; 23.34) are of a different order and are treated separately below. 8.19 is probably a positive use, 13.52 and 23.34 certainly so.

There remain to be discussed the three paralleled (Mt./Mk) uses of 'scribe' alone (7.29; 9.3; 17.10).

In 7.28f. Matthew has 'the multitudes were astonished at his teaching, for he taught them as one having authority and not as *their* scribes' in place of Mark's 'not as *the* scribes' (Mk 1.22). Taken on its own, this verse would be an insufficient basis for a theory of the Matthean *Sitz im Leben*, for which it is frequently used.[49] However, the alteration to the genitive pronoun may be significant for our own investigation since it directly concerns the way Matthew uses the term scribe itself. This appears to be a specification, albeit a broad one, of the same order as we have observed in cases where Matthew indicates the Pharisaic association of the scribes in question. Here, as in 2.4, Matthew is speaking of 'the scribes of the people' (γραμματεῖς τοῦ λαοῦ [2.4] and οἱ γραμματεῖς αὐτῶν, whose genitive personal pronoun refers back to οἱ ὄχλοι [7.28f.]). In both cases we have a strong element of comparison—in 7.29 Jesus teaches not as the scribes of the multitude, and in 2.4 the chief priests and scribes of the people are aligned with Herod, and identified with the forces of evil conspiring against Jesus and his 'camp' in the shape of the Magi.[50]

The scribes who wield authority both at the time of the birth of the Messiah and at the time of the instruction in righteousness by Jesus are the scribes who hold sway in the religious affairs of Palestine, namely those who though held in public esteem are blind to the will of God, the 'Pharisaic scribes'.[51] It is no accident that Matthew uses αὐτῶν in 7.29, and there is certainly no hint that he is confused here. And again he avoids any possible implication that scribes *per se* are under criticism.

Mt. 9.3 (// Mk 2.6) is, according to Cook (p. 25), the 'only' time that Matthew reproduces a Markan reference to scribes 'in a manner implying that Matthew knows who they are—and such a reproduction could result from mere copying.' Cook resorted to similar argumentation for the mention of Herodians in 22.16 (see my n. 29), and if anything it is even less persuasive in relation to this verse. In 9.3-4 Matthew is in his usual way improving on Mark's style, tightening up Mark's loose and pedestrian Greek and omitting what he finds theologically dubious or not in accord with his own theological or christological concerns. Thus, in place of Mark's inelegant 'But there were certain of the scribes sitting there and reasoning in their hearts' (ἦσαν δέ τινες τῶν γραμματέων ἐκεῖ καθήμενοι καὶ διαλογιζόμενοι ἐν ταῖς καρδίαις αὐτῶν), Matthew has 'And behold, certain of the scribes said within themselves' (καὶ ἰδού τινες τῶν γραμματέων εἶπαν ἐν ἑαυτοῖς); and Matthew omits the explicit contrast between Jesus and God in Mark's 'who can forgive sins but one, even God?' (Mk 2.7) (cf. Matthew's avoidance of the same issue by altering Mark's 'none is good, save one, even God' [Mk 10.18] at 19.17). So it is very clear that Matthew is alert and on good form precisely at this point. Yet he retains—indeed this is *all* he retains here—'certain of the scribes' (whereas Luke, interestingly enough, changes to 'the scribes and the Pharisees' [Lk. 5.21]). Why? Surely not because of 'mere copying'! We have noted above that Matthew is apparently concerned to specify the scribes who oppose Jesus as 'Pharisees' rather than allow them the honorific label of 'scribes'. But here he has no need to do so since Mark already exonerates the scribes *per se*—it is only *some* (τινες) of them who are accusing Jesus of blasphemy; and so he can retain this part of Mark's wording—it is quite compatible with his own view of the scribes.

The mention of the scribes at 17.10 (// Mk 9.11; Luke omits this pericope) is another which Matthew has taken over from Mark without change. This is in fact the only time he uses οἱ γραμματεῖς absolutely (i.e. without qualification or juxtaposition to another group-term). 'The disciples asked him, saying, "Why then say the scribes that Elijah must first come?"' In this case, the scribes referred to are not present, but are merely given as the source of a piece of eschatological doctrine. Jesus in the subsequent verse accepts this teaching, with the addition that 'Elijah has already come' (17.11). There is no implication that Jesus, or Matthew or his community has any quarrel with the accuracy of the doctrine of these scribes. From the point of view then of Matthew's reputed anti-scribism, either (1) we have a case of Matthean inconsistency (perhaps due to another 'mere copying'!), or (2) he concedes they are not always wrong (and in view of Matthew's omission of the commendation of the scribe in Mk 12.34 [cf. Mt. 22.34ff.] it may not be his concern to give this impression), or (3) the doctrine derives from *scribes of a different sort*, non-'Pharisaic' scribes. Rabbinic literature provides a number of parallels to this usage.

In Mishnah, it is the norm for a piece of doctrine or halakhah to be introduced by a formula stating its source: e.g. 'R. Judah says . . .'; 'the School of Shammai say . . . ' Where there has been disagreement, the final, definitive ruling is very often given in the form 'the Sages say . . . ' (e.g. *m. Ber.* 6.4; 7.5). Now although the exact phrase 'the Scribes say . . . ' is not found,[52] Mishnah also preserves the formula 'the words of the Scribes' (דברי הספרים) to designate binding rulings of an earlier generation, whose authority is unassailable (cf. e.g. *m. Sanh.* 11.3: 'Greater stringency applies to [the observance of] the words of the Scribes than to [the observance of] the words of the [written] law . . . If a man . . . adds to the words of the scribes he is guilty'; and *b. Ber.* 1.4: 'The words of Torah . . . include commands both of light and weighty importance, but the words of the scribes [דברי ספרים] are all weighty . . . The words of the elders [*j. Sanh.* 10.3 has 'the words of the scribes'] are weightier than the words of the prophets . . .').[53] The scribes (Soferim) are reputed to have received the oral law by a direct line of tradition from Moses on Sinai. Their word carries absolute authority.

Furthermore, fragments of early teaching about the return of Elijah are preserved in traditions ascribed in Mishnah to a similar source:

R. Joshua said: I have received as a tradition from Rabban Johanan b. Zakkai, who heard from his teacher, and his teacher from his teacher, as a *Halakhah* given to Moses from Sinai, that Elijah will not come to declare unclean or clean, to remove afar or to bring nigh, but to remove afar those [families] that were brought nigh by violence and to bring nigh those [families] that were removed afar by violence ... And the Sages say: Neither to remove afar nor to bring nigh, but to make peace in the world, as it is written [Mal. 4.5f.], *Behold I will send you Elijah the prophet ... and he shall turn the heart of the fathers to the children and the heart of the children to their fathers.*[54]

The earliest record of such a doctrine (evidently based on Mal. 4.6) is found in Sirach, the eminent Second Temple *scribe*, at Sir. 48.10: '... you [Elijah] who are ready at the appointed time ... to restore the tribes of Jacob ... ' (cf. Mt. 17.11).

It seems reasonable, then, on the strength of this circumstantial evidence to suggest that the phrase 'the scribes say ... ' in Mk 9.11 (Mt. 17.10) is of a similar kind: 'the scribes' who 'say' that Elijah must first come are the authoritative Soferim of an earlier generation.[55] If this is so, then Mark has made a false link with Jesus' opponents, 'the scribes' who argue with the disciples directly after the pericope in ch. 9 (v. 14, cf. v. 11). This looks likely on general grounds, too, since the scribes in dispute in this unruly crowd scene are scarcely identifiable as the honoured source of an authoritative eschatological doctrine.[56] Matthew, however, recognizes the doctrine of the Soferim for what it is and therefore retains it, without qualification or alteration. Since these are scribes *par excellence* (and not necessarily Pharisaic), he has no need to specify any association with the Pharisees. Indeed, he is at pains to avoid such a specification because they are quite other than the run-of-the mill contemporary *ḥakhāmîm/* Pharisees mentioned in Mk 9.14. On this occasion, out of literary considerations Mark has let himself be misled into making a tenuous thematic link on the basis of the term γραμματεύς; Matthew understands the situation better. We find, therefore, that option (3), which in any case best fits the pattern of Matthean usage that we have discerned elsewhere, is the best explanation for Matthew's treatment of the scribes at this point. Far from being ignorant of and confused by the scribes, Matthew is well enough acquainted with them to be able to distinguish between various *types* of scribe![57]

In the light of this, Mt. 23.2 is open to another explanation, as we indicated above. The καθέδρα of Moses may be both abstract and physical.[58] This was an actual stone seat reserved for the authoritative teacher—'usually a scribe'[59]—at the front of the synagogue. Renov[60] claims that the seat was not actually sat on but was reserved for the scrolls and that the main significance of the expression is the sense of legal authority inherited, in rightful succession, from Moses. In the abstract, metaphorical sense, the teacher took both the place of Moses as instructor and guide of the community, and imparted 'Moses' (i.e. the Law of Moses)[61] to his hearers. In so doing the scribes assume the Mosaic mantle and authority. Hence Jesus can recommend the observance of the teachings of the scribes *insofar as they faithfully propound the Torah of Moses*.[62] The scribes predominating in Matthew's purview (and/or of Jesus' time) happen to belong to the Pharisaic party; therefore Matthew is able to portray Jesus as including 'the Pharisees' with 'the scribes' as being the ruling authorities with respect to the Law. (It would surely have been nonsense to suggest that the Pharisees *per se*, or as a party, sit on Moses' seat—such a depiction can only apply to Pharisees who are scribes, and then only by virtue of a line of scribal succession.) We have noted above the similar usage of 'the scribes and the Pharisees' in 12.38, where the presence of the scribes in the group is associated with a mitigation of the opposition presented by the group. We would suggest that here too it is the scribes *qua* scribes who in Matthew's view merit the authority associated with the 'seat of Moses', while it is the scribes of the dominating Pharisaic party that are hypocrites, tantamount to usurpers of this authority. We may, by way of summary, loosely paraphrase 23.2f. thus:

> The scribes—including the incumbent Pharisaic scribes—are authoritative teachers of the Law of Moses, standing in the genuine scribal tradition that represents Moses. Their scribal authority makes their rulings binding on you; but don't fall into the trap of hypocrisy like the Pharisaic scribes.

Here again, as in 17.10, 'the scribes' are the authoritative *sôferîm*, the traditional mediators of the Law of Moses. And again, this would accord with the rabbinic confirmation of the authority of the ancient Soferim whom they trace back to Ezra, in clear contradistinction to the *sôferîm* of their own day. *M. Sota* 9.15 and other tannaitic references (e.g. *Sota* 15a; see further Strack-Billerbeck I, p. 80) are good indicators that the passing of the golden age of the Soferim proper was regretted.[63]

So far we have drawn out two quite distinct usages of the term γραμματεύς in Matthew. The majority of cases concern the Pharisaic scribes to whom Jesus, his disciples and Matthew's community are vigorously opposed, and whom Matthew usually specifies by explicit association with the Pharisees. Others, however, show a consistent concern to exonerate the scribes *per se* from outright condemnation and indeed to portray them in an altogether better light. Misdemeanours are attributed instead to 'Pharisees', to *Pharisaic* scribes, to 'some of' the scribes, or to scribes united with a consistently opposing group; and often when 'the scribes' as such are mentioned (even with Pharisees) they are given a more sympathetic treatment (9.3; 12.38; 17.10; 23.2) than the Pharisees. The scribes are treated as experts in the Law and (from the point of view of intellectual debate) on a comparable footing with Jesus (though of course Jesus always wins); explicitly in 23.2 and implicitly in 17.10 the authority of the scribes as rightful teachers of Israel is endorsed. Matthew is clearly not averse to *introducing* the scribes at appropriate points (e.g. 12.38) as well as deleting them where inappropriate (e.g. Mk 9.14). Far from there being evidence of confusion here, as Cook suggests, we have found a consistency which indicates that Matthew has a clear notion of who the scribes are, and *what they should ideally be.*

I take 13.51f. and 23.34 to be key passages for Matthew's positive concept of the scribes. They require a full contextual exegesis of their own, which will be attempted in Part III, in the light of our investigation of background concepts of the scribe. There remains one other instance of the term scribe in Matthew to be discussed here: Mt. 8.19f.[64]

In view of the single parallel in Luke (9.57ff.), this brief pericope is usually thought to derive from Q; it is seen as basically a son-of-man logion (or double logion) preserved as an apophthegm (pronouncement story). In the Q version there was evidently no framework, so that Luke (9.57) and Matthew (8.18) each provide one and choose their own setting (Matthew: Galilee; Luke: Samaria). However, the wording of the double question and answer remains so similar in the two versions that the divergences, seen from a redaction-critical perspective, are potentially quite significant.[65] First, while Luke has 'a certain man' (τις), which is frequently regarded as more original (since Q, it is assumed, was not interested in persons and places but in the sayings themselves), Matthew has instead *introduced* 'a/one scribe' (εἷς γραμματεύς). Bauer lists εἷς in this verse as equivalent to the indefinite article, with 21.19 and 26.69 as further examples in Matthew. The usage is relatively unusual. It is still possible that Matthew means to imply that *only* one, exceptional, scribe made such an offer to follow Jesus. This would certainly be in accordance with his usage if for Matthew the scribe belongs to the opposing party of Pharisaic scribes (cf. the qualification of the scribes in 9.3 with τινες). The more significant point is that Matthew sees fit to call this enquirer a γραμματεύς at all. Second, it is notable again (cf. on 12.38 above) that the introduction of the scribe is associated (1) with a courtesy address, διδάσκαλε (also introduced) and (2) with teaching (a riddle?) that has the 'son of man' as its main content (cf. 12.40).[66] Matthew clearly thought it appropriate to make a 'scribe' the recipient of teaching involving son of man terminology and a 'disciple'[67] the recipient of a challenge to radical discipleship. Third, the implication in 8.21 appears to be that the scribe is in some sense a 'disciple' (since Luke's [Q's] 'another' [ἕτερος] becomes Matthew's 'another of the disciples' and the word to the scribe also is concerned with the rigours of discipleship).

In the vast literature devoted to this passage, scholars are more or less evenly divided over whether Matthew's scribe and/or his disciple here are to be taken as accepted or rejected by Jesus.[68] In the absence of information regarding the subsequent course of events it is impossible to be sure. Nor is it apparent that this can have been completely clear to Matthew or Luke (or even to the compiler of Q!): the double logion is preserved for what Jesus says, not for the example (positive or negative) presented by the enquirers. Perhaps there is a hint of the outcome (in Matthew's view) in the immediately following 8.23—'the disciples followed him'.[69] It is possible, however, to say something more concrete about Matthew's presentation of this scribe, which is in any case our concern here.

Without wishing to anticipate the conclusions of our exegesis of 13.52, we may draw attention to the obviously positive portrayal of the disciples in 13.51 and the logion linking the disciples with the 'discipled' scribe in v. 52. The linguistic similarities to 8.19f. are equally obvious. In 13.51f. the question-answer format is again operative, though there Jesus himself poses the question; and again the focus of attention is upon the logion itself. For our purposes, however, the most significant point to draw from this comparison is that the link between scribes and disciples for Matthew is both close and positive. In view of (1) Matthew's consistent defence of the scribes *per se* which we have noted in the other texts discussed above; (2) the similar treatment of this scribe in the aspects we have just noted; (3) the links with 13.51f., it would be hard to avoid the conclusion that the scribe in 8.19 is seen in a positive light.[70] If we are right, incidentally, then this pericope (perhaps seen together with 13.52) is effectively a counterpart to, and replacement for, the 'omitted' commendation of the scribe in Mk 12.28, which, as we have seen, had to be reworked to fit in Matthew's context (ch. 22).

We may conclude this review of Matthew's knowledge and treatment of the scribes with the following summary of our findings:

If there is any substance to Cook's charge that Matthew's knowledge of the scribes is minimal, indeed utterly dependent on Mark's understanding of them, then evidence for it is not to be found in any 'confusion' in their treatment by Matthew. On the contrary, Matthew displays a consistent regard for the scribes which strongly suggests that he has a clear notion of who scribes are: he seeks to exonerate them from strident opposition to Jesus by characterizing scribes who do so as unrepresentative of scribes *per se*, hence always linking *opposing* scribes with known opponents of Jesus, especially Pharisees, or qualifying them as only 'some of' the scribes; he portrays them positively by removing suggestions that they 'tempt' Jesus and by making them courteous learners and genuine enquirers; he is aware that the scribes carry a genuine authority; he shows they are treated with respect by Jesus; only the Pharisaic scribes, who culpably distort the honoured picture of the scribe by their hypocrisy and false leadership, bear the full brunt of Jesus' criticism. We conclude that everything points to Matthew's having a positive and firm concept of the scribes.

It follows from this that, from Matthew's perspective at least, scribes and Pharisees are *not* synonymous, except when the terms are used as a hendiadys. The fact that Matthew sees Pharisaic scribes as *Pharisees* rather than as scribes, which provides grounds for Cook's and Rivkin's view that they are synonymous,[71] is actually an evidence of the contrary. It is precisely because Pharisees are *not* 'scribes' in the ideal sense that Matthew calls them Pharisees rather than scribes; they may be the same people, but the *terms* are not synonymous for Matthew.

If we have made a plausible case for a consistently positive concept of the scribe in Matthew (in addition to the undisputedly positive uses in 13.52 and 23.34), can this be supported by reference to similar concepts in comparable literature? It will be our concern in the following chapters to investigate the likely background to such a view of the scribes in the first century before returning in Part III to consider Matthew's other scribe texts in the light of this investigation, with a view to forming as clear a picture as possible of Matthew's concept of the scribe.

Chapter 2

THE SCRIBE IN THE OLD TESTAMENT
AND IN THE SECOND TEMPLE PERIOD

If, as we have argued in Chapter 1, there is such a consistency in
Matthew's use of the term 'scribe' that—as Michael Goulder puts
it[1]—'it is hard to think that so regular a picture is without
significance', we are bound to ask, Is such a firm, positive concept
unique to Matthew, or is a similar stance found elsewhere in Jewish
literature? Our concern here is to investigate the background
perceptions of the scribe that may have guided Matthew's use of the
term. We are not attempting a socio-historical account of the scribes
in this period (which in any case, being dependent on the texts,
would have to be preceded by a study of the *use* of the term in the
texts), our prime interest being only in the way scribes, individually
and as a class, are presented in the texts. That is, we are interested in
perceptions of the function/role and the authority of scribes.
Occasionally, however, the presentation or even the signature of
historical scribes in the texts may suggest possible socio-historical
inferences.

To my knowledge there exists no full study devoted to the scribes
as a distinct class or profession, whether to the γραμματεῖς of the
hellenistic and NT environments or the *sôferîm* of rabbinic lore
from the period of Ezra onwards; nor one dealing specifically with
their socio-religious position and function in the societies of the
Second Temple period.

In the limited studies concepts of the scribe to date[2] it has been
usual to seek a background in perhaps the more obviously formative
literature, especially the Old Testament (which offers Ezra, Baruch
and a few less renowned 'scribes'[3] as possible models), the books of
Maccabees (which make brief mention of influential groups of

'scribes' [γραμματεῖς] at 1 Macc. 5.42, 7.12f. and 2 Macc. 6.18), and Sirach (which indeed offers a graphic picture of an eminent scribe of ca. 200 BCE). This composite picture is then usually supplemented by recourse to a more contemporary (though strictly later) perspective in rabbinic literature, which has in particular been heavily drawn upon to elucidate Matthew's 'scribal' features. The fact is, however, that some potentially highly informative materials in this respect, especially apocalyptic literature, but also the Targums and the Dead Sea Scrolls, have been largely overlooked or ignored by expositors of Matthew's Gospel,[4] and Part II of this study will be devoted to a detailed study of some significant parts of this material. We begin, however, with a necessarily brief discussion of concepts more frequently acknowledged as a relevant background to the scribes of the NT period.

1. The Exilic and Post-Exilic Periods

In a study of this scope and compass we do not aim to make a thorough study of OT concepts of the scribe, but are concerned simply to draw out some of the main factors influencing concepts of the scribe in the Second Temple period, the period in which, after all, concepts of the scribe developed which were operative in the first century BCE.

A. 'Ezra the Scribe' and the Chronicler

The still standard study of concepts of the scribe, centred on the eminent OT scribe, Ezra, is that of H.H. Schaeder, *Esra der Schreiber* (Tübingen, 1930). Schaeder argues that Ezra, in the Aramaic letter of Artaxerxes called 'scribe of the law of the God of heaven' (Ezra 7.12, 21), was 'secretary of state for Jewish affairs'[5] in the Persian government (the text preserving his authentic Persian title). To the Chronicler Schaeder ascribes a shift in meaning as he reinterprets the title in the strictly Jewish sense—looking back no further than the restoration of the Jewish community—of expertise in Torah; hereby the *Schreiber* (highly educated, eminent administrative official) becomes the *Schriftgelehrte* (expert in the Law of Moses). The implication is then that thenceforward the סופר/ספרא title in

Jewish usage invariably carries the latter meaning, the earlier, not strictly Jewish, senses of *Schreiber* being lost.[6] This may be true in the context of the Chronicler's interests.[7] But there is no reason to assume from this that the Chronicler's emphasis determined the sense of the word, so restrictively, for posterity, or that external influences from societies where the scribe/wise man was legal expert, political adviser, diviner, composer and author, should no longer have affected usage in Second Temple Jewish society. Our study of the intertestamental literature will show the falsity of this *a priori* assumption.

In order to understand the concepts of 'scribe' embodied in Ezra we need some appreciation of (1) the role and function of scribes in the courts of the ancient Near East and of (2) the role and function of the Jewish Torah-experts. If the Aramaic letter is genuine, and if it does ascribe a secular Babylonian office to Ezra, Ezra's role is composite, indeed unique, and we cannot expect him necessarily to be a representative example of the Jewish scribes of the Second Temple period. Indeed Ben Sira the scribe, in conspicuously omitting all reference to Ezra in his Praise of the Fathers (Sir. 44ff.), offers silent evidence that the scribal tradition was not *dependent* on Ezra as its model. Nonetheless, at least in later periods Ezra was clearly taken to be the prototype, the model, of the Jewish scribe—though naturally he may increasingly have been seen in the image of the later scribes—whether rabbinic or apocalyptic (see on Ezra in Chapter 4).

(1) It would be well outside our brief to make a detailed examination of concepts of the scribe in the ancient Near East, but here we may note a few possibly significant points.

'Scribes' in ancient Near Eastern courts—'scribes' here will embrace a number of terms[8]—are generally of high rank. This will have to do, partly, with the fact that they were educated well beyond the level of most members of the society. But they also have political significance, functioning in close association with other high officials and political advisers.[9] They are the wisdom-school experts in ancient writings and the sciences, including the divinatory skills of astrological, dream and omen interpretations. The early parts of the book of *1 Enoch* and the book of Daniel reflect something of the Babylonian influence in particular on Jewish concepts of the role of the scribe. The civilization which educated Ezra also educated

'Daniel', and the image of its god Nabu the heavenly scribe (among other, especially Mesopotamian, scribal ideals) may well have contributed to the apocalyptic picture of Enoch (see Chapter 4 below). This background was the seed-bed of the traditions surrounding Daniel and *Nebu*chadnezzar and *Nabo*nidus. To be a scribe in Babylon, as indeed in Egypt, in Assyria, and in Sumer beforehand,[10] was in large part to be an eminent interpreter of mysteries for the benefit of the court and ultimately for the nation, though the art itself remained largely esoteric. Ben Sira also witnesses to the influence of the background on the scribal art of his day. Clearly the Babylonian inheritance, as far as the scribal legacy in Second-Temple Judaism is concerned, did *not* end with Ezra, even if there was some shift in meaning reflected in the Chronicler's report of Ezra as Torah expert. Indeed, the much later representations of Ezra himself in the apocalyptic literature, which depict him as a visionary and as an inspired author of revelations, bear a fascinating similarity to facets of the ancient Babylonian mantic scribes.

(2) Ezra is called 'a scribe skilled in the law of Moses . . . ' (Ezra 7.6) and 'learned in matters of the commandments of the Lord and his statutes for Israel' (7.11), and his programme is 'to study the law of the Lord, and to do it, and to teach his statutes and ordinances in Israel' (7.10). It is this description of his role that was particularly influential on certain subsequent (especially rabbinic) concepts of the role of the scribe, and indeed it is what Schaeder understood as the new Torah-centred role of the *Schriftgelehrte*. However, four qualifications need to be made of this simple view.

First, this role is ascribed to Ezra 'the priest and scribe', and (despite Ezra 7.6) some at least of it (teaching, knowledge of statutes) will also be inherent part of the *priestly* role that was his too. But a clear distinction is not possible here, since the functions of priest and scribe commonly overlap in the Second Temple period (see Part II); and the function can be scribal even if the functionary is a priest.

Second, according to the Chronicler's picture, the scribal role announced in Ezra 7.10 (cf. v. 25) is actually performed, in practice, by the *Levites* (Neh. 8.7ff.)—it is they who 'teach' the people (Neh. 8.9) and 'help them to understand' (Neh. 8.7, 8). We may gather that the named Levites in Neh. 8.7 were the 'teachers of the law' of the period. A similar role is ascribed, perhaps anachronistically,[11] to the Levites during the monarchic period (2 Chron. 17.7ff.; cf. 19.8ff.;

35.3); and the Chronicler actually uses the term *sôferîm* of them (2 Chron. 34.14). It is generally thought likely that the Chronicler himself was a Levite. In view of his high regard for Ezra and the Levites and his use of the term 'scribe' for both, it may be that he saw his own role also as specifically that of a *sôfēr*.[12] We would suggest, therefore, that the model of the scribe to be found in the Chronicler extends beyond the eminent figure of Ezra himself to the teachers of the community (the Levites and possibly himself), and perhaps to the authorship of religious writing (his own work).

Third, in addition to the Babylonian and secular associations of the term scribe implicit in the title brought with him by Ezra ([1] above), the Chronicler also preserves the term as the title of an official in Samaria, Shimshai the Scribe (Ezra 4.7ff.), whose competence may be in legal and diplomatic matters of state, but certainly not in the interpretation of the Torah for Israel.

Fourth, again in addition to the specifically Babylonian background of the scribe, account needs to be taken of the ancient and thoroughly *Jewish* tradition of the scribe. This already includes association with high office, with the court, the temple, and the schools—and the *literary* practice of the scribal art. (For examples see note 3 above, and on Jeremiah, below.)

The Chronicler's composite picture of the scribe shows then, that he associated the scribe, first, with eminence in society: (a) as a high secular official whose work involves diplomacy and letter-writing in or to the imperial courts (Ezra in Babylon, Shimshai in Samaria); (b) as a national political figure (Ezra and Shimshai). Second, he associates the scribes with expertise in diplomacy, writing, and with the highest Babylonian education—which, as we have seen, includes the whole range of interpretative sciences. Third, for the righteous community the scribes (Ezra *and* the Levites), are the indispensable interpreters of the law of righteous living. Fourth, it may well be that the Chronicler, sympathetic—to say the least—to the work of both Ezra and the Levites, sees his own written contribution as in some way also an exercise of the scribal art. Certainly a main aim of his work is didactic, the same function he ascribes to these teachers of Israel;[13] his exegetical techniques, moreover, often described as 'midrashic', are thoroughly scribal.[14] Furthermore, the Chronicler may, in his role as a historian, have something of a 'prophetic' self-consciousness, an aspiration common to many 'inspired' scribes.[15]

B.   *The Scribes of Old Testament Prophecy*

It is notoriously difficult to separate the 'prophetic' from the 'scribal' in the later parts of the prophetic corpus. We shall give further attention to the question below, as it impinges on the book of Daniel in particular. But the notion of scribal or prophetic 'schools' preserving and developing the prophecies of (Second) Isaiah, Jeremiah (Baruch/ the deuteronomistic school?), Ezekiel, Zechariah and Joel (in apocalyptic vein) and even Amos before them (cf. also e.g. the final redaction of Hosea) is now widely accepted.

The limitations of this investigation prohibit us from a full study of the scribal aspects of all the later prophetic parts of the OT. But in view of (1) Matthew's special interest in both scribes and the book of Jeremiah[16] and (2) the high-profile role of scribes in Jeremiah, it may be particularly valuable to focus briefly on Jeremiah as a relevant part of the background to Matthew's concept of the scribe.

Jeremiah

Jeremiah is one of those prophets[17] who intended some of their prophecies to be presented in literary form from the beginning (cf. e.g. Jer. 29.1-28; 30.2ff.; 36.4ff.; 51.60). Indeed it has been suggested that Jeremiah's own *profession* (his prophetic activity obviously not bringing in an income) was that of a *scribe*. Certainly his social position, the references to his writing (above; cf. the images used in 17.1, 13; 22.30; 31.33) and his close association with scribal families such as the families of Shaphan (see note 3) and Baruch would be consistent with this.[18] This is a fascinating possibility in view of the many other links between scribalism and prophetic inspiration which we shall have cause to note in the course of this investigation. However, it was specifically and primarily Jeremiah's secretary, Baruch the Scribe, who was entrusted with making the record of his prophecies (36.4ff.). It is notable that Baruch's role as scribe is seen as an extension of the prophetic activity of Jeremiah the prophet. The two are a team: when Jeremiah is instructed to write a prophecy on a scroll (36.2, 28), it is in fact Baruch who writes at Jeremiah's dictation; he deputizes for Jeremiah in reading to all the people the words of the Lord from the scroll in the temple (36.5f.); and he is liable to be persecuted with Jeremiah as being responsible with him for the unpalatable prophecies (cf. 36.26). True, at least as far as prophecy is concerned, Baruch is second in rank to Jeremiah (cf. 36.8), but he is intimately involved in the prophetic ministry.

Baruch is not the only scribe to be involved with Jeremiah's prophecies. Seraiah, Baruch's brother, who is almost certainly also a scribe,[19] is responsible for writing and preserving the prophecy in 51.59ff. (obviously making two copies, since one has survived [cf. 51.63]!). Eminent scribal families (Shaphan's, Neriah's) are prime characters in the action surrounding Jeremiah's largely political prophecies; professional and family rivalries are also involved in the conflict of (prophetic) scribes (and true prophets) against (official) scribes (and false prophets) (cf. Jer. 8.8 and note 3 above). The analogy with Matthew's situation may extend to this also (cf. our comments on Mt. 23.34 in Chapter 6).

On another level, the book of Jeremiah as we have it is evidently the product of scribal enterprise, whether by the deuteronomic 'school', or by a single 'biographer', possibly Baruch himself, or by *both* of Jeremiah's prime disciples, providing the alternative arrangements of the book in MT (Seraiah, in Babylon) and LXX (Baruch, in Egypt).[20] It is difficult to avoid the conclusion that Baruch at least played some part in the formation of the book, and it is reasonable to suppose that this activity was compatible, indeed commensurate, with his function as a scribe—the writer, collector, preserver, reader and champion of the teachings and prophecies of Jeremiah. Perhaps Baruch was the mainstay and founder of a 'Jeremianic school', similar to the (likely) Isaianic school, Ezekiel school, and so on. The evidence in each case is found in the collation, preservation and presentation of the prophecies; it is also seen in the *contribution* to the prophecies themselves that has apparently been made by these prophetic scribes. According to Lundbom, both Baruch and Seraiah have immortalized themselves in typical scribal fashion by the extensive use of the colophon form in Jeremiah.[21] In particular, Baruch has authored ch. 45, which concludes the book (less ch. 52) in the LXX, and Seraiah's colophon (51.59-64) concludes the MT version (less ch. 52). It seems clear that scribes are responsible for the compilation of the book as a whole and for the authorship of at least certain summary statements of Jeremiah's prophecies (the colophons). Baruch is almost certainly responsible for more than just ch. 45; Lundbom sees 36.1-8 as another of Baruch's colophons, and it is possible that much of the narrative derives also from him. In any case, the end-product (to whomever the particular components are to be ascribed—ch. 52 will be by later scribes, for example) is largely a scribal work (entirely so, if Jeremiah was a scribe!). That is, in Jeremiah we have a prophetic text effectively composed by scribes.

Other Prophets

Similar circumstances may surround the composition of other prophetic works. In the case of Joel, for example, it has been suggested that some of the 'prophecies' are almost midrashic, prophetic compositions made at a literary level using other prophetic texts. Wolff writes:[22]

> Here [in Joel] we are hearing a 'literary prophet' in the strictest sense, insofar as he reads prophetic writings and writes prophecy. He belongs to those who study the literary transmissions of the prophets '. . . with the passion of those tormented. They gain from it conclusions that become new revelation for them' [cited from G. Quell, *Wahre und falsche Propheten* (1952), p. 133] . . . Thus we are confronted here with a 'learned prophecy' that takes up the received eschatological message with a burning passion for knowledge, and with the help of sapiential training, and gives it new expression in intense expectation of Yahweh's future.

This is similar to the scribal activity we found in the Chronicler, but is especially close to that of the 'apocalyptic' texts—both those of the late works of the OT and the apocalyptic works proper (see Part II). But more than this: this scribal activity, of prophecy at a literary level—frequently associated with wisdom features—is often barely distinguishable from that of the prophet himself. Perhaps some of the prophets are scribes; but conversely, too, the scribes are authors and composers of prophetic texts. They therefore deserve greater recognition than the lowly designation of 'redactors' and 'compilers' generally implies. They, too, are 'prophets'.[23]

Psalms

The Psalms, too, witness to the close relationship between scribal and prophetic inspiration; indeed psalms are a feature of many of the prophetic books. The canonical Psalms have very often been regarded as prophecy (cf. e.g. the use of the Psalms in the Gospels as proofs of the fulfilment of prophecy in Christ), and have more recently been examined in terms of prophecy by modern scholars,[24] while they were also evidently subject to scribal influences.[25] Many others have both scribal and prophetic features and are, interestingly, associated with Levites (e.g. the sons of Korah). Common to prophecy and psalmody, of course, is that essential ingredient of good poetry and rhetoric: 'inspiration'. That prophecy and literary inspiration are sometimes almost interchangeable concepts is evident, for example, in the work of Ben Sira the Scribe (cf. Sir. 24.33, which we shall discuss below). Psalms are an expression of inspiration in the Hodayoth of the Teacher of Righteousness (1QH), the Qumran Psalms (cf. esp. 11QPs[a]DavComp, discussed below, which talks explicitly of scribal 'inspiration') and in various parts of the New Testament; and often they are expressly associated with OT prophecy. While it would be too much to claim that the writing of Psalms is exclusively the domain of the scribes, it is clear that the scribes, immersed in the prophetic writings and fully equipped academically for the task, are the obvious candidates for the composition of inspired and inspirational works. It is, incidentally, quite natural that the OT Levites should be both temple-singers and *sôferîm*; probably many (perhaps including the Chronicler) will have been both.

We shall have further cause to discuss the relationship between scribes and prophecy at various points in our investigation; in particular see on the Targums below and on Ben Sira in Chapter 3. But it should already be clear that the literary output of the biblical scribes is frequently closely associated with prophetic inspiration.

C. *The Wisdom Scribes*

The scribal art of the wisdom writers is a subject deserving of a more thorough treatment than is possible within the scope of this book. Indeed, it is quite well served with studies already.[26] Moreover, our concern is to point up other relevant aspects of the scribal background affecting first-century Judaism. However, a few observations should be made at this point.

Scribes are commonly equated with the members of the wisdom schools. In sections A and B above we have stressed the prophetic, eminent, poetic, creative and didactic aspects of scribal models; but 'wisdom' is certainly also a prime domain of the scribe, and much of the wisdom material of the OT has to be credited to *sôferîm* as well as *ḥakhāmîm*—where indeed such a distinction is at all valid or possible.[27] We have mentioned, above, the scribal schools of the ancient Near Eastern courts through which eminent persons graduated. The scribal education in court circles was international, and the cross-fertilization of forms and themes in wisdom literature is a proof of the extent of this influence. Clearly some of the OT writers had such a background or were closely acquainted with it— Ezra/the Chronicler and the author of Daniel, as we have mentioned, but also the authors of wisdom material proper, members of the deuteronomic school and contributors to the book of Proverbs, for example. These are the archetypal 'scribes', the educated and well-read intelligentsia of many generations and cultures.

The wisdom teachers are invariably designated as scribes and wise men. The wisdom literature is the tangible legacy of these scribes, and the title scribe is completely appropriate for the authors of this literature. Throughout Near Eastern antiquity wisdom was perceived as the domain of the scribe, and scribe is an honorific title which its bearers were not reticent about glorifying. This is reflected in all the ancient cultures of the area. As Smith notes, scribes were very much occupied with themselves: 'They projected their scribal activities on high, on a god who . . . was a teacher in his heavenly court. They hypostatized the scribe and scribal activities in the figure of Divine Wisdom'.[28] Clearly this applies, for example, to the authors of Proverbs 1-9, the Wisdom of Solomon and by implication to the authors of Job and Qoheleth, as well as it does to the authors of apocalyptic works. The Psalms called 'Maskil', and the Psalms of the Sons of Korah, are in general self-consciously Levitical and scribal in form and interest, features practically indistinguishable from the wisdom characteristics of these psalms. The 'pen of the ready scribe' in Ps. 45.1 is the author's metaphor for the manner of his own poetic inspiration.[29] The scribes are careful to leave their mark in their literature.

Indeed, the most influential extra-/deutero-canonical wisdom author, Ben Sira, both elevates and emulates the current (early 2nd cent.) ideal of the scribe. But Ben Sira is of a kind with other wisdom writers of his day; the relative paucity of extant, similar and contemporary idealizations of the scribe in Palestine should not lead us to think otherwise. It is now becoming increasingly recognized that Ben Sira is not so far removed from the 'apocalyptic' scribes as was once thought;[30] in particular the case for a dichotomy between Ben Sira and the contributors to the book of Daniel is demonstrably flimsy.[31] The points of contact between Ben Sira and the wisdom authors of other late parts of the OT are even more evident.[32] Duesberg and Fransen are quite right to include the authors of Proverbs, Job, Qoheleth and the Wisdom of Solomon alongside Ben Sira as 'inspired scribes'.[33] Comparisons are also possible with the Chronicler, for example in respect of Sira's interest in history. This is not to say that this varied literature is in any sense monolithic, nor that it all derives from a narrowly definable social group of scribes. Rather, we acknowledge the thorough scribal training and the sense of inspired purpose and creativity that unites these authors. There is no doubt that these works exhibit a sense of inspired authority that goes beyond the simple belief that 'wisdom comes from Yahweh'; in this respect they are little short of prophetic in the classical sense.[34]

We have seen, too, that the contacts between scribal wisdom and the composition of the prophetic works, indeed the scribal/wisdom influences on the original prophets themselves, are close and numerous. As prophecy diminished and 'ceased', of course, the possibilities of influence were restricted more to the prophetic upon the scribal than vice versa, and prophetic claims became expressed in a lower key. Nonetheless, the urgency of an inspired and authoritative message worth proclaiming remained and found expression in a wide variety of scribal forms, whether in the reinterpretation and proclamation of Torah, the composition of pious poetry, the presentation and interpretation of the messages of the prophets, or in the theological and philosophical search for a theodicy or a hope for the future.

The First Evangelist demonstrates considerable expertise in a variety of scribal forms and methods,[35] many of which he will have learned from the canonical wisdom literature, as well as (probably) Sirach and other wisdom-influenced scribal literature whose relevance to Matthew will be brought out in Parts II and III of this study. Wisdom's influence on Matthew may be pervasive: as in Proverbs 8, Wisdom 7 and Sirach 24, Matthew's wisdom teacher/scribe (Jesus) speaks in the name of Wisdom. Matthew appears implicitly to present Jesus as Wisdom/Torah in 11.25-27, 11.19 and 23.34 (cf. Lk. 11.49). This is entirely a scribal feature, and is significant for our understanding of Matthew's Gospel as a scribal product, as well as of Matthew's perception of Jesus. But as we have already seen, and will show more fully in Part II, important as it is the OT wisdom literature is by no means the *only* likely source of scribal influence on Matthew.

D. *The Classical Soferim*[36]

Since we are here concerned with perceptions, rather than with socio-historical reconstructions, of the scribe, a full discussion of the issues associated with such reconstructions falls outside our scope. We shall, however, review briefly the literary traditions concerning the historical scribes of this period.

In historical terms, very little is known of the Soferim in the period in which, according to rabbinic tradition, they flourished (between Ezra [late 5th or early 4th century BCE] and Ben Sira [early 2nd century BCE]). The mishnaic references are often vague and quite diverse, and do not inspire the historian's confidence, particularly so in the wake of Neusner's work, which has placed a bold query against historical judgments based on pre-70 CE traditions in rabbinic literature.[37] And it is apparent that (at least in later times) the term *sōferîm* can be applied to various generations of scholars.[38] However, whatever their precise characteristics in an obscure period of Jewish history, we would continue to give credence to the basic notion of a flowering of authoritative Soferim in this period, since (a) the tradition of a body of men responsible for the early foundations of Judaism is so widespread in rabbinic literature and so deep-seated, (b) the notion coheres well with independent data, such as Nehemiah 8–10; Sirach, which presupposes a (conservative) tradition of scribalism; traditions of the LXX; the actual development of the 'Oral Law'; the compilation of large parts of the OT; known wisdom influences of the period, etc., and (c) the notion cannot be dismissed on the grounds of the varied use of the word *sōferîm* in Talmud, nor on the grounds of the lack there of specific attributions of laws to the period.

It is quite possible that the 'Men of the Great Synagogue' referred to in the chain of tradition given in *Pirke Aboth* (1.1) are to be associated with the historical Soferim, particularly in view of their similar role, according to rabbinic tradition, in 'making a fence around the Torah' by giving legal rulings on the implementation of the Law (cf. the 'words of the scribes').[39] In fact, in respect of the *tiqqûnê sôferîm* the midrashim explicitly make this identification (see note 64, below). There are problems surrounding the authenticity of traditions of the 'Great Synagogue' as a formal institution[40] and it is now widely asserted that the notion derives solely from the account given in Nehemiah 8-10, where the 'Great Assembly' is simply the people who gather to receive the Law from Ezra. However, the association, on the one hand, of the Great Synagogue with the interpretation of the Law in rabbinic tradition, and on the other, of the interpretation of the Law *to* the Great Assembly by the Levitical scribes under Ezra (see section A, above) makes it possible that the tradition (loosely) reflects a genuine, continuous line of Soferim from Ezra to the time of Simon the Just and beyond.[41] Our suggestion is that the phrase 'men of the Great Assembly' originally *did* relate to the Nehemiah 8-10 occasion, but that it designated *the Levites who instructed* the 'Great Assembly' of the people. Their usefulness can scarcely have been exhausted on this one occasion, and they would surely have continued to operate as interpreters of the Law. In fact, though many scholars suspect some anachronism, the Chronicler and the Deuteronomist indicate an already long-established tradition of instruction by the Levites (cf. e.g. 2 Chron. 35.3; Deut. 33.8-10). As such they would have become an institution (though not necessarily a formal, legislative governing body)[42] which would accord closely with what is known of the Soferim of the same period. Of known figures these are in any case surely the best candidates for identification with the Soferim between Ezra and Ben Sira.[43]

If this is so, there may be more to the rabbinic tradition that the 'men of the Great Synagogue' 'wrote' some late biblical books (Ezekiel, the Twelve Prophets, Daniel, Esther, Ezra and Chronicles)[44] than at first appears: we have already noted the scribal and Levitical contributions to some of these. In the absence of hard evidence and in view of the range of alternative explanations of the 'Great Synagogue' which have already been expressed,[45] however, in this context we claim no more than plausibility for this view.

The fact is, however, that rabbinic tradition saw the Soferim as filling a large gap in a significant period in the development of Torah interpretation, the basis for later Judaism, and held them in the highest regard. While the rabbis saw the continuation of the chain in the *Zugoth*, the 'pairs' of proto-rabbinic sages beginning with Antigonus of Sokho, the classical Soferim were always regarded as a class apart. The evidence of the books of Maccabees may indicate, as Hengel concludes,[46] that these Hasidic Soferim are the intellectuals responsible for the cultivation of new ideas that give rise to the apocalyptic and Essene movements as well as, ultimately, the Pharisaic and rabbinic. In this respect at least, their significance can hardly be overrated.

E. γραμματεύς *in the Septuagint*

Josephus calls the seventy elders who translated the Hebrew Scriptures into Greek 'interpreters of the law' (ἐξήγηται τοῦ νόμου, *Ant*. 12.2.13) rather than scribes.[47] But the LXX translation itself apparently favours the term γραμματεύς, and one suspects that the sympathy of these translators for the role of the scribe may have influenced their usage. While the LXX consistently uses γραμματεύς for סופר (ספרא), it also quite frequently uses it to render שׁטר (prince, officer—15 ×) and occasionally for the terms שׁפט (Ezra [2 Esdr.] 7.25), (possibly) על־הבית (LXX^A, Isa. 22.15) and (probably) מחקק (Sir. 10.5). Since the instances of ספרא/סופר are dealt with above (sections A–C) we shall restrict our brief comments here to the less common usages.

(1) γραμματεύς for שׁטר. The שׁטרים are the 'officers', leaders of the people who act as administrators and instructors (often in a military context). Thus in Exodus 5 (vv. 6, 10, 14, 15, 19) they are overseers of the Hebrew slaves and report to Moses and Aaron; in Joshua they pass on Joshua's commands to the people (Josh. 1.10; 3.2; 23.2; 24.12) and are among the leaders present at Joshua's writing and reading of the Law to the people (9.2 [8.33]). In Num. 11.16 they are assembled as leaders with the elders, to whom Moses' spirit is to be given; and in Deut. 20.5, 8, 9 they are charged with instructing the people, here again, as in 1 Chron. 2.7 also, in a military context. Finally, in 1 Chron. 23.4 and 2 Chron. 19.11 they are classed among Levites who have judicial responsibility.

The common factors here are the high official rank and the authority of these γραμματεῖς. They are overseers, instructors and judges; they bear Mosaic authority and are connected with Levites and the implementation of the Law.

(2) γραμματεύς for שֹׁפֵט (Ezra 7.25). שֹׁפְטִים (judges) are commonly mentioned alongside שֹׁטְרִים and it is quite understandable that sometimes the distinction between them should be blurred, particularly in view of their similar role (see [1] above). Scribes often played a judicial role (cf. e.g. Sir. 38.33).

(3) γραμματεύς for מְחֹקֵק. The only instance of this in the LXX[48] is in Sir. 10.5, where it agrees with later Palestinian usage. According to Vermes,[49] it reflects a contemporary situation in which the 'rulers' of the nation are also scribes (*sōferîm*). See on targums, below.

The LXX also uses γραμματεύς in a few instances which have no extant Semitic *Vorlage*, notably in the books of Maccabees: in 1 Macc. 5.42 the 'scribes of the people' act as army officers controlling the people for Judas (γραμματεῖς have a strikingly similar role in LXX Josh. 1.10f.; 3.2f.; cf. LXX 1 Chron. 27.1); in 1 Macc. 7.12 a 'synagogue of scribes' is apparently equated with leaders of the Hasidim who sue for peace with Alcimus and Bacchides; and in 2 Macc. 6.18, Eleazar, 'one of the scribes in high position', is publicly humiliated and martyred. These appear to be leading figures amongst the Hasidim; but exactly who they were is a historical question we cannot broach here. The references tell us little of what their function was, except that it seems to have involved politics and diplomacy as well as moral leadership. They are probably not to be identified with the classical Soferim, who antedate them; but they will stand in the same scribal tradition.

2. Scribes in the Targums and Rabbinic Literature

A.   ספרא and מחקק

As we mentioned above, rabbinic literature has to be treated with great reserve for traditions relating to the pre-70 period, and we do not propose to use it to construct a picture of the *sōferîm*. However, the very diversity of the usage of the term there is an interesting *sequel* to the period with which we are concerned and is of value in comparison. Like Bowker, we do maintain a distinction between rabbinic literature and the targums, however, which—though here too the problems of dating are notorious—are potentially more informative for the pre-70 period than are Mishnah and Talmud; the Isaiah Targum, for example, has recently been reassessed as informative for the NT background.[50] In any case, as we shall see, the concept of the scribe in the targums is quite homogeneous and presents an independent Jewish understanding of the scribe which has affinities with non-rabbinic notions, including that found in Matthew's Gospel.

The targums, paraphrastic Aramaic translations or 'interpretations' of the Hebrew Bible, were of course designed to make the difficult, even foreign, text of Scripture accessible to lay people. The work of the meturgeman (= 'interpreter') is classically the interpretation of the Law. If the LXX translators have a preference for the use of γραμματεύς in relation to the MT, we might expect something similar of the targumists. This is indeed the case.

An interesting departure from the usage of the LXX is that, in addition to maintaining the equation ספרא = סופר, the meturgemans introduce the term ספרא almost invariably where the MT has מחקק (ruler/sceptre)[51] and frequently where it has נביא (prophet). We mentioned above that LXX Sir. 10.5 renders מחקק as γραμματεύς. Vermes suggested[52] that this equation emerged as the text was adapted to the contemporary situation where the Soferim were the nation's rulers. In a sense, this was also true of the tannaitic period, which saw as binding the Oral Law of the Soferim and which produced the Targums. There, the מחקק of the MT is either interpreted as Moses, the Great Scribe, or as other scribes. From (all) the Targums to Gen. 49.10 and Pss. 60.9; 108.9,[53] it is clear that the scribal role is of teaching and interpretation of Torah. When applied to Moses (e.g. Targums to Num. 21.18; Deut. 33.21)[54] the reference is evidently more to the giving, or mediation, of the Law (in Midr. Isa. 33.22 the Lord himself as *Teacher* and lawgiver is the מחקק),[55] but is also associated with prophecy (Tgs Deut. 33.21). In all cases, the מחקק/ספרא is the one who makes the Torah accessible to Israel. As Vermes notes, the sense is identical to the interpretation of מחקק (Num. 21.18) as the Interpreter of the Law in CD 6.2-11. Thus the targumic ספרא is equivalent, in some contexts at least, to the Qumranian דורש־התורה.

In the Damascus Document the royal sense of מחקק is also retained, and is present in its application to the figure who will 'teach righteousness at the end of time'—the 'messianic' teacher of righteousness. This eschatological connection (cf. Targum to Joel 2.23) is, interestingly, found typically among the scribes of apocalyptic literature, notably Enoch,[56] but also in relation to the rabbinic expectation of the return of Moses.

Firm conclusions from these data are difficult. But it seems that (1) from the second century BCE there was an established Palestinian understanding of מחקק as having to do with *giving or interpreting the Law*, and for the Tannaim this was equivalent to the role of the respected Soferim; (2) דורש־התורה is practically synonymous with ספרא and γραμματεύς in the appropriate contexts; (3) the sense of 'ruler'—both contemporary (ruling Soferim of the theocratic period) and eschatological—is maintained in association with the authority of the eminent interpreter (e.g. Moses and the Teacher of Righteousness).

B. ספרא *and* נביא

Another interesting feature of the targumic use of ספרא is its representation of נביא, prophet. This is a much more radical and significant step in the direction struck by the LXX translators, for here not only do scribes abound, assimilating other functions, but frequently they actually directly replace the *prophets*. Thus Targum Jonathan to Isaiah 9.15 renders 'the prophet who teaches lies' as 'the scribe who teaches lies':[57] false prophet = false scribe! Similarly, for Isa. 3.2 'the judge and the prophet' taken into exile are in the Targum 'the judge and the scribe'. 'The priest and the prophet' who 'reel with strong drink' (Isa. 28.7) become 'the priest and the scribe'.[58] Though the critique remains, it is readdressed. Why should this replacement be so consistently made? (1) Is the meturgeman keen to exculpate prophets and place blame rather on the more mundane, perhaps more political and more secular scribes? (2) Or is the consideration that he sees the scribal role (perhaps his own) as in a sense prophetic, and thus wishes to tighten the connection between prophet and scribe in the text? (3) Or does he have a genuine understanding of the close historical ties between cult prophets and scribes? The liberties taken with the MT in other cases militate against possibility (3): historical corrections are no part of his brief. Possibility (1) cannot apply since the targums agree in designating Moses himself as 'scribe', and also see other scribes positively, as is clear from the translations of מחקק discussed above, and from such cases as the following:

the Lord hath cast among you the spirit of error, and hath hidden
from you the prophets; the scribes and the teachers who taught you
the instruction of the law hath he hidden. And all prophecy is
become unto you as the words of a book which is sealed (Tg Isa.
29.10).

Here, scribes are closely associated with the prophets. Indeed, ספריא
actually replaces 'seers' (חוזים) here, though this may be determined
less by the correspondence of the term 'seer' with 'scribe' than by the
context, especially the natural identification with the 'learned' who
should be able to read the 'sealed book' (29.11f.).[59] The Targum has
maintained the sense that there is no one left to interpret; but has it
adapted it to a more contemporary situation in which 'prophecy' and
'the instruction of the law' are now 'hidden', because the *scribes*, as
well as the prophets, are hidden. Scribes are portrayed as the genuine
and *sole* interpreters of the prophets. This may be particularly
illuminating with regard to our understanding of the meturgeman,
whose own concern is precisely the interpretation of the prophets! In
contrast, it is interesting that both Mark (7.5ff.) and Matthew
(15.6ff.) report Jesus' use of this passage in *rebuke* of the *Pharisees
and scribes* who culpably 'hide' ('make void') the word of God. The
Gospel perspective is antagonistic to the Pharisaic scribes. But the
basic concept of the scribes as actually bearing the authority and
responsibility for scripture interpretation is common to both
traditions, as is the lament that the period of their reliability is
past.

Thus it seems, at least for the meturgeman of Isaiah, that scribes
are positively associated with prophets. If, therefore, he sees his own
role as scribal, his equations and associations of prophets with scribes
must be a further indication[60] of the proximity of the scribal and the
prophetic roles in his understanding (= possibility 2 above). We have
already seen that he is by no means alone in this.

Is it possible to be more precise as to the nature of the association
between prophets and scribes in the targums? It is stated quite
frequently in rabbinic literature that the spirit of prophecy ceased
with Haggai, Zechariah and Malachi, the 'last' of the prophets, and
that from then on responsibility for Israel's spiritual welfare was
assumed by the scribes or the sages.[61] From the mishnaic perspective,
in which the Law was perceived as superior to the prophets (who in
fact were concerned primarily with teaching the law), and in which

the custody of revelation was perceived as having been maintained in an unbroken line via the Mosaic tradition of the *sōferîm*, there was in any case no need for new 'revelation'; humanity's prime goal, and the very foundation of Judaism, was obedience to the Law as interpreted by the sages. This is reflected very clearly in the use of the word 'revelation' in rabbinic literature; it is almost exclusively used of the revelation to Moses on Sinai, and never of new revelation. This in striking contrast to both Qumran and the NT (cf. e.g. CD 3; 1QS 8; 1QH (*passim*); 1 Cor. 14.26ff.; Mt. 16.17). The *sōferîm* were thus the natural successors of the prophets and could be associated with them.

Since the prophets were long since gone, perhaps the meturgeman in interpreting them for his contemporaries considered it desirable to bring them more up to date. But then why did he not use the term 'sages' at these points, a term which his rabbinic colleagues[62] were using of themselves? The answer seems to lie in the tradition of the authority of the Soferim. From the early post-prophetic period onwards, סופרים typically designated the rightful successors of the prophets; hence authoritative interpreters, be they the classical Soferim or the authors of later interpretative material (such as the targums themselves), merit the label 'scribes'. The 'sages', meanwhile (as the NT silently attests), are generally post-70 rabbinic scholars whose authority is only derivative from the *sōferîm*. The targumists would not have made the equation *sōferîm* = *ḥakhāmîm* which we find in the talmudic *dibrê haḥakhāmîm*.[63]

We have hinted strongly above that the targumists may have understood their own role as that of the ספרא/סופר. The main indications of this are three. First, the correspondence between the role of the ספרא as interpreter of the law and the prophets and the role of the meturgeman as interpreter of the same. The underlying principle is identical, even though the medium is different. Second, the relative frequency of the term ספרא, like the frequency of γραμματεύς in the LXX. Third, the positive use of the term in the targums for Moses, Enoch, the prophets and other authoritative 'rulers'. As we shall see in Chapter 4, similar features attend the use of the word 'scribe' in apocalyptic literature whose authorship is undoubtedly 'scribal'. Jonathan ben Uzziel, author of the Prophets Targum according to *b. Meg.* 3a, is the nearest thing to an apocalyptic scribe in rabbinic literature; significantly, there is some criticism here of his 'revelation of secrets'. It may be significant, too, that the Prophets Targum is in *b. Meg.* 3a credited to the inspiration of Haggai, Zechariah and Malachi—the last of the inspired prophets in rabbinic tradition and *the direct predecessors of the 'Men of the Great Synagogue'* (the Soferim; *m. Aboth* 1.1). Here implicitly (though of course anachronistically) the meturgeman ('Jonathan ben Uzziel') is associated with the classical Soferim! In the targums we thus have a glimpse of a strong and longstanding tradition concerning the quasi-prophetic authority of the interpreting ספרא. It is a tradition which was certainly maintained in first-century Judaism and is thus of considerable relevance to the study of Matthew's scribes.

C. *Other sōferîm in Rabbinic Literature*

By far the majority of mishnaic and talmudic references to *sōferîm* occur in the formula *dibrê sōferîm* (see note 39 above); like the midrashic references to the *tiqqûnê sōferîm*,[64] these relate in all probability to the classical Soferim reputedly responsible for these halakhic and textual decisions, though the link is slightly less compelling with those responsible for the *tiqqûnê sōferîm*, who look rather pale in comparison with the more original thinkers who produced the Oral Law. However, some other references relate to *sōferîm* of other, more contemporary, generations, being apparently equated with the *ḥakhāmîm*, the sages of tannaitic and amoraic times.[65] Although some rabbis attempted other derivations,[66] the basic association is with books (ספרים), so that the סופר may be one who binds books,[67] but especially one who *writes* books—a scholar.[68] While there is a degree of correspondence between the mishnaic usage and that of earlier generations, the usage is much less homogeneous in Mishnah and Talmud (in distinction from the targums and some midrashim) and has to be treated with some reserve, particularly in view of the late date of the mishnaic formulation of the references. Indeed the palpable nostalgia of some for times when *sōferîm* held real esteem and eminence[69] is lent authenticity by this lack of homogeneity: not only has prophecy ceased, but genuine scribalism has also disappeared! This is, we shall argue, Matthew's concern too.

3. Philo and Josephus

Philo of Alexandria has only a single reference to a γραμματεύς (*Flacc.* 1.4), in the sense of a political adviser. Though Philo's art as an interpreter of scripture is undoubtedly scribal and of some general relevance to the background study of Matthew's Gospel, especially in his high regard for wisdom and Torah, the data are an insufficient basis for a discussion of his concept of the 'scribe' *per se*. In the context of our discussion of Moses as scribe (Chapter 4 section 1.B[4]) we shall, however, observe the overlap in his thinking between the scribal and the prophetic roles (Moses and the LXX translators, for example, are 'prophets').

Josephus uses the term rather more frequently (29 times). In the majority of cases (e.g. *Ant.* 7.110, 293, 319, 364) he follows the LXX in reference to biblical scribes. He occasionally supplements these by introducing them into his narrative, e.g. at 6.120 (cf. 1 Sam. 14.33), where they report to the king on the cultic impurity of the Israelite army. They also occur as high-ranking officials: Diophantus, a royal γραμματεύς with an acknowledged skill as a forger (*Wars* 1.529; *Ant.* 16.319), other royal scribes (e.g. *Ant.* 11.272, 287), temple scribes (e.g. *Ant.* 11.128; 12.142) and eminent persons including those mentioned in the books of Maccabees (*Wars* 5.532; *Ant.* 20.208f.). He reports, too, Chaeremon's description of Moses as scribe (*Ag. Ap.* 1.290). His usage thus does not depart significantly from that of the LXX, except that there is no hint of a delight in the usage that we find there and in the targums: there is no explicit evidence that Josephus consciously applies the term to himself. However, we must bear in mind that in Rome at least, γραμματεύς was becoming used in quite a humble sense,[70] so that contemporary usage may have discouraged his applying the ancient honorific title to himself; in fact, he aspires rather to a *prophetic* function (see below). It is worth noticing, as Neusner points out,[71] that Josephus, a self-confessed Pharisee, never uses the term γραμματεύς of a Pharisee and never associates Pharisees with the 'scribes' he mentions. For Josephus, evidently, 'Pharisees' are a sect, while scribalism is a profession (*ibid.*, p. 269). Matthew also makes such a distinction (though for Matthew the term 'vocation' might be more appropriate than 'profession').

As a concession to his Gentile readership, one assumes, Josephus makes use of the terms ἱερογραμματεύς and ἐξηγητής where one

60   *The Understanding Scribe*

might have expected to read γραμματεύς. ἱερογραμματεύς is used almost exclusively in connection with Egypt: in *Ant*. 2.205, 209, 234 it refers to a high-ranking Egyptian who predicts the birth of Moses (by divination); 2.205 explains that the ἱερογραμματεῖς are 'persons with considerable skill in predicting the future'. These diviners are also political advisers: in *Ant*. 2.255 they incite Pharaoh to murder Moses, and in *Ag. Ap*. 1.289 Phritobautes (or Phritiphantes) the ἱερογραμματεύς tells the king what to do. They also, however, have Hebrew counterparts: *Ant*. 2.243 speaks of the ἱερογραμματεῖς of 'both nations' (Egyptian and Hebrew) as leaders having political concerns; and in *Ag. Ap*. 1.290 Moses as γραμματεύς and Joseph as ἱερογραμματεύς are the adversaries of Phritobautes. The latter situation is taken from Chaeremon, whose record Josephus is criticizing, but the use of the term is *not* criticized; indeed it accords both with *Ant*. 2.243 and the other, non-Egyptian mention of ἱερογραμματεῖς in *Wars* 6.291, who correctly interpret the portents presaging the destruction of the temple.

High rank, correct interpretation of omens and prediction here characterize the ἱερογραμματεύς. The word in this sense adequately reflects the Old Testament's depiction of Joseph as an interpreter of dreams, predictor of the future and high-ranking official in Egypt. It also corresponds of course to ancient Near Eastern usage in general (cf. the beginning of this chapter and on Daniel as scribe, below). In view of the proximity of the sense of the word to prophecy, in which Josephus is very interested (ca 370 mentions of prophets/prophecy!), and to which he aspires,[72] Josephus may himself have more sympathy for the title—particularly as it involves custody of and training in sacred literature—than for the wider and now less prestigious term γραμματεύς; but he does not expressly apply it to himself.

In *Ant*. 17.149, 214, 216 he uses the term ἐξηγῆται (τῶν [πατριῶν] νόμων)—interpreters (of the laws [of the fathers]) (also however called σοφισταί, 'sages'), to describe Judas and Matthias, eminent teachers and experts, whose concern is with obedience to the Law, and who forfeit their lives in attempting to correct Herod. ἐξηγητής here appears to be more a description of a function than a title, a function corresponding to that of the דורש התורה whom we find at Qumran. Again, Josephus does not apply the term directly to himself.

Josephus does, however, claim to be regarded by his compatriots as 'a *wise man* who is fully acquainted with our laws, and is able to interpret their meaning; on which account, as there have been many who have done their endeavours with great patience to obtain this learning, there have yet hardly been so many as two or three that have succeeded therein' (*Ant.* 20.264). For Josephus those who are experts in and interpreters of the law are those given wisdom by God and may be called 'wise' (σοφός)—so, Ezra (*Ant.* 11.129) when he appoints judges (and scribes) who know and will teach the law (cf. *Ant.* 18.82; 20.264). He is very sparing in his use of σοφός, while the rabbinic scholars with whom he disagrees are merely σοφισταί. Thus Josephus is interesting as one who, like many another eminent scribe, associates his role with that of the 'wise men'. His usage should not lead us to conclude that his own role is not that of the eminent *sôfēr/grammateus*; on the contrary, as 'prophetic' and 'wise', he certainly aspires to the status of the inspired scribe[73] whom we find in the Chronicler and Ben Sira, for example.

This said, Josephus's actual presentation of the scribe is multi-faceted, and it may be a false procedure to use both this and his *own* office and role to inform our picture of first-century concepts of the scribe. However, Josephus certainly *is* a scribe of a high order and an appropriate use of this insight would be—in another context—to examine his work from this perspective. Here, however, we conclude our brief review of 'scribal' literature in the broad sense and move to an examination of literature that specifically honours the role of the *grammateus* and the *sôfēr*.

PART II

THE 'APOCALYPTIC' SCRIBE

Chapter 3

BEN SIRA AND THE MODEL SCRIBE

1. **Ben Sira's Ideal Scribe**

The Wisdom of Jesus Ben Sira is a crucial source for knowledge of
the scribal profession in Palestine. But our comments here must
remain brief. Ben Sira's concept of the scribe is not a controversial
area of scholarly debate—unlike the matter of his position with
respect to Hellenism and the matter of his religio-political colours;
being quite explicit in the text, it is a relatively straightforward
matter. Furthermore, this has been the subject of an important
recent monograph to which, in this context, we have little by way of
correction to add: H. Stadelmann's *Ben Sira als Schriftgelehrter*.[1]
One of our prime concerns throughout this study is to help plug
some of the more desperate gaps in previous study of the scribes.
However, Ben Sira may be highly relevant in our search for the
background to Matthew's concept of the scribe, and his work clearly
merits at least a brief discussion of its own in the present context.[2]
We shall have reason in subsequent chapters to return to the book.

Most scholars treating the concept of the scribe in Judaism rely
heavily on Ben Sira for their picture of the Jewish scribe. This is
entirely appropriate for the Second Temple period in which he wrote;
furthermore, his work may well have been assumed reading for later
scholars in many Jewish schools (though evidently not all, since some
actually banned his work).[3] He can also inform us to some extent
about previous generations of scribes:[4] his anti-hellenistic critique[5] is
but one aspect of his conservatism, and the Wisdom of Jesus ben Sira
gives every indication of standing squarely within an established
scribal tradition, in its historical awareness, its regard for moderation
and the preservation of long-cherished moral and religious values,
and in its use of traditional literary forms. However, we shall see that

Ben Sira's ideal scribe is no mere conservative scholar; rather, he is original and creative, even 'prophetic', to use the author's own terminology.

In a work so shot through with autobiographical reflections it is not always easy to keep separate the portrayal of the scribal office on the one hand and of its exercise by the illustrious author himself on the other. Our distinction between the two can only be loose. Nor would we expect Ben Sira's depiction to be an objective one: the author's standing in society is probably only exceeded by his aspirations (cf. e.g. 39.9ff.; or the autobiographical colophon to the Praise of the Fathers, 50.27). But an explicit depiction of the scribe *per se* we do have; and it is the fullest we possess in all Jewish literature.

Sir. 38.24–39.11, to which the opening phrase 'the wisdom of the scribe' (σοφία γραμματέως/חכמת סופר) is effectively a title, turns on a contrast between the social roles of skilled tradesmen on the one hand and the scribe on the other. Unlike the less sensitive, indeed satirical, piece on which it may be based, the work of the Egyptian scribe Douaf,[6] there is no evidence of crass intellectual snobbery in this passage. But the contrast is nonetheless emphatically made in 38.33:

> Yet they [the artisans] are not sought out for the council of the people
> nor do they attain eminence in the public assembly.
> They do not sit in the judge's seat,
> nor do they understand the sentence of judgment;
> They cannot expound discipline or judgment,
> and they shall not be found using proverbs (ἐν παραβολαῖς οὐχ εὑρεθήσονται).

The clear implication of the contrast is that the scribe *does* fulfil this eminent role in society: he is an expert in legal matters and is thus in demand as an authority in the ἐκκλησία and in the courts. But already in this verse the scribe's *own* preoccupations are plain, over and above his acknowledgment of his social ranking with respect to other professions: his concern is to 'become wise' (38.24), hence he must 'understand', be able to 'expound' and be adept in the use of παραβολαί. These skills are the heart of the scribe's occupation and are more fully brought out in 39.1-11. It may be useful here to quote this passage in full.

(1)   On the other hand he who devotes himself to the study of
the law of the Most High
will seek out the wisdom of all the ancients,
and will be concerned with prophecies;

(2)   he will preserve the discourse of notable men
and penetrate the subtleties of parables;

(3)   he will seek out the hidden meanings of proverbs
and be at home with the obscurities of parables.

(4)   He will serve among great men
and appear before rulers;
he will travel through the lands of foreign nations,
for he tests the good and the evil among men.

(5)   He will set his heart to rise early to seek the Lord who made
him,
and will make supplication before the Most High;
he will open his mouth in prayer and make supplication for
his sins.

(6)   If the great Lord is willing,
he will be filled with the spirit of understanding;
he will pour forth words of wisdom
and give thanks to the Lord in prayer.

(7)   He will direct his counsel and knowledge aright,
and meditate on his secrets,

(8)   He will reveal instruction in his teaching,
and will glory in the law of the Lord's covenant.

(9)   Many will praise his understanding,
and it will never be blotted out;
his memory will not disappear,
and his name will live through all generations.

(10)   Nations will declare his wisdom,
and the congregation will proclaim his praise;

(11)   if he lives long, he will leave a name greater than a
thousand
and if he goes to rest, it is enough for him.

The key term here is *'understanding'*. The word itself (σύνεσις)
occurs as the prime faculty extolled in the climactic v. 6, and it is for
this that the scribe will be remembered (v. 9). But also a whole series
of verbs in the passage indicates the scribe's fervent search for
understanding: διανοουμένου (38.34c/39.1), ἐκζητήσει (39.1),
συνεισελεύσεται (v. 2), ἐκζητήσει (v. 3), (τὴν καρδίαν αὐτοῦ)
ἐπιδώσει ὀρθρίσαι (πρὸς Κύριον) (v. 5), διανοηθήσεται (v. 7); and

the nouns show the difficulty of his subject-matter: 'the law of the Most High' (38.34c), 'the wisdom of all the ancients' (v. 1), 'prophecies' (v. 1), 'the discourse of notable men' (v. 2), 'the subtleties of parables' (στροφαῖς παραβολῶν, v. 2), 'the hidden meanings of proverbs' (ἀπόκρυφα παροιμιῶν, v. 3), 'the obscurities of parables' (αἰνίγμασι παραβολῶν, v. 3), 'his [the Lord's] counsel, knowledge and secrets (ἀποκρύφοις)' (v. 7), 'the law of the Lord's covenant' (v. 8). All this (cf. again 38.33) serves to emphasize that the scribe's occupation is with understanding matters, especially religious ones, that are in some way 'hidden' from others. He is a professional 'understander'. As a result, he naturally enjoys a high social reputation (vv. 4,[7] 9ff.); but this is deserved, because not only does he have an important social role during his own lifetime (e.g. in the courts and in politics) but he is also a teacher whose authoritative pronouncements will continue to carry weight long after his death. In all these respects, he closely resembles the scribes we have called above the 'classical Soferim'—who indeed must have been his immediate predecessors—whose prime task was 'to help the people to understand'.

As the catalogue of scribal concerns indicates, the 'parable' in its various forms is the special focus of the scribe's intellectual energies. Wise sayings, proverbs, riddles, prophecies, and parables of all kinds are deemed to have *hidden* meanings that require to be dug out. *The scribe's prime task is to understand parables.*

An almost incidental quality of the scribe is his exemplary piety (vv. 5, 6b, 8b), which is clearly part and parcel of his occupation with scripture. It is almost taken for granted that the scribe is a 'righteous man'. Here one is reminded particularly of the near contemporary depiction of Daniel as such a one (cf. Dan. 6.10f.; 9.3ff.), and of the hymns of the Essene Teacher of Righteousness; both of them bear many scribal features (see especially Chapters 4 and 5). Wisdom and righteousness are two sides of the same coin in much wisdom-influenced Jewish literature; and Ben Sira is the first writer who clearly identifies Wisdom and Torah. The expert interpreter of the law and the wise man, similarly, are united in his picture of the *scribe*. This is but one of many respects in which Ben Sira's concept of the scribe finds echoes throughout apocalyptic literature (cf. e.g. Dan. 12.3).

Verses 6ff. indicate the results of the scribe's understanding.

We shall frequently have occasion to refer to affinities between Ben Sira and Qumran literature, and will have especial cause to do so when we discuss the latter in Chapter 5. Such reference can hardly be avoided when the topic is inspiration and prophetic self-understanding—a matter of great concern to both. Here the two literatures can be mutually highly illuminating. The connection between 'inspired' righteous teaching and prayer and thanksgiving is frequently made in Qumran literature. The Teacher of Righteousness virtually epitomizes the scribe as defined in Sir. 39.6-8:

> I thank Thee, I thank Thee!

> What am I, that Thou shouldst [teach] me
> > the counsel of Thy truth,
> and give me understanding
> > of Thy marvellous works;
> that Thou shouldst lay hymns of thanksgiving within my mouth
> > and praise upon my tongue,
> and that of my circumcised lips
> > (Thou shouldst make) a seat of rejoicing?

> I will sing Thy mercies,
> > and on Thy might I will meditate all day long.
> I will bless Thy Name evermore.
> I will declare Thy glory in the midst of the sons of men
> > and my soul shall delight in Thy great goodness (1QH 11).

Stadelmann (p. 184) criticizes Maier's[8] comparison of Ben Sira with Qumran and apocalyptic literature, claiming that in the latter, revelation succeeds prayer while in our passage in Sirach, the sequence is the reverse. But the comparison is entirely justified. In fact the 1QH 11 passage agrees with Sirach's order. Repeatedly, the Teacher of Righteousness 'recounts' God's wonders and 'gives thanks' on the *basis of his special insight* (cf. e.g. 1QH 7 [*bis*]); indeed the typical pattern of the Thanksgiving Hymns is to thank God, lyrically, precisely for the already granted special revelation. Not only is this order borne out in several passages in Sirach (e.g. 15.9f.; ch. 51), but it is also a feature of the saying preserved in Q (Mt. 11.25-27 // Lk. 10.21-22) which, as has often been noted, bears striking resemblances to Sirach 51. We shall argue below that the Teacher of Righteousness is best understood as scribe in the elevated sense here expressed in Sirach. As we shall see, some of the 'Q' and special Matthean sayings in Matthew's Gospel (e.g. 11.25ff.; 13.52) exhibit identical features and look *scribal* in the same sense.

It is further noticeable that the scribe here functions exactly as does the Maskil at Qumran in 'preserving' received teaching (συντηρήσει, 39.2) and in testing the understanding of others (ἐπείρασεν, 39.4b). Attention will be given to these and other links in Chapter 5.

To return to Sir. 39.1-11, it is notable, as the RSV indicates by its division of the text at this point, and as Stadelmann argues at length, that a distinction is drawn between the scribe in vv. 1-5 and the scribe in vv. 6ff. 'If the great Lord is willing, he will be filled with the spirit of understanding . . . ' (v. 6a,b). Perhaps (contra Stadelmann) Ben Sira is talking of the same person in both sections; but the implication is that generally speaking, the scribe is *not* 'filled with the spirit of understanding': only the exceptional scribe, or the scribe on exceptional occasions, in any case the *ideal* scribe, enjoys this kind of inspiration.

Inspiration is certainly in view here: when filled with this spirit, the scribe 'pours forth' wisdom and 'gives thanks to the Lord in prayer'. Following verses leave no doubt that this is autobiographical (cf. 39.12ff.) (see section 2 below); but it is specifically and fully associated with his role as *sôfēr*. In view here is special insight that is given to the eminent, righteous scribe—'revelation', one might call it (cf. already ἐκφαίνει in v. 8) for the benefit of others: it is 'prophetic' or 'apocalyptic' in this sense. We shall see in Chapters 4 and 5 that this feature recurs with some regularity in apocalyptic literature with reference to other scribes. And at Qumran, the phrase 'spirit of understanding' *itself* occurs in a strikingly similar context (the 'prophetic' 'inspiration' of a *sôfēr*) (cf. 11QPsᵃDavComp—discussed in Chapter 5, below). Since portions of Sirach are represented among the finds at Qumran and Masada it may be that the striking affinities between the two representations of the scribe here are by no means coincidental,[9] though direct literary dependence is not finally demonstrable. But it would be wrong to suppose that the notion of the prophetically inspired scribe was restricted to Sirach and Qumran: our next chapter will draw deserved attention to some of the wealth of other intertestamental literature that paints a similar picture.

The passage under discussion, which relates explicitly to the *sôfēr*, is a sufficient basis for a graphic view of Ben Sira's ideal scribe; but there is clearly an overlap between the 'scribe' and the 'wise man' in Sirach, so that some brief mention should be made of other texts in a similar vein which concern those whose business is wisdom and correspond in general and in matters of detail to the picture of the scribe expounded in 38.24–39.11. Compare, for example, 6.34-37; 8.8f.; 9.15-17; 10.1-5—here the 'person of the scribe' (προσώπῳ γραμματέως, v. 5) is identified as a 'wise magistrate', an 'understanding man' (v. 1) and a ruler with 'understanding' (σύνεσις, v. 3); 14.20f.; 15.9f.; 18.29; 21.13, 15, 17; 24.23-27, 32-34; 32.15; 33.3; 34.9-11; 37.23-26. Similar scribal qualities are praised in chs. 44-50, of the 'famous men' who were

> leaders of the people in their deliberations
>> and in understanding of learning for the people,
> wise in their words of instruction;
> those who composed musical tunes,
>> and set forth verses in writing.
> Peoples will declare their wisdom
>> and the congregation proclaims their praise (44.3-5, 15).

These words would be equally at home in the picture of the ideal scribe in 39.1-11. Ben Sira himself is faithfully and unmistakably mirrored in them. Though not all the worthies listed may be most appropriately designated as scribes (several of them are prophets, others patriarchs and kings), nonetheless various scribal functions shine through in Moses (45.5), Aaron (45.17), David (47.8) and especially Solomon (47.14-17) (contrast Rehoboam, v. 23). It is of course notorious that Ezra is conspicuously absent from the list. And it is indeed intriguing that the founding Scribe of Second Temple Judaism—according to our books of Ezra and Nehemiah—is passed over in silence by his professional heir. However, there are various possible explanations for this omission, and I do not propose to add to them here. In any case Ben Sira's sympathies apparently lie rather with Nehemiah, whom many scholars now regard as more significant a figure for Israel than the *historical* Ezra. Of interest, however, is the double mention of Enoch (44.16; 49.14), in view of the contemporary apocalyptic preoccupation with Enoch as scribe. The oddly cryptic mentions of Joseph, and especially Shem, Seth and Adam, alongside Enoch in the second context (49.14-16) are suggestive of some esoteric *sous-entendre* that may have been intelligible to certain scribes.

2. **Ben Sira as Scribe**

Ben Sira's catalogue of famous men concludes, as we have mentioned, with an autobiographical note:

> Instruction in understanding and knowledge
>   I have written in this book,
> Jesus the son of Sirach, son of Eleazar, of Jerusalem,
>   who out of his heart poured forth wisdom (50.27).

By his (unusual)[10] signature (however the textual problem here is resolved), Ben Sira clearly hopes—highly successfully, as it turns out—that 'Many will praise his understanding, his memory will not disappear, and his name will live through all generations' (39.9; cf. v. 10). An echo of the previous verses also reverberates here: 'He will reveal instruction in his teaching' (39.8) and 'he will pour forth words of wisdom' (39.6) '. . . and give thanks to the Lord in prayer' (39.6; cf. ch. 51!). The earlier autobiographical note in 34.9ff., where key terms are travel and understanding, is clearly reflected in the passage concerning the scribe (cf. 39.4, 6, 9, etc.), and it hardly requires demonstration that Ben Sira himself corresponds to functions of the scribe detailed in 39.1-5. The whole book shows this. But it is also clear that Ben Sira regards himself in the terms of vv. 6-11: the use of the first person singular in 39.12 makes this quite plain—'I have yet more to say, which I have thought upon, and I am filled, like the moon at the full' (cf. again 1QH 11). Ben Sira regards himself as an inspired scribe. As a record of his wisdom, the book itself thus purports, by implication, to be inspired; certainly it is a self-conscious piece of writing (50.27; cf. 44.5). The written word is his main medium by which to leave his wisdom to posterity, and as a polished work of literature it speaks for itself as a testimony to his scribal art and artistry.

In view of the connections between scribes and prophecy that we noted in some of the OT (and targumic) literature discussed above (Chapter 2) it is very interesting that Ben Sira appears to regard his inspired scribal activity in a prophetic light. This topic is given a full and important treatment by Stadelmann in his third chapter ('Prophetentum und Schriftgelehrsamkeit bei Ben Sira' [pp. 177-270]), to which the reader is referred.[11]

It has long been noticed that Ben Sira uses a variety of prophetic forms. W. Baumgartner[12] noted, for example, the 'announcement of judgment' (32.22-26), the 'prophetic invective and threat' introduced by a 'woe' (2.12ff.; 41.8), the references to God's faithfulness in the past (2.10; 16.7-10). He saw these as *imitations* of prophecy rather than the genuine article. But, as Stadelmann correctly recognizes, the 'ganz eigenartige Vermischung zwischen Prophetie und Weisheit' which Baumgartner notices in the forms Ben Sira uses is not merely superficial, as Baumgartner supposes, but is a feature of the prophetic self-consciousness that pervades the book at a deeper level. The notion of inspiration (e.g. in 39.6ff.) is surely no mere 'imitation' of the prophetic, nor is this at all suggested by the mention of the scribe's preoccupation with prophecies in 39.1.

The suggestion that the Hebrew underlying the verb in 50.27c cited above was ניבא (prophesied) rather than ניבע (poured forth) cannot be demonstrated.[13] But the notion of 'pouring forth' wise sayings is in any case at least quasi-prophetic, for in another autobiographical reflection in 24.32f., Ben Sira announces in the name of Wisdom:

> I will again make instruction shine forth like the dawn,
>> and I will make it shine afar;
> I will again pour out teaching like prophecy,
>> and leave it to all future generations.

The Syriac reads '*in* prophecy' here: if this is the more original reading, we have to do with much more than a comparison—the prophetic aspirations go beyond the simple attempted emulation of prophecy, and the inspiration is seen *to be* prophetic. But even if the Syriac version does not reflect the original reading, the verse remains crucial for an understanding of Ben Sira's consciousness of his role, since it still directly compares it (ὡς) to the prophetic. Further evidence of Ben Sira's interest in the prophetic vocation is found in other parts of the book—the 'Praise of the Fathers', for example, details many of the prophets, emphasizing their prophetic contributions, evidently as models for the scribe, as well as honouring men 'giving counsel by their understanding [= the scribal role expounded throughout the book] and proclaiming prophecies' in his encomiastic introduction to the section (44.3; cf. v. 4).

Again the question of the relationship between prophecy and scribalism arises—in this case: In what sense can the role of Ben Sira as scribe be described as 'prophetic'? Is it simply that the scribe makes capital of the fact that the prophets have become extinct, using an appeal to prophetic authority as a means of bolstering his own, perhaps in the interest of a polemic against the incursions of Hellenism?[14] Or is he simply interested in them as the authors of the prophecies with whose interpretation he is occupied (39.1; cf. 36.15f.)? Or does he genuinely see his role in Israel's society as of the same order as that of the prophets? If so, in what respects—political, professional, or perhaps exercising a similar charismatic inspiration?

As Stadelmann correctly acknowledges, the key passages are 39.6ff. and 24.30ff. And there, as we have already noted, the notion of the (prophetic) *inspiration* of the scribe is quite explicit. Like the apocalypticists, Ben Sira appropriates the terminology of prophecy to describe an experience of a scribe's special inspiration. It is instructive here again to draw attention to a quite remarkable parallel between Ben Sira and the Teacher of Righteousness, precisely at the point of their self-understanding as prophetic teachers. The passage Sir. 24.30-33 is so closely mirrored in 1QH 8 that a common source, if not a direct dependence, must be considered likely. In the latter the imagery is more fully developed, though the language is at many points almost identical. Absolutely identical, however, is the assertion, by means of this imagery, of prophetic inspiration in the Scribe's/Teacher's teaching. The Qumran passage reaches its climax with:

> But Thou, O my God, hast put into my mouth
>   as it were rain for all [those who thirst]
> and a fount of living waters which shall not fail.
> When they are opened they shall not run dry;
> they shall be a torrent [overflowing its banks]
>   and like the [bottom]less seas.
> They shall suddenly gush forth
>   which were hidden in secret . . .

Perhaps genuine OT prophecy is different from scribal inspiration in intensity rather than in kind, as Hengel suggests.[15] It should in any case be remembered that special inspiration, revelation, divination, prophecy, whatever the precise terminology used in particular instances, is a feature of the scribe's art throughout the ancient Near East. To judge from the proviso 'if' in 39.6, not all scribes of Ben Sira's day could lay claim to this gift—certainly not all at one time— but nonetheless it is a thoroughly *scribal* phenomenon. The ease with which the targums replace 'prophet' with 'scribe', the 'prophetic' aspirations of Josephus, possibly the Chronicler, and, as we shall see, evidently those of the apocalypticists and the Qumran teacher(s), are among the many independent pieces of evidence that the scribe-prophet connection was naturally made in Judaism—over a long period. A prime reason for the ease with which the connection was made seems to be the common factor of *inspiration*.

It is in the moment of inspiration indicated by Sir. 39.6 that the eminent scribe fulfils his potential and his vocation. In his full-time occupation (cf. 38.24) with the scriptures and with other wisdom, the scribe has schooled his wisdom, and has eventually *understood* parables, prophecies, and the like (cf. e.g. 8.8f.). So far this reflects the level of achievement portrayed in 39.1-5. But then, on the basis of the understanding already achieved—and presumably this is fully bound up with concentration on interpreting the secrets of the scriptures—the ideal scribe according to Ben Sira is *given special insight*, a 'spirit of understanding'. This new inspiration prompts a prophetic or quasi-prophetic role in which the scribe becomes highly creative, as the author of authoritative teaching (cf. 24.33) and as an inspired source of wisdom, expressed in poetic praise as well as in teaching, oral and written. It is thus on a phenomenological level that we see the roles of scribe and prophet overlapping. The ideal scribe is not a mere epigone of the prophet; in entering in to the hidden wisdom expressed by the prophets, he empathizes with their inspiration to such a degree that in the end he shares it. In the end, in fact, the scribe—especially in an age of eschatological fervour—as interpreter of the prophets is actually superior to them, in the sense that he understands what they did not (cf. the 'wise' of Dan. 12.8-10 compared with Daniel; the Teacher of Righteousness [1QpHab 2, 7] and the disciples of Jesus [Mt. 13.17] compared with the prophets).

We shall see in Part III how the concept of the idealized scribe with special understanding recurs significantly in Matthew's Gospel. However, we must first turn our attention to an extensive area of study which offers an important source of much-neglected information relevant to the background of Matthew's concept of the insightful scribe: the literature more usually acknowledged as 'apocalyptic'.

Chapter 4

SCRIBES IN APOCALYPTIC LITERATURE[1]

It cannot be without reason that the role played by 'scribes' in the apocalyptic literature is uniformly a central one. Since most of the seers of apocalypses are pseudonymously characterized as eminent 'scribes' of Jewish antiquity, rather than strictly as prophets, priests or kings, there is clearly some significant factor inherent in the standing of 'scribes' that marks so many of them out as suitable recipients of direct divine revelation. In addition there may be grounds for supposing that the glorification of the scribe has a discernible *Sitz im Leben*: namely in a social struggle for dominance between two parties, at least one of which is a scribal party. This in any case is the kind of setting often postulated for the rise of apocalypticism itself.[2] We shall therefore consider the role of the 'scribe' in the framework of the apocalyptic literature, before we, secondly, attempt an analysis of the ('scribal') authorship of the material.

1. **Eminent Scribes in Apocalyptic Literature**

A. *Enoch as Scribe*[3]

(1) *Jubilees and the Earlier Enoch Literature*

The traditions concerning the figure of Enoch, some of them very ancient,[4] kept alive and developed most extensively in apocalyptic circles, are most important in regard to a special use of the term 'scribe'. For the figure of Enoch himself, in later traditions associated and even equated with the 'Elect One', the 'Son of Man' and other heavenly figures such as Metatron, is primarily referred to in the early traditions as 'scribe'.

The simple title[5] 'scribe' appears at *1 Enoch* 12.3 and 92.1 (probable reading) and 'scribe of righteousness' at 12.4, 15.1 (and frequently in later Enoch literature), with the title ספר פרשא prevailing in the Aramaic Enoch fragments (see below).[6] The fragments of the Book of Giants found in Cave 4 at Qumran and published by Milik[7] prove the antiquity of this term as employed in *Ethiopic (1) Enoch* and the later Enochic writings. Furthermore, the application of the title to Enoch in the Targum Ps.-Jonathan[8] to Gen. 5.24 may indicate that this idea is unlikely to have been confined to 'sectarian' spheres of speculation but was in all probability a well-established and widespread idea over a long period, including the first century.

In what sense is Enoch, the recipient and mediator of divine revelations, a 'scribe'? It is not immediately obvious why Enoch was *originally* given this title. Certainly, it fits broadly with his 'scribal' role in heaven: his recording of human deeds in preparation for God's judgment. (It is probably this function that gave rise to *Metatron's* title 'Great Scribe'; see below.)[9] It also fits, and certainly more obviously so, with his authorship of many books (such is the ascription in *Chronicles of Jerahmeel* 26.20[10]). It agrees, too, with his role as 'teacher'. It is very likely that in time, Enoch's scribal title was seen to be worked out in all these functions and may even account for some of them. However, as we shall see, like the biblical Ezra's title and that of the biblical Baruch, Enoch's scribal title seems to be *presupposed* before his special functions are related. From *1 Enoch* 12.3f. and 15.1 it also seems to be an honorific title applied to one who is far more than 'literate': Enoch was *inspired* to write down what was revealed to him through his special insight. And like those of the apocalyptic Ezra and Baruch, the books he writes are divinely appointed (even dictated) 'scriptures'. Our contention will be, therefore, that in the literary apocalyptic context the scribe epithet is always related to the eminent, spiritual and charismatic role of the figure, as the *recipient and mediator of divine revelations*. In other words his scribal role entails above all the exercise of a special gift of understanding for the benefit of others; moreover, this is by far the most dominant facet of his scribal qualities and functions.

It is true, of course, that Enoch is credited with expertise in writing, and this is indeed an important, even indispensable, part of his function as a scribe. However, in the case of Enoch, as in other telling cases we have investigated in Chapters 2 and 3 above, the title 'scribe' carries a far fuller and more significant import than the designation of 'copyist' or even 'author'.

The following passage from *Jubilees* contains an early[11] and quite comprehensive indication of the sense of the term 'scribe' as it was applied to Enoch, though *Jubilees* itself does not use the term. (My italics draw attention to the various aspects of Enoch's work of which the majority, as we shall see, are entirely characteristic of the various eminent 'scribes' throughout the apocalyptic literature.)

> Enoch was the first among men that are born on earth who *learnt writing and knowledge and wisdom* and who *wrote down the signs of heaven* according to the order of their months in a book, *that men might know* the seasons of the years according to the order of the separate months. And he was the *first to write a testimony*, and he *testified to the sons of men* among the generations of the earth, and *recounted the weeks* of the jubilees, and *made known to them* the days of the years, and *set in order* the months and *recounted the Sabbaths* of the years *as we made (them) known to him*. And *what was and what will be he saw in a vision* of his sleep, as it will happen to the children of men throughout their generations until the day of judgment; he *saw and understood everything*, and *wrote his testimony*,[12] and *placed the testimony on earth for all the children of men and for their generations* (*Jub.* 4.17-19).

It is clear from this picture that writing alone does not adequately characterize his activity. First of all he *learns* writing and knowledge and wisdom before he writes anything, and when he does write, it is to record and recount astronomical, calendrical and eschatological data that have first been revealed to him 'so that men might know'. Verse 19 conveniently summarizes his activity: he has visionary insight and his writing is a medium for the communication of the resulting revelations for the instruction of further generations.

The passage continues as follows:

> (20) And in the twelfth jubilee, in the seventh week thereof, he took to himself a wife, and her name was Ednî, the daughter of Dânêl, the daughter of his father's brother, and in the sixth year in this week she bare him a son and he called his name Methuselah. (21) And he was moreover with the angels of God there six jubilees of

years, and *they showed him everything* which is on earth and in the
heavens, the rule of the sun, *and he wrote down everything*. (22)
And he *testified to the Watchers* who had sinned with the daughters
of men, and Enoch *testified against* (them) all. (23) And he was
taken from amongst the children of men, and we conducted him
into the Garden of Eden in majesty and honour, and behold *there
he writes down the condemnation and judgment of the world*, and all
the wickedness of the children of men. (24) And on account of it
(God) brought the waters of the flood upon all the land of Eden; for
there he was set as a sign and that he should *testify against all the
children of men*, that he should *recount all the deeds of the
generations* until the day of condemnation. (25) And he burnt the
incense of the sanctuary, (even) sweet spices acceptable before the
Lord on the Mount.

The passage reiterates the process of heavenly (angelic) revelation
preceding committal to writing. Then the new information given
here includes, first of all, the claim that Enoch is closely related to
that other eminent wise man of prehistory, Dan'el (v. 20); secondly,
that after his exaltation (v. 23) he assumed the role of heavenly
recorder; and thirdly, the indication that he has a *priestly* role (v. 26),
a trait that is held in common with other eminent scribes.[13] It is
generally accepted that *Jub.* 4.17-19, cited above, draws on earlier
traditions of Enoch the scribe found in *1 Enoch* (the Book of
Watchers, the Astronomical Book, the Book of Dreams, and possibly
the Epistle of Enoch). The statements about Enoch's work *after* his
translation to heaven (including *Jub.* 4.23-26), however, are not
based on *1 Enoch* and appear to represent a new development in the
tradition (possibly dependent on other sources). Thus they present a
picture of Enoch that goes beyond his original role as 'scribe'. In the
case of the role as heavenly recorder, the origin should probably be
sought in similar ideas expressed elsewhere in ancient Near Eastern
mythology, which recur also in later apocalyptic material.[14] This is
not to say, of course, that the new functions necessarily have no
application as a backdrop to NT ideas, since they still predate the
New Testament by two centuries, but we need to recognize that the
heavenly scribe idea is an expansion on what the early authors of the
'books' of Enoch saw as Enoch's role.

It should be mentioned that a further 'scribal' function is accorded
Enoch in *Jubilees*, namely as an author of particular halakhoth (*Jub.*
7.38f.; 21.10). Noah, too, is credited with the creation of such rulings;

VanderKam[15] notes that 'The two men who walked with God have, it seems, assumed in some traditions the function of instructing others exactly how to do the same'. It is the task of the 'righteous man' to instruct others in righteousness; it is also typically the task of the 'scribe of righteousness' (see below).[16] But no mention is made of the 'scribe' title in connection with these rulings.

In the early parts of *1 Enoch*[17] on which the book of *Jubilees* depends, Enoch is first referred to (1.2) as 'a righteous man whose eyes were opened by God' (cf. Num. 24.3f., 15f.); as such, he 'saw the vision of the Holy One in the heavens, which the angels showed me, and from them I understood as I saw, but not for this generation, but a remote one which is for to come' (cf. Num. 24.17).

This characterizes Enoch immediately as the elect recipient of divine revelations, mediated by him (in writing) to a particular group of spiritual descendants living in a significant future period (clearly the eschatological period in which the author sees himself). The epithet 'scribe' is not used at this point, but already here the content of Enoch's role is clear, even before the specific mention of his actual writing down of the revelations. When the title or appellation 'scribe' first appears in 12.3f. it must relate to the earlier statement that he 'understood for a remote generation' (1.2) (unless it depends on a still earlier tradition of Enoch no longer preserved).[18] It is, of course, understood that the revelations to a 'remote' generation (i.e. that of the apocalyptic writer) have been mediated in writing, but the writing itself does not appear to be the only or even the principal basis for the use of the epithet 'scribe'. He is a mediator of revealed knowledge; in the terms of *1 Enoch* 1.2 his role is to *understand for* the eschatological generation; and this, in the framework of *1 Enoch*, is the background to the use of the term 'scribe'.[19]

Indeed, after the 'blessing' in 1.1 (cf. Deut. 33.1), what is said of Enoch in the introductory chs. 1–5,[20] is related exclusively to his reception and mediation of divine (or angelic) revelations. In its language and form, the passage is highly reminiscent of the Balaam narrative, Numbers 23f., on which it may well be consciously modelled.[21] The Book of Watchers (BW) calls Enoch 'scribe', but it is plain that he is seen to stand in (or at the head of) the spiritual tradition of the ancient *seers and prophets*.[22]

Enoch is called 'scribe' in BW not simply because he is able to write and functions as a clerk, or a copyist, or even as an author;[23]

rather, he is chosen to write down the revelations given him for his posterity because he is a scribe in the respected, authoritative sense. Like Ben Sira's model, he is one who 'understands' (cf. *Jub.* 4.19; *1 Enoch* 1.2; 14.2f.; 81.2 etc.), and can interpret and mediate divine communications, an inspired visionary.

After all, even strictly in his function as writer or copyist, this scribe writes down nothing but what has been revealed to him. He is not a clerk or recorder of administrative or other data, but a mediator of revealed mysteries. 'Scribe', in Enoch's case, is an appropriate appellation[24] for what is in modern terms (and *only* in modern terms) usually called an 'apocalypticist': one who mediates revealed mysteries in writing.

According to Dexinger, the emphasis on the scribal role of Enoch reflects the self-understanding of the apocalyptic author:

> Der anscheinend so nebensächlich wirkende Titel Henochs, 'der Schreiber',[25] gibt einen tiefen Einblick in die Vorstellung, die man sich von dieser Gestalt machte; vielleicht muß man richtiger sagen, daß die Konzeption Henochs eigentlich das Selbstverständnis des hinter diesem Text stehenden pseudonymen Autors reflektiert (p. 149).

This is a reasonable assumption, and if accurate, we have here a further indication of the self-understanding of an apocalyptic author, or community of authors, as 'scribe'. The use of the term 'scribe' in this literature may say at least as much about its authors as about conceptions of the figure of Enoch. Almost certainly, the authors of the apocalyptic literature would have regarded themselves as 'scribes' (though clearly not 'heavenly scribes'), whether or not the application of the title 'scribe' itself to their apocalyptic hero in fact represents a sublimation of their own role.[26] The very fact that they write apocalyptic material, presenting the revealed communications first vouchsafed to Enoch, is a sufficient indication of this. It is quite clear that they regarded their products as inspired and revelatory scriptures and that *their* contribution was to mediate the mysteries in writing and by interpretation to those of their own and future generations who are able to 'understand'.

We now move to a more detailed examination of the *title* 'scribe' as it occurs in the Enoch literature.

The Simple Title 'Scribe' (*saḥāfi*; אפסא; γραμματεύς)
It is certain that the epithet 'scribe', unqualified, was used of Enoch
in the Enoch literature. Unfortunately, the Aramaic text corresponding
to *1 Enoch* 12.3 (4QEn^c 1v)[27] is too fragmentary at this point for
certainty as to whether the simple title 'scribe' stood there, and Isaac
omits it in his translation of the Ethiopic.[28] Knibb, however, accepts
it,[29] also adopting the simple title in his translation of 92.1.[30] The
word 'scribe' certainly belongs here, despite Charles's and Isaac's
paraphrastic translations.[31] It is reasonable to assume that the simple
title 'scribe' was used in addition to the fuller titles such as 'scribe of
righteousness'. It is instructive to compare the use of both simple and
expanded titles in relation to Ezra in Neh. 8.1, 4, 9; 12.26, 36; Ezra
7.6, 11 (simple); Ezra 7.6, 12, 21 (expanded). There, the expanded
titles spell out in what sense the simple title is to be taken.[32]

The use of the title 'the Great Scribe' in reference to Enoch (cf.
Tg. Ps.-Jon. to Gen. 5.24)[33] is difficult to assess. It is hard to be sure
whether the title referred to Enoch's exalted, heavenly role (the
passage identifies Enoch with Metatron), or whether it ultimately
derives from traditions about the earthly Enoch the seer. Apart from
the mention of Metatron at this point,[34] which could be a late
intrusion, there is no indication that the Enoch who is designated
'Great Scribe' is any other than the earthly Enoch.[35] It is quite
possible that, on the basis of the MT, without necessarily drawing on
the earlier Enoch literature, the meturgeman could call Enoch
'scribe' because of the special insights and revelations he would
expect the latter to have gained when taken up to heaven by God.[36]
However that may be, the targumic usage testifies further to the
ascription of the title 'scribe *par excellence*' to Enoch.

First and foremost, then, in the apocalyptic literature and the
broad sphere of targumic influence, Enoch is called 'the Scribe'.

The Heavenly Scribe
For our purposes it is not crucial to establish where the title 'scribe'
in the apocalyptic literature originated, since how the figure was
originally understood may not necessarily have much significance for
first-century conceptions.[37] This is almost certainly true as regards
the probable origin of some of the apocalyptic heavenly scribe
notions in the Mesopotamian mythologies. Nonetheless, it has to be
acknowledged that the correspondences between the post-exaltation,

transcendent figure of Enoch the (heavenly) scribe and other mythical figures of the ancient Near East are very close in many respects, and we must consider the possibility that the underlying notion of a heavenly administrator or even judge[38] was still closely associated with the term 'scribe' in the period in which we are interested. Certainly these associations were self-evident for those Jews who maintained and developed the Enoch/Metatron traditions and speculations, although there the heavenly (angelic) figure assumes increasing importance and authority, emerging at one stage as the 'Lesser Yahweh' (cf. *3 Enoch* 12.5), while the specifically 'scribal' activities are performed by numerous other, angelic or less significant figures (unnamed at e.g. *1 Enoch* 97.6; 98.6-8; 103.3; 104.1, 7; later a range of named figures, e.g. Seraphiel, Radweriel, cf. *3 Enoch* 26; 27; 33.2). These figures, however, probably owe more to angelological speculation about the administration of the heavens than to concepts of 'scribe' as such. This is true also of other 'scribal' figures in rabbinic literature, such as Elijah, who on translation becomes an 'angel' and records human deeds (see below, n. 68).

The 'heavenly scribe' idea has a diversified but full ancient Near Eastern background. The role of Hermes/Thoth in passing on to his posterity mysteries, also in writing, received from the gods, is strikingly similar to Enoch's—particularly so when one considers his ascent to heaven and his role there as 'recorder' (ὑπομνηματόγραφος) of the gods.[39] But in *1 Enoch*, at 89.68ff., 76; 90.14, 20, 22, for example, Enoch is only associated, and not identified, with the celestial scribe, who may be Michael. The *heavenly* scribe idea may be based ultimately on either Thoth (Hermes) or the Babylonian scribe-deity Nabu,[40] though apparently Yahweh himself is also cast as a scribe in Ps. 87.6. In any event, *it does not apply to Enoch* in *1 Enoch*.

The primeval king Enmeduranki in Babylonian lore[41] is particularly interesting in view of his parallel position to Enoch in some of the antediluvian lists[42] as the seventh after the first man, taken up to heaven and shown secrets by the sun god—cf. the solar interest evidently implied in Enoch's 365 years.[43] But unlike Nabu, though he spends his time in the company of the gods and assumes some angelic qualities, Enmeduranki is an earthly seer and not a heavenly 'scribe' as such.[44] It lies beyond the scope of our study to unravel the precise threads that link these ideas in the figure of Enoch. Very probably the Enochic writers themselves were quite unaware of the extraneous and long-forgotten influences that had affected the traditions they received. Nonetheless, it would be a mistake not to acknowledge these influences; and it remains possible that the works of Berossus, the third-century Babylonian priest and scribe, which record the traditions about Xisouthros and Enmeduranki, were read by second-century scribes in Palestine.[45] For our purposes it is sufficient to note where the contacts with Enoch's scribal role lie, and these are closest in the case of Enmeduranki the human *seer* (*barû*) rather than with the scribe-deity Nabu.[46]

According to Charles,[47] the role of 'heavenly scribe', in *1 Enoch* 89 and 90 probably identified with Michael (in light of 90.14, 22),[48] has 'devolved on Enoch' in 12.3f., 15.1 and 92.1 (and on Ezra in *4 Ezra* 14.22-26 and on Vretil in *2 Enoch* 22.11ff.). Charles does not expand on this statement, however, and makes no suggestion as to the nature and means of this 'devolution'. Presumably he means that an earlier heavenly scribe concept has become associated with the earthly Enoch as the latter gained in eminence. But the grounds for this view are elusive; there is no reason to see in 12.3f., 15.1, and probably not in 92.1 (see below), a specifically heavenly scribal role for Enoch in the sense that we have later, when Enoch is himself an exalted, angelic figure.

In fact there seems to be a constant cross-fertilization of ideas over a very long period. VanderKam[49] points out the possibility that ancient traditions in surrounding Near Eastern countries could contribute to the Jewish picture at various points in the course of the formation of the Enoch traditions. It seems that Metatron 'usurped', so to speak, some of Michael's functions also;[50] and Enoch and Metatron may have been identified, or even become 'rivals' for honours, because of a close similarity in their originally distinct roles. Enoch himself is in disfavour in the rabbinic literature proper, while 'scribal' honours—though significantly the *title* scribe appears nowhere in relation to them apart from Tg. Ps.-Jon. to Gen. 5.24— are shared between Metatron, Elijah and the Messiah.

The intermingling of such a variety of ideas associated with an increasingly revered figure (cf. esp. the astonishing number of different roles eventually ascribed to Metatron in *3 Enoch*) means that we should not expect to find a totally consistent picture of Enoch in what is, after all, a composite work whose final form postdates its earliest parts by at least two centuries. Nor should we expect to be able to determine with confidence the precise nature of the interrelationships between the various elements of the tradition.

Clearly, the 'scribe' title has both celestial and terrestrial connotations in this literature. The evidence of the Enochic *texts* as they stand seems to suggest that the prime application is to human beings. There is no doubt of this in the case of Baruch, whose selection for veneration in the apocalyptic literature is because of his reputation as an earthly scribe and not because of association with a heavenly scribal figure.[51] His most important role, for his pupils and descendants, is his authorship of the 'epistle and scroll' which constitute the book of *2 Baruch* itself and which form an important scripture for meditation in the 'congregations' (*2 Bar.* 86.1ff.). He is an author of a religious work based on visionary experience and divine inspiration; the biblical Baruch the Scribe (Jer. 36.26, 32), who is furthermore closely associated with a classical prophet, is an eminently suitable identity for the author of apocalyptic material.[52]

The same is very probably true of Ezra, who, in any case, even in his scribal role in *4 Ezra* 14, is not a heavenly figure, nor yet situated in heaven when he writes his inspired works, which are specifically intended for 'the wise among the people' on earth (*4 Ezra* 14.26, 46; cf. Dan. 11.33; 12.9-11). Like Enoch, he is evidently modelled to some extent on the mysterious figure of Balaam the seer, but specifically as 'scribe': The addition to *4 Ezra* 14 in the Syriac (cf. also Eth., Arab. 1 and Arm. versions) reads 'At that time Ezra was caught up and taken to the place of those who are like him, after he had written all these things. And he was called the Scribe of the Knowledge of the Most High for ever and ever.' This powerfully recalls Num. 24.16, which speaks of Balaam as one who 'knew' the 'knowledge of the Most High'—*the only occurrence of the phrase in the MT*. And here it is of the revelations vouchsafed to him by special understanding and inspiration that Ezra is 'scribe', and not of the 'righteous deeds' or otherwise of those subject to judgment in a forensic context.[53]

The case of Enoch, it is true, is complicated in the later material by his apparent identification with the Son of Man and the Elect One in *1 Enoch* 71. But the Son of Man/Elect One is not referred to as scribe nor given a 'scribal' role, which is reserved for the human Enoch alone. Enoch is, nonetheless, shown the 'secrets of righteousness' here,[54] which may account in part for the title 'scribe of righteousness', discussed below.

The Interpreting Scribe

As we noted above (note 44), according to Zimmern, the 'scribal' feature of Enoch's role could derive from Enmeduranki in that both are scribes by virtue of their reading the heavenly tablets. VanderKam's objection[55] is that the scribe's activity is not adequately characterized by the *reading* of written material. However, it is a significant part of Enoch's role in *1 Enoch* that he has access to the *written* mysteries in heaven. What is more, these, alongside his visions and the oral and visual revelations by the angelic guides (cf. e.g. 93.2), provide a major source for the revelatory instruction of his sons.[56] In 81.1ff., for example, Enoch 'observes', 'reads' and 'marks' the heavenly tablets; then, having '*understood*' everything (cf. *Jub.* 4.19), he is taken to 'declare', 'show', 'teach' and 'testify' to his sons on this basis; in 93.1ff. Enoch 'recounts from the books'; and in 103.2ff. (cf. 106.19; 107) Enoch's instruction is also derived from these works (heavenly tablets and holy books).

In the Enochic fragments found at Qumran in Aramaic, Enoch's usual title is ספר פרשא, found at 4QEnGiants[b]ii14 and reconstructed by Milik at ii22 (p. 305), 4QEn[c]2 (line 2) (pp. 236f.), 4QEn[g]1ii (line 22) (= *1 Enoch* 92.1);[57] Milik translates this variously as 'the distinguished scribe' and 'the scribe of distinction'. The usual meaning of פרש, apart from the basic meaning 'to separate', is 'to make distinct', as in Ezra 4.18.[58] Compare the similar sense in the Hebrew in Neh. 8.8, precisely of the activity of the Levites, who with Ezra the priest and scribe (8.9) 'helped the people to understand the law ... and they read from the book, from the law of God, distinctly (or, with interpretation); and they gave the sense, so that the people understood the reading' (8.7, 8). In both cases (Ezra 4.18 and Neh. 8.8), the verb is used in connection with the essentially scribal activity of clear explanation or interpretation.[59] This has nothing to do with the 'distinguished' nature of the scribe,[60] but rather with his interpretative role. Indeed, the most obvious meaning of פרשא, though infrequently attested, is that given by Levy (II, p. 303b), namely, 'Erklärung, Auslegung', with reference to Tg Deut. 17.18— concerning the explanation of teaching. This reading of the text is made so much the more likely by the fact that in one of the two

certain occurrences (4QEnGiants[b]ii14) the text reads לספר פרשא חלמא
ויפשור לנא; it is the role of this scribe to interpret (in this case,
dreams). The same would seem to apply to lines 22f. 4QEn[c]2 (line 2)
would not contradict this understanding.

In the only other certain reading of ספר פרשא (4QEnGiants[a]8, line
4) the text immediately following the phrase is lost; however, that the
following passage is intended to be an exposition seems likely from
the beginning of line 6 (ידיע להוא—Let it be known to you) and from
the use of the word פרש in line 13. Milik thus seems to be assuming
alternately too little and too much from the texts when he claims
(p. 262) that the epithet ספר פרשא, 'the scribe of distinction',
qualifies Enoch 'as a professional, "distinguished" copyist who writes
"distinctly, clearly", and perhaps, at the same time, as a redactor of
laws which have the force of judges' "decisions"'. The suggestion
that follows 'perhaps' in Milik's claim has no visible basis and
appears to apply uncritically a rabbinic conception of the *sôferîm* to
Enoch; the first part of the statement is inadequate—the title 'scribe'
can hardly mean 'professional . . . copyist' in reference to Enoch.
Enoch is, amongst other things, a 'scribe of exposition/explanation',
and this would appear to be the sense of ספר פרשא in the Book of
Giants and possibly in the Apocalypse of Weeks (*1 Enoch* 92.1).

Finally, an expository understanding of the expression in the
notoriously difficult *1 Enoch* 92.1 is possible both in Milik's
reconstructed Aramaic[61] ספר פרשא (as in the above cases) and in the
Ethiopic, which has 'the scribe of all the wondrous deed(s) of
wisdom'. The meaning of the latter phrase seems to imply at least the
ascription of special knowledge and expertise to Enoch and probably
entails the notion of an interpretative role.[62] Dexinger (p. 117) rejects
Milik's (Aramaic) reconstruction of 92.1, though he does accept
(p. 110) the word *saḥāfi* (ספר) as original here, preferring to supply
ספר קשטא, 'Schreiber der Gerechtigkeit', in accordance with 12.4 and
15.1 (p. 178). Knibb, as mentioned above, translates with the simple
title 'Enoch the scribe'. It is hazardous, in view of the textual
difficulties, to draw firm conclusions from this verse, but we need
briefly to examine the possibility that it refers to Enoch's role as
judge.

The Judging Scribe?
In Charles's translation of 92.1, followed by Knibb, it is 'this

complete doctrine of wisdom' that merits the designation 'a judge of all the earth', and VanderKam agrees that this correctly represents the best Ethiopic versions (against Milik). Charles refers to 84.3, where, he claims, Wisdom is seen as the πάρεδρος (assessor) of God (cf. Wis. 9.4, from Prov. 8.30 LXX). But is it possible that in this verse a judicial role is ascribed to Enoch himself? Dexinger implicitly accepts this in his translation (which follows Beer; cf. p. 111) as does Milik in his reconstruction of the Aramaic, though neither scholar discusses the point. VanderKam accepts Milik's reconstruction,[63] arguing that חכים followed by אנשא is more likely to have referred to Enoch himself than to wisdom (feminine anyway) or teaching (which is grammatically possible). However, in the rest of the early Enoch literature, Enoch is never given the role of judge,[64] which is reserved for the Elect One and Son of Man in the Similitudes[65] and for Raphael and Michael elsewhere (cf. *1 Enoch* 10.4-8, 11-13). It would thus be rather hasty to assume that Enoch the scribe was given the title 'judge of all the earth' at this stage.[66] It is easy to see how this notion might eventually enter the ever-expanding conception of Enoch in view of the fact that Enoch is imagined, at an early stage, to be seated in heaven recording deeds for the purpose of human beings' eventual judgment (cf. *Jub.* 4.24). On the basis of the latter passage, VanderKam[67] even gives Enoch the title 'scribe of judgment', though without explanation and without indicating that the title is nowhere attested. In the mystical sphere, where the angelic mediators of revelation (cf. Michael and Gabriel in Daniel, Michael again in *Ascension of Isaiah*, Uriel in *4 Ezra*, etc.) are seen as scribal figures[68] and also function as agents of justice (cf. *1 Enoch* 10), it is a short step to the identification of the seer, who already 'feels united' with one of these figures, with all aspects of that figure's role. But, significantly, this secondary fusing of roles is not accomplished in the early Enoch literature. There, Enoch's role is a continuing one: he writes down human deeds as they are done (*Jub.* 4.24; cf. *2 Enoch* 53.2), and not, as in the case of Hermes/Thoth, only in the judgment scene itself.[69] In later popular conceptions Enoch clearly evokes a mixture of fear and hope because of his awesome authority in choosing what to record and what to wipe out.[70] But it is clear that the judgment still lies ultimately in the hands of Yahweh, who may overrule him.[71]

We conclude, then, that in the early Enoch literature and the book of *Jubilees*, Enoch's scribal role does not extend to the responsibility for passing judgment.

Dexinger, however, apparently supposes that the title 'scribe of righteousness', which he finds in 92.1, would be in keeping with such a role, and we shall need briefly to consider this title of Enoch.

The Scribe of Righteousness

This title is well attested.[72] *1 Enoch* 12.3f. in the Ethiopic text reads:

> The Watchers called me—Enoch the scribe [*saḥāfi*]—and said to me: 'Enoch, thou scribe of righteousness [*saḥāfi sedeq*], go, declare to the Watchers of the heaven who have left the high heaven . . . ye shall have no peace nor forgiveness of sin'.

Similarly, in 15.1, before a similar commission to censure the fallen angels, we read: ' . . . I heard His voice, "Fear not, Enoch, thou righteous man and scribe of righteousness"'. The Greek versions of the Book of Watchers (= *1 Enoch* 1–36) also witness to the title, variously rendering it as γραμματεὺς τῆς δικαιοσύνης (δικεόσυνης) (12.4) and ἄνθρωπος ἀληθινὸς καὶ γραμματεὺς τῆς ἀληθείας (15.1). In the Aramaic texts, Milik states[73] that Enoch may be called ספר קשטא, 'the scribe of righteousness'. It has to be said, however, that there appears not to be any clear instance of the Aramaic title in any published Aramaic fragment; but in view of the widespread agreement in the above texts, as well as in a number of later texts (cf. especially *T. Abraham* 11.3 [Rec. B][74]), Milik's reconstruction is probable. The corresponding Hebrew title would then have been סופר צדק(ה),[75] which bears a close resemblance to the title מורה צדק, 'teacher of righteousness', used of the honoured leader (and founder?) of the Qumran community.[76]

The latter title, it is true, may be translated as 'the Righteous Teacher',[77] since in Hebrew, as in Aramaic, the use of an abstract noun in an objective genitive construct is indistinguishable in form from its adjectival use; but in view of the weight of opinion in favour of 'Teacher of Righteousness' as the most appropriate translation of the title it seems that Milik is a little hasty to assume that the term 'scribe of righteousness' simply 'underlines his moral rectitude (in line with "Enoch the righteous man" of En 1.2)'.[78] This would in any case produce an uncharacteristic tautology, especially at 15.1 quoted above (where the phrase is too prosaic to be a synthetic *parallelismus membrorum*).

A similar criticism might be directed to Charles, who states[79] that the epithet is used 'because he is himself a righteous man, 15:1, 17:14-16, and declares the righteous judgment that is coming, 13:10, 14:1, 3, 81:6, 82:1 &c.'. Certainly, that Enoch is a righteous man is implied in the expression, but is the *role* of the scribe of righteousness best characterized in his declaring coming judgment? There is some association of his scribal role with admonition, it is true: in 13.10 and 14.1, words of righteousness are spoken by Enoch in the context of reprimand for the Watchers; but these 'words of righteousness'[80] are more than simply admonitory—repeatedly the emphasis in Enoch is on teaching, albeit ethical teaching, on the authoritative basis of the scribe's revelatory insight.[81] The 'words of righteousness' in 13.10 are explicitly equated with the recounting of what has been revealed to Enoch in his visions. And 14.1 equates the words of righteousness with the announcement of the revelations (in book form) 'so that man may have understanding with his heart'; God has in fact given Enoch the 'word of understanding' (14.3) that is the basis for his reprimands; the emphasis is still on authoritative insight. Like the title 'scribe of interpretation', 'scribe of righteousness/truth' characterizes Enoch largely as an author/tradent of revelations; spiritual insights are inextricably interwoven with authority in ethical matters.

Van Andel[82] correctly observes that Enoch's role is contrasted with the action of the fallen Watchers whose untimely and unauthorized revelation of mysteries to humans is condemned: Enoch 'walked with God', and in this privileged position he enjoyed authorized access to the divine mysteries, including the 'secrets of righteousness'. This privilege of access is ascribed also to the Elect One (49.2), with whom Enoch is identified in 71.14, and to the righteous ones in heaven (58.5) for whom Enoch is the illustrious forerunner and model. As scribe of righteousness, Enoch stands in a mediating position between the one who preeminently 'has' righteousness (46.3; 71.14) and has the keys to the store of the secrets (cf. *1 Enoch* 46.3; cf. *3 Enoch* 10.6; 48c.3), and the righteous posterity who in turn pass on the revealed secrets (cf. e.g. *1 Enoch* 81.1-7). He learns and he transmits; as scribe he is primarily a teacher of religious insights, a 'teacher of righteousness' in this sense.[83]

The whole point of the revelations to Enoch, according to the Astronomical Book (*1 Enoch* 72–82), is that they be taught to Methuselah and his posterity for the positive benefit of future generations (82.1), who will thus be encouraged to walk in the 'way of righteousness' (e.g. 82.4; 91.19). In 81.6, Charles's other example of Enoch's declaration of coming righteous judgment, Enoch is given a year with his son to 'declare everything', 'give his last commands', to 'teach his children and record (it) for them' and to 'testify to all his children'. Part of this task is sobering and admonitory: he is to 'show' to all his children 'that no flesh is righteous in the sight of the Lord . . .', but the overall thrust of this teaching of righteousness is clearly a positive one. There is in fact no talk of judgment here (except to mention the general dogma that even the righteous shall die on account of the deeds of humankind [v. 9]). And the next verse (82.7) encourages Enoch to 'take heart', because when he is taken from his children 'the good shall announce righteousness to the good; The righteous with the righteous will rejoice, And shall offer congratulation to one another'.

If, therefore, as seems likely, Charles is correct to assume that this very early section of *1 Enoch* has influenced the content of the 'scribe of righteousness' title, then we must take full account of the positive emphasis on the teaching of revealed knowledge and of righteousness for posterity, especially of course for the communities associated with these particular writings. Reprimand of the Watchers is part of Enoch's task as 'scribe of righteousness' but should certainly not be understood as the only or even the major aspect of his role. The important point is that as 'scribe of righteousness' Enoch is seen as the mediator of revelation and instruction in righteousness for a community of the faithful righteous.

Significantly, Charles does not call upon his 'heavenly scribe' concept to illuminate the content of 'scribe of righteousness', despite his presumed 'declaration of coming righteous judgment', for clearly the term itself does not carry a judicial sense, even if Enoch does (in *Jubilees*) write down human deeds in the heavenly court.

In the later, but still probably pre-Christian *Testament of Abraham* (Recension B), there is a vigorous rebuttal of any speculation as to Enoch's role as judge;[84] and it is precisely in this context that he is called '*the teacher of heaven and earth and the scribe of righteousness*' (11.3f.). It is Abel who is presented as the witness and judge, while 'it is not Enoch's business to give sentence; rather, the Lord is the one who gives sentence, and it is this one's [i.e. Enoch's] task only to write' (11.7; cf. 11.1-10): in the forensic context he has no more responsibility than to 'record the sins and the righteous deed of each person' (11.4).That part of his function as scribe of righteousness which goes beyond his purely secretarial activity in the heavenly court is here specified, in line with the main elements of his role in *1 Enoch*, as *teaching* heaven (i.e. presumably the 'reprimand' of the fallen angels, cf. *1 Enoch* 13; 14 etc.) and earth (i.e. Methuselah and his posterity), by means of his writings, which are for instruction in righteousness.[85]

We have discovered evidence of the following aspects of Enoch's role as 'scribe of righteousness':

1. By implication, Enoch's moral standing as a righteous man is re-emphasized. The tone is similar to that in which the same qualities are described of Ben Sira's ideal scribe (cf. p. 68 above).

2. He is a 'teacher of heaven'.[86] Speaking 'words of righteousness' that depend on his revelatory insight, he is entrusted with the admonition and positive exhortation of the fallen Watchers to restore themselves to their former unimpeachable righteous status.

3. As 'teacher of earth', (a) he functions like the eminent wisdom teachers such as Ben Sira the scribe, whose concern, we recall, was also constantly the 'understanding' and the 'righteousness' of his pupils; (b) he passes on the mysteries (= secrets of righteousness) he has received by revelation through the mediation of the angels and through his access to the heavenly books, orally to Methuselah and his sons; (c) he commits these revelations to writing in books (= the various 'Books of Enoch') which are for the righteous instruction of his posterity that will be able to 'understand'; (d) his role also coincides to a significant extent with that of the Essene Teacher of Righteousness.

In *Jubilees* and *Testament of Abraham* Enoch has the additional 'scribal' role of recording the deeds of humans during their lifetime as documentary evidence to be used by God (or Abel) in the judgment.[87] But it is not at all clear that this role has any bearing on the title 'scribe of righteousness', which must in any case antedate the 'heavenly scribe' idea as applied to Enoch. The title 'scribe of righteousness' has not been found to contain the idea of 'judge' in the literature we have discussed.[88]

Enoch a 'Classical Sofer'?

At some points the notion of Enoch as scribe bears comparison with rabbinic conceptions of the authoritative Soferim, the official heirs of the oral teaching ascribed to Moses and the authors of individual halakhoth.[89] Such passages as *Jub.* 7.38-39 and 21.10 ascribe particular halakhoth to Enoch (others are ascribed to Noah;[90] cf. *T. Zeb.* 3.4 [vt]).[91] This is not to say that the rabbis conceived of Enoch as a 'Sofer' any more than they did the authors of Qumranic halakhoth. Clearly not, since Enoch predates Moses, the author of all halakhoth according to rabbinic tradition.[92] Nor is the title Sofer given to other biblical figures in Mishnah and Talmud who are credited with the introduction of certain halakhoth (e.g. Joshua, Samuel, David, Solomon, Hezekiah and Daniel). But it does indicate that at a pre-rabbinic date some halakhoth were being ascribed to ancient figures who in effect were prototypes of the Soferim[93] (Enoch at least may even have been honoured in some circles as superior to Moses).[94] In *1 Enoch* itself, however, where there is no emphasis on the introduction or interpretation of halakhoth, there is no reason to suppose that anything corresponding to rabbinic notions of 'Soferim' authority is implied in Enoch's titles.

To summarize, then, the picture of Enoch as scribe in *1 Enoch* and *Jubilees*: Enoch is the 'scribe', 'the scribe of interpretation' and 'the scribe of righteousness/truth'. His scribal role is indeed connected with writing, and especially of the books containing the divine secrets revealed to him in heaven, so that an emphasis on the *inspired* nature of his writings is dominant. As 'scribe of interpretation' he is also an expert in religious matters, being skilled also in divination as well as exegesis, and he passes on his insights into mysteries to his righteous posterity. As 'scribe of righteousness' he preaches to the Watchers both in admonition and exhortation, and gives revealed instruction in righteousness to the righteous of future generations via his writings. He is given a secondary 'scribal' role in heaven as a recorder of human deeds, providing documentary evidence to be used for judgment; he is not, however, given a judicial role himself. It is possible that his authorship of a small number of halakhoth may also give further appropriateness to the title 'scribe' in relation to him.

As an eminent righteous man, a *ṣaddîq*, Enoch is acclaimed as an ideal man of God, like Noah; but specifically as 'scribe of righteousness' he prefigures a line of teachers of righteousness including the eminent founder of the Qumran community, and their expected eschatological leader (if the two are not to be identified), who are given special revelations for their adherents living in the eschatological age; he prefigures also the eminent 'Teacher' of the Gospels, especially of Matthew, as the authoritative transmitter of revealed mysteries and the author of the call to true righteousness.

(2) *Enoch as Scribe: The Later Enochic Literature*

Since the dating of the composite writings now called *2 (Slavonic) Enoch* and *3 (Hebrew) Enoch* is in both cases much disputed and probably mainly post-Christian,[95] we shall not be able to draw on them for firm evidence of distinctive ideas that were influential in the period with which we are mainly concerned. However, insofar as they witness to a continuity in the ideas surrounding the figure of the eminent scribe they may be helpful in establishing the relative importance attached to these ideas throughout the period of their transmission and development.

2 Enoch[96] describes Enoch as a 'wise man', 'a righteous man' and a 'great scholar',[97] whom the Lord took away to be a 'witness' of God and of the marvels of the heavenly places. He functions in similar ways to 'Enoch the Scribe' of *1 Enoch* and *Jubilees*, though given the actual title 'scribe' only at 36.3 (in the previously unpublished manuscript A now translated by Andersen).[98]

According to 36.3 (shorter recension, MS A), the Lord says to Enoch:

> because a place has been prepared for you, and you will be in front of my face from now and forever. And you will be seeing my secrets, and you will be *scribe* for my servants, since you will be writing down everything that has happened on earth and in the heavens, and you will be for me a witness of the judgment of the great age.

The relative age of this manuscript is at present impossible to ascertain,[99] but it is quite conceivable that this passage represents an early reading. In any case it is of value as a comparative datum for the purposes of our study. If it is as late as the bulk of the *3 Enoch* material, it both documents the use of the epithet 'witness' for Enoch (in common with *3 Enoch*) *and* the continued use of the title 'scribe' in reference to Enoch (in contrast to *3 Enoch*; see below). But it could be much earlier, since it presupposes no more than is derivable from *Jubilees* and *1 Enoch*; it probably reflects a transitional stage in the very long period between the early Enochic literature and *3 Enoch*.

It is interesting that in this one distinct usage of the epithet scribe, the term is expanded to explain its precise content. First, Enoch is to be scribe 'for my servants', which appears to indicate that his role is envisaged as finally for the benefit of the righteous in all generations on earth—in other words he is in a sense a mediator.[100] Secondly, his role is physically to commit matters to writing. Thirdly, the content of these writings is revelatory, namely the record of 'everything that has happened on earth' (to include human deeds, but also, one must assume, God's deeds; nothing is left concealed from the scribe-seer) 'and that exists on earth and in the heavens' (corresponding to the content of the geographical, cosmological and astronomical mysteries commonly revealed in the apocalyptic writings). This picture of Enoch as apocalyptic scribe corresponds very closely with that presented in the earlier Enochic literature.

In *2 Enoch*, *Jubilees* and *Testament of Abraham*, Enoch writes down the deeds of everyone, but here before creation as well as continuously (53.23 [J]). His manuscript will never be destroyed (53.3 [A]). Enoch teaches his children how to 'walk' before the Lord (66, preface, and 66.2),[101] instructing them in righteousness (36[39]-66).[102] He has put all this teaching down in writing 'so that you ['his children'] might read it and think about it' (66.8) and the books are to be cherished, passed on and explained to others (48.6f.; 54, etc.). In heaven for sixty days, he writes notes about God's creatures, authoring 366 books for his children on earth (23.6; 68.2). Again, this written material depends on revelations to Enoch given by virtue of his special righteousness and understanding. Vrevoil, the exceptionally wise heavenly recorder, is instructed to give Enoch access to the divine books and to give him materials to record them under dictation (22.10f.). Honoured above the angels, who lack his special understanding (24.3),[103] he is required to sit on the Lord's left with Gabriel (24.11) and is given individual instruction in 'my secrets' by the Lord himself (24.2f.). Enoch's understanding is again emphasized

(33.3), in contrast to those who are undiscerning and do not understand (48.8). The books are then written that his children will 'read and understand . . . that they may carry out all your instructions and study the books in your handwriting accurately and attentively' (36.1; 33.8f.; cf. 66.8).

Thus, although the actual title 'scribe' is not ostensibly an important one in *2 Enoch*, and although a number of minor details are added to the picture of Enoch given in *1 Enoch*, there is a fundamental continuity with the earlier material in regard to the picture of Enoch as scribe in heaven and on earth, as the recipient and mediator of revealed secrets for the benefit of his posterity on earth. He is still a seer, an interpreter and a scribe/teacher of righteousness as well as a recorder and inspired author of cherished scriptures.

3 Enoch[104] maintains the essential traits of the Enochic character as depicted in the earlier Enochic literature, but the picture is very much affected by the new formal identification of Enoch with Metatron, so that he is fundamentally a heavenly figure.

God has 'committed to him wisdom and intelligence more than to all the angels' (48c [K]; Odeberg, *Enoch*, p. 166); he is the 'Knower of secrets' to whom God has declared 'all mysteries in uprightness'; to him are committed 'all the treasuries of wisdom' (48d.2), and his role is 'to give wisdom to all the wise of the world and understanding and knowledge to all who understand [Dan. 2.21 is here quoted; Dan. 11.33 and 12.9f. are likely to be in mind] . . . to reveal to them the secrets of my words and to teach the decree of my righteous judgment' (48c.9). This is precisely the role of elect mediator of revealed mysteries that is ascribed to Enoch in the earlier literature, where the Danielic allusions abound, in terms of the 'scribe of interpretation' and 'scribe of righteousness'. With Enoch's formal identification with Metatron, however (cf. *3 Enoch* 4.2), the title 'scribe' itself seems to have fallen out of favour, since the exalted Enoch-Metatron is not specifically called *sôfēr* in this literature.[105] A multiplicity of 'scribes' now appear, who, with the unsurprising exception of 'Ezra the Scribe' (*3 Enoch* 48d.10), are heavenly figures: one 'scribe' has a position below the Lord, and some manuscripts witness to another above the Lord (*3 Enoch* 33.2); *sôferîm* read the books given to the Holy One by Radweriel (27.2); the figure named

Seraphiel is called 'swift scribe' (26.1); and two further important figures named Sopheriel (18.23ff.) are 'appointed over the books' of the living and the dead respectively, and are clearly to be taken as scribes also.[106]

It seems that at this later stage in the tradition, and/or the esoteric circles responsible for the literature, the term *sôfēr* is being understood (with the exception of the single occurrence of the fixed biblical title of Ezra the Scribe) in the simple sense of 'clerk', 'bookkeeper' or 'notary' in the heavenly court.[107] Enoch-Metatron is not specifically said to be engaged in any writing (unlike the earlier Enoch), although Odeberg[108] suggests that in *3 Enoch*, Enoch-Metatron is 'defined as Scribe-Witness in agreement with Book of Jubilees 4:21 seqq. and Targ. P. to Gen. 5:24'. We have already seen that the probably earlier MS A of *2 Enoch* includes the titles 'scribe' and 'witness' in parallel (*2 Enoch* 36.3), but Odeberg of course does not mention this passage. By the time of *3 Enoch*, however, the *epithet* applied to Enoch is in fact that of 'witness' against his own generation at *3 Enoch* 4.3, 5 (cf. *Jub.* 4) and not 'scribe'; at 48c.2, where he is taken to heaven, again, 'my witness', the latter term is not expanded upon, but his appointment, according to the next verse, 'over all the treasuries and stores in every heaven' (i.e. of wisdom, understanding, etc.) and his custody of the keys to them (48c.3; cf. 8.1ff.; 48d.2, 10) is very much like the honour accorded to him in the earlier literature where as 'scribe' (15.1, etc.) he sees the secrets of the various treasuries (e.g. *1 Enoch* 17; 18; cf. *2 Enoch* 36.3 [A]). So the title 'scribe' in reference to Enoch seems to have been superseded at this point by 'witness', while the 'scribal' role of Enoch-Metatron has become reduced, accordingly, to that of heavenly administrator (or recorder: *b. Hag.* 15a).[109] We thus have a tacit confirmation of our finding that the title 'scribe'/'scribe of righteousness' in the *earlier* literature contains a much broader range of meaning than can be accounted for simply on the basis of a narrow association of the title with 'writing', to which, however, the title seems to have reverted in the later literature. Elements added to the role of Enoch by virtue of his association with Metatron include his judging of the heavenly household, conferring of authority on princes, expecting their obedience (12.5; 48c.8); his seventy names give him a position of glory and eminence, and while he can still be called 'my servant' (48c.3; 10.3) he is 'Prince of the Presence and Knower of Secrets', and even 'the Lesser YHWH' (48c.7). His judging role is evidently a corollary of his elevated position and does not belong to the concept of 'scribe' *per se*; indeed the lack of the title in *3 Enoch* may indicate the perceived inadequacy of the title at the time of the book's composition to indicate judicial authority. In his vast eminence in *3 Enoch*, Metatron in fact no longer *records* sins at all—indeed, it is Satan, the Accuser, who writes down Israel's sins (26.12).[110]

3 Enoch appears to reflect a period (or periods) when the title 'scribe' was again low in prestige.[111] However, the peculiarly 'scribal' character of some of the main functions of the ancient visionary is maintained, particularly at the level of access to and administration (mediation) of the mysteries, with the important difference that he does not write books,[112] nor yet keep records. Above all, he 'gives wisdom', 'reveals secrets' and 'teaches' (see esp. 48c).[113]

In sum, we have seen that the title 'scribe' is associated in the early literature with ideas of the reception and transmission of revealed mysteries which function not only as mystic insights for the subsequent righteous community but also as encouragements to righteous living. In the much later literature of *3 Enoch*, the title 'scribe' has lost its eminent standing and fallen out of favour, and it seems to be more narrowly associated with ideas of writing and book-keeping, functions performed by (heavenly) persons other than the now vastly elevated heavenly figure of Enoch-Metatron, so that Enoch has largely lost his specifically scribal role.[114] The reference to Enoch as scribe and witness in *2 Enoch* seems to reflect a middle stage in the development of the concept, between *1 Enoch* and *3 Enoch*.

B. *Other Scribal Figures*

(1) *Daniel the Maśkîl as Scribe*[115]

Daniel is not called 'scribe' (ספרא/סופר) in the canonical book that bears his name. We must therefore be circumspect in our use of his description in Daniel to elucidate concepts of the scribe, particularly since by contrast Ben Sira, roughly contemporary with the Daniel material, uses the term as a matter of course. However, since the broad affinities between the apocalyptic heroes are self-evident

Daniel has to be considered as a comparable figure. Furthermore, there is a considerable overlap between the *maśkîl* and the *sôfēr*, as we have already seen in the course of our review of Ben Sira's concept of the scribe and as we shall see in our examination of the evidence of Qumran and Matthew (Chapters 5 and 6 below). The appropriateness of the title 'scribe' in relation to Daniel is, meanwhile, indicated by the following points.

First, it is striking that in Daniel he is not described as a 'prophet',[116] though in its concern with the 'true' meaning of prophetic texts, the work is clearly preoccupied with prophecy.[117] In a real sense, Daniel is primarily an interpreter, both as an exegete of scripture (cf. e.g. the use of Isaiah in chs. 10–12) and as an interpreter of other revelatory material (dreams and cryptic graffiti, e.g. ch. 9). His role as a visionary, a recipient and transmitter of mysteries, is consistent with this.

Daniel is portrayed as a 'wise man' (חכימא; cf. 2.12, 13, 18), 'skilful in all wisdom, endowed with knowledge, understanding learning'[118] (1.4), given a three-year education in the 'letters and language of the Chaldeans' (1.4, 6);[119] in addition God 'gave' him and his companions 'learning and skill in all letters and wisdom'[120] and Daniel 'had understanding (הבין) in all visions and dreams' (1.17; cf. 9.22); he is the recipient of 'revealed mysteries' (cf. 2.19-30, 47, etc.);[121] he has 'light and understanding and wisdom',[122] 'an excellent spirit, knowledge, and understanding to interpret dreams, explain riddles, and solve problems'[123] (5.11f.; cf. 5.14); he 'reads' writings (5.17, 24f.) and gives 'interpretation' (cf. 5.16f., 24ff., and *passim*); he 'writes down' the content of his dream (7.1); he is engaged in detailed biblical study (9.12, 13), which is the basis of his curiosity concerning obscure matters; he is given instruction from heavenly books (12.4, cf. 12.2); he has charge of words which will be 'understood' at the end of days (12.9ff.), and which are to be identified, presumably, with the book of Daniel itself (cf. Rev. 22.10, in reference to the book of Revelation). All this paints the unmistakable picture of the mantic scribe that we saw already in Ben Sira and especially in the Enochic literature.

Perhaps the most characteristic quality of the figure of Daniel as represented in the book is his consuming desire for and possession of 'understanding' (שכל, בינה); see for example 8.15; 9.22f.; 10.1, 12, 14, in addition to the references given above. As we have seen, this precisely characterizes the *sôfēr* according to Ben Sira in 38.24–39.5 and above all the inspired scribe in 39.6ff. Furthermore, as *maśkîl*, his role is to instruct in righteousness, by making people 'understand' (11.23; cf. 12.3).[124]

The correspondence between this picture and the description of the scribe found in Sir. 39.1-11 is very close; certainly there is a greater emphasis on dream-interpretation and divine revelation in Daniel, but we have seen that such 'apocalyptic' elements are not alien to Ben Sira's ideal scribe, especially according to 39.6ff.[125] Indeed the 'wisdom of the *Maskilim*'[126] is actually in many respects closer to the 'wisdom of the scribe' in Ben Sira than to wisdom in the Wisdom of Solomon.[127] Collins's statement (p. 57) that 'the *maskilim* of Daniel have little in common with the scribes of Ben Sira's type' entirely overlooks the 'mantic' aspects of the latter; though he is correct (pp. 56ff.) to distinguish to some extent between proverbial and mantic wisdom (as Ben Sira himself does), he is wrong to see them as mutually exclusive.

The elevated social standing of the eminent scribe according to Ben Sira, including the specific statement that the scribe will 'serve among great men and appear before rulers' (Sir. 39.4), also applies to Daniel.[128]

Finally, as Lacocque points out,[129] Daniel is introduced (Dan. 1.4) in a 'pronounced priestly context'; here as elsewhere in the Old Testament (e.g. Pss. 1; 19; 119) the sacerdotal and sapiential domains overlap.[130]

As we have seen, virtually all these details are reiterated, with minor variations, concerning Enoch the Scribe in the apocalyptic literature. The Enochic title 'scribe of interpretation' would have been a particularly appropriate one for Daniel. The only significant scribal role performed by Enoch and not by Daniel is that of heavenly recorder, and this is hardly a surprising matter since like Ezra in *4 Ezra* and Baruch in *2 Baruch*, Daniel is not transported into the heavenly realms.[131] In addition, Dan'el, the primeval wise man and king to whom the biblical figure of Daniel seems to owe a good deal (mentioned in Ezek. 14.14, 20; 28.3 and in Ugaritic literature) is closely associated with Enoch, both by reference to him in *1 Enoch* 6.7 and 69.2 and especially in *Jub.* 4.20 (where the latter is said to have married Ednî, Dan'el's daughter).[132]

The scribes Ezra and Baruch (as represented in *4 Ezra* and

2 Baruch) are also closely modelled on Daniel, who, furthermore, is called *maśkîl* and *ḥākhām*, 'wise man' (rather than prophet) at a time (early second century BCE) when contemporary works indicate a close interrelationship between the titles 'wise man' and 'scribe'.[133]

Daniel is certainly a 'seer' and a 'wise man', but it is important to note the appropriateness, in the *apocalyptic frame of reference*, of the title 'scribe' for Daniel; not only do the form and language of the book of Daniel exert an enormous influence on the ideas of later apocalyptic writings, but the figure of Daniel himself plainly has an important impact on the portrayal of the scribal figures on which most of the apocalyptic literature is focused.

We have not argued for an exact one-to-one correspondence between *maśkîl*, *ḥākhām* and *sôfēr*. This would be to tend towards the reductionist synonymizing that we have criticized in other studies.[134] Rather, our aim has been to show the essential compatibility between the terms, and to point out the relevance of the Danielic model to a full understanding of the background to concepts of 'scribe', even though his actual designation is *maśkîl* rather than *sôfēr*.[135]

(2) *Ezra as Scribe in 4 Ezra*[136]

Ezra and his Titles

The titles of Ezra in Ezra–Nehemiah, 'Ezra the scribe' (Neh. 8.2, 4, 13), 'Ezra the priest' (Ezra 10.10, 16, etc.) and 'Ezra the priest and scribe' (Neh. 8.9), or 'Ezra the priest, the scribe ... ' (Ezra 7.11, 12, etc.)[137] are not reproduced exactly in *4 Ezra*.[138] Indeed, there is only one scribe title in *4 Ezra*: 'Scribe of the knowledge of the Most High', which, though missing in the Latin text, concludes ch. 14 (and the book) in the Syriac, Ethiopic, Arabic 1 and Armenian versions.[139] This title may be based on the Aramaic letter of Artaxerxes (Ezra 7.12, 21: ספר דעתא די־אלה שמאיא) although the specific phraseology 'knowledge of the Most High' recalls Num. 24.16 (but cf. also 1 Esdr. 8.19) in the context of Balaam the seer.[140] Ezra is addressed only as 'Ezra' (6.10; 7.2, 25; 8.2; 14.15, 38), which name is actually introduced as an alternative to 'Salathiel'[141] in 3.1, and no title is used in the addresses (unlike *1 Enoch* 12.3f.; 15.1).

The introduction to *5 Ezra* and the completed *2 Esdras* credits Ezra with the title 'prophet' (2 Esdr. 1.1), which is a significant departure from the biblical texts. According to Knibb[142] this 'reflects the fact that 2 Esdr 1–2 has the form of a prophecy'.[143] Chapters 15–16 are also styled a prophecy (cf. 15.1), so that it does look as if the 'prophet' epithet is at home in the later material,[144] while 'scribe', found in the non-Latin versions of 14.50, is an earlier idea derived from the biblical record. On the other hand, in 12.42 Ezra is hailed as the last of the prophets. Myers[145] suggests that he is thus called as a way of bolstering the people's hope. But we should perhaps rather regard this as a further instance of fluidity between the designations 'prophet' and 'scribe' that emerges from the recognition of the 'prophetic' character of the role of the authoritative scribe.[146] There is no reason to see the use of the title 'prophet' in relation to Ezra as an indication that the 'scribe' epithet was regarded as so inferior as to warrant exclusion, nor that the titles are mutually exclusive. We must conclude that *4 Ezra* still has Ezra the Scribe in view.

In an apparently autobiographical note,[147] the author refers to the insights he has acquired through his extensive travels (3.33), and this is precisely part of the distinctive function of the scribe according to Sir. 39.4 (cf. 34.9-12), and is untypical of the prophets; thus we may have even here an implicit, albeit unintentional, indication both of 'scribal' authorship and of the ascription of scribal characteristics to Ezra.

If, as we have suggested, Daniel was recognizably a scribe, this might have facilitated the identification of the apocalyptic figure of Ezra the Scribe as Daniel's 'brother' in *4 Ezra* 12.11.[148] For Ezra, the model scribe in the OT writings, maintains his specifically 'scribal' role in the apocalyptic literature as well as the 'Danielic' role of the seer and mantic wise man. In a sense, Ezra is seen as superior to Daniel in understanding,[149] and thus in authority, since the latter was not able to have insight into the things now revealed to Ezra (12.12), who alone is worthy to learn the 'secret of the Most High' (12.36; cf. 7.44; 13.53). (This may have been inferred from Dan. 12.8-10 itself.) As in Daniel's case, there is little emphasis on scholarly expertise in respect of the Law; rather the scribe's qualities in this area are simply presupposed and the accent is placed on his spiritual or mantic insights and receptivity to revelations.

As with Ben Sira's treatment of the ideal scribe, the author's most pressing concern is with Ezra's *understanding*. It is this, coupled with his attention and obedience to the Law (cf. also 6.31f.; contrast 7.72), that is given as the reason for his special enlightenment (13.53f.). His initial revelation begins with a heavenly question as to his understanding of 'the way of the Most High' and his affirmation, 'Yes, my lord' (4.2f.);[150] his actual ignorance is then displayed (4.10f., 21) in order to demonstrate that his natural 'power of understanding' (4.22) will never be enlightened without a divine revelation of what is inherently hidden from human beings. He 'strives to understand' (5.34) and when in communication with heaven he gains 'the spirit of understanding' (5.22—the very phrase that indicates the moment of the scribe's inspiration in Sir. 39.6) but is repeatedly dismayed by his lack of understanding (10.30-37; cf. 8.4f.; 12.8f.). He is progressively given insights into hidden things by means of 'interpretation' or 'explanation' of parables and dreams (4.47; cf. 12.10ff., 35; 13.21, 25, 53), and matters are 'shown' to him as he can bear them (cf. 6.30, 33; 7.44, 104, etc.).

Ezra's fundamental commission is to

> write all these things that you have seen in a book; and you shall teach them to the wise among your people, whose hearts you know are able to comprehend and keep these secrets (12.37).

Accordingly, he promises to 'write everything' under the inspiration of the Holy Spirit (14.22) and the 'lamp of understanding' is then 'lit' in his heart for the duration of the writing process (14.25). After drinking a potion,[151] he says, 'my heart poured forth understanding, and wisdom increased in my breast . . . and my mouth was opened' (14.40f.). The 'mantic' understanding is also given to the men who take the dictation: 'the Most High gave understanding to the five men, and by turns they wrote what was dictated, in characters which they did not know' (14.42). The seventy esoteric, apocalyptic books in particular then contain 'the spring of understanding, the fountain of wisdom, and the river of knowledge' (14.47). This looks like a simple, clear declaration of the inspiration of these works. It is then on the basis of his 'having written all these things' that Ezra is 'called the Scribe of the Knowledge of the Most High for ever and ever'.

It is clear that Ezra's visionary experiences chronicled here are built largely on Daniel's in the biblical book.[152] (It will be remembered of course that Daniel's questioning and progressive revelation through dream and interpretation are themselves based on prophetic scripture [cf. Dan. 9.2].) And the pattern of the visionary's lack of understanding, followed by revelation, interpretation and understanding, is also taken from Daniel. The principal difference here is the emphasis on the writing down of the revelations (though this is also implied in Daniel) and the explicit title 'scribe' rather than *maśkîl*; 'understanding' or 'insight' is equally the fundamental concern of both functions. While Daniel 'shuts up the words and seals the book until the time of the end' (Dan. 12.4, 9), when 'the wise shall understand', it is Ezra's specific duty to 'write all these things' (12.37; 14.50; cf. Dan. 12.7) and teach them to 'the wise among your people, whose hearts you know are able to comprehend . . . ' (12.37; cf. Dan. 11.33; 12.10). This is also precisely the interpretative, mediatory role given to Enoch as scribe in the earlier literature, as we have seen. There is clearly a close coherence between the roles of Daniel as mantic *maśkîl* with scribal features, Enoch as scribe-seer and righteous wise man, and Ezra as Danielic scribe-prophet. The authorship of each work is germane to the others, representing as they do the work of apocalyptic scribal groups; and this is reflected in the similarity between the ideal figures at the centre of each work, who are essentially 'inspired', 'charismatic', model scribes.

(3) *Baruch as Scribe in 2 Baruch*[153]

Like the biblical Ezra, the biblical Baruch is associated with a good deal of literature, both apocryphal and apocalyptic. Similar to 1 Esdras, the apocryphal book of (1) Baruch is a fairly unimaginative reworking or 'transcription' of biblical material, which Keerl[154] rather uncharitably compares to 'the rhetorical practice of a feeble schoolboy, who composes an opusculum out of all sorts of passages'. *2 Baruch*, on the other hand, is a much more 'inspired', distinctive and innovative work, whose proximity to *4 Ezra* in a number of respects (not least the clear literary dependence at many points— though possibly on a mutual source) makes it especially interesting that 'Baruch' is associated with it as 'Ezra' is with *4 Ezra*: for both figures are of course important, model 'scribes' of the OT.[155]

In none of the Baruch literature does Baruch appear to be given a title, though in the titles given to the book of Baruch itself, he is variously called 'Prophet' (Coptic; in addition the Old Latin and Vulgate versions of Baruch style the book as the 'Prophecy of Baruch') and 'scribe' (Syriac). Since Baruch is expressly identified with Baruch, son of Neriah (cf. e.g. *2 Bar.* 1.1), who in Jeremiah 36 is called 'the scribe', and since there is some emphasis on his writing of revelatory material (cf. e.g. 1 Bar. 1.1), it seems reasonable to suppose that the literature (1, 2 and *3 Baruch*) regards him both as scribe and—in view of the fact that as a chosen recipient of special revelations he is on a par with or even superior to Jeremiah the prophet (cf. *2 Bar.* 2.1; 5.5; 9.1; 10.2; but cf. 33.1f.)—as a prophet (cf. also the prophetic introduction, *2 Bar.* 1.1). But it is important to note that the biblical title 'scribe' is neither revoked nor superseded. Baruch is evidently still seen as a scribe, even though his role is largely a 'prophetic' one. This is further evidence of a fluidity between the two titles and roles.[156]

Baruch in *2 Baruch* is in many ways the exact counterpart of Ezra the scribe in *4 Ezra*, and what we have observed concerning his scribal role there applies here also.

First, Baruch has the function of a letter-writer. In 77.12 he is requested to write 'to our brothers in Babylon . . . a letter of doctrine and a roll of hope', to fill the gap left by the 'shepherds of Israel', the 'lamps' that are 'extinguished', and the 'fountains' that have dried up (77.13). Clearly this refers to authoritative, prophetic teaching.[157] Chapters 78–87 are presented as the content of the letter, which consists largely of a revealed 'word of consolation' (81.1, 4; 82.1; cf. 78.5), an encouragement in view of the national calamity and an exhortation to keep the Law (cf. e.g. ch. 84) and to prepare for the last times. The letter is to be given with 'the traditions of the Law to your children after you . . . ' and to be 'read carefully in your assemblies'. It is obviously designed as a religious writing to be cherished by the faithful, an authoritative, didactic scripture. Baruch is given this commission forty days before being taken up to heaven (76.2, 4), in the following terms:

> Go, therefore, now during these days and instruct the people as much as you can so that they may learn lest they die in the last times, but may learn so that they live in the last times (76.5).

This is above all the classical role of the scribe (cf. e.g. Neh. 8.1-8), and we have seen it to be typical of the apocalyptic scribes Enoch and Ezra.[158] In 31f. also, Baruch is depicted as the authoritative teacher of the assembled people (cf. Neh. 8.1ff., 13; Ezra 10.1, 7f.), exactly as Ezra is in both OT and *4 Ezra* (cf. *4 Ezra* 5.18; 12.40ff.). Speaking to the assembled elders and leaders again in 44-46, Baruch instructs them to 'admonish the people as much as you can. For this is our work. For, when you instruct them, you will make them alive' (45.1, 2). The future succession of 'wise men' will then be guaranteed (46.4), and their authority is final: '. . . be subject to those who are wise and understanding with fear' (46.5).[159] We have noted the literary (inter)dependence between *4 Ezra* and *2 Baruch*; it applies especially to passages such as this, where the function of the eminent figures coincides to a large degree: two different figures from different times and situations can be given the same role because they share the same (quasi-prophetic) scribal authority.

Finally, like the other apocalyptic scribes we have discussed, Baruch is concerned both with the understanding of the Law and with the purposes of God in the unfolding of future events, through revelation and interpretation. It is because the Lord enlightens 'those who conduct themselves with understanding' (38.1) that Baruch can ask for and receive the explanation of his vision (38.3; 39.2). (It is clear that, like Ezra and Enoch, he is specially chosen for enlightenment; cf. 48.3.) Indeed, he is charged to 'understand that which has been revealed to you because you have many consolations which will last forever' (43.1). As in *1 Enoch* and *4 Ezra*, the understanding that is stressed is closely associated with righteousness,[160] and it is only those who both 'understand' and keep the Law (these seem to be mutually dependent qualities) that have any hope for the future (cf. 44.14; 51.3f., 7; 66.2; cf. 15.5f.; 46.5). The apocalyptic Baruch, like these other figures, might equally have merited the titles 'scribe of righteousness' and 'scribe of interpretation'.

Baruch the scribe, then, has the following roles: (1) apocalyptic seer of visions; (2) chosen recipient of revelations and explanations; (3) authoritative teacher of the people, concerned with spiritual insight and righteousness; (4) author of religious material based on divine revelation, for use by future generations; (5) a quasi- or fully prophetic role. In these he corresponds closely to Enoch and Ezra. It is noteworthy, however, that although like these two he is to be taken up to heaven before his death (cf. 46.7), he is, like Ezra, and indeed like Enoch in the earliest traditions, not specifically given a role in heaven: his scribalism, though a medium of divine revelation, is exclusively earthly. And it is notably only the peculiarly visionary function (1) that clearly distinguishes his role from that of the inspired scribe as represented in Sirach.

(4) *Moses as Scribe*

Targum Onkelos to Deut. 33.21[161] describes Moses as the ספרא רבא
דישראל, Israel's scribe *par excellence* (cf. the appellation of Enoch in
Tg. Ps.-Jon. Gen. 5.24).[162] Clearly, this is related at least partially to
the fundamental belief in Moses' authorship of Torah (written and
oral)—Moses is the Great Scribe because he is the author of the
Great Book. But Moses' entitlement to the appellation rests on
broader grounds than this.

Later generations of Jewish scholars would elaborate on Moses'
scribal expertise, suggesting, for example, that he wrote thirteen
scrolls of the Torah,[163] and elaborating on Moses' work as a student
and expositor of the law, on his outstanding wisdom and intelligence
and his role as teacher and judge of Israel.[164] But the author of
Targum Onkelos, broadly contemporary with other instances of a
general association of scribes with prophets (see Chapter 2), may also
have had in mind the notion of Moses as an apocalyptic scribe in a
similar sense to the depiction of Ezra in *4 Ezra* and *5 Ezra* and of
Baruch and especially Enoch in the apocalyptic literature that bears
their names; for to Moses is ascribed an apocalyptic Testament, the
Testament of Moses,[165] in which the primary traits of the eminent
apocalyptic scribes are also present. Here Moses instructs Joshua to
'take this writing so that later you will remember how to preserve the
books which I shall entrust to you' (1.16), and to 'keep these words
and this book' (10.11), the genre of which is correctly described as a
Testament. The form of the book itself is typical of that wisdom/
apocalyptic genre, its farewell speech involving a historical projection
of the future history of Israel in periods divisible by seven. In
particular, it is very similar in both form and content to the
Testaments of the Twelve Patriarchs and *1 Enoch* (esp. 97–107),
2 Baruch (cf. esp. 84), *4 Ezra* 14, *inter alia*. Indeed, there are several
close connections between the portrayals of the apocalyptic scribes
Ezra, Enoch and Baruch, and that of Moses in *T. Moses*. These
include the mention of the *revelatory* function of the latter in
mediating revelations in writing under inspiration: *T. Moses* 3.11,
'is this not that which was made known to us in prophecies[166] by
Moses'; 3.12; cf. 1.12-14, '[the Lord of the world] did not make this
purpose of creation openly known from the beginning of the
world. . . . But he did design and devise me, who (was) prepared from
the beginning of the world, to be the mediator of his covenant.

Therefore I shall speak plainly to you.' Moses is 'the divine prophet for the whole earth, the perfect teacher in the world' (11.16).[167] Again, like Enoch, Daniel and the other eminences of apocalyptic, in later Jewish literature Moses also has a heavenly counterpart, a 'teacher'/'scribe', namely Zagzagel 'scribe of the angels' (also like Enoch identified with Metatron),[168] who instructs Moses 'in all the secrets of the Torah', and is responsible for giving him the 'rays of majesty'.[169]

Such connections could be catalogued at length, but the point need not be laboured. It is interesting to note, however, that even Philo holds a comparable view of Moses' function. Moses is 'king, lawgiver, high priest and prophet' (*De Vita Mosis* 3.39). While Philo does not give Moses the title 'scribe', he does appear to acknowledge him as 'interpreter' (1.1), though clearly he thinks Moses is much more than this; the rest of the scribal characteristics emerge under Philo's four major categories. Educated in Egyptian philosophy and language, Assyrian literature, Chaldaean astrology and Greek learning, as well as music and mathematics (1.5), Moses can be 'inspired, and full of the spirit of prophecy' (1.36); and at the end of his life, quite transcendent, he is transformed 'into a most sun-like mind . . . wholly possessed by inspiration', a description which could almost have been taken directly from apocalyptic literature itself.[170] The LXX translators, incidentally, whose task it is to 'explain the sacred account', 'like men inspired, prophesied', as 'not mere interpreters but hierophants and prophets'.[171] It is clear from this and from his description of Moses as 'prophet' that Philo's category of 'prophet' largely overlaps with the apocalyptic concept of the 'scribe', an overlap we have seen to be common in Early Judaism.[172]

It is true that Josephus (*Ag. Ap.* 1.290) pours scorn on Egyptians who see Moses and Joseph as 'scribes' (Moses a *grammateus*; Joseph a *hierogrammateus*). In context, though, Josephus is giving no quarter in his argument against a highly tendentious, apparently anti-Jewish, account by Chaeremon of the exodus ('expulsion'!) of the Hebrews from Egypt, and his main criticism here is that Chaeremon has linked Joseph and Moses, who should be separated by 'four generations'. But this would accord with our observation in Chapter 2 that for Josephus γραμματεύς is a humble, mundane term. The Egyptians he criticizes may well retain a high ideal of the scribe. After all, the Egyptian royal adviser, Phritobautes, is given the same title (ἱερογραμματεύς, *Ag. Ap.* 1.289).[173]

But the scribal function of Moses is already emphasized in the deuteronomistic account; chs. 32 and 33 of Deuteronomy are perhaps themselves early examples of this testament genre; their wisdom connections are evident (cf. e.g. 32.28f.; 34.9). Deuteronomy 32 is presented as the 'Song' of Moses, which he is instructed by Yahweh to 'write down' and to 'teach to the people of Israel' as a 'witness' against them (31.19, 21f.; cf. vv. 24, 26, 28; cf. the roles of Enoch, discussed above). The Deuteronomist's work seems generally to be self-consciously scribal.[174] The whole context is one of the communication or 'mediation'[175] of the Law to the people, which is the province of the *scribe*.

We need not deal with the question of the historical Moses as scribe (though there would be plenty of scope for possibilities of a typical royal, Egyptian scribal education between Exod. 2.10 and 11),[176] nor with the wider field of Jewish traditions concerning Moses. We are here concerned to point out simply that (a) Moses is portrayed as a scribe in all but name by the Deuteronomist; (b) the context of this portrayal is scribal in both form and content; (c) the scribal nature of Moses' work is reiterated in other scribal contexts; (d) in later works, Testaments and Apocalypses, broadly contemporary with Matthew's Gospel, and marked by scribal characteristics, the scribal functions of Moses are presented with an apocalyptic emphasis on the transmission of revelatory material. It is possible that the targums also are acquainted with such ideas. At any rate, the fact that in the targums the title is otherwise used only of Enoch the (apocalyptic) scribe is highly suggestive of this.

We must conclude that Moses was regarded as an eminent, model scribe in intertestamental and Early Judaism and that, together with the other eminent scribes we have reviewed, he forms an important part of the background against which concepts of the scribe in the NT period should be seen.

We may build upon the results of this survey of the eminent scribes in the apocalyptic literature—which has revealed a remarkably consistent picture—in the following discussion of the apocalyptic authors' view of themselves as scribes.

2. The Apocalyptic Authors as Scribes

Study of the *Sitz im Leben* of apocalyptic literature and of the socio-religious and political groups responsible for it is hampered by a lack of hard evidence beyond what my be gleaned from the literature itself;[177] the various groups that produced and venerated the literature cannot be confidently identified. Even where historical names and propensities may be *plausibly* matched up with literary products (such as the putative association of the *Hasidim* of 1 and 2 Maccabees with the 'early/proto-apocalyptic' circles responsible for the book of Daniel),[178] no certainty can be attained.[179] Such is the case not only for the 'dark age' in which Jewish apocalyptic first emerged, especially in the third century, but also for later periods: no consensus has yet been reached, for example, on an identification of the particular groups responsible for *4 Ezra* and *2 Baruch*[180] (though there is more general agreement on their dates). Our *historical* sources are simply not adequate to give us the precise contours that we would desire for socio-religious classifications.

This does not mean, however, that no socio-historical conclusions may be drawn;[181] only that the literature itself must first be thoroughly sifted for its own evidence. What kinds of information, then, does the literature afford in respect of the persons and 'communities' from which it sprang?

1. *The content of the literature is bound to reflect to a large degree the concerns and aspirations of its authors and the community for which it exists.* Most religious works have a serious and quite functional purpose. In the case of apocalyptic literature the material is not only 'revelatory', catering for the particular intellectual needs of a community threatened by a crisis of faith and theology, but hortatory, serving both as an encouragement to personal perseverance and fortitude and as a unifying bond for the community as a whole. The community is clearly expected to *see* itself *in* the literature: physically, in the direct line of tradition unbroken since Enoch first delivered it to Methuselah, or Ezra to his amanuenses; but also in the central figure of the work as an eminent, prime example of the kind of *homo religiosus* that is the individual member of the community.

Our suggestion is that the authors and venerators of the literature were pleased to identify with the *scribal* characteristics of the central figure; they would be sure to seek to emulate his example, and if, as in Enoch's case, he was 'the scribe', they would aspire to the same high office, albeit on a lower plane. This would be particularly appropriate to them if by force of circumstance or dogma other religious *cadres* (e.g. the priestly or the prophetic) were barred to them.

It is of course not always the case that the central figure(s) of a piece of literature will reliably reflect an accurate image of the person and role of its author; however, it often seems to be the case in Jewish religious literature. The levitical allegiance of the Chronicler is almost certainly a factor in his portrayal of the significance of that group among the Jewish leadership,[182] and it is legitimate to regard the Chronicler as probably a Levite himself.

Similar conclusions may be drawn from the portrayal of Daniel and the other heroes in the book that bears his name as *maśkîlîm*. Here, as in the Chronicles, the group to which the author owes allegiance is named.[183] In Daniel 11 and 12 the eschatological group for whom the writing is intended (probably largely identical with the collectors and authors of the Danielic material) may not be *maśkîlîm* in precisely the same sense as the heroes of the court-tales (Daniel 1–6; cf. e.g. 1.4, 17), but they will certainly have identified with them nonetheless.[184] The link is clearer in the revelation that causes Daniel to 'become wise' (Dan. 9.22, 25). At a further remove from Daniel 1–6 we see the same phenomenon reappearing at Qumran, where the respective Maskil of each Essene group clearly owes his title and the major part of his function to the Danielic model, even if the Essenes were not *the same people* as the *maśkîlîm* of Daniel.[185] F.F. Bruce states,[186] 'The Qumran community appears to have stood in the direct succession of those faithful *maskilim*'.

The exact nature of the relationship between the central figure and his venerators is difficult to determine, especially as psychological, phenomenological and anthropological issues are also involved. And the complex question of pseudonymous writing is tied up with this. Some recent studies of the apocalyptic phenomenon suggest that the relationship is so close that the seer 'feels united' with the central worthy with whom he is concerned, to the extent that he may 'identify himself'[187] with that figure. Thus the phenomenon of pseudonymity may rest less on a deliberate strategy of archaizing deception or self-legitimation by identification with an eminent figure of the past than on the phenomenological laws of the apocalyptic process itself: the apocalyptic writer, in writing down Enoch's revelations, for example, effectively *is* Enoch writing down the revelations. In Russell's view, pseudonymity in apocalyptic is explicable on psychological grounds. In *4 Ezra*, for example, the close coincidence between the depiction of Ezra and the presentation of Moses in Exodus reflects a 'psychological situation' in which 'Moses himself is seen to be identified with Ezra, who in turn is identified with the author of the book'.[188] Furthermore, the veneration of a particular man's name may involve the writer's seeing himself 'as in some way an "extension" of his personality'.[189] Russell associates these factors with the mooted Hebrew idea of 'contemporaneity' (a telescoping of an ancient time into the present in the author's perception), which he posits by analogy with Wheeler Robinson's concept of 'corporate personality'. The latter notion has been seriously questioned,[190] reconstructions of psychological processes in ancient figures are of course fraught with difficulties, and Russell's position may require modification. However, I find myself in agreement with Russell's finding that

> The apocalyptic writers, like the ancient seer in whose name they wrote, stood within the apocalyptic tradition, shared the same visionary experiences and received the same divine revelations. The sameness of their respective experience would make it possible for them to associate, to the point of coincidence, their own circumstances with those of their worthy predecessor and to see in them, as it were, a spiritual reproduction of his own.

C. Rowland, taking up J. Lindblom's assessment of the visionary phenomenon as due to an *alter ego* experience,[191] suggests the possibility that, in the apocalypses, the visionary accounts may involve a 'linking of the visionary's *alter ego* [anonymous] in the literary account of [genuine] visions with a figure of the past, whose visionary prowess was renowned'. To write in the name of the ancient figure was 'the only way in which [the apocalypticist] could do justice to the nature of his experience'.[192] When it comes to precise definitions, no certainty is achievable, and both Russell and Rowland admit the tentative nature of their conclusions. But scholars agree that in some way, the apocalypticists *identify* with the central figure in whose name and of whose experiences they speak. The apocalypticist groups could *see* themselves in the venerated figures. If Daniel, for example, was 'wise' and 'lettered', so were they;

if interested in *pesher* interpretation, so were they; if concerned to understand the course of significance of world history, so were they; if involved with prophetic, visionary revelations and dream-interpretations, so were they. Daniel was their heroic exemplar, their ideal. And if the primary role of their exemplar was as scribe-seer, we may expect the apocalypticists to have viewed themselves as such also.

It is true, of course, as we have mentioned, that the apocalypticists *also* saw themselves *explicitly* referred to in the literature, as the 'wise and understanding', the *maśkîlîm* and the 'righteous' to whose charge the revelations were entrusted. We have already had occasion to note the close relationship between the seer and the 'seen' figure and between the seer and the 'wise and understanding' readership of the (contemporary) 'future'. (A parallel relationship may pertain between the seer of the narrative—the eminent ancient—and the *angelic* revealer; if *alter ego*s are indeed involved in this, the phenomenon may be one dimension more complex than Lindblom and Rowland allow!) The apocalypticists themselves are everywhere present in their literature.

2. Our second point rests on the perhaps self-evident observation that a piece of literature is the product of an author, who is bound to project himself in some way into that literature. The apocalyptic literature is unmistakably the work of authors who are interested in understanding their place in history and their physical environment, in understanding scripture, in writing and studying books, and in visionary experiences. This does not of itself make the authors themselves visionaries, but *it does make them scribes* in the sense we have discerned both in Ben Sira and in the eminent figures portrayed at the centre of the apocalyptic literature. In writing down the revelations to Enoch, Ezra and the others they are, like them, mediators and interpreters; in their very evident expertise in the law and the scriptures they are 'understanding' scribes (cf. Sir. 38-39); like Baruch, or like Ezra and his amanuenses they are inspired writers; like Enoch, Daniel and the 'righteous' for whom 'Enoch' and 'Daniel' write, they are concerned to instruct the faithful in righteousness. Indeed, in all aspects other than the specifically heavenly role of judicial notary and witness, they are scribes in much the same way as the eminent central characters.[193]

A. *The Apocalyptic Works as Scribal Products*

Scholars have long recognized the 'scribal' character of apocalyptic literature, which, however, they tend to see primarily, if not exclusively, in the 'rabbinic' sense which we have seen to be an inadequate understanding of the scribal art according to Ben Sira and the apocalyptic heroes: namely that the authors are scribes because they are experts in interpreting the law and the scriptures. Thus Vielhauer, for example, can state programmatically that 'Die Apokalyptik ist Buchweisheit',[194] and Janssen can state that since the apocalyptic authors derive much of their 'visionary' material *midrashically, from the OT*, 'Das bedeutet, daß die Apokalyptiker Schriftgelehrte sind'.[195]

In a section devoted to the apocalyptists as scribes, Janssen also notes that the names given to the apocalyptic books 'sind durchweg Weise und Schriftgelehrte'.[196] He does not specify in which of the two categories Enoch is at home; if 'Schriftgelehrter' or both 'Schriftgelehrter' and 'Weiser', then surely not in the same sense as the apocalyptic writers unless there is rather more content to the term than simply 'expert in the scriptures'; one suspects that a too easy equation of ספור/γραμματεύς with 'Schriftgelehrter' is operative here, which with few exceptions[197] has persisted since Luther. And we have seen in the Enoch literature, to name but one example, that this is not the primary sense of the word *saḥāfi*/ספרא—it would hardly do justice to Enoch here to designate him simply as a Schriftgelehrter.

In addition to these factors, Janssen notes various specifically scribal concerns in the literature: e.g. its adaptation of a contemporary cosmology from the perspective of a belief in creation,[198] its historical perspective, which adapts the hellenistic view of history into a salvation-historical framework, and its concern with determinism. This is not, says Janssen, the product of a sectarian piety but is 'einwandfrei Anliegen schriftgelehrter Arbeit'.[199] His concern, however, to rehabilitate apocalyptic in the direct line of authoritative tradition between the prophets and the rabbis has created what may be a false dichotomy here. The commoner fallacy is to posit a fundamental dichotomy between apocalyptic and scribalism. Janssen successfully overcomes this point of view, only to succumb to the equally fallacious notion that scribalism and Pharisaism/rabbinism are necessarily of the same order. However, Janssen is justified in arguing for the scribal character of apocalyptic literature on the grounds that (a) the central figures reflect distinctively scribal interest, (b) the issues that occupy the authors are typically 'scribal', and (c) the methods employed by the authors (midrashic exposition on a scriptural base) are also scribal. The present study would add that the 'scribal' nature of the literature also carries with it the visionary or revelatory qualities of the scribal figures whom the literature reveres. Like them, the apocalyptic authors are purveyors of revelation; they are inspired interpreters (of scripture, dreams, history and the signs of the times); they are teachers of the righteous; and their literary products are 'inspired' and revelatory (hence their common self-designation as, or equation with, 'prophecy'). This observation would extend to all the classical apocalyptic material from Daniel through the whole intertestamental period. We would suspect its presence too in the NT—for example in the synoptic 'Little Apocalypse' and the book of Revelation.

John of Patmos as Scribe; Revelation as a Scribal Product
We may at this point expand briefly on our observation above that the scribal character of apocalyptic is evident in the book of Revelation. We noted the similarity between Ezra as scribe and author of 'prophecy' in 2 Esdras and John as witness (cf. 1.2) and author of 'prophecy' in Revelation.[200] If the apocalyptic authors are 'prophetic' 'scribes', this would appear to be an eminently appropriate way also to understand the author of the Johannine Apocalypse. Indeed it is difficult to see any substantive point at which John can be seen to differ in role, experience and perceived authority from the scribe figures of Jewish apocalyptic literature. Though the book is probably not pseudonymous, it matches *4 Ezra, 2 Baruch, 1 Enoch* and Daniel in its whole ethos of revelatory experience and piety. The coincidences extend beyond its varied apocalyptic interests and language: the visionary at the centre has a similar role and status in each; above all he is a mediator in writing of revelatory material, an inspired, pious interpreter.

In fact, the self-consciously repeated references to the 'writing' of 'this book' in Revelation, with its 'words of prophecy', may themselves indicate that the author saw himself as a scribe of prophetic words (to coin a phrase) rather than simply as a 'prophet'. As in the case of Jewish apocalyptic works, the book is a record of revealed mysteries which the author is commissioned to write down (cf. e.g. 1.11; 21.5; 22.19);[201] references to writing are very common (γράφειν in various forms occurs 29 times in Revelation), while the use of βίβλιον in the book accounts for as many as 23 of the NT's 34 occurrences (with a further two uses of βίβλος). Since most of the references concern the apocalyptic writing itself (as do similar references in the apocalyptic literature), the natural inference would be that scribal influences and concerns are quite probably operative here too. This claim could also be supported by reference to the *Schriftgelehrter*-role of the author in respect of the 'charismatic exegesis' of scripture (see below), especially of Daniel. In all this 'apocalyptic' literature we are clearly dealing with the work of scribes who saw their role as in some sense 'prophetic'. One might justifiably call them 'mantic scribes'.

An interesting view of the mechanics of the scribal origins of the visionary material of Revelation has been expressed by A. Farrer.[202] He reminds us that the rabbis issued grave warnings about the dangers of meditating on the Merkabah passage (Ezek. 1), which is a practice in which the author of Revelation clearly indulged; this rests on the recognition that meditation on the scriptures can *give rise* to visionary experiences. In Farrer's view this process is most acute when the subject is *writing*: 'he meditates into vision what he writes, and feels the presence of the mysteries he describes'.[203] This is tantamount to a claim that the scribal art (meditation, interpretation, composition) is a natural environment and medium for 'apocalyptic' revelation.[204] There are indeed good grounds for this view. After all, is this not precisely what the scribe 'Daniel', for example, was doing with the scriptures of Jeremiah and Isaiah before him? Certainly it is a trait of apocalyptic literature that the visions and interpretative material are steeped in allusions to the scriptures;[205] clearly this is a result of extended and intensive meditation on them. In Revelation, as in pre- and non-Christian Jewish apocalyptic proper, the greater part of the material is midrashic in spirit, if not in genre, and is fundamentally exegetical. It builds on a deep and intense reflection on the OT, especially the prophets. Indeed L. Cerfaux describes the book as 'une traduction en clair, dans la lumière du Nouveau Testament, des prophéties de l'Ancien Testament'.[206]

This is not to contest in any way the correct recognition of the prophetic features of the book, nor the 'prophetic' role of the original seer. Rather, our concern is to point up the scribal character of the development from original prophetic vision to its expansion and presentation in literary form, a factor which has not been adequately considered in the 'apocalyptic versus prophecy' arguments concerning the nature of the book. If the book of Revelation is *scribal* in the apocalyptic sense, it is also mantically inspired, so that the whole 'apocalyptic versus prophecy' debate (even if it was justifiably conceived of in the first place) turns out to be a false dilemma.

Once again, the terminological question poses itself (cf. our discussion of scribes and prophecy, Chapters 2 and 3 above): Is John of Patmos actually a *prophet* employing 'scribal' techniques and skills, like the latter OT prophets and their interpreters; or is he first and foremost a *scribe*, whose charismatic insight means his work is in a real sense 'prophetic'? In John's case it has to be recognized that the terms overlap and the respective functions largely coincide. The author of Revelation does not refer to himself as 'scribe' (though comparable apocalyptic authors, as we have seen, do carry this self-understanding); on the other hand, he does not (even in 22.6) refer to himself as a 'prophet' (though the prophets are his 'brethren' [22.9; cf. the similar angelic acknowledgment of Ezra's role in *4 Ezra* 12.11]). Prophets, when operating in a 'scribal' mode, are in practice barely, if at all, distinguishable from charismatic, inspired scribes. The principal common factor is divinely granted insight. The author of Revelation is equally at home in both categories, and the acknowledgment of the scribal character and authority of his work in no way implies a detraction from its prophetic authority.

B. *'Charismatic Exegesis'*

This brings us to the delicate question of the existence and nature of 'charismatic exegesis'[207] and its relation to apocalyptic literature and prophecy. The constraints of this study preclude a detailed survey of exegetical methods and hermeneutical principles operative in apocalyptic literature, Qumran and the NT, which is in any case now well-trodden ground.[208] Rather, we are concerned with an underlying principle which has to do with the interpreter's *authority* (and hence creative freedom) in relation to the interpretation of the text, that is, the spiritual factor that connects interpreter and text.

M.E. Boring, in a discussion of the Johannine Apocalypse as early Christian prophecy,[209] describes the author's relationship to the OT thus:

> The prophet does not operate deductively, quoting the Old Testament and then giving the Christian meaning, but by inspiration, operating in an almost organic union with the Old Testament text which he does not perceive as an object of his reflection, but the vehicle which forms a living unity with his own message.

We shall have cause to discuss this view of apocalyptic-prophetic inspiration in respect of Matthew (Chapter 7). Boring in fact explicitly differentiates Matthew from the 'pneumatic-apocalyptic' hermeneutical stance; he sees Matthew as an example of the 'scribal-rabbinic' stance which 'distinguishes clearly between the word of Scripture and the word of the interpreter' (see Chapter 7, note 18). Some of Matthew's methods and some of his hermeneutical principles may indeed differ from those of the authors of Revelation and the apocalypses in certain respects, but we shall argue that the foundation on which he operates is very much the same: he is a scribe whose authority rests on his 'inspired' spiritual insight.

At this point, it is sufficient to note that scriptural exegesis need not be regarded as on a lower plane than pneumatic revelation. For the later OT prophets at least, such a role was part and parcel of the prophet's function, as has been amply demonstrated by Ellis.[210] At least from the exile onwards, there is no scriptural prophecy that does not take its point of departure from earlier scriptures, which provide both inspiration for new revelatory material and insight into God's dealings with the believing community. In Aune's words, 'Divine illumination into the true meaning of the OT . . . cannot be separated from other forms of spiritual discernment; all are based on the presence and activity of the Spirit of God.'[211] Our point is that the intuitive, 'inspired' or 'charismatic' use of the OT both by the *apocalypticists*, Jewish and Christian, and by *prophets*, Jewish and Christian, is fundamentally a *scribal* art. For the 'divine illumination' of the genuine, understanding scribe is an essential part of his function and indeed amounts to a seal of his authority. And any scribe worth his salt will practise this art for the benefit of God's people.[212]

The lack of such a study has obliged us to examine the scribal concepts and concerns in the apocalyptic literature in some detail. My suggestion that this literature is of import for the discussion of concepts of the scribe in early Judaism and Christianity has, I hope, been vindicated to the extent that we have been able to observe a firm basis of agreement throughout this literature with regard to Jewish concepts of the scribe in the intertestamental period. While there is certainly no rigidity in the use of the term 'scribe', and not all scribes exercise precisely the same functions to the exclusion of all others, nonetheless there is a large measure of consistency in the usage. Typically in this literature the concept of the scribe involves: (1) social eminence and religious authority of the scribe—as in Ben Sira and the OT; (2) occupation with hidden meanings, of scripture, visions, prophecies and 'parables'—as in Ben Sira; (3) a concomitant emphasis on 'understanding', especially divinely inspired insight, and on 'interpretation'—as in Ben Sira and the levitical scribalism of the OT; (4) function as a mediator of revealed insights, a writing teacher of contemporary and future generations, whose concern is to cause others to understand—like Ben Sira; (5) a 'prophetic' or quasi-prophetic charisma and vocation—like some of the OT scribes (and their representation in the targums) and once again Ben Sira. We shall find this general concept of the scribe to be very significant for a full understanding of Matthew's own concept of the scribe, as also of his Gospel.

The Qumran literature remains to be investigated with the same concerns in mind.

Chapter 5

SCRIBES AND QUMRAN LITERATURE

1. Scribes in Qumran Literature

It is a curious fact that the title 'scribe' is not found as an overt self-designation among the authors of the materials discovered at Qumran, especially in view of the currently prevailing concept of the Qumran community which envisages it as a 'scribal' community with its 'scriptorium'[1] and distinctive scriptures and school of exegesis. There is no doubt that many if not all of the activities that are traditionally regarded as being 'scribal' were practised by the Essenes and the Qumranites, for which the scrolls themselves are ample evidence (particularly if they wrote them, of course;[2] but also by virtue of their preservation of the literature, which is in itself a scribal task). Indeed, Qumran is an obvious place to look for scribal 'models', and it was natural for Stendahl to take Qumran as a paradigm for the activity of the Matthean 'school'.[3] It is understandable, too, that a scholar should be tempted to essay a solution to the discrete problems of the identity of the NT 'scribes' and of the surprising absence of the Essenes from the Gospel narratives: hence the interesting but untenable view of J. Dampier.[4]

We propose, then, to look at eminent 'scribes' in the Qumran literature and then at the roles of the corresponding scholars and teachers among the Essene communities as represented in their writings.

We have already discussed the use of the term 'scribe' in relation to *Enoch* in the Aramaic fragments of Enoch literature found in Qumran Cave 4. 'Scribe of righteousness' and 'scribe of interpretation' are relatively well attested titles of Enoch here, as we have seen. Exactly how the Enoch literature relates to the concerns and beliefs of the Qumran community is a matter of some debate;[5] but unless the Qumran cache of MSS was merely a repository or genizah, of unrelated (or only very loosely related) materials,[6] it is clear that at the very least the Qumran Essenes regarded the Enoch materials as worthy of copying and preservation. It is possible that they, or their direct 'hasidic' forerunners, were precisely the authors of some of this material. In any case, the Essenes certainly saw Enoch as an eminent scribe, and presumably one worthy of emulation.

From the remaining fragments of Sirach found at Qumran and Masada it is clear, too, that the work was held in high esteem by the Essenes. It is unfortunate, however, that the sparse remains do not include the relevant 'scribal' passages of chs. 38f., so that we cannot be certain that these were known to the Qumran community, although there is a good likelihood of this.[7] What is of particular interest, however, is the brief writing included on the Psalms scroll of Cave 11 (on which, five or six columns earlier, there is also a Hebrew writing identified with Sir. 51),[8] which Sanders labelled as 11QPs^aDavComp.

A. *David as Scribe in 11QPs^aDavComp*

The text of this well-preserved passage in Sanders's edition runs as follows:

l. 2	ויהי דויד ישי חכם ואור כאור השמש וסופר
l. 3	ונבון ותמם בכול דרכיו לפני אל ואנשים ויתן
l. 4	לו יהוה רוח נבונה ואורה ויכתוב . . .

(. . . there follows a list of his compositions, of interest because of the calendrical implications of its 364 daily tamid songs and 52 sabbath corban songs . . .)

l. 11	כול אלה דבר בנבונה אשר נתן לו מלפני העליון

Translation:

David son of Jesse was a wise man and a light like the light of the sun, and a scribe, and understanding and perfect in all his ways before God and men.

And Yhwh gave him a spirit of understanding and brilliance, and he wrote (. . .) All these things he spoke in prophecy which was given him from before the Most High.

Sanders translates וסופר in line 2 as 'and literate', with a note offering
the alternative 'scholarly', with reference to 1 Chron. 27.32 and *b.
Ber.* 45b. In both these cases, however, a noun is called for in
translation, and in both 'scribe' would seem eminently suitable
(Jastrow [*s.v.*] suggests 'scholarly man' for *b. Ber.* 45b, since there
the סופר stands in opposition to the בור, the illiterate man; Ben Sira
teaches us however [cf. Sir. 38] that this is a perfectly appropriate
contrast to make concerning the 'scribe'.) In any case we are dealing
with the same word, and for the sake of consistency[9] I would
translate (along with Vermes, Hengel, Stadelmann, *et al.*) with
'scribe'.

This very interesting passage has close affinities with both Ben
Sira and apocalyptic literature. Stadelmann attributes it to the 'der
Apokalyptik nahestehenden "Offenbarungsweisheit"'.[10] It is close to
Ben Sira in juxtaposing the qualities of the *sôfēr* with those of the
ḥākhām (cf. Sir. 38.24) and in particular in stressing the 'understanding' of the scribe (cf. Sir. 38.33–39.9). Further, in a phrase that
corresponds precisely with the picture of the divinely inspired scribe
in Sir. 39.6, David is here credited with the divine 'gift' of the 'spirit
of understanding' on the basis of which he 'wrote' the psalms and
songs attributed to him, which 'he spoke in prophecy which was
given him from before the Most High'. The closest thing to the
רוח נבונה in the OT is found in Isa. 11.2, again concerning a
descendant of Jesse on whom the Spirit of the Lord rests; Sanders is
also right to draw attention to 2 Sam. 23.2 and 1 Sam. 16.18, which
again of course concern David. But it should be noted that the exact
phrase is found only in Sir. 39.6 (where it is entirely in keeping with
the rest of the book; cf. e.g. 24.25ff.; 50.27; 51.20) and in certain more
overtly 'apocalyptic' writings (*4 Ezra* 5.21; *1 Enoch* 49.3; *Ps. Sol.*
17.42; *T. Levi* 2.3; 18.7),[11] where the context is always one of special,
messianic authority or revelation to an eminent personage (in
1 Enoch, *Psalms of Solomon* and *T. Levi* 18 a messianic figure, as in
Isa. 11).[12] The 'spirit of understanding' is in practice inseparable
from and co-terminous with the 'spirit of the Lord' that rests on
those who are privileged to see divine mysteries, understand hidden
things and to speak, teach or write things under 'inspiration'.[13] That
the privilege is specifically accorded to the 'scribe' in Sir. 39.6 and
our passage here (cf. also Ezra in *4 Ezra* and the Elect One [=
Enoch] in *1 Enoch*)[14] says a good deal about current understandings

of the ideal scribe. The inspired scribe, endowed with this spirit, enjoyed authority equal to that of the prophet and fulfilled a comparable role. David, wise man and scribe, is inspired to speak 'in prophecy', while Ben Sira, scribe, speaking in the name of Wisdom 'will pour out teaching like (or 'in'—Syr.) prophecy and leave it to all generations' (Sir. 24.33; cf. 18.29; 39.6ff.; 50.27).[15] In both cases, the resultant words of the scribe are inspired and 'prophetic' and are due to a special gift of 'understanding' (cf. also *Ps. Sol.* 17.48f.). When in the realm of inspired wisdom and apocalyptic literature, we are squarely within the realm of the quasi-prophetic, eminent scribe. The revelatory quality of the insight from which all these figures derive their authority is the same; and it is explicitly a *scribal* authority.

With Stadelmann, one hesitates to label this passage 'apocalyptic' in the narrowest sense, but its affinities with the style and content of apocalyptic material are strong enough for us to relate it to what we have observed concerning the eminent scribes of that literature. In this and all the cases we have discussed, the eminent scribe is endowed with special understanding and is inspired by God to produce sayings or writings which have a quasi-prophetic role in the righteous instruction of the scribe's posterity.[16]

B. *The Teacher of Righteousness, the Maskil and the Scribe*

The term *sôfēr* is not used of the Essene leader in the extant scrolls. Rather, he is referred to as 'the Teacher' (cf. e.g. CD 14) or the 'Teacher of Righteousness'—one who 'rains righteousness' (cf. 1QH 8.16). He teaches with great personal authority, as the one 'to whom God made known all the mysteries of the words of His servants the Prophets' (1QpHab 7 [Vermes]); his words come 'from the mouth of God' and must therefore be followed (1QpHab 2, etc.). Essentially, his role is that of the *dôrēš hattôrâ*, the Interpreter of the Law,[17] whose revelatory interpretation of the Law determines the understanding of the Law as it is to be followed by the Qumran community. He is both a 'discerning interpreter of wonderful mysteries' (1QH 2.13) and a trainer and teacher in whose heart God has 'put teaching and understanding, that he might open a fountain of knowledge to all men of insight' (1QH 2.18).

Now it is clear that the incumbent[18] Teacher of Righteousness is essentially a single, revered figure, and that his interpretation of the prophets and his teaching are seen as determinative of the life of the whole community. We should therefore see him as an eminent 'Teacher' with supreme authority, a creative genius, and not simply as a prime representative of a class of teachers of the law or 'scribes' *in this sense*. But his role bears comparison with that of the 'eminent scribe' that we have seen in each of a number of branches of the apocalyptic literature:

First, he is endowed with special 'understanding' (בינה, 1QH 1.22; 2.10, 17f.; 14.8; cf. 15.12, etc.), 'knowledge' (דעת, 1QH 4.27; 7.27; etc.) and 'wisdom' (שכל, 1QH 9.31; etc.).

Second, his role is to interpret and teach mysteries to the wise, *causing them to understand* (1QH 2.13, 18, etc.; cf. 1QS 9; CD 1.1; 2.2ff., 14ff.).[19]

Third, the teaching based on his interpretative gift includes halakhic rulings that are *'revealed'*,[20] and thus carry divine authority. By contrast, his opponents, who clearly offer halakhah that is at variance with his, are described as 'teachers of lies and seers of falsehood' (1QH 4); they do not share his illumination and will thus 'perish without understanding' (1QH 4).

Fourth, it is clear from the authorship of many of the Hodayoth (and possibly other of the Qumran texts) that the Teacher himself exactly matches the Davidic model, discussed above, as represented in 11QPs³DavComp: he too is an author (in 11QPs³ the specific term is סופר) of introspective and pietistic psalms that come of direct, divine inspiration.[21]

Fifth, it is evident from the whole range of the material that the teaching of the Teacher was seen as definitive and permanently determinative of the whole community.[22]

It should be added that the Teacher of Righteousness is a priest, indeed *'the* Priest' (CD 14.7, emphasis mine).[23] Not all priests were of course scribes, nor all scribes priests; but most scribes of high standing will have been either priests or Levites. We have already noted the priestly credentials of Ezra the priest, the scribe (also, incidentally, of the Zadokite line [Ezra 7.2]) and the priestly connections of Ben Sira, Enoch, Daniel and Baruch. (Ezekiel and Jeremiah, too, we recall, have priestly and scribal functions.) A priestly heritage is no guarantee, it is true, of a scribal or even a teaching function (though a levitical heritage may be—cf. e.g. CD

13), but it is additional, circumstantial evidence for the likelihood of the Teacher's scribal role in the community.

We have drawn attention to those aspects of the role of the Essene Teacher which most obviously bear a close correspondence to the role of the apocalyptic scribe as we find him in the figure of Enoch, Ezra or Baruch. But these also appear to be the essential characteristics of the Teacher's role, so that the parallel with the apocalyptic scribe is more than just a superficial one. Indeed it is difficult to avoid the conclusion that the earthly, 'righteous' figures of the chosen and inspired apocalyptic scribes and authors and the venerated Teacher of Righteousness are viewed by their followers in an altogether similar light.

There are two further factors in his role: the founding of a community (cf. CD 1; 4QpPs 37); and, possibly,[24] the final proclamation of righteousness at the end of days. Strictly speaking, the former concerns the 'building' of the community and may be compared with the establishment of a distinctive righteous community as we find at least implicitly attributed to each of the ancient figures venerated in the apocalyptic literature, and indeed in particular to Ezra the scribe according to Ezra–Nehemiah. It is interesting that the title given at this point (4QpPs 37) is 'the Priest, the Teacher of Righteousness', in view of the similar epithet applied to Ezra, 'the Priest, the Scribe', in Ezra 7.11f., 21. The similarity may be no more than coincidental, since the Qumran commentaries otherwise show no special indications of influence from Ezra–Nehemiah, but in any case the similarities in the respective roles of Ezra the Scribe (= דרש את תורה יהוה in Ezra 7.10; cf. CD 6.7; 7.18; etc.) and the Teacher of Righteousness as priest and teacher/interpreter of the Law (as well as builder of a righteous community) are close enough to warrant the suggestion that the Teacher of Righteousness, like Ezra, may have been regarded as an 'eminent scribe'. The major element in each leader's role is the authoritative (inspired) interpretation of scripture, and this precisely characterizes both on the one hand Ezra (cf. e.g. Ezra 7.6 with 7.10, 11) and the Levites who aid him (Neh. 8.7-9, 13), and on the other hand the Essene Interpreter of the Law and those (Levites?—cf. 1QSa 1-2) who constantly study the Law (דרש תורה; cf. 1QS 6). It is some indication of the proximity between the two that it has even been argued[25] that the Essene Teacher of Righteousness and Ezra are in fact to be identified historically.

R. Leivestad,[26] whose concern is actually to separate the Teacher of Righteousness from any identification as a 'prophet' figure, is surely correct in asserting that

> Er is sich bewußt, der wahre Lehrer zu sein, und das heißt, der glaubwürdige, vom Geist inspirierte Ausleger der heiligen, prophetischen Schriften. Sein Prototyp ist eigentlich weder Elia, noch Mose, sondern Esra der Schriftgelehrte. Der heilige Geist macht ihn nicht zu einem Propheten, sondern zu einem die Geheimnisse der prophetischen Schriften durchschauenden Interpreten, *melîz*, ἑρμηνευτής (1QpHab. vii).[27]

There is no substantive difference, we would argue, between the 'teaching of righteousness' and the 'interpretation of the law'.[28] in practice they are identical activities which precisely characterize the essential function of the authoritative scribe in the literature we have reviewed.

What Leivestad does not mention, and what is very interesting in this connection, is the use of the term *mehōqēq* with reference to the Teacher of Righteousness/Interpreter of the Law. In CD 6.2-11 the *mehōqēq* of Num. 21.18 'is the Interpreter of the Torah'. This corresponds closely to the Fragment, Ps.-Jonathan and Onkelos Targums to the same verse, according to which the *mehōqēq* who 'dug' the 'well' (= Torah) becomes 'Moses and Aaron, the *scribes* (ספריא) of Israel'; a similar equation (*mehōqēq* = *sôfēr/safrā'*) is made elsewhere in the Targums (see Chapter 2) and in Sirach (Sir. 10.5: מחקק rendered as γραμματεύς). What Qumran calls 'Interpreter of the Law', then, is evidently identical with what the targums call 'scribe'.

Furthermore, the Teacher of Righteousness refers to himself in the Hodayoth as Maskil (cf. 1QH 12), the title also of the *mebaqqēr* or 'Guardian' (Vermes) of the camp, responsible for instructing the members of the community, who has a high profile in the Community Rule (1QS).[29] Vermes distinguishes the Teacher of Righteousness who founded the community from the Interpreter of the Law/Maskil in 1QS.[30] What is clear is that those who expounded the Law to the community (this may have applied to one in each company of ten—cf. 1QS 6—and certainly to each successive Maskil) were concerned with instructing them in righteous living: 'to do according to all that has been revealed from age to age' [Leaney: 'is revealed from time to time'] (1QS 8.15; cf. 9.13; 1.7ff.).

This entails fundamental instruction in how to apply and keep the Mosaic Law; for the halakhic-type rulings given precisely in 1QS itself are presented as applications of the Law in concrete terms for the governing of the life of the community (cf. e.g. in 1QS 5.14f. the grounding of isolationist economic practice in the legal principle, 'Keep away from all that is false' [Exod. 23.7]). Anyone who enters the community is obliged to

> undertake by a binding oath to return with all his heart and soul to every commandment of the Law of Moses in accordance with all that has been revealed of it to the sons of Zadok, the Keepers of the Covenant and Seekers of His will ... (1QS 5.7ff.).

The 'men of falsehood', by contrast, 'have neither enquired nor sought after Him concerning His laws that they might know the hidden things in which they have sinfully erred; and matters revealed they have treated with insolence' (1QS 5.10ff.). The Maskil, charged with the instruction of the community, thus has great authority; those who do not precisely follow *his* 'revealed' instruction *cannot* be keeping the Law properly.[31] The Maskil's halakhic rulings, then, have an (implicit and explicit) claim to *revelation*; the Maskil himself is one who, in his diligent searching of the scriptures, receives revelations, thus enjoying an elevated, charismatic authority in his interpretation of the Law and the Prophets.

As instructor and authoritative interpreter of the Law, the Maskil certainly has scribal functions; as the recipient of revelations and the revealer/concealer of these he also recalls, and evidently emulates, the eminent scribes of apocalyptic veneration. Furthermore, he has the special access to revelations that also typifies those figures. Perhaps, too, to him belongs the credit for the authorship, or compilation and composition, of some at least of the scrolls themselves. Certainly, the distinctive exegetical principles evident in the composition of the Qumran biblical commentaries, and the thorough familiarity with the text of the scriptures shown in CD, 1QS, 1QH and the other literature, are indications of a professional and accomplished scribal authorship. Like Daniel himself, the Qumran Maskil is scribe in all but name; the titles Maskil, Interpreter of the Law and Teacher of Righteousness, severally and together, equate to that name.

As noted above, the function of righteous instruction accords exactly with the (briefly characterized) role of the *maṣdîqîm/maśkîlîm* in Daniel 11 and 12: the *maṣdîq*, who turns people to righteousness (by teaching and example) is the *maśkîl* who by special enlightenment 'understands' what has been revealed in the inspired scriptures. The *maśkîlîm* of the book of Daniel, for whom Daniel himself is the eminent ideal, are those who 'will understand' at the end of days, and who will moreover 'turn many to righteousness'. Clearly Daniel is a model for the Teacher of Righteousness and his followers:[32] in 1QH 12, knowledge, wisdom, and the understanding of mysteries are the qualities ascribed to himself by the Maskil, and the corresponding 'understanding' of those in his charge is closely connected with righteousness and correct living—in exactly the parallelism that characterizes *maśkîlîm* and *maṣdîqîm* in Daniel. If Daniel is the Maskil *par excellence* and his followers the *maśkîlîm*, so too the Teacher of Righteousness is the eminent Maskil and his 'understanding' followers are *maśkîlîm* or *ḥakhāmîm* (and 'doers of the law'). This idea will be developed in our exegetical study of Matthew 13, but for the moment we make, in summary, the following suggestion.

The Teacher of Righteousness functions as the apocalyptic eminent scribes of apocalyptic literature function, namely as a specially chosen human recipient and communicator (teacher and writer) of the divine revelation of mysteries. In this fundamental respect he is of a kind with Enoch, Ezra and Baruch and is akin to the inspired scribe of Sirach 39.[33] In addition, he is evidently consciously modelled on Daniel the Maskil, whose functions we have also seen to be of a 'scribal' nature in the apocalyptic eminent scribe sense. We may further surmise that the Qumranic 'David' of 11QPs[a], himself conceivably modelled to some extent on Daniel, and specifically a 'wise man' and 'scribe' with the divine 'spirit of understanding', was also an example for the Teacher of Righteousness as an inspired author of 'Hodayoth', or was at least seen in similar terms by his followers. While the term 'scribe' is not specifically used of Daniel or the Teacher, their common designation as 'Maskil' coincides with the 'scribal' role of the eminent scribe in the intertestamental literature, to such an extent, indeed, that it would be clearly wrong to insist on a substantive distinction between scribe and *maśkîl* in this literature simply on the basis of divergent terminology. A scribe by any other name is still a scribe; *maśkîl*, co-terminous with 'interpreter of the law' at Qumran, is the Danielic and Qumranic[34] counterpart (one might even say, equivalent) to the 'scribe' in Sirach and apocalyptic literature. Similarly, the title *mēlîṣ*, interpreter (1QH 2, etc.) is entirely appropriate as an alternative to *sôfēr*; and the equation between חקק and Interpreter of the Law (CD 6) is precisely the equation *meḥōqēq = safrā'/grammateus* found in the targums and Sirach. The Teacher of Righteousness, like Enoch, is a scribe of righteousness.

2. The Essene Interpreters as *maśkîlîm*/Scribes

The Qumran manuscripts show that the Qumran Essenes venerated Enoch as scribe of righteousness / scribe of interpretation; they honoured David as inspired scribe and wise man; they read and preserved the writings of Ben Sira the classical scribe; and they especially revered the book of Daniel, maintaining and emulating the practice of its pesher-exegesis, and probably seeing in themselves the understanding scribal *maśkîlîm* of the last days. We have argued, too, that the Teacher of Righteousness, the Maskil and the Interpreter of the Law had their nearest analogy in Daniel and the eminent scribes of the intertestamental literature, so that they can, without fear of misrepresentation, be classed as comparable examples of eminent scribalism. Since the Teacher of Righteousness (unlike the eminent mythological figures of Enoch, and perhaps Daniel, certainly Ezra and Baruch) is an actually remembered figure in the community preserving the literature about him, there is clearly a socio-historical connection *between* him and that community; the members carry on the instruction and the revelations that he initiated, and the institution of the Maskilim is designed to maintain this.[35] If the Essenes are at all faithful to his teaching and example they will be likely to perform a similar role, which we have characterized as scribal. Is this actually borne out by the texts? In what sense, then, if at all, can the ordinary Qumran Essenes be conceived of as 'scribes'?

It will be clear from the foregoing study that it would be quite inappropriate to view them as 'scribes' simply on the basis of their apparent role[36] as diligent copyists of manuscripts in the Qumran 'scriptorium'. It is at this level that many modern concepts have unfortunately maintained their usage, largely because of the supposed archaeological evidence to this effect.[37] But we have seen from all the literature, not least Qumran's own 'Davidic Compositions', that the scribe-sofer is of a higher calibre than this.

An alternative fallacy has been to regard the Dead Sea scrolls as a monolithic sectarian library of documents, belonging to a single sect and following a single doctrinal line (that of the founding Teacher of Righteousness), and to see its socio-religious setting as a single 'school' of exegesis (cf. Josephus' own classification of Essenism as a 'philosophy'). But this view, too, is a simplistic one. The scrolls witness to a lengthy history of compilation and redaction, with shifts of emphasis and direction in halakhah, exegesis and theological viewpoints; more than one branch of 'Essenism' is almost certainly represented there. A 'school' of exegesis may perhaps be traced in the sense in which the 'Johannine school' is understood: fairly uniform hermeneutical principles guide the exegesis in the biblical commentaries (pesharim), for instance, with similar examples in the other Qumran literature, and the character of the exegesis is marked by the same attachment to the 'Teacher of Righteousness', in awareness of his eschatological significance. This is like a 'school' in this sense, but the self-awareness appears to be one of *community* conviction rather than theological stance. It has to do with the fulfilment of a particular role in the historical and eschatological plan of God.

The hermeneutical principles we have mentioned are to some extent comparable with rabbinic *middôt*;[38] but the pesher itself, with its confident self-identification as the eschatological community that is the specific object (and sole comprehender) of the import of Israel's prophetic legacy, is of a different order. It is not so much that the resultant exegesis is distinctive, nor that this particular group uses an alternative list of hermeneutical principles, but rather the distinctiveness of the *type* of exegesis in the pesharim ultimately lies in its *pedigree*. It is of a kind with the Danielic interpretation of dreams, visions and cryptic writing, and with the self-aware authorship of the book of Daniel itself. A whole array of connections between the book and the Qumran literature makes the assumption of a direct line from the *ḥasîdîm* or *maśkîlîm* of Daniel a very reasonable one. Moreover, the Essene movement itself in all probability emerged from the circles of *ḥasîdîm* (whether or not this is taken to designate a distinct sect or movement) from which, perhaps in reaction to the new apocalypticism, the Pharisaic movement also derives; and most scholars place the writing of Daniel in this context.[39] It is not our concern here to discuss in detail the difficult questions of apocalyptic origins and Essene origins. For present purposes it is sufficient to note the undoubted apocalyptic impetus that is common to the rise of apocalyptic ideas, particularly from the third century BCE onwards, the composition of the book of Daniel, and the politico-theological concerns of apocalyptic literature and the Essene documents.[40] It is an impetus of apocalyptic and eschatological fervour; but it derives demonstrably from the scribal circles in which mantic wisdom flourished. Qumran stands in this scribal tradition.

The 'pedigree' of the Essene interpreters, as we understand it, lies in their appeal to the special *revelations* granted to members of the community, from the Teacher of Righteousness and the Maskil (and Interpreter of the Law) onwards, on the basis of their divinely granted spiritual *insight*. By definition, these members of the Essene brotherhood are *maśkîlîm*: they, being 'wise', 'understand' and on this basis give instruction in righteousness. They are honoured successors of the prophets, like Daniel, Ezra (Daniel's 'brother'; *4 Ezra* 12.11), and Baruch; like these and Enoch the Scribe and the ideal scribe according to Ben Sira, their special understanding is their prime quality, and interpretation and teaching of mysteries their role.

The Teacher of Righteousness, the Maskil, the Interpreter of the Law, as we have seen, are best viewed in this light. The leading members of the community or communities in which the documents belong and to which they refer clearly claim the same pedigree, the same authority. The search of the scriptures that gave rise to the pesharim is, to borrow Patte's term, 'inspired'.[41] There may be particular hermeneutical principles guiding aspects of the interpretation, but at base the motivation for all this is not simply the pursuit of an academic, scholastic exercise in religious terrain, such as is frequently (though not exclusively) found in rabbinic exegesis, but a deep and sure conviction of close contact with the divine purpose being worked out, marvellously, among their own community. This deep sense of urgency and conviction cuts right across the academic principles (though for the most part these are undoubtedly learned), making their exegesis and their composition largely intuitive, even 'prophetic' in Ben Sira's sense, 'inspired' by the same spirit as the compositions of David the Scribe. In interpreting the scriptures with such authority they demonstrate insight into the 'mysteries' and the 'hidden things' that are obscured from others; this is, to them, evidence of their own chosenness and inspiration.

We have referred, above, to the 'charismatic exegesis' that characterizes the Essene writings. It is an appropriate term for the 'inspiration' that prompts their interpretations. And we have seen that it is of a kind with the mantic interpretations of dreams, visions and prophecies such as are found in Daniel, Enoch and the other apocalyptic literature.[42] In addition, we have drawn attention to the close contacts between the emphasis on inspiration and the idealized capacities of the scribe according to Ben Sira. We have seen, too, that Qumran stands squarely within the aegis of such enthusiastic, perhaps mantic, concepts of revelation and interpretation. It is in this sphere of application that the term 'scribe' has meaning for the Qumran interpreter. The interpreter at Qumran—be he one who copied and 'corrected' the biblical manuscripts,[43] one in a group of ten 'studying the Law',[44] one receiving and sharing a word of 'revelation', a Levite standing in as expert expositor, an author of one of the pesharim or another interpretative document,[45] the incumbent Maskil instructing and testing the 'understanding' of the community members, or the Interpreter of the Law or the Teacher of Righteousness himself—in each case, he is a 'scribe' as such is presented, with considerable uniformity, in the late biblical and pseudepigraphal literature and, classically, in Sirach. Certainly, the leading Essenes were scribes; and their closest analogies should not be sought in the post-Pharisaic rabbis, but in the earlier and the contemporary literature that formed them, and which has been the subject of our discussion in Chapters 4 and 5.

We hope already to have established that the picture of the scribe that is commonly portrayed by a wide range of authors from Ben Sira to the Qumran Maskilim and the authors of various apocalyptic works is consistent enough to be potentially a very instructive comparison on which to draw in examining other Jewish works contemporary with much of the literature and germane in their eschatological and especially apocalyptic and scribal interests. Such a work we take the First Gospel to be, and our next task will be to discover what bearing this comparable material may have on our understanding of the scribes presented in that Gospel.

PART III

MATTHEW AND THE SCRIBAL IDEAL

Chapter 6

THE SCRIBAL IDEAL AND MATTHEW'S DISCIPLES

In Chapter 1 of this study we saw that, far from being 'confused' as to the term γραμματεύς which he found in his sources, Matthew in fact, as our redaction-critical survey established, variously uses and 'omits' the term in the service of a consistently positive presentation of the scribe, thereby showing that he *does* have a firm perception of the 'scribe'. Implicit criticism of the scribes *per se* is avoided by his characterizing Mark's negatively portrayed scribes as 'Pharisees' or as 'scribes-and-Pharisees'; and scribes *qua* scribes are introduced by Matthew in a fully positive light in 8.19f. and 23.2. We noted, further, that the term scribe is used positively in 13.52 and 23.34; and it is to these very important texts that we now turn.

1. Mt. 13.51-52

'Have you understood all these things?' They answered him, 'Yes!' And so he said to them, 'Thus every scribe who has become a "disciple" with respect to the kingdom of heaven is like a man who is a householder, who produces new things as well as old things from his treasure-store' (translation mine).

These verses, to understate the case rather, have been subjected to many and varied interpretations,[1] but it is not necessary for our present purposes to treat all of these in detail. A full bibliography is included in the list of works consulted at the end of this study.

According to all the Synopses and commentaries, Mt. 13.52 is unparalleled in the canonical Gospels. It is thus invariably attributed either to Matthew's special material (M) or to his free redactional activity.[2] That it evidences the hand of its author is taken to be demonstrated by the mention of 'every scribe discipled to the Kingdom of Heaven', which is seen, sometimes perhaps a little hastily, as a cryptic signature alluding to the author or to his (scribal) community (see however Chapter 7 below). Further evidence for its redactional formulation is adduced from the thoroughly Matthean language used: διὰ τοῦτο, μαθητεύειν, βασιλεία τῶν οὐρανῶν, ἄνθρωπος qualified, οἰκοδεσπότης, θησαυρός and ἐκβάλλειν are all either unique to Matthew or are significantly more common in Matthew than in the other Gospels.[3] There are, then, serious questions as to the authenticity of the saying as it stands, and there is every indication that Matthew the redactor has made at least some contribution to its composition. In Chapter 7 section 2 we shall attempt to elucidate the rationale behind his creation and to discover the mechanics of the composition of this piece of scripture and the nature of the materials used. For the present, however, our concern is with an exegesis of the saying in its context, with a special interest in the content of the term scribe in the light of the background literature we have examined.

First, a few remarks about context and structure. Mt. 13.52 concludes the parables discourse: v. 53 uses the formula καὶ ἐγένετο ὅτε ἐτέλεσεν ὁ Ἰησοῦς τὰς παραβολὰς ταύτας, which, with minor variations, concludes all five of the major discourses in the Gospel (cf. 7.28; 11.1; 19.1; 26.1); with such a clear division, indeed, that it has been taken to support the influential theory that the Gospel was intentionally constructed as a five-book work on Pentateuchal lines.[4] Clearly, v. 52 is intended to sum up the discourse in some way, and in fact we find parables with a Matthean stamp concluding the Sermon on the Mount (7.24-27), the 'ecclesiological discourse' (18.23-35—the parable of the debtors, which begins with several linguistic parallels to 13.52) and the 'eschatological discourse' (25.31-46—the apocalyptic vision of the Son of Man judging the sheep and the goats). A recent thesis[5] sees in these four parables a distinctive Matthean genre of 'summary parables'. Any evaluation of 13.52 should therefore (and this is frequently overlooked) keep in mind the structure and concerns of the book as a whole as well as those of the chapter.

Curiously enough, analyses of Matthew 13 as a whole frequently give only cursory treatment to v. 52, which in a chapter of kingdom parables is something of a misfit, despite the common use in kingdom parables of its language and motifs—βασιλεία τῶν οὐρανῶν, ὅμοιός ἐστιν ἀνθρώπῳ . . . ὅστις, οἰκοδεσπότης, θησαυρός—because ostensibly (to judge by the subject of the sentence) it is not *about* the kingdom of heaven but about the *scribe*. The fact that it is somewhat incongruous amongst kingdom-parables has led certain interpreters to suppose that it is not a parable at all. Thus, we are told, within vv. 1-50 we have a typically 'rabbinic' device in a collection of seven of a kind: the sower being followed by the wheat and the tares (vv. 24-30), the mustard seed (vv. 31f.), the leaven (v. 33), the hidden treasure (v. 44), the pearl (vv. 45f.) and the dragnet (vv. 47-50), making a neat seven in total, to the exclusion of v. 52.[6] This overlooks the fact that if v. 52 is not strictly a kingdom parable, then neither is the 'parable' of the sower, which lacks the typical opening, 'The kingdom of heaven is like . . .' Furthermore, regardless of whether v. 52 is about the kingdom, the fact that a metaphorical picture is used indicates that this is a 'parable'—a *mashal*—of some kind, and the kingdom-parable language and motifs it uses suggest it might have been intended, chameleon-like, to blend in with the kingdom-parable background. The theory[7] that we have here an original kingdom parable (e.g. 'The kingdom of God/heaven is like a householder who brings out of his storeroom things new and old'), originally linked with the dragnet parable to make up a third pre-Matthean pair, though perfectly possible, is very difficult to support in the light of the thorough re-working which on this reading Matthew has given it. The present analysis in any case is concerned to view the logion as it is now intended to be read: in its redacted or newly composed form. A solemn, summary statement is being made, and kingdom-parable and possibly allegorical language (cf. 20.1) is being used as a literary device to weld it to its context and in order to balance it with the sower parable which opens the chapter.[8]

As it stands, the subject of v. 52 is the scribe who is 'trained', 'instructed' or 'discipled/made a disciple', 'in', 'about', 'to', 'for', or 'with respect to' the kingdom of heaven.[9] Exegetical scholarship on this verse has concentrated its efforts largely (1) on finding an appropriate translation for this phrase and (2) on elucidating the significance of the 'new and old things'. It is common to find exegetes characterizing the scribe here as the 'Christian scribe',[10] thereby placing him, and therefore the saying, firmly within Matthew's Christian community, and playing down the Jewishness of the term 'scribe' itself. The phrase μαθητευθεὶς τῇ βασιλείᾳ τῶν οὐρανῶν is generally taken as a christianization of the Jewish scribe: the scribe in this verse is a (former) Jewish scribe who has become a disciple of Jesus, a Christian. Thus the emphasis in the verse is found in the Christian qualification of the scribe rather than in his role *as a scribe*. This then dictates the exegesis of the cryptic phrase 'new things and old things': since the scribe has become a disciple (a new thing) he brings out of his storehouse new things appropriate to his being a Christian disciple, such as new interpretation of the Old Testament, or the sayings of Jesus himself, or 'the Gospel', or even the 'New Testament'. Now it will, we trust, be evident from our whole preceding investigation of perceptions of the scribe in a wide range of Jewish literature that there the term carries considerable weight in its own right. In view of the great probability that a Jewish scribe has himself had a hand in the formulation of the saying, we should, I submit, pay full heed to this background in exegeting the passage— not, of course, to the neglect of the saying's own context.

A. *The Disciples as Understanding Scribes and maśkîlîm*

Agreeing broadly with Wenham's analysis of the structure of the chapter, we have noted a balance between the parable of the sower and the scribe saying. We have suggested that the saying is itself a parable in the broad sense, a *mashal*, since by its difficulty and its parabolic and cryptic terminology it is evidently intended to invite attempts at interpretation. The balance in structure with the parable of the sower invites a connection to be made with that parable and its interpretation, which in the Markan *Vorlage*, it will be recalled, is a key stage in Jesus' test of the disciples' comprehension of his own role (and perhaps the 'messianic secret'). There, though in principle the disciples are given the mystery of the kingdom (Mk 4.11), they still fail to understand. As is well known, Matthew in general paints a more complimentary picture of the disciples than Mark does, and the contrast between Mark and Matthew on the matter of the understanding of the disciples is often seen as part of this overall tendency in Matthew. However, we find that Matthew's concern with 'understanding' is quite separate from any interest in flattering the disciples and is more consistently expressed (the disciples continue to lack faith, for example, in Matthew, while their understanding is repeatedly asserted).[11] Moreover, for Matthew, understanding is intrinsically linked with the hidden meanings of parables and the appropriate role of the interpreting scribe. The telling verse is actually v. 51, in which the understanding of the disciples is emphatically announced, and which leads on immediately into the saying of v. 52; and we must take the two verses together in our exegesis.

On the supposition that Matthew sometimes uses the linking phrase διὰ τοῦτο in a less than obviously logical sequence,[12] it is often assumed that the phrase is no more than a literary device introducing a logion, giving it some superficial connection to what has gone before, and in this particular instance ensuring that the reader understands that the logion was spoken to the disciples;[13] alternatively, the phrase is seen as a vestige of an earlier source whose logical force is now lost in the new context.[14] But perhaps there is more force in the term than is generally supposed. In the nine occasions when Matthew has διὰ τοῦτο on the lips of Jesus, (a) there is always some more or less evident connection with what has gone before, and (b) the phrase introduces a solemn and resounding logion (or parable, cf. 18.23) of Jesus. 6.25 and 12.27 have exact Lukan parallels and may derive from Q; at 12.31 and 21.43 we have the solemn διὰ τοῦτο λέγω ὑμῖν, which in the former case replaces Mark's ἀμὴν λέγω ὑμῖν (there is no parallel to 21.43); διὰ τοῦτο is peculiar to Matthew in the parables context (13.13), where it introduces the highly significant statement of the purpose of the parables, and is additional to Lk. 21.40 in the urgent Son of Man saying of 24.44; διὰ τοῦτο in 18.23 occurs in the clause διὰ τοῦτο ὡμοιώθη ἡ βασιλεία τῶν οὐρανῶν ἀνθρώπῳ βασιλεῖ, very similar in form to our 13.52, introducing a parable with a serious and impassioned call to the ἀδελφοί to forgive one another; finally, there is the quasi-prophetic διὰ τοῦτο ἰδοὺ ἐγὼ ἀποστέλλω πρὸς ὑμᾶς προφήτας καὶ σοφοὺς καὶ γραμματεῖς of 23.34, spoken by 'the Wisdom of God' in the Lukan parallel (11.49) and with clear classical-prophetic as well as wisdom resonances in form (cf. e.g. Jer. 8.10, 17; 9.7), again within a context of judgment and apocalyptic ideas.[15] A comparison of these usages reveals that the phrase διὰ τοῦτο in Matthew is used most frequently *in a position of climax*, when, with some intensification of emphasis, Jesus makes a portentous statement, either with reference to judgment on his opponents (12.27: 'they shall be your judges'; 12.31: 'the blasphemy against the Spirit shall not be forgiven'; 13.13: concealment of the mysteries from the crowds, through parables; 21.43: 'the kingdom of God will be taken away from you'; 23.34ff.: 'upon you will come all the righteous blood shed on earth') or gives a warning to his followers in the light of the coming judgment (24.44; 18.23ff.). The only exception to this is 6.25 ('Therefore, I tell you do not be anxious'), which appears as a reassuring logion to the disciples (cf. Lk. 12.22). We are surely justified then in suspecting both a logical force to διὰ τοῦτο in 13.52 and a high degree of emphasis in the summary pericope that follows; there is likely to be a definite link to the subject of the preceding verse and chapter, which has been the understanding of the mysteries of the kingdom declared by Jesus in parable.

On a superficial reading, Jesus speaks the logion of 13.52 to the disciples because they have understood his teaching about the kingdom in the parables they have just heard (i.e. 'all these things' = 'all these parables'); that is, they have understood the point of the parables. The reader will recall that a concern with 'understanding' hidden meanings of dark sayings is paramount in the story of Daniel (whom we have characterized also as a scribe); 'parable' language is used in relation to revelations to Enoch (the Scribe) in *1 Enoch* 37–71, where it is evidently based on a (scribal!) connection made with Balaam the seer's 'parables' in Numbers 24; the concern of Ezra the Scribe and Baruch the Scribe in *4 Ezra* and *2 Baruch* is with the understanding of mysteries revealed to them, some of them in parabolic form of one kind or another; but above all, the understanding of parables we found to be the prime concern of the typical *scribe* according to Ben Sira—the measure of the worth of a scribe is precisely the skill with which he can understand the hidden meanings of *parables*, 'proverbs', 'dark sayings' and other *mᵉšālîm* (Sir. 38.33–39.3). The close connection between parables, understanding and scribes in this literature is highly instructive for any informed interpretation of Mt. 13.52, and its model in Sirach and the apocalyptic literature has hitherto been virtually overlooked.[16] Matthew's Jesus can use the term 'scribe' in relation to the disciples precisely *because they understand parables*! However, as we shall see, the intertestamental Jewish literature may offer yet more insight into the significance of these verses for Matthew.

We have seen that διὰ τοῦτο generally means more than a simple, logical 'therefore' to Matthew (which would be sufficient for the reading above, which we have called 'superficial'). And the chapter is concerned with rather more than Jewish scribes' skills in parable- and riddle-solving. For it is not only the parables which the disciples understand, but to them it is 'given' to know the *'mysteries'* of the kingdom (13.11); they see and hear 'things which many prophets and righteous men desired to see and hear and did not' (13.16, 17), and they understand 'the word of the kingdom' (13.19) or 'the word' (13.23). All this is in contrast to 'them' (v. 11), who do *not* understand and do not see and hear (v. 13) and whose blind inability to understand is in specific fulfilment of scripture. This, then, is an eschatological moment that merits its own full formula quotation (vv. 14, 15). The understanding of the disciples, over against the culpable blindness of the opponents of Jesus, is a vibrant motif, if not a major theme, in the First Gospel.[17] As we have already remarked, this fact is frequently overlooked by commentators wishing to see the understanding of the disciples in a favourable, even 'idealizing' light by comparison with Mark. Whether this is the case or not,[18] Matthew has a particular and fundamental concern to make clear that the disciples have understanding (σύνεσις), and that others, especially the Pharisaic scribes who should have it, do not.

So much is clear even from a statistical analysis of the terminology. The verb συνιέναι (συνίειν), to understand, comprehend or gain (an) insight into (Bauer, *s.v.*), representing בין and שכל in the LXX, occurs nine times in Matthew,[19] of which no fewer than six instances are found in ch. 13 (vv. 13, 14, 15, 19, 23, 51), where the verb is first used. (This compares with six occurrences in Mark, four in Luke and none at all in John.) Matthew's remaining three usages come in fairly quick succession. In 15.10 (paralleled in Mk 7.14) Jesus calls 'the people' to him and calls out 'Hear and understand!';[20] Matthew adds the point that the Pharisees are offended at his saying and has Jesus call them *blind* guides (15.12, 14; cf. ch. 23). In 16.12 the disciples are said to understand Jesus' warning to beware of the teaching of the Pharisees and Sadducees (no parallel: Mk 8.21 ends the pericope with 'Do ye *not* yet understand?').[21] In 17.13 the disciples are said to understand that Elijah and John the Baptist are one (no parallel in Mark 9). 16.9 lacks the dominical castigation of Mk 8.17, 'Do you *not* understand?' Even the inclusion of the Markan 'Are you without understanding (ἀσύνετοι)?' (Mk 7.18) in 15.16 qualifies the question heavily with ἀκμήν (peculiar to this verse in the NT), and the emphatic position of καί—it is still clear that the term *really* applies to the Pharisees rather than the disciples. Barth[22] has convincingly argued along similar lines, and the point could be further elaborated by an analysis of the use of τυφλός and συνετός/ σοφός in the Gospel, but it should already be clear that Matthew is at some pains to present the disciples as understanding, and that ch. 13 marks the beginning of the references to their understanding. It is quite specifically from ch. 13 onwards, and especially from 13.51 onwards, that the disciples are depicted as those who understand.[23] In view of this, Kingsbury is correct, though for inadequate reasons, in seeing ch. 13 as the turning-point in the Gospel.[24] It is indeed the moment when the two camps are separated definitively and Jesus' complete rejection begins.

The contextual pride of place given to the pericope within the chapter and within the Gospel as a whole, taken together with our review of Matthew's solemn use of διὰ τοῦτο, permits us to state that the pronouncement of Jesus in 13.52 is given at a point of climax: the disciples have *understood*, that is, they have acceded to the insight into the mysteries of the kingdom of heaven, which is the dominant theme, if not the full significance of the chapter (cf. vv. 3, 9, 10-17, 19, 23, 34f., 36, 43). The point of climax may be usefully compared to Peter's confession in 16.15ff. In very similar terms to 13.51, Jesus there asks a question of the disciples, and an answer is given which is then commended in a pronouncement as being inspired by divine revelation. True, Peter is a special case in 16.15ff.,[25] but in 13.51f. the point is very similar: the disciples have received insight through divine revelation (cf. 13.11; 11.25-27), and this is cause for an important pronouncement by Jesus. Like all Jewish disciples, they are subject to *testing*,[26] and they have passed the test. But in the case of *these* disciples, they have not merely learned something by rote; they have been selected for the divinely imparted gift of wisdom and therefore understand (cf. 13.11). They stand in direct contrast to the so-called 'wise and understanding' (11.25) from whom 'these things' (ταῦτα, cf. πάντα, v. 27) have been 'hidden' (cf. 13.35) and stand in the apocalyptic tradition as those—typically *scribes*—to whom the divine mysteries are revealed.

Barth, rejecting the notion of the idealization of the disciples by Matthew, says of the Gospel's emphasis on the understanding of the disciples that 'this is not a matter of bias in favour of excusing the disciples, of deleting what is unfavourable to them, but it is a firm construction of the first evangelist which has a quite different background'.[27] Unless we are to assume that Matthew has just made a poor job of an intended idealization of the disciples but an oddly good job of emphasizing their understanding, we are bound to agree. What, then, is this background to Matthew's concept of 'understanding'? It is unfortunate that in an otherwise masterly study of this subject, Barth states syllogistically that because Matthew uses a series of other expressions for 'understanding' or 'not understanding' (γνῶναι [13.11], βλέπειν and ἀκούειν [13.13-17], παχύνειν [13.15], ἀσύνετος [15.16], νοεῖν [15.17; 16.9, 11] and ἐπιγιγνώσκειν [17.12]), 'The thought of "understanding" cannot therefore be explained by a study of *sunienai* in the rest of the New Testament or in the LXX. Matthew is here solely conditioned by Mark, whose conception of the disciples' understanding he alters in a characteristic way. Hence we are confined entirely to the statements of Matthew himself.'[28] Had Barth indeed examined the LXX more closely he would have found, for example, that Sirach, whose concerns for the scribe in any case suggest the comparability of his work to this context, attaches far greater significance to the term σύνεσις than any other author preserved in the LXX: σύνεσις occurs no fewer than 30 times in Sirach, as compared with 10 times in Proverbs, and σύνετος a further 18 times (9 times in Proverbs); this in addition to the frequent use of σοφός (26 ×) and the occasional use of φρόνιμος (9 ×), φρόνεσις (5 ×) and the verb νόειν (3 ×).

It will come as no suprise to the reader that I hold Matthew's concept of understanding, and ch. 13 and vv. 51f. in particular, to be best explained with reference to the late Old Testament and the intertestamental literature, specifically the book of Daniel and Ben Sira, and that in this respect Matthew stands in a broad Jewish tradition which is also represented in the literature of Qumran.

We have already noted that Matthew sees the blindness of the opponents of Jesus as the eschatological fulfilment of the scriptures (13.14f.). My suggestion is that he probably also sees the understanding of the disciples as the eschatological fulfilment of the scripture, namely Daniel 11 and 12, identifying the disciples with the *maśkîlîm*.

With reference to the Markan Apocalypse, Jan Lambrecht[29] has pointed out the coincidence of quasi-Danielic terms in Mark 13, including ταῦτα and πάντα (separately or conjoined), συντελεῖσθαι and the 'accomplishment' of ταῦτα πάντα in Dan. 12.7 (Mk 13.4, 23, 29, 30). In that chapter also care is taken to point out the necessity of understanding what is going on in terms of the fulfilment of the Daniel prophecy (13.14, 'Let the reader understand');[30] explicit reference is made to the abomination of desolation (13.14), and other terms such as the tribulation (v. 19) and the Son of Man (v. 26) have their background in Daniel. It is notable that Matthew both *expands* the apocalyptic language in his version of the chapter, making the reference to Daniel explicit in 24.15, and also introduces many of these precise Danielic terms as well as a number of additional Danielic allusions into his parables chapter (Mt. 13), that are absent in Mark's: for example, the 'furnace of fire' (vv. 43, 50; cf. Dan. 3.6, etc.), 'the close of the age' (vv. 39, 49; cf. 'the latter days' and 'the time of the end' in Daniel), the revelation of 'mysteries' (v. 11; cf. Dan. 2.17, 19, 29, 30), the interpretation of 'parables' (cf. Dan. 5.12, etc.), understanding 'the word' (vv. 19, 23; cf. Dan. 10.1; also 12.4, 9), the 'shining' of the righteous (v. 41; cf. Dan. 12.3) and the hope of the 'kingdom' (e.g. v. 41; cf. Dan. 7.18). In view of all this, it should not be surprising that we find in our v. 51 two further Danielic terms, namely 'understand' (συνήκατε) and 'all these things' (ταῦτα πάντα). In Dan. 12.7 the man clothed in linen[31] is indicating the eschatological moment when 'all these things' (כל־אלה) will be 'accomplished' (cf. Mt. 24.34); the very next words (Dan. 12.8a) are 'I heard but I did not understand (לא אבין)', and the man explains that 'the words are shut up and sealed until the time of the end', then 'none of the wicked shall understand, but the wise (המשכילים) shall understand'. The striking similarities to our passage in Matthew can hardly be accidental, in view of the apocalyptic concerns of the chapter.

Ταῦτα πάντα appears to be a semi-technical term in the First Gospel. Its comprehensiveness may make it seem a little vague but what is clear is that its meaning is not exhausted by reference to the items mentioned immediately before it in the text, and that in particular there is some apocalyptic[32] content to it. Even in Dan. 12.7 the term may already be semi-technical: compare the deuteronomists' Deut. 4.30 ('When you are in tribulation and all these things come upon you in the latter days . . . ') and 30.1 (cf. also 1 Chron. 17.19; Zech. 8.12). *Jub.* 1.6 (cf. 23.14); *4 Ezra* 6.33 (cf. v. 30); and 12.37

(perhaps also *2 Bar.* 83.23) provide similar instances of Daniel-inspired apocalyptic usage of the phrase. Matthew uses it twelve times (Mark 2 × [13.4, 30], Luke 6 ×, John 1 × [but cf. John's comparable use of ταῦτα and πάντα in separation, in relation to revealed things]). Four of these occur in the apocalyptic section (23.36; 24.2, 8, 34) and three in our parables chapter (13.34, where Jesus speaks 'all these things' to the crowds in parables; 13.51, now under discussion; and 13.56, where it refers to Jesus' special wisdom evidenced by his teaching [cf. v. 54]). The remaining four usages (4.9; 6.32; 6.33 [*bis*] and 19.20) are possibly loaded with an ironical *double entendre*.[33] Be that as it may, the very least we can say is that the phrase is very frequently used of the things *revealed* by Jesus to the disciples with eschatological or apocalyptic reference. We might also look to 11.25-27 for exactly the same associations of the words ταῦτα and πάντα. We suggest, therefore, that when Jesus asks the disciples in v. 51 whether they have understood 'all these things', he is not merely asking whether they have got the point of the parables. He is asking whether they have received insight into the eschatological mysteries themselves (cf. v. 11), which, like Daniel, many prophets and righteous men longed to see and did not (v. 17). The moment when they have understood (aorist, συνήκατε) and can answer 'Yes!' is thus a resounding climax. This is the moment at which the disciples identify themselves as the *maśkîlîm* of Dan. 12.10, who 'understand',[34] and is itself an eschatological event, in direct fulfilment of scripture.

Lest it be thought that such a connection would be too far-fetched to be the conscious design of an author like Matthew, we may refer again to the eminently comparable Qumran scribes who made a similar connection, to the extent of institutionalizing their *maśkîlîm* (see further below). Similar self-identification with Danielic events is clearly intended in other 'apocalyptic' texts; Matthew was by no means the only Jewish or Christian writer of his generation to see Daniel's prophecies as being fulfilled.

In other contexts this fulfilment of scripture might have been an occasion for another formula quotation, and it might be objected that Matthew would surely have made his allusion explicit here. To this we must answer that: first, apocalyptic lends itself far better to allusion than to quotation (cf. Mt. 24.15); secondly, the understanding of the disciples expressed proleptically and in other words in v. 11 is already, by implication, responded to in the formula quotation from Isa. 6.9-10 (vv. 14f.); thirdly, in v. 51 the whole passage has arrived at a peak of significance, and the authoritative word at the end of a discourse comes quite naturally from the lips of Jesus, rather than from a scriptural quotation (which might have marred the dramatic effect); fourthly, as we shall argue in Chapter 7 below, it may be seen as delightfully appropriate that in v. 52 itself we have a scribe's product—an example of the 'new things' produced from the scribe/householder's treasure-store.

B. *Matthew's Disciples as maśkîlîm*

It has already been suggested—by others—that the disciples in *Mark* are intended to be understood in the light of the Danielic *maśkîlîm*.[35] We would argue that the degree of correspondence there is far exceeded by that in Matthew's portrayal of the disciples.

The disciples are called 'scribes' in Matthew at the moment they gain insight into the mysteries. It is suggestive that later (23.34) as scribes they are ranked with those other mantics, the 'prophets' and the 'wise men'. Perhaps the term σοφοί in the latter instance reflects a Semitic *Vorlage* of משכילים. Even if the Semitic term is actually חכמים we are still evidently dealing with mantic wise men (see below), who in Daniel and in Qumran are called *maśkîlîm*. We have noted several instances of סופר overlapping with חכם or משכיל in the intertestamental literature.

The *maśkîlîm* of Daniel 11 and 12, besides their effulgence in 12.3 (cf. Mt. 13.43),[36] have a dual role: (1) to 'understand' in the last days (12.10), and (2) to exercise the missionary, or at least pastoral/didactic function of 'causing many to understand' (11.33) in a time of national and religious distress. In Chapter 5 of this study we saw that the Qumran Maskil and Teacher of Righteousness exactly fits Ben Sira's description of the inspired scribe of Sir. 39.6ff. Just like the Danielic *maśkîlîm*, the Qumran *maśkîlîm* are also appropriately characterized as scribes. In fact there the inspired scribe and the *maśkîl* have practically identical roles.[37]

The role of the Maskil at Qumran was basically threefold: (1) *to instruct* the 'saints' (Danielic language)—also called the 'sons of light' and the 'sons of righteousness'—*in righteousness and understanding*, passing on to them knowledge that had been revealed to him;[38] (2) *to test the understanding* of those in his charge:

He shall separate and weigh the sons of righteousness according to their spirit . . . He shall judge every man according to his spirit. He shall admit him in accordance with the cleanness of his hands and advance him in accordance with his understanding (1QS 9);

(3) *to keep his insights obscure* from the unrighteous ('He shall conceal the teaching of the Law from the men of falsehood, but shall impart true knowledge and righteous judgment to those who have chosen the Way' (1QS 9); 'I will impart/conceal knowledge with discretion and will prudently hedge it within a firm bound' (1QS 10). These functions as described in the Community Rule match very well the concerns of the author of the *Hodayot*, who repeatedly thanks God for the insight into the mysteries that God has given him, and for the 'understanding' of the 'disciples' (Vermes's translation), 'men of insight', 'wise men', etc. to whom he has passed on his wisdom, while emphasizing that by contrast, the 'mysteries' have been 'hidden' from the 'false interpreters', the 'seekers of smooth things' and the 'children of men' in general.

> These things I know by Thy understanding (מבינתך), for Thou hast unstopped my ears to marvellous mysteries (1QH 1.21) . . . Thou hast made me a banner, and a discerning interpreter of wonderful mysteries, to try those who seek truth and to test those who love correction . . . They have cast towards the Pit the life of the man whose mouth Thou hast confirmed, and into whose heart Thou hast put teaching (תלמד) and understanding (בינה), that he might open a fountain of knowledge to all men of insight (מבינים) (1QH 2.13-18) . . . Thy mercy is towards the sons of Thy goodwill. For Thou hast made known to them the secret of Thy truth, and hast taught them (השׂכלתם) Thy marvellous mysteries (רזים) (1QH 11.9-10).

Here the Teacher acknowledges that through him his disciples have had God's mysteries revealed to them. The mention of the role of testing disciples is repeated. And the appropriateness of imagery such as that found in Isa. 6.9f. is clearly as evident to the Essene author as to Matthew. It is true, of course, that the Qumran literature abounds with such language. It would be premature to argue for any dependency here. However, the fact is that the portrayal of the Maskil and his disciples at Qumran is very strikingly similar to the portrayal of Jesus and his disciples in Matthew 13. Furthermore, both portrayals are quite evidently heavily dependent on the

Danielic model. And we have seen that in both Daniel and Qumran *maśkîl* is an equivalent term for the understanding scribe.

It will be evident that the comparison with our passage in Matthew could take us well beyond our immediate concern with the portrayal of the disciples as scribes and *maśkîlîm*, since the role of the Maskil/Teacher of Righteousness finds a veritable *Doppelgänger* in the Teacher portrayed in this chapter of Matthew. The connections frequently made between the Teacher of Righteousness and Jesus are most justifiable in Matthew. Even W.D. Davies, at pains to stress the differences between Jesus and the Teacher of Righteousness, can say in connection with the Sermon on the Mount that 'Matthew has draped his Lord in the mantle of a teacher of righteousness'.[39] This is a considerable subject on its own; for the present we may note that the disciples in Matthew are commissioned to continue Jesus' teaching role. If the Teacher's disciples are *maśkîlîm*, the disciples' Teacher is bound to be a Maskil!

One further Qumran text should be cited in this context, one which we think conclusively demonstrates the probability of our suggestion that the depiction of the disciples as *maśkîlîm* is in conscious emulation of the Danielic model. Drawing on the same Danielic language—and in passing showing remarkably similar concerns to Matthew's—the Maskil says in 1QH 13.11-14:

> They [those instructed by the Maskil] will recount Thy glory throughout all Thy dominion, for *Thou didst make them see* (הראיתם) that which not [. . .] before. And to create *new things* (חדשות), to invalidate (הפר) the established things of old, and to (raise up?) the things of eternity. For (Thou art from the beginning) and wilt be forever and ever. And in the *mysteries of Thy understanding* (וברזי שכלך) Thou didst appoint *all these things* (כל אלה) to *make known* Thy glory. (And what is he) a spirit of flesh to *understand all these things* (להבין בכול אלה) and *to have insight* (ולהשכיל) *into the my(stery* of Thy) great (name)?

(Echoes of the Danielic language found also in our passage in Matthew are italicized.) This passage is all the more remarkable for the fact that in addition to using the language of 'understanding' 'mysteries'/'all these things' it apparently ascribes to those who have received revelation of mysteries through the Maskil's teaching the creative role of producing 'new things'—just as does Mt. 13.52! Once again, the depiction applies equally well to the inspired scribe, who on the basis of his revealed understanding 'recounts' God's glory (cf. e.g. Sir. 15.10; 39.6, 14ff.; 51) and produces wise sayings of his own (Sir. 39.6ff.; cf. 15.21; 18.29).

The disciples of the Maskil—both the Qumran Teacher, and, if we may call him a Maskil, Matthew's Teacher—whose understanding is so important and to whom mysteries are revealed, are themselves *maśkîlîm* like their teacher (cf. Mt. 10.25). It follows that those brought to such understanding themselves assume the role of *maśkîlîm* as those who both understand and cause others to understand, and it is perhaps in these terms that we should see the Great Commission of 28.19f. For Matthew's disciples are those who understand; to 'make disciples', therefore, in large part, is to 'cause to understand', and the disciples thus assume the pedagogic role of their master (cf. 28.20). Aware of the risks of circularity in the argument, I venture to suggest that herein also lies the sense of μαθητευθείς in 13.52. To be 'discipled' to the kingdom or 'made a "disciple" with respect to the kingdom' is—for Matthew—conceptually equivalent to 'being given to know the mysteries of the kingdom' (13.11). Thus a disciple in this sense is one who has genuine, *revealed* insight, and whose understanding has been tested and has been vindicated by the teacher. This is, moreover, entirely appropriate in the context of both the 'scribe' and the 'Maskil', whose methods of inculcating understanding also include the test of understanding (see text of 1QS 9 cited above), while specifically looking, as we saw in Ben Sira's scribe and the scribes of apocalyptic literature, for a special divine gift of understanding.

In Matthew 13 the disciples are scribes and *maśkîlîm* because they have God-given understanding, and their role is now to use it both to interpret (making people understand) and to exercise creativity on the basis of this inspiration.

C. *The Imagery of 13.52*

If our general exegesis of Matthew 13 and of the connection between 13.51 and 52 is correct, how does this affect our appreciation of the imagery of 13.52?

The saying, as we have noted, has broadly parabolic form—and parable is the domain of the scribe in Sirach and apocalyptic literature. But it is not typical of the dominical kingdom parable in its transparency. The *Bildhälfte* merges so far into the *Sachhälfte* that the image is only superficial. οἰκοδεσπότης is a term Matthew introduces to colour the bland term ἄνθρωπος in 21.33 (cf. Mk 12.1 and Lk. 20.9), and in ch. 13 itself it is used secondarily to colour in v. 27 the ἄνθρωπος of v. 24. The ἄνθρωπος οἰκοδεσπότης of 20.1 is characterized as ἀγαθός in v. 15. We shall attempt to demonstrate in Chapter 7 that Matthew may well have used the source of 12.35 as part of his *Vorlage* for 13.52. If this is correct, it was perfectly natural that he should render ὁ ἀγαθὸς ἄνθρωπος as ἄνθρωπος οἰκοδεσπότης; the non-parabolic ἐκβάλλει ἐκ τοῦ ἀγαθοῦ θησαυροῦ ἀγαθά requires very little redaction to give the ἐκβάλλει ἐκ τοῦ θησαυροῦ αὐτοῦ καινὰ καὶ παλαιά of 13.52, and the sentence as a whole then forms an almost exact parallel to and a possible *Vorlage* for our verse. The *Bildhälfte* of the 'parable' is thus so thin as to be almost totally transparent. The ἄνθρωπος οἰκοδέσποτης then means little more than 'a man' or 'a good man'[40] and θησαυρός has the sense not primarily of a physical storeroom—which would be unique in the New Testament—but of the repository of wisdom and understanding, the 'heart'. This is the sense of θησαυρός in 12.34, which Matthew seems to be using at this point; cf. 6.21. Compare Sir. 1.25 'In the treasuries of wisdom are wise sayings' (ἐν θησαυροῖς σοφίας παραβολὴ ἐπιστήμης!); 20.30; 41.14; 50.27; Col. 2.2f.[41] This is clearly part of the picture of the *scribe* rather than of a householder. Furthermore, it is hardly typical of a householder that he brings out of his storeroom new and old things. But it is precisely typical of the *scribe*, inspired by his God-given *understanding*, that he 'out of his heart pours forth wisdom' (Sir. 50.27) and 'pours forth words of wisdom' (Sir. 39.6).

Thus 13.52 is a saying about scribes, appropriate to the context because of the emphasis on the revealed understanding of the disciples, the primary ideal of the scribes. In view of its Matthean stamp in language and interests, it looks very much as if a Matthean scribe has created it. And creativity of this sort, the production of new parables, new wise sayings from the store of divinely granted insight, is precisely the role to which the disciples, as scribes, are enjoined in this passage. Of course, the old things are there too, for it is important that the scribe be conservative before he is innovative—he is custodian and interpreter of a vast treasure in the scriptures; but the emphasis here is on the freshness of revelation and inspiration. The author evidently sees himself in the same light.

Small wonder that his concerns are at odds with those of the ruling religious parties, and that his affinities lie overwhelmingly with the 'revelatory' material of apocalyptic literature (this surely includes Sir. 39.6ff.) and Qumran.

In Chapter 7 we shall consider in greater detail the nature of the composition of the Matthean Gospel in the light of this passage. There now remains one further text in Matthew which presents 'scribes' in a positive light, and we need first to look at it briefly.

2. Mt. 23.34

> Therefore, behold I send you prophets and wise men and scribes: some of them shall ye kill and crucify; and some of them shall ye scourge in your synagogues, and persecute from city to city: that upon you may come all the righteous blood shed on earth, from the blood of Abel the righteous unto the blood of Zechariah son of Barachiah, whom ye slew between the sanctuary and the altar. Verily I say unto you, All these things shall come upon this generation (23.34-36).

There is a vast literature on these verses, which indeed bristle with problems for the exegete. We are interested here solely in the use of the term scribe in the passage and will have to pass over many of these problems, though of course our discussion is informed by the various debates that surround the verses.

Matthew's version of this saying differs significantly from Luke's (11.49-51) in a number of respects, not least in relation to the identification of the speaker. While Matthew's speaker is clearly Jesus—since the saying runs on without any indication of a break following the anti-Pharisaic polemic immediately preceding it in the text—Luke's is identified as 'the wisdom of God'. In Matthew, the Pharisees are directly addressed and accused by the saying; in Luke the attack is expressed in the third person. Further, while Matthew speaks of prophets, wise men and scribes, Luke speaks of prophets and apostles; Matthew's fuller version speaks explicitly of crucifixion (unless the reference is due to a gloss) and of some kind of persecution ('from city to city' and 'scourging in the synagogues'); 'righteous blood' is twice mentioned in Matthew's version; Zechariah is identified as 'son of Barachiah'; and for Matthew, the shed blood will not simply be 'required' of this generation, but rather 'all these things shall come upon this generation'.

It is sometimes argued that Matthew here is identifying Jesus with the figure of Wisdom since, assuming—as most scholars do—that Luke's version more closely reflects the original at this point, it is taken that Matthew simply recognizes this prophetic Wisdom saying as being spoken on Jesus' own authority and quite naturally equates the two figures. It is indeed common in the wisdom literature for the hypostatized Wisdom to make pronouncements in the first person, so that even without express reference to Wisdom Matthew may still imply that Jesus and Wisdom are to be identified. The same thing may be implied in other sayings recorded in Matthew, including 11.25-30 and 11.19. The problem in the present instance is of course that Matthew does not mention Wisdom here; he may simply be *replacing* the Wisdom attribution with the attribution to Jesus, assuming his readers will have access only to, or pay regard only to, his version of the saying. In any case the identification is not explicit enough for the text to be convincingly used to argue for a 'wisdom christology' in Matthew.[42] However, we have noted that in Sirach, the scribe and the figure of Wisdom speak in unison; in particular, Ben Sira himself in his aspirations to prophetic inspiration is indistinguishable in tone from the similarly inspired figure of Wisdom in ch. 24. Wisdom is the idealized scribe there; perhaps like Ben Sira the inspired Teacher in Matthew's Gospel naturally uses first-person wisdom language. It is difficult to be sure.

Though the saying may ultimately derive from a wisdom source,[43] as the text stands in Matthew, Jesus, the Teacher of the disciples, is the speaker. His solemn introductory words, favourites of Matthew's, which we found to be redactional in 13.52—διὰ τοῦτο (ἰδοὺ ἐγὼ ἀποστέλλω)[44]—give the saying the prophetic ring of the 'Thus saith the Lord' proclamations of judgment in the prophets. In particular the wording strongly recalls Jer. 8.17, the LXX version of which reads διότι ἰδοὺ ἐγὼ ἐξαποστέλλω εἰς ὑμᾶς ὄφεις .... (Mt. 10.16, which has a similar idea and similar wording, combines the 'serpents' [ὄφεις] of Jer. 8.17 with the 'wise' idea [here φρόνιμοι] in application to the sent disciples, and is thus practically a doublet of 23.34.)[45] Jesus' authority is heavily accentuated. The sending of 'prophets'—in the OT always the prerogative of Yahweh—facilitates this association. Perhaps, too, there is a reminiscence at least of the incident recently reported in 22.15ff., where the Pharisees—whom Jesus is here haranguing—'send (ἀποστέλλουσιν) to him *their disciples* with the

Herodians' in order to tempt or 'ensnare' him (22.15, 18), and Jesus calls them 'hypocrites' (22.18) as in the present context. Perhaps the idea is that Jesus, rather than the Pharisees, is the one with the authority to *send*, to initiate mission. If so, this would support the identification of the 'prophets, wise men and scribes' mentioned here as disciples of Jesus rather than figures from the past, such as the OT prophets.

Those sent by Jesus are prophets, wise ones and scribes. Matthew has a special interest in all three of these eponyms, along with 'little ones' and 'righteous ones'.[46] It is difficult, perhaps misguided, to attempt to draw clear divisions between all of these designations as if they necessarily referred to identifiable distinct groups within Matthew's own community. We have seen how in Sirach (and elsewhere) the terms 'wise man' and 'scribe' are practically interchangeable, and how there the scribe's role can be characterized as 'prophetic'; the roles of prophet and scribe we saw overlapping already in Jeremiah, perhaps also in the Chronicler, at Qumran (David's Compositions), in apocalyptic literature (Ezra, Baruch), and with great regularity in the targumic literature. These are thoroughly Jewish categories, and there is actually no compelling reason to assume—as most scholars do—that the scribes here are merely *Christian* scribes, specifically of the Matthean community, or that the 'prophets' must be either the OT prophets or 'Christian' (i.e. no longer specifically 'Jewish') prophets. Matthew, we consider, is quite happy to present the disciples in traditional Jewish terms; in fact here the essential continuity between Jesus' envoys and the OT figures is expressly brought out. True, the disciples of Matthew's own experience are Christians—this is one implication of the reference to crucifixion in 23.34 (if that is not a gloss)—but he consistently presents them in entirely Jewish terms. In 13.52, as 'scribes made disciples with respect to the kingdom of heaven' they are fully Jewish too.

How does the term 'scribe', our special interest in this verse, function in the context of the passage? The 'scribe' of 13.52 is a 'disciple'; and the prophets, wise ones and scribes sent out by Jesus in 23.34 are clearly his disciples. They are sent, as we have seen, with the same Jeremianic commission (ἰδοὺ ἐγὼ ἀποστέλλω . . .) and similar warnings as in ch. 10. Like the serpents of Jer. 8.17, they are evidently agents of judgment (23.35f.). Here we have a scene typical

in Matthew's literary art, in which a dramatic reversal is played out.
The scribes-and-Pharisees have been castigated as hypocrites, blind
guides, those who only *appear* to be 'righteous', and as the 'offspring
of vipers'. All this despite the fact of their acknowledged authority as
scribes (23.2; see our discussion in Chapter 1). The reversal comes
when Jesus' own disciples are sent to the scribes-and-Pharisees, just
as the Pharisees *'sent their disciples'* to Jesus (22.16). Moreover, they
are sent as *'prophets'* to those who recognize only the *dead bodies* of
the prophets (23.29; and perhaps also the 'false' prophets, cf. e.g.
7.15), for whose blood they are already responsible (23.30-32); they
are sent as *'wise men'* to those characterized elsewhere ironically as
the 'wise and understanding' (11.25) and here as *'blind* guides'; they
are sent (if the link with 10.16 is acknowledged) as wise *serpents* to a
brood of *vipers*!; they are sent to give their 'righteous' blood to those
who claim but only appear to be righteous (23.28); and they are sent
as *scribes* to those 'scribes' who are keeping people out of the
kingdom of heaven, rather than using their 'key of knowledge' (cf.
Lk. 11.52) to let people in (23.13f.).

Thus in 23.34 the term scribe is used polemically and artistically
first and foremost. We cannot expect *a priori* to learn a great deal of
Matthew's concept of the *scribe* from his usage here. The term may
well be to some extent stylized.[47] The trio of prophets, wise ones and
scribes, incidentally, appropriately balances the opposing trio of chief
priests, elders and scribes retained in the Passion narrative and its
prediction (cf. e.g. Mt. 27.41; 16.21).[48] We do not consider it prudent,
therefore, to drive too firm a wedge between the three designations
on the basis of this grouping of terms, and to argue, for example, that
the 'prophets' are the Christian prophets, proclaimers of the
kerygma; the 'wise men' are those exercising other charismatic gifts
in the church; the 'scribes' are the Christian teachers. Rather, all
three figures represent facets or modes of the 'prophetic' or
'charismatic' role. They are those who bear witness to the kingdom
on the basis of their God-given insight.

It is interesting that Luke has 'apostles' for 'wise ones and scribes',
as if (assuming Matthew's version is more accurate at this point—
again commonly agreed) the notion of 'sending' were specially
appropriate to them, or as if the 'apostles' were' typically wise ones
and scribes (such as Paul?). We have noted in the apocalyptic
literature the frequent references to the commissioning of scribes. In

1 Enoch, for example, when Enoch is first mentioned as scribe the context is one of sending: 'Enoch, scribe of righteousness, go and make known to the Watchers . . . ' (12.4) (cf., of Baruch, *2 Bar.* 4.7; of Ezra, *4 (5) Ezra* 2.33; 14.20, 23, 27). There the commission almost always entails the teaching of righteousness by some means, on the basis of revelation. Such a sending of scribes is entirely at home in apocalyptic literature in particular. It is a quasi-prophetic character-ization of the scribal role.

A number of features thus emerge to supplement and confirm the picture of the scribe we have found in the other mentions of the term in the Gospel.

First of all, scribe is here a vigorously *positive* term. It effectively recalls the mention of scribes in 23.2, where the principle of (in this case, abused) scribal authority is boldly acknowledged. It is used of Jesus' disciples in the language of a *prophetic* commissioning.

Secondly, the juxtaposition with prophets makes it likely that the scribes here spoken of are seen by Matthew in a compatible light— either as prophets themselves or, like many other scribes we have investigated in the intertestamental Jewish literature, as what we have called quasi-prophetic scribes. This is further supported by the simultaneous juxtaposition with wise ones, who for Matthew are those with special spiritual insight.

Thirdly, the scribes figure prominently in the eschatological fulfilment of prophecy: in 'filling up the measure of your fathers' (23.32) the scribes-and-Pharisees are seen as squarely in the mould of those who rejected and who were challenged by the classical OT prophets; the disciples as prophets, wise ones and scribes are in the corresponding prophetic party—the prophetic situation thus finds its eschatological fulfilment here, with the persecution of the 'prophets' culminating in the definitive destruction of the holy city. Although the context of 13.52 is very different, being spoken to the disciples themselves, there is still in this respect a conceptual link with this verse. There, the disciple-scribes are those who fulfil the Danielic prophecy of those who understand in the last days; here they are those who are agents in the fulfilment of all the judgment foreseen by the prophets. The linguistic link is there too: in the prophetic/apocalyptic διὰ τοῦτο; and while in 13.51 the disciples 'understand' 'all these things', here they are agents in the bringing about of the eschatological 'all these things' upon the scribes-and-Pharisees.[49]

Fourthly, tentatively it may be suggested that the role of these scribes in the prelude to judgment is typical of the judicial role of the Jewish scribe—in his expertise in the right implementation of the law, in passing judgment (cf. e.g. Sir. 38.34; Enoch in the later Enochic literature) or, especially as in the apocalyptic literature, in simply playing a part as a witness in the preparation of the evidence for the prosecution.

It remains to consider why Matthew should specifically include scribes amongst those named as suffering severe persecution in the synagogues and 'from city to city'. It is common for a connection to be made here—as in the case of ch. 10—with the *birkat ha-minim*, supposedly instituted as a means of ostracising and effectively removing Christians from the synagogues at the time of the Jamnian conference from ca 85 CE.[50] We cannot here engage in a full discussion of this much-debated topic. We would simply point out that there is ample evidence that it was not necessary always for zealous Pharisees to use such oblique means of disposing of significant opposition or competition: witness Paul the Pharisee's own persecution of 'the church' (Acts 8.1; 9.1ff.),[51] well before this date, and the possible persecution of those other 'scribes', the Essene community, also presumably by the ruling Pharisees and/or Sadducees. Presumably in neither of these persecutions was there any notion that what was being conducted was anything other than a rectification of erroneous teaching and/or practice *within* Judaism. We are not arguing that the persecution spoken of in Matthew 23 is to be identified with any of these particular persecutions—here the announcement evidently refers to the future. It is merely that this confrontation could in principle be *seen* as entirely *intra muros*, that is, an internal Jewish affair. There is nothing at all in the language of this passage (aside from the dubious mention of crucifixion—though even this is not exclusively a Christian fate) to suggest that a specifically *Christian* group is to be persecuted. The terms used are solidly traditional Jewish terms. Those who claimed to be prophets *might* be persecuted by the Jewish religious authorities; certain scribes found their writings banned (even Ben Sira suffered this fate at one stage)[52]—especially the authors of certain targums and authors of other 'outside books', *sifrê mînîm* and *gilyônîm*.[53] The rabbinic references to these measures of control may not refer to the identical situation facing Matthew's own community; but they do eloquently demonstrate the total Jewishness of confrontations comparable to that depicted in Matthew's account. We must repeat, therefore, that it may well be misleading to refer to Matthew's positive scribe and prophet terminology as relating to '*Christian*' offices in the church. Matthew's categories are thoroughly Jewish.

3. The Scribal Role of the Disciples in Other Matthean Contexts

If our appreciation of scribes as an appropriate characterization of the disciples according to Matthew is correct, we might reasonably expect to find some support for it in other parts of the Gospel, perhaps where the term scribe is not itself used. Is this in fact the case?

We cannot in this context discuss in full Matthew's picture of the disciples, which continues to be the subject of much debate.[54] But it may be valuable to draw attention very briefly to one or two texts (in addition to those discussed above; cf. also the discussion of 8.19 in Chapter 1) which appear to bear out our observation that Matthew presents the disciples as ideal scribes.

It is quite striking that in *5.19f.* the teaching of righteousness is brought into close association with the criticism of the scribes-and-Pharisees. The disciples to whom the saying is addressed are expected to have a righteousness beyond that of the latter; ch. 23 of course expands the idea further. Evidently they are mirrored in *5.10ff.* as those persecuted for the sake of righteousness (cf. our discussion of 23.34ff. [where the persecuted disciples are *scribes* as well as prophets and wise men]). Their scribal role is more obvious in the emphasis on their right *teaching* of (Jesus'?) commandments (5.19).[55]

We have already noted the link between these verses and the Great Commission that closes Matthew's Gospel (*28.18-20*). There the disciples are sent out—as in Mt. 23.34ff.—and given the specific task of *teaching* Jesus' own commandments as well as 'making disciples' (cf. discussion of 13.52). Like the eminent scribes of apocalyptic, Jesus is 'given all authority in heaven and earth' (cf. e.g. Enoch as 'teacher of heaven and earth' in *T. Abr.* 11.3); the disciples, who are to be like their master (10.25), are to continue his own role as teacher of righteousness. The passage is reminiscent of other apocalyptic texts in which the departing figure is a scribe commissioning his posterity to continue to teach understanding and righteousness in accordance with his revelations. Compare, for example, *T. Levi* 13.2, 9; and especially (as noted and cited in Chapter 4 above) *2 Bar.* 76.2-5, where the mountain-top location for the departure of the Scribe after forty days from this world to a continuing existence elsewhere prompts a strikingly similar commission. (Cf. also *1 Enoch* 105.)

The disciples effectively have custody of the teaching of the kingdom of heaven: it is they alone who have insight into its mysteries (13.11). And specifically as scribes they bear an important relationship to the custody of the mysteries of the kingdom (13.52). As true but persecuted scribes in 23.34ff. they effectively contrast with the scribes-and-Pharisees of 23.13 who 'shut' people (including themselves) out of the kingdom, while they should be using their 'key of knowledge' to let them in. '*Theirs* is the kingdom of heaven' (5.10). The disciples are indeed appropriately characterized as scribes if the term bears any resemblance to the understanding of the scribes in Sirach and the apocalyptic literature we have examined, who typically are renowned for their insight into mysteries.

Again in the account of Peter's confession (*16.13-20*) there is a close connection between the *revelation* to Peter of the insight concerning the mystery of the identity of Jesus (16.17) and the giving of the 'keys of the kingdom of heaven' to Peter (16.19). The allocation of the keys (cf. 23.13; Lk. 11.52) and of the authority to 'bind and loose' (16.19; cf. 18.18) is evidently the proper authorization of a scribe.[56] In view of what we have seen in the apocalyptic literature (where, incidentally, some scribes even have the comparable custody of the treasuries of wisdom)[57] it is striking that this scribal language is used of a disciple with specially given insight—exactly like the ideal scribe and his 'spirit of understanding' in Sir. 39.6; 11QPs^{a}DavComp (cf. *T. Levi* 2.3; 18.7 etc.). Significantly, Matthew reapplies this authorization to the disciples as a whole in his doublet of 16.19b in 18.18; the scribal aspect of the community's life is not left out in Matthew's collection of 'ecclesiological' teachings (cf. also 18.6).

The conflict between the 'blind' official scribes and those with true scribal insight underlies the Matthean text at many points. It is a recurrent theme in the contrast between Jesus' own insight and the lack of insight of the Pharisaic scribes, which is a topic we cannot go into here. We would mention briefly, however, the contrast between

Herod's scribes in 2.4 and the Magi. The former are confused, lacking understanding; the latter, unlikely though they might be in terms of religious pedigree, are nonetheless possessed of genuine spiritual insight. We do not here wish to speculate on their background—whether they may have been Essene wise men,[58] for example, or Iranian astrologers. But it is interesting to note that their role here—the right interpretation of omens and dreams—is exactly that of ancient Near Eastern mantic wise men and scribes (cf. Joseph, Daniel, Ahikar and a whole host of others), so that they certainly have a likely *conceptual* background. Their insight puts the official 'scribes' to shame (as in fact it does in the stories of Daniel and Joseph of course); it comes as a special divine gift. And is there perhaps a hint of what is to come in 13.52 as these wise men 'open up their treasures (τοὺς θησαυροὺς αὐτῶν)' (2.11)?

We must curtail our discussion at this point in order to summarize our findings with respect to Matthew's perception of the scribes as evidenced in his depiction of the disciples in scribal terms.

4. Conclusion

Matthew has a clear perception of what a scribe is; and this perception is reflected in his presentation of two basic types of scribe, those with true insight and true teaching of righteousness, and those without. We have discerned an ideal of the scribe whose pedigree ultimately derives from a joint Jewish and ancient Near Eastern—especially Babylonian—background, surfacing in Ezra, the Levites and the later prophets, and in a wide range of intertestamental scribal literature, especially Sirach, apocalyptic literature and Qumran. This literature is found to demonstrate a high degree of common ground as to perceptions of the scribe in the Second Temple period and on into the first centuries of the common era. This ideal of the scribe involves the following elements:

(1) the exercise of wisdom and the gift of special 'understanding' or insight; typically this is evidenced in the understanding of 'parables' and 'mysteries';

(2) the notion of authority, in the custody and maintenance of religious values, or true 'righteousness' in the Jewish community;

(3) hence the notion of righteous teaching, including the right interpretation of the law and the prophets—the object being to inculcate 'understanding' in others;

(4) a close association with true prophecy: the ideal scribe is a mantic, sharing the mission and commission of the prophets as well as their insights;

(5) related to (4), a sense of inspiration—the scribe perceives that he has a creative, 'prophetic' contribution to make, whether in the composition of hymns, particularly of inspired thanksgiving, or in the creation of new 'wise sayings' as a means of passing on his new insights.

Matthew's presentation of the two basic manifestations of the scribe corresponds quite remarkably with this common Jewish ideal—an ideal most positively and clearly expressed in non-rabbinic and non-Pharisaic sources. Pharisaic scribes are heavily criticized by Matthew because they do not measure up to his ideal of the scribe. They lack 'wisdom and understanding', lacking insight into the divine mysteries (even if occasionally they do understand parables at a more superficial level; cf. 21.45). They reject the continuing validity of the 'prophetic'. Their teaching of righteousness is flawed since they attend to the outward form of the law rather than to its spirit, thereby nullifying it. They are thus hypocrites. Hence their proper function is thoroughly vitiated: though they enjoy the public respect and traditional social standing of the scribes, and the right as scribes to occupy the 'seat of Moses', they are unable to interpret correctly the eschatological mysteries being revealed to others around them. Not understanding, they are blind guides of the people, shutting them out of the kingdom of heaven into which they have no insight.

The ideal scribe, however, Matthew finds to be an appropriate concept for use in his depiction of Jesus' disciples. The correspondence between Matthew's portrayal of the disciples as scribes and the 'apocalyptic' portrayal of scribes is in any case too great to be put down to coincidence: clearly Matthew shares with apocalyptic literature a thoroughly positive notion of the insightful scribe. It would be difficult to draw the precise limits of Matthew's use of the scribal ideal in his presentation of the disciples. Terminology for the apocalyptic scribe is being used of the disciples; but we have such a consistent, ideal picture of the scribe in Matthew, as expressed most graphically in ch. 13, that one is moved towards the conclusion that the disciples are in Matthew *being made to conform to this ideal*, not vice versa. Indeed Matthew may do more than read into the *disciples* this ideal of the scribe: their express model is to be found in their own Teacher, who may himself be understood in Matthew as—amongst other things—Maskil and Scribe.

The scribes/disciples are those who understand. The object of their understanding is the content of Jesus' parables and the underlying mysteries of the kingdom of heaven which the parables simultaneously conceal and reveal. Their insights are given by special divine revelation. In being commissioned to teach Jesus' commands and teach rightly, exercising as well as teaching true righteousness (cf. 5.19f.; 23.3), the scribes/disciples have the traditional quasi-prophetic role of the divinely sent scribe. Like the prophets, they are a testimony to those who need correction (cf. 10.18ff.) and will face persecution as a result (5.10ff.; 10.17f.; 23.34). They are invested with Jesus' own authority (28.18) and are entrusted with the custody and promulgation of Jesus' teaching (5.19f.; 28.20; cf. 23.3). Last, but by no means least, they have the prophetic authority also to produce 'new things' (13.52).

In our final chapter we shall, by way of a postscript, give attention to some of the 'new things' produced by the First Evangelist himself in an attempt to understand some principles of his writing and to offer suggestions as to the senses in which Matthew may himself be meaningfully characterized as a scribe.

Chapter 7

MATTHEW AS SCRIBE

It is generally agreed that in 13.52 the First Evangelist indulges in some self-reference. Thus P.J. Becker suggests the author has 'sich als wahrer *grammateus* . . . ein Denkmal gesetzt'; J. Dupont describes the author as 'un bon exemple' of the scribe depicted in the verse; and Goulder in particular in his chapter entitled 'The Scribe Discipled' gives many reasons for seeing Matthew's own reflection here.[1] Some scholars have even maintained that there is a cryptic signature in the word μαθητευθείς (in which the name Ματθαῖος may be discerned)—comparable to the supposed cryptic signatures of the authors of John's Gospel (the 'Beloved Disciple') and Mark's Gospel (the enigmatic young man of 14.51f.). This would certainly be in keeping both with the scribe's love of riddles and wordplays and with the conventional signature of the scribe in colophon literature. In any case, there is a great deal of evidence that the author has received a thorough training in Jewish exegesis and writing, the most tangible aspect of the traditional art of the scribe. Indeed this has been the basis of a number of interpretations of Matthew's literary art, not least R.H. Gundry's recent commentary, Goulder's discernment of a lectionary in the Gospel, and Cope's exegesis of certain passages as the work of 'a scribe discipled to the kingdom of heaven'.[2]

Michael Goulder, in the chapter cited above, has argued that Matthew is a 'scribe' in the tradition traceable through the Chronicler, Ezra and Ben Sira and the first-century 'rabbis' Hillel and Shammai. He takes the type of scribe Matthew was, to be that represented by Levi ben Sisi in *j. Sheb.* 36d: a leading figure in society who combined the roles of *sôfēr, ḥazzan* (= 'a sort of super-verger'), teacher, preacher and judge, as head of a Beth ha-Midrash. But

> Matthew does not of course think of himself as a humble provincial copyist-schoolmaster, a mere scribe as opposed to the rabbis or Learned Ones ($h^akhāmîm$): in his eyes he is the Christian inheritor of the noble title borne by a line of servants of God from Ezra to Ben Sirach and Hillel and Shammai, but betrayed by their Pharisaic descendants (p. 13).

Furthermore, Matthew's literary and hermeneutical art is comparable to the rabbinic, as Goulder shows in some detail from a whole range of features of Matthew's art. Finally,

> the weight of the case that Matthew was a scribe, lies not so much in his familiarity with Jewish Torah or with sayings of the rabbis, which might be due to matter he took over, or even with his scribal theology, though this is sufficiently striking, as with the thoroughly rabbinic manner in which he sets out his book (p. 24).

In a brief review of Matthew's use of the term 'scribe' (pp. 13f.), Goulder finds, as we have found, that Matthew considers that 'Scribes as such are fine people, but the persecuting scribes of Judaism are a monstrosity' ... 'Scribes in principle are a divine institution'.[3] Goulder goes on to say that Matthew 'draws a line between good Christian scribes and bad Jewish scribes'.

There is much here with which we can agree. However, the main problem lies in Goulder's choice of literature to compare with Matthew. Certainly there are many aspects of Matthew's style that are shared with rabbinic style; a number of hermeneutical principles are held in common also. And in a few individual figures who are called *sôfēr* in rabbinic literature there are possible comparisons to be made with Matthew. But Goulder regrettably ignores both Qumran literature—which many commentators now acknowledge as the closest comparable literature in hermeneutical technique as well as in specific legal concerns—and apocalyptic literature, whose affinities with Matthew's scribal concerns we hope to have amply demonstrated. Matthew's vigorous and deep-seated rejection of things rabbinic and Pharisaic should give one pause before this choice is made. Furthermore, though in the matter of literary style this is a less serious criticism than in the matter of theological concerns and hermeneutical method, it should always be remembered that in rabbinic literature we have material which is very much later than the First Gospel, and of very uncertain usefulness as a source of data regarding the first century, while the Qumran and apocalyptic literature is for the most part no later than contemporary with the Gospel.

It follows that we should not take the 'rabbi' as a model for Matthew's work[4]—nor 'rabbinic' as a characterization of it—any more than we should other offices such as the *ḥazzan* for which there is no basis in the text of the Gospel nor in the contemporary and extant literature of the first century. And as we have already argued in Chapter 6, there is no need to supply the completely new category of 'Christian scribe' by which to contrast Matthew with the Pharisaic or 'Jewish' scribes. Goulder has himself sought to demonstrate that Matthew is a 'Jewish' scribe. Certainly there the scribe 'discipled with respect to the kingdom of heaven' is fundamentally different from the leading Jewish 'scribes' associated with the Pharisees, but the whole Matthean controversy with the Jewish authorities rests on the rivalry between the two claims to the divine authority within the Jewish heritage. It is a type of rivalry which clearly was well established before 'the disciples were first called Christians' (Acts 11.26), since it is implied in much of the apocalyptic literature and explicit in the Qumran literature.

Now the scope of our study has been restricted to *perceptions* of the scribe in Jewish literature of earlier and comparable date to Matthew's. The study of literary technique as such and the tracing of theological ideas and hermeneutical principles—while eminently worthwhile pursuits and important corollaries to our study—have lain outside this scope. However, it belongs to the investigation of *perceptions* of the scribe to deal with ideological matters. We mentioned earlier the *pedigree* of the work of the ideal scribes in Sirach, apocalyptic literature and Qumran that distinguishes it—in its authors' eyes at least—from other interpretative material. We found that the principle underlying *true* scribalism—once again in the eyes of its representatives—is that the teaching offered by the true scribe derives from divine revelation; it is a matter of inspiration. This is reflected constantly in the emphasis on God-given insight, the claim to special access to the divine mysteries (these are the trademarks of 'apocalyptic' literature, if we may use the term in Rowland's broad sense), and on the ideal scribe's commission to instruct his posterity in understanding and true righteousness. There is generally also an explicit claim to inspiration, whether in terms of 'prophecy' or in terms of the divine granting of understanding in extraordinary measure (especially as the 'spirit of understanding'). Finally, the principle of inspiration extends necessarily to the resultant medium by which the revelatory material is passed on: first in the personal instruction of family and/or pupils (at least as regards Sirach and Qumran); secondly, and in the end much more significantly, in the scribes' written legacy—the 'apocalyptic' literature itself.

If Matthew, like the disciples he portrays in ch. 13, is himself a scribe who stands in this 'apocalyptic' tradition, then the corollary is surely inescapable that he regards his own work as authoritative and based on revelation: as inspired instructional literature.[5] What has been recognized in apocalyptic literature and at Qumran as 'charismatic exegesis' may in principle be part of Matthew's *modus operandi* too. As we saw in Chapter 4, charismatic exegesis depends on the scribe's total preoccupation with the hidden meaning of scripture—its *actual* (i.e. contemporary, eschatological) meaning—coupled with a sense of special understanding. This is exactly what Matthew credits the disciples with. In understanding the parables through Jesus' instruction they have gained insight into 'all these things' spoken of in the scriptures, promised to the 'wise' at the end of days. The authors of Daniel 11 and 12 are themselves evidently reflected in those original 'wise'; the author of Matthew 13, we suggest, is reflected with equal clarity in the latter-day embodiment of these figures in that chapter.

The principle of the scribal role in the *mashal* of Mt. 13.52 is to produce *new things* as well as old (emphasis Matthew's!)[6] from his treasure-store of special understanding. The principle may be worked out in charismatic, creative interpretation of the scriptures in the light of the scribe's understanding of the eschatological events going on around him. But the principle is also one of quasi-prophetic creativity: to produce material which, though based on the old, is altogether *new* because it rests on a living experience of revelation.

How is this creativity expressed in practice? In Matthew there are several areas in which this may be discerned: perhaps in the formation of his version of the birth narrative, for example; or perhaps in the readaptation of certain miracle accounts into doublet pericopae; or in the colouring of the passion events with detail from the scriptures. We cannot investigate these possibilities here. Instead, we propose to examine a few dominical sayings as a test of the sense of creative authority, the 'newness' which might be expected of the scribe of 13.52. The ideology of the ideal scribe as expressed in Sirach involves, as we saw, the 'adding' to wise sayings and parables, and 'pouring forth words of wisdom'.[7]

1. Matthew's Production of 'New Things'

Much recent discussion of Matthew's art has been concerned with the applicability of the term 'midrash' to it, particularly as regards the composition of the birth and infancy narrative, but also as a general principle for the composition of the book as a whole. Reaction to the views of Gundry and Goulder in particular has demonstrated that the wholesale application of the generic term 'midrash' to the First Gospel is problematic; but that some use of midrashic techniques cannot be confidently discounted.[8] 'Midrash' strictly (i.e. in the rabbinic sense at any rate) relates to the exegesis of OT scripture;[9] though other contemporary concerns may be brought in to the exegesis, the biblical text determines the course of the midrash itself. This is a problem for both Goulder's and Gundry's view. The more general term 'exegesis' does not have this problem, however, and this is the term preferred by Graham Stanton.

In an article entitled 'Matthew as a Creative Interpreter of the Sayings of Jesus',[10] Stanton argues that Matthew should be thought of as an exegete, or 'creative interpreter', who adapts and expands his sources, thus forming ostensibly 'new' sayings of Jesus (Stanton consistently places the word 'new' in inverted commas). These should not, however, be seen as creations *de novo*. With approval he quotes D. Senior,[11] commenting that 'in the Passion narrative Matthew is not an innovator but a creative redactor', and H.J. Held, who writes that 'the retelling (sc. of Mark's miracle stories) is in many cases fashioned in the light of a saying of Jesus in the pericope and brings it firmly into prominence. Thus the guiding thought in the interpretative retelling is already in the tradition itself.'[12] On the basis of a number of specific examples of logia, Stanton proceeds to claim that the Matthean expansions demonstrate that 'Matthew is creative but not innovative: he is committed to the traditions at his disposal, but he endeavours to elucidate them for his own community'. Finally, he claims (p. 287) that 'The expansions we have observed are not the work of a Christian prophet, but of an "exegete"'.

As his examples, Stanton takes a number of passages where Matthew has added expansions to sayings of Jesus in Mark, Q and so-called 'M'. At 9.13 and 12.7, for instance, Matthew has incorporated a quotation from Hos. 6.6, 'I desire mercy and not sacrifice', into a dominical saying taken from Mark, in line with his own emphasis on the theme of 'mercy', which is prominent throughout his redactional work.[13] Stanton continues (p. 275):

> In both passages the evangelist himself created 'new' words of Jesus as part of his elucidation and exposition of the Marcan pericopae. As in the other passages where the OT is quoted, Matthew is not reinterpreting Scripture in the light of Jesus, but rather citing Scripture in order to interpret the actions and teaching of Jesus.

This is clearly an accurate description of what Matthew is doing. But it appears to undermine Stanton's case for preferring Matthew's characterization as 'exegete' in these instances. The activity just described is hardly what is usually meant by exegesis; it may, and evidently does, presuppose some kind of exegetical training and skill, but to the extent that it involves innovation—and putting a saying into the mouth of Jesus for the first time can hardly be less than this—it is composition and not simply exposition.

Another of Stanton's examples is Mt. 21.41c, 43 (cf. Mk 12.9, 11f.). He begins by asserting his agreement with the widely accepted view that 21.43 is the evangelist's own composition. The verse provides a basis for Matthean expansions of the parable at vv. 34 and 41c (additional reworking of καιρός and καρπός). 21.43 itself is intended by Matthew, says Stanton, to be his elucidation of Mk 12.9-11, especially καὶ δώσει τὸν ἀμπελῶνα ἄλλοις and the citation of Ps. 118.22f. Now the epilogue of the parable begins (v. 42) with the question also found with slight variation in Mark's version, οὐδέποτε ἀνέγνωτε, 'Did you never read . . .?', a favourite Matthean phrase that is in keeping with his scribal interests and use of the OT. Suggested by 12.3, it is also introduced in 12.5 and evidently prompts the Bible-study that results in the expansion in 12.7 taken from Hos. 6.6, mentioned above. Here, as elsewhere,[14] a reference to the scriptures in Mark prompts Matthew to carry out his own Bible-study and reflection and include a further saying of Jesus that calls upon an OT scripture. It may indeed be that 21.43 itself is the result of meditation on and reinterpretation of Dan. 2.44f.[15] In a sense, exegetical procedures are being employed; but the 'method' is at a rather more sublime level: by meditation, through association and allusion, on the basis of spiritual insight (with which Matthew credits the disciples and by clear implication himself) a logion has developed which has to be seen as *new*. While there always remains the *possibility* that the verse derives from a separate source, the cumulative evidence of the vocabulary, content and location of the expansions in the Gospel makes it very likely that this verse too is redactional.[16] Furthermore, while it may, and surely does, result from meditation on Mark and the OT, it is a *new* saying and goes beyond the work of a simple exegete.

Is it necessary, then, to return to the commonly supposed avenue of 'sayings of the risen Lord', the 'Christian prophets', in order to explain the authority by which sayings have come into existence, when it is clear that they are not verbatim sayings of the historical Jesus? No. Stanton, Aune, Hill and others are surely right to reject this view. The composition of these sayings is on a literary level. But in Matthew's presentation of the disciples—and evidently his own work—in terms of 'apocalyptic' scribalism we see continuing a traditional (intertestamental Jewish) sense of quasi-prophetic authority among religious authors and exegetes. The 'apocalyptic' *scribe*, with his divine commission, continues to exercise the authority ascribed to his master. It is the 'apocalyptic' scribe who has the authority to formulate dominical sayings.

2. The Composition of Mt. 13.52

In the 'charismatic exegesis' of apocalyptic literature (in which we include the book of Revelation) and Qumran (see Chapter 4), the 'method' involves the writer's thorough immersion in the text of the OT. In some cases scriptures are cited verbatim as part of the writing; in others, it is clear that the writer has a particular passage of scripture in mind but contents himself with allusions, some self-evident, some no more than echoes and reminiscences. The First Evangelist's task differs in some obvious respects from that of the apocalyptic writers': his general purpose is different and his Gospel as a whole fits no apocalyptic genre. But his allusive use of scripture is very similar. Matthew's use of Daniel in the background to ch. 13 is of the same order as that found in both apocalyptic literature and Qumran. As Gundry pointed out,[17] 'recent researches in the Qumran scrolls have shown that in the NT period the interweaving of scriptural phraseology and one's own words was a conscious literary method'.[18] In the non-biblical Qumran texts 'we rarely find a whole or even a half-verse, but mostly only splinters of verses ... it is natural to find not only single words but idioms and phrases from the OT used in them'. Further, 'one might almost say that allusive quotations are more revealing than formal quotations, for "the least direct allusion testifies to the firmest grasp and appreciation of a subject"'.[19]

The working assumption in the following reconstruction is that Matthew, like apocalyptic and Qumran writers, uses a similar technique with regard to the extrabiblical sources he uses, Mark and Q in particular. He uses this technique, I believe, to produce new sayings on the basis of this insightful immersion in the scriptures and in the sayings of Jesus.

It is not original to suggest that Matthew has made creative use of a source (a section of 'Q') which Luke followed much more closely in Lk. 6.40–7.1; indeed I.H. Marshall calls this suggestion of Schürmann's 'broadly convincing'.[20] The present reconstruction suggests that the *Vorlage* for Mt. 13.52 is found in its Lukan form in Lk. 6.40 and 6.45.

Most of Matthew's version of the section appears in ch. 7: Lk. 6.41-44 in Mt. 7.3-5, 16-18; Lk. 6.46 in Mt. 7.21; and Lk. 6.47–7.1 in Mt. 7.24-28, where both conclude a discourse section.

There are two recognized exceptions to Matthew's placement of material from this section in his ch. 7:

1. The source-text underlying Lk. 6.40a ('The disciple is not above his teacher') is taken word for word into Mt. 10.24a and expanded redactionally in vv. 24b and 25 (where οἰκοδεσπότης represents the teacher-master[21] with whom the disciple is compared).[22] Luke, on the other hand, has a totally different and probably more original form of an addition in v. 40b. The present suggestion is that it is this addition (Lk. 6.40b) which provides the *formal* basis for Matthew's construction in 13.52a:

| *Everyone* | *fully trained* | *will be like* | *his teacher.* |
| *Every scribe* | *discipled* | *is like* | *a householder.* |

(There is also a possible linguistic link between Lk. 6.40a μαθητής and Mt. 13.52a μαθητευθείς.)

2. The other Matthean parallel to this Q section that is not found in ch. 7 is the parallel to Lk. 6.45, which is placed at Mt. 12.34f. There the order is changed (v. 45c is put before v. 45a as Mt. 12.34b), as is the reference of the saying in context (in Lk. 6 it is about ethical fruits, while in Matthew it becomes related to evil speaking—the Beelzebul accusation). But most interestingly, his version of the wording of Lk. 6.45a,b differs from Luke's with respect to phrases which he will re-use almost verbatim in 13.52b. That is, ἐκβάλλει corresponds to Luke's προφέρει and recurs in 13.52b; the neuter singulars in antithetic parallel, ἀγαθόν . . . καὶ . . . πονηρόν, become neuter plurals ἀγαθά . . . καὶ . . . πονηρά in 12.35 and correspond to the neuter plurals καινὰ καὶ παλαιά in 13.52b. Meanwhile, Lk. 6.45's expansion of θησαυροῦ, τῆς καρδίας, is omitted both in Mt. 12.35 and 13.52b; τοῦ θησαυροῦ is retained in both; and ἄνθρωπος is retained in both.

The development may be set out as follows:

(1) Lk. 6.40a   οὐκ ἔστιν μαθητὴς ὑπὲρ τὸν διδάσκαλον
     Mt. 10.24   οὐκ ἔστιν μαθητὴς ὑπὲρ τὸν διδάσκαλον

     Lk. 6.40b   κατηρτισμένος δὲ πᾶς ἔσται ὡς ὁ διδάσκαλος αὐτοῦ
     Mt. 10.25   ἀρκετὸν τῷ μαθητῇ ἵνα γένηται ὡς ὁ διδάσκαλος αὐτοῦ
     Mt. 13.52a   πᾶς γραμματεὺς μαθητευθείς. . . ὅμοιός ἐστιν ἀνθρώπῳ οἰκοδεσπότῃ

(2) Lk. 6.45   ὁ ἀγαθὸς ἄνθρωπος ἐκ τοῦ ἀγαθοῦ θησαυροῦ τῆς καρδίας
     Mt. 12.35   ὁ ἀγαθὸς ἄνθρωπος ἐκ τοῦ ἀγαθοῦ θησαυροῦ
     Mt. 13.52b   ἀνθρώπῳ οἰκοδεσπότῃ. . . ἐκ τοῦ θησαυροῦ αὐτοῦ

     Lk. 6.45   προφέρει τὸ ἀγαθόν (καὶ . . . τὸ πονηρόν)
     Mt. 12.35   ἐκβάλλει ἀγαθά (καὶ . . . πονηρά)
     Mt. 13.52b   ἐκβάλλει καινὰ καὶ παλαιά

In view of Matthew's well-known practice of combining materials from different sources in a new context (e.g. in the discourses) it should occasion no surprise that he merges two verses that are separated by a paragraph in his *Vorlage*. In any case, in the separating paragraph between Lk. 6.40 and 45 there is the verb ἐκβάλλειν, found three times in v. 42, which Luke prefers not to use in 6.45, but which Matthew appropriates for use in both 12.35 and 13.52.

The disadvantage with an analysis such as this is that it attempts to explain in concrete terms, at a textual level, something which is in principle operating on a different plane. What we see here are the tangible, largely fragmentary, word-products of a much more subtle and complex process in the author's mind, to which of course we have no direct access. It resembles in difficulty attempts to explain a joke or a piece of music. Matthew may not himself have been fully aware of the *mechanics* of his own method, since it plainly operates on an intuitive level, involving a high degree of lateral thinking and unconscious allusion (what Schürmann calls 'sprachliche Reminiszenzen'). For Matthew the exercise is certainly not an academic one, some kind of word-game, or even a rabbinic-type exegesis; it is a product born of extended reflection and meditation on the written words of scripture and of his Jesus-sources.

If this reconstruction is correct, then Matthew has by no means lost sight of the main point of the saying in Lk. 6.40: rather, from 6.45 he makes an expansion illustrating the way in which the (understanding) disciple is 'like his teacher'. When he is 'fully trained' or 'made a disciple', like his teacher, the οἰκοδεσπότης *par excellence*, he can bring 'good things out of his treasure'; Matthew's new point is that these things are *new* as well as old.

Stanton's finding that the main point of a saying is maintained in Matthew's version but elaborated and expanded to suit his own emphasis is confirmed. But we are not simply left with the old saying in a new version. When the pedigree of a saying is a little more complex, as in this verse, such a 'montage' (to use D.E. Garland's term), plus such an 'expansion' (Stanton's term) can mean the birth of *a new logion*; and here, appropriately enough, the logion is a new 'parable', the *mashal* that is the prime domain of the scribe. It is important to note that the end product is considerably greater than the sum of its parts.

This is not simply the work of an exegete, though charismatic exegesis is certainly a feature of his method; it is the product of a writer who shows awareness of his own authority and of the worth of his own creative output—an 'inspired scribe'.

3. Implications of this Study

We have already summarized the main findings of this investigation at the end of Chapter 6. Here we wish to indicate briefly some of the related and dependent areas which, we suggest, require further investigation in the light of these results. The reader may identify others.

First, interpreters of Matthew's Gospel have too long been content either to ignore altogether Matthew's affinities with apocalyptic literature or to note them and not make appropriate inferences from them. We hope to have demonstrated that Matthew in some essential respects—in his sense of vested authority and mission, in his apocalyptic understanding of scripture and in his insight into the essence of Jesus' instruction in understanding the mysteries of the kingdom and the will of God for the righteous—sees Jesus, the church and himself standing squarely in the tradition of the prophets and in the quasi-prophetic tradition of the apocalyptic scribes (including Qumran's). This is a necessary corrective to the notion of Matthew as a 'rabbinic' author, and to some instances of 'parallel-omania'[23] with reference to the use of rabbinic literature in illumination of the First Gospel.

Secondly, Matthew's at-homeness with this very broad but essentially non-Pharisaic branch of Jewish life and thought suggests the desirability of further investigations of relationships between Matthew and Qumran (now that the excesses of the 1950s are long past), between Matthew and apocalyptic literature[24] and between Matthew and Sirach.

Thirdly, in suggesting a tradition of creative 'charismatic' exegesis and composition in which to see the work of the First Evangelist, we hope to have offered a new direction in the debate concerning the pedigree of 'inauthentic' or 'redactional' dominical sayings. The recognition of the quasi-prophetic creative authority of the insightful scribe in relation to the 'redactor' or 'composer' of the Gospel offers a new level of appreciation of his art, in a way not fraught by the inadequacies and complexities of the 'Christian prophecy' theory.[25]

Fourthly, our attempt in this chapter to analyse the mechanics of the scribe's production of a new saying in terms of his immersion in the scriptures and the Jesus-sources and his confident reformulation of dominical material is a first step in a possible new way of dealing with the question of sources in Matthew. If, for example, a particular

'M' saying is found to be derivable from Matthew's other sources to the extent that 13.52 is, the possibility must in each case be raised whether it is not in fact a scribal creation. Each uncertain saying will need careful consideration on its own merits.

Fifthly, the consideration that the composer of the First Gospel has a sense of the apocalyptic authority of his own 'true' understanding and interpretation of scripture and the mysteries of the kingdom of heaven may be applicable to other NT writers also. In Chapter 4 I suggested Daniel and Revelation might be seen as the products of 'apocalyptic scribes'. I hope other scholars will join me in exploring the usefulness of this concept for understanding other parts of the biblical text.

NOTES

Notes to Chapter 1

1. The collection of controversy pericopae in Mk 2.1–3.6 is generally thought, since Albertz (M. Albertz, *Die synoptischen Streitgespräche* [Berlin, 1921]; cf. more recently J. Dewey, *Markan Public Debate* [Chico, 1980]), to be a pre-Markan collection of traditions in which the common factor is precisely the context of controversy with the Jewish scribes (Mk 11.15–12.40 comes from another). Though the collection itself may have a *Sitz im Leben* in the church, and Albertz himself admits there are indications that redactional hands have played a part, he still asserts that the narratives preserve a deposit of historical authenticity (p. 64). In any case, there are particular sayings here which are classifiable as authentic on other grounds (e.g. Mk 2.27, a sabbath saying whose controversial content and antithetic parallelism are in chiastic form, which are good indications of authenticity; cf. also Mk 7.15; see the discussion by Jeremias, *New Testament Theology*, I, pp. 208-11). Lohse (art. σάββατον, *TDNT*, VII, p. 22 n. 172), asserts: 'the fact that Jesus Himself before the community was engaged in conflict regarding the Sabbath regulations is to be regarded as one of the best established parts of the tradition. . . ' For a discussion of the issue from a sceptical viewpoint see M.J. Cook, *Mark's Treatment of the Jewish Leaders* (Leiden, 1978), esp. pp. 77-97; he provides a bibliographical note on representatives of the various positions on pp. 80f.

2. For a convenient statistical analysis of all the group labels in the synoptics see A.F.J. Klijn, 'Scribes, Pharisees, High-Priests and Elders in the New Testament', *NovT* 3 (1959), pp. 259-67. In the following analysis, which is based on Klijn's, but is not exhaustive, possible sources are roughly indicated in parentheses; however, the sources themselves may not of course always be directly responsible for the labels as redacted and reapplied by the evangelists; we do not attempt to distinguish pre-Markan sources.

Pharisees are mentioned as a separate group in all three synoptics (as well as in John): (Mk) Mk 2.18 // Mt. 9.14; Lk. 5.33; Mk 2.24 // Mt. 12.2; Lk. 6.2; (Q) Mt. 9.34; 12.24 (cf. Lk. 11.15); Lk. 11.37-39, 42f.; (M) Mt. 15.12; (L) Lk. 7.36; 13.31; 16.14; 17.20; 18.10-11; 19.39. *Scribes* are mentioned independently less frequently by Luke and Matthew than by Mark: (Mk) Mk 1.22 // Mt. 7.29; Mk 2.6 // Mt. 9.3; Mk 2.16 (scribes of the Pharisees); 3.22; 9.11 // Mt. 17.10; Mk 9.14; 12.28 (// νομικός in Mt. 22.35 and Lk. 20.25); Mk 12.32 (cf.

Lk. 20.39); 12.35, 38 //Lk. 20.46; (Q) Mt. 8.19; (M) Mt. 13.52. *Sadducees* are mentioned on their own only at Mk 12.18 // Mt. 22.33; Lk. 20.27. *Elders, captains* and *Herodians* never appear on their own.

3. That groups appear in combination or association does not necessarily mean that no distinction between them is implied, though this is clearly the case in some instances (such as the 'scribes and Pharisees' hendiadys of Matthew 23) as we shall see; this has to be determined exegetically in each case.

Scribes and Pharisees appear together more frequently in Matthew and Luke than in Mark: (Mk) Mk 7.1, 5 // Mt. 15.1; Mt. 23.1 (cf. Mk 12.38); Lk. 5.21, cf. v. 17 (cf. Mk 2.6); Lk. 5.30 (cf. Mk 2.16); Lk. 6.7; Mt. 12.38 (cf. Mk 8.11); (Q) Mt. 13.38; 23.13, 15, 23, 25, 27, 29; (M) Mt 5.20; cf. (L) Lk. 7.30 and 14.3 (Pharisees and νομικοί). *Pharisees and Herodians* appear together in (Mk) Mk 3.6; (8.15, vt); 12.13 // Mt. 22.15-16. *Pharisees and Sadducees* appear together only in Matthew's redaction of (Q) Mt. 3.7; (Mk) Mt. 16.1, 6; (M) Mt. 16.11-12. In addition, *scribes, high-priests and elders*, in various combinations, are mentioned at (Mk) Mk 8.31 // Mt. 16.21; Lk. 9.22; Mk 10.33 // Mt. 20.18; Mk 14.1 // Lk. 22.2; Mk 14.43, 53; 15.1, 31 // Mt. 27.41; also Lk. 20.19 (cf. Mt. 21.45f.); Lk. 23.10. The remaining combinations are not of interest to us in this context.

4. Cf. e.g. (scribe) Mt. 8.19ff.; (ruler of the synagogue) Mk 5.22 (// Mt. 9.18; Lk. 8.41); (Pharisees) Lk. 7.36ff. (cf. Jn 3.1); cf. Lk. 11.37ff.

5. Klijn's statistical analysis notes at the outset that there is 'remarkable disagreement' between the evangelists in their use of these labels (*op. cit.*, p. 259).

6. It may be that Matthew himself was perplexed by this designation. Even in Mark they are only mentioned in connection with the Pharisees. But see note 29.

7. Luke mentions the Pharisees as in the crowd at the triumphal entry into Jerusalem (19.39); Matthew mentions them once after the crucifixion (27.62); John mentions them as partly responsible for Jesus' death (18.3). Otherwise they are conspicuous by their absence from the passion accounts.

8. Compare our discussion in Chapter 6 (p. 158).

9. Cf. e.g. C.L. Mitton, 'Matthew's Disservice to Jesus', *Epworth Review* 6/3 (1979), pp. 47-54. Tilborg (S. van Tilborg, *The Jewish Leaders in Matthew* [Leiden, 1972]), clearly saddened by Matthew's portrayal, states in his Preface: 'the results of my investigation have also led me to ask how one can reconcile the anti-Jewish mentality of the Gospel of Matthew with the gospel as the good news of the coming Kingdom... Matthew was the mouthpiece of a community with a pronounced anti-Jewish atmosphere. The knowledge and (partial) experience of the sad history of the Jewish people, in which an ideologization of (among other things) some of Matthew's

statements played an unhappy role, ought to keep us from an all too naive apology. The negative tone of the Mt gospel should not tempt us into pronouncing a negative judgment on Judaism.' Tilborg's judgment, it should be noted, depends on labelling Matthew as a Gentile editor and on classing as non-Matthean such texts as present Jewish groups in a favourable light, e.g. Mt. 23.34.

10. For instance, in his transfer of the 'woes' in Q, originally—it is supposed—addressed to two distinct groups (as in Lk. 11.42-44, 45-52), apparently to a single group of scribes-Pharisees in Mt. 23.13-36. It is also seen as symptomatic of this that Matthew tends to replace 'scribes' in his Markan *Vorlage* with 'Pharisees', as if he does not appreciate a difference between them. However, as we shall see, this is not the best interpretation of the data.

11. For an attempt to isolate pre-Markan traditions from the Markan redaction, see Cook, *Mark's Treatment of the Jewish Leaders*.

12. Cook (*Mark's Treatment of the Jewish Leaders*, esp. pp. 58-67) argues that the majority of Mark's references to scribes (11 out of 16) are redactional, 'each such mention being the result of Mark's having shifted his Jerusalem-based personnel back into earlier scenes of the drama, so as to knit together the two distinct units of his composition (chs. 1–13 and 14–16), and to sow the seeds of hostility between Jesus and his Passion narrative enemies as early as feasible in that first unit (which actually only had Pharisees and Herodians in this role)' (p. 63).

13. There is also, however, only one Markan reference (Mk 12.18 // Mt. 22.33; Lk. 20.27) to the Sadducees on their own.

14. Scribes and Pharisees are mentioned together in the typical synoptic way in the non-Johannine pericope usually placed at Jn 7.53-8.11 (v. 3).

15. Some of these, despite an aura of scholarship, have not been accepted generally as even worthy of rebuttal and will thus not be listed here. In the early days of Qumran scholarship it was frequently suggested that Essenes actually formed the nascent Christian community (which would explain to some degree the lack of reference to them as a separate group in opposition to Jesus, since the church was that group); the idea was expressed in various forms by J.L. Teicher, A. Dupont-Sommer, J.M. Allegro, H. del Medico and many others, and has recently been reworked in a highly ingenious and elaborate form by B.E. Thiering (*Redating the Teacher of Righteousness* [Australian and New Zealand Studies in Theology and Religion; Sydney, 1979]; *The Gospels and Qumran. A New Hypothesis* [same series, 1981]; *The Qumran Origins of the Christian Church* [same series, 1983]). We mention this for two reasons: (1) the basic hypothesis has particular relevance to the First Gospel, which has even been called 'The Gospel to the Essenes' (the title of an article by C.U. Wolf, *Biblical Research* 3 [1958], pp. 28-43); (2) the problem of the identity of the NT scribes has been linked with the question

of the absence of the Essenes from the NT, in particular in J.H. Dampier, 'The Scrolls and the Scribes of the New Testament', *BEvThS* 1.3 (1958), pp. 8-19. Dampier's article argues that 'the scribes' in the Gospels are to be identified with members of the Essene party. Neither Wolff nor Dampier has demonstrated his case; to do so would require massive documentation, which is neither provided nor available. However, it is hoped that the present study may open up a new avenue of possibilities in this area too. The Essenes were certainly a predominantly scribal group.

16. *Wars* 2.8.2ff. devotes a proportionately great amount of attention to them. While Josephus puts the number of Pharisees at 6000, Philo (*Quod omnis probus liber*, 12) puts the Essene strength at 4000.

17. See e.g. his *The Rabbinic Traditions about the Pharisees before 70 C.E.* (Leiden, 1971). On the rabbinic evidence and its interpretation, see Chapter 2 below.

18. J.W. Bowker, *The Targums and Rabbinic Literature* (Cambridge, 1969), p. 55 n. 1. In private correspondence, Professor Bowker explained to me that a major shift in his field of study brought him away from his declared intention. Indeed, he supported my own intention to deal with scribal concepts in this study rather than with the socio-historical problem.

19. The Fourth Evangelist, though he also has clear Jewish connections, does not show interest in the religious parties of Jesus' (or his own) day. For him there are 'the Jews', who are responsible for Jesus' death, and who appear to be simply representative, almost a symbol in dualistic terms, of those who reject Jesus. The 'Pharisees' to whom he refers several times appear to be similarly stereotyped. The scribes (outside the non-Johannine pericope Jn 7.53ff.) are not even mentioned.

The *Tendenz* of Luke's redactional activity with respect to the Jewish leaders is clear, if inconsistent: his overriding literary concern is that he should be understood by a Gentile readership unfamiliar with the specifics of Jewish religious hierarchy (as indeed he may be himself) and accordingly employs Roman legal terminology, avoiding the term γραμματεύς where possible (leaving 14 occurrences compared with Mark's 21, usually in contexts paralleled either in Matthew or Mark, with one or two insignificant exceptions). He does not always represent γραμματεύς and Φαρισαῖοι with νομικοί and νομοδιδάσκαλοι but uses all four terms with some apparent arbitrariness. (The references to the 'scribes of the Pharisees' party' [Acts 23.9], and 'the Pharisees and their scribes' [Lk. 5.30] probably depend on Mk 2.16's 'scribes of the Pharisees', whose difficulty of interpretation has evidently given rise to the considerable degree of textual variation at this point.)

Mark, in the opinion of most scholars, would seem to provide the nearest thing to a substantial historical source for the nature of the Jewish leaders (as for much else) that we may find in the Gospels, by dint of the fact that Mark maintains a certain consistency of usage in keeping the terms 'scribes' and 'Pharisees', 'elders' and 'chief priests' largely distinct; also in view of the sense that can be made of Mark's redactional activity in this respect when specific sources underlying the Gospel are discerned. But Mark, even if his own background was Jewish, was clearly not writing for Jews or Jewish Christians to the extent that Matthew was.

20. For an attempt to confront this common perspective, see D.A. Carson, 'The Jewish Leaders in Matthew's Gospel: A Reappraisal', *JEvThS* 25/2 (1982), pp. 161-74.

21. Relevant works are listed in the bibliography at the end of this volume. Reviews of the discussion may be found in R. Marcus, 'The Pharisees in the Light of Modern Scholarship', *JR* 32 (1952), pp. 153-64; and, more recently, M. Silva, 'The Pharisees in Modern Jewish Scholarship', *WTJ* 42 (1979), pp. 395-405. Numerous works have been devoted to a discussion of the relationship between Jesus and the Pharisees.

22. Cf. e.g. S. Westerholm, *Jesus and Scribal Authority* (CBNTS, 10; Lund, 1978).

23. Cf. e.g. J. Le Moyne, *Les Sadducéens* (Paris, 1972).

24. Cf. B.W. Bacon, 'Pharisees and Herodians in Mark', *JBL* 39 (1920), pp. 102-12; W.J. Bennett, Jr, 'The Herodians in Mark's Gospel', *NovT* 17 (1974), pp. 9-14; H.H. Rowley, 'The Herodians in the Gospels', *JTS* 41 (1940), pp. 14-27.

25. Cf. e.g. E.E. Urbach, *The Sages. Their Concepts and Beliefs* (ET Jerusalem, 1975); *idem*, 'The Derasha as the Basis of Halakhah, and the Problem of the Soferim', *Tarbiz* 27 (1958), pp. 166-82; E. Rivkin, 'Defining the Pharisees', *HUCA* 40 (1969-70), pp. 205-49; *idem*, 'Scribes, Pharisees, Lawyers, Hypocrites. A Study in Synonymity', *HUCA* 49 (1978), pp. 135-42; *idem, A Hidden Revolution* (Nashville, 1978).

26. Hence a host of essentially apologetic studies dealing with the supposed anti-Semitism in Matthew. A recent example of this concern is N.A. Beck, *Mature Christianity. The Recognition and Repudiation of the Anti-Jewish Polemic of the New Testament* (London and Toronto, 1986), esp. pp. 136-65. See also note 9 above.

27. Of some relevance to parts of our study are also S. van Tilborg, *The Jewish Leaders in Matthew*; D.E. Garland, *The Intention of Matthew 23* (Leiden, 1979); R. Hummel, *Die Auseinandersetzung zwischen Kirche und Judentum im Matthäusevangelium* (Beiträge zur evangelischen Theologie, 33; 2nd edn; München, 1966)—a particularly influential work; S. Westerholm, *Jesus and Scribal Authority*; S. Légasse, 'Scribes et disciples de Jésus', *RB* 68 (1961), pp. 321-45, 481-505; J. Hoh, 'Der christliche γραμματεύς (Mt., XIII,52)', *BZ* 17 (1925), pp. 256-69. Important studies of Matthew's own scribal art, which will be our focus in Chapter 7, are: O. Lamar Cope,

Matthew—A Scribe Trained for the Kingdom of Heaven (CBQMS, 5; Washington 1976); M.D. Goulder, *Midrash and Lection in Matthew* (London, 1974), esp. Chapter 1. The present work is, as far as I am aware, the first full study of the scribes in Matthean perspective.

28. This is not the place to go into an assessment of Cook's main thesis, in particular his argument that *Mark himself* is confused by the variant usage in his sources of the titles 'Pharisees' and 'scribes'. Cook argues that Mark has attempted to perpetuate the distinction, being unable to see that they are actually identical, the distinction extending to terminology alone (hence his care not to introduce Pharisees into his passion narrative—where the tradition spoke only of scribes—and his retrojection of scribes from there into the early chapters as preparation for their role in the passion account). It is doubtful whether Cook has demonstrated his case (see e.g. W.R. Telford's review in *JTS* 31 [1980], pp. 154–62).

29. *Mark's Treatment of the Jewish Leaders*, pp. 19f. Matthew's apparent lack of interest in the Herodians, however, may have nothing at all to do with his knowledge of scribes (or Pharisees)—even if Cook is correct to suggest that Matthew is actually ignorant of the Herodians. But there are several alternative ways to account for Matthew's omission of Herodians in 12.14 (cf. Mk 3.6) and replacement with Sadducees in 16.6 (here the variant reading of Mk 8.15 may in any case not have been available to Matthew). Furthermore, Matthew *retains* the Herodians in 22.16. That the latter is 'likely the result of inadvertent copying' (p. 20 n. 17, with an appeal to W.L. Knox, *The Sources of the Synoptic Gospels: Vol. 1 St. Mark* [Cambridge, 1953], pp. 9-10, 57 n. 1) sounds like special pleading; it is probably no more intrinsically likely than that the omission in 12.14 is an inadvertent omission—certainly Cook has not shown that it is.

30. Cook does not consider the matter of the term 'apostles': is Matthew equally perplexed by this term, which he uses only once (10.2) in a quoted passage? Cf. W. Trilling, 'Amt und Amtsverständnis bei Matthäus', in *Mélanges bibliques en hommage au R.P. Béda Rigaux* (Gembloux, 1970), pp. 40f.

31. Cf. e.g. E. von Dobschütz, 'Matthäus als Rabbi und Katechet', *ZNW* 27 (1928), pp. 338-48 (ET in G.N. Stanton [ed.], *The Interpretation of Matthew* [Issues in Religion and Theology, 3; London/Philadelphia, 1983], pp. 19-29), and, more recently, M.D. Goulder, *Midrash and Lection in Matthew* (esp. ch. 1). Cf. Cope, *Matthew, a Scribe Trained for the Kingdom of Heaven*.

32. Cf. Goulder in *Midrash and Lection*; R. Mohrlang, *Matthew and Paul* (Cambridge, 1984).

33. Cf. e.g. K. Stendahl, *The School of St. Matthew and its Use of the Old Testament* (Philadelphia, 1968).

34. G.W.E. Nickelsburg reflects this in his inclusion of a section on

Matthew in his *Jewish Literature between the Bible and Mishnah* (London, 1981).

35. Cook makes the total 23, but he appears to count Mt. 23.2 twice (at p. 25 n. 39, Mk 12.38 is counted as one of the 10 mentions Matthew retains [in 23.2, presumably], and 23.2 is then mentioned as one of Matthew's 13 non-Markan mentions).

36. Strictly speaking the figure should be 12, to accommodate Mk 12.38. But as Cook himself implicitly acknowledges, the change to 'the scribes and the Pharisees' in Mt. 23.2 (see previous note) does not amount to an omission.

37. Cf. the way Matthew overrides Mark's similar thematic link in Mk 9.14 (see on this verse and Mt. 17.10 below).

38. It is notable here that Matthew's literary (contextual) requirements have caused him to change a question regarding traditional eschatological teaching derived from the Soferim ('How say the scribes?—see on Mt. 17.10 below) into a direct question to the Pharisees ('What do *you* think...?'). Matthew has *not*, however, simply assumed that scribes = Pharisees. He recognizes that what is under examination is not the teaching of 'the scribes' (Mk 12.35) but the understanding of the contemporary Pharisees concerning the Messiah, and has restructured the pericope accordingly. There is no longer a danger that readers might understand Jesus to be critical of established scribal doctrine.

39. Although 'scribes' are specified again at 26.57—and it is not easy to see why here in particular (we may have to admit some inconsistency, unless, as in the case of some later MSS at 26.3, 'scribes' have reentered the text in line with the Markan parallel)—and at 27.41, which may be a literary expedient, providing a trio of opposing groups. In rabbinic literature 'scribes' and 'elders' are sometimes interchangeable. Cf. *j. Ber.* 1.4; *j. Sanh.* 10.3 (*m. Sanh.* 11.3), etc. Matthew, notably, does not make the error of replacing scribes in the trial account with the Pharisees, who, *qua* Pharisees, had no such power (though he sees it is legitimate for them to be concerned later [27.62] with possible error).

40. See on Mt. 17.10 below, where we argue that Matthew detects and removes an inconsistency in Mark's usage (the scribes here are quite different from those other 'scribes' with whom Mark links them—Mk 9.11 // Mt. 17.10). A further possibility is that Matthew simply omits it as part of the Markan editorial addition (9.15) which has dubious relevance to the pericopes which precede and follow.

41. Wisdom is a recurrent Matthean motif, the virtue being a distinguishing mark between those who have insight into the kingdom and those opposed to Jesus. The contrast is evident especially in ch. 13 and 11.25ff. but also underlies other passages (see on 13.52, Chapter 6).

42. Here we have to disagree with R. Hummel's analysis of Matthew's usage of the term, which he describes as 'neutral' (*Die Auseinandersetzung zwischen Kirche und Judentum in Matthäusevangelium* [München, 1966], p. 17). The thrust of the present study is to demonstrate the uncompromisingly *positive* associations of the title for Matthew.

43. Cf. e.g. J. Klausner, *Jesus of Nazareth* (London, 1925), pp. 334f.; J. Jeremias, *Jerusalem in the Time of Jesus* (London, 1969), p. 231 and n. 41; Goulder, *Midrash and Lection in Matthew*, p. 14.

44. Except for his addition of 'elders' at 27.41, which I suggest is a clarificatory improvement of Mark because although 'elders' automatically includes 'scribes', the reverse is not necessarily the case.

45. It is not completely clear why Matthew should have retained the mention of scribes here rather than omit as he did in the instances discussed above. Perhaps we have a hendiadys here as (probably) in 5.20 and 23.13ff., since the article is omitted (diff. Mk 7.1, 5). It would then be evident that these are specifically Pharisaic scribes, and thus subject to Jesus' full criticism (15.3, 7, 14); this is in any case the impression given (cf. esp. 15.12).

46. Scribes are, unusually, added to the 'Pharisees' of Mk 8.11 here, perhaps in part as a concession to the mention of them in Mk 9.34 (= Pharisees in Mt. 12.24). But other changes are also made: The phraseology is similar to that in 23.2; here, as there, some honour is accorded them by Matthew (12.38: omission of Mark's πειράζειν [Mk 8.11] [which is retained for Pharisees and *Sadducees* in the doublet Mt. 16.1; cf. 19.3; 22.35; 22.18— the *hypocrites* tempt]; the added courtesy address, Διδάσκαλε; and qualification of the critics by τινες [cf. on 9.3, below]). Matthew apparently thinks the added teaching on the Sign of Jonah (a *mashal*) is appropriate brain-teasing material for scribes to listen to as well as the Pharisees. This would accord very well with the instruction of the 'scribes' by 'parables' in Matthew 13; see Chapter 6 below.

47. In passing, we may note here a further possible explanation for Matthew's confident use of Φαρισαῖοι and οἱ γραμματεῖς καὶ Φαρισαῖοι, namely his semitic understanding of the sense of 'interpreter', from the root פרשׁ, often mentioned by scholars as a likely origin of the term *perûšîm* in addition to the reference to their physical separation into levitically pure fellowships. After all, it is both the practice *and* the teaching of the Pharisees that are so strongly criticized in Matthew. And in this case γραμματεῖς and Φαρισαῖοι would be almost true synonyms (some support for this may be found in the Qumran references to the 'seekers of smooth things'). However, I acknowledge the speculative nature of this observation, which is not essential to the argument.

48. The scribes and Pharisees are crucial foils to Jesus' teaching of righteousness according to Matthew. If Mk 12.38ff. alone is responsible for

this view of the Pharisaic scribes, then Matthew has drastically rethought his own appreciation of Jesus' central teaching on rather a flimsy basis! In 5.19f. the essence of righteous living and teaching is at stake, not the issue of hypocrisy and ostentation.

49. Seen together with the mention of 'their synagogues' in 4.23; 9.35; 10.17 (cf. 23.34), it can be taken as an indication that the Matthean community is still smarting from a split from within Judaism.

50. It is consonant with Matthew's presentation of wisdom as a virtue of the disciples that the Magi (archetypal 'wise men') are seen in such an entirely positive light (despite, and possibly partly because of, their unorthodox background) in contrast to Herod's scribes. The contrast is the stronger for the parity of their roles in society (throughout the ancient Near East 'scribe' was an equivalent title to *magus*).

51. In 2.4 perhaps the scribes are not Pharisees; but the parallel of 7.28f. makes it likely that 'scribes of the people' is an equivalent term. According to Josephus, the Pharisees were popular with the people; the priestly groups including the Sadducees, by virtue of birth and upbringing, would have been more aloof from the people, even allowing for the exclusivistic rules of *ḥabûrâ* which many of the Pharisees practised.

52. As far as I have been able to determine. However, *ḥakhāmîm* and *sôferîm* are at times synonymous (cf. Rivkin, 'Defining the Pharisees'; but see my criticisms of his overall argumentation, note 71), there being some fluctuations in the usage, so that this is hardly a problem for our argument at this point.

53. Cf. *m. Kel.* 13.7 (= *t. Yom.* 4.6): 'R. Joshua said: The Scribes have invented a new thing, and I cannot make an answer [to them that would gainsay them].'

54. *M. Eduy.* 8.7. Cf. also Justin Martyr, *Dial. Tryph.* 8 (citing a Jewish tradition) and *Sifre Deut.* 33.1 342 (142a) (quoted in Strack–Billerbeck IV/2, p. 787). *4 Ezra* 6.26f. witnesses to a similar tradition (Elijah is implicit in this passage).

55. I do not mean to imply that the *sôferîm* responsible for the דברי סופרים in Mishnah are necessarily the *same* people that formulated the doctrine regarding Elijah. The *sôferîm* probably flourished over a period of generations (cf. e.g. 'the rest of the scribes' dated to the time of Alexander Jannaeus [104–78 BCE] in *Meg. Ta'an.* 12 and the contemporary reference to them in the 18 Benedictions. See Chapter 2 section 1 D). I merely wish to argue that the mishnaic use provides evidence of the acknowledgment of the long-established authority of statements by Second Temple *sôferîm*, whoever they were exactly, and that Mk 9.11 //Mt. 17.10 can be profitably seen in this light.

56. In any case, it is evident from other references (cf. Mt. 16.14; Jn 1.21)

that the expectation of the eschatological return of Elijah was already firmly entrenched in popular belief.

57. It is true that on our reading there is a change of subject in v. 12—the 'they' who 'did not know' 'Elijah' (= John the Baptist) cannot be identified with those to whom the eschatological teaching is ascribed in v. 10. But this is clear in any case, because in v. 12 Jesus changes the identity of Elijah also, and refers to contemporaries who have no insight into the things of the eschaton or of the Son of Man, for whose persecution they will be responsible. The disciples, meanwhile, have this eschatological insight (v. 13)—the characteristic of the ideal scribe, as we shall see in Chapter 6.

58. Cf. E.L. Sukenik, *Ancient Synagogues in Palestine and Greece* (London, 1934), pp. 57-61.

59. D. Hill, *The Gospel of Matthew* (London, 1972) p. 310.

60. I. Renov, 'The Seat of Moses', *IEJ* 5 (1955), pp. 262-67.

61. Cf. P. Bonnard, *L'Évangile selon Saint Matthieu* (Neuchâtel, 1970), p. 334; Lk. 16.29; 24.57. The tone of Mt. 23.2f. recalls Deut. 17.10f., where Moses directs that obedience should be given to the decisions of the *Levitical* priests and judges.

62. In view of vv. 15ff., the ὅσα ἐάν of v. 3 can only be a loose term here and need not be taken as referring to all halakhic teachings of the Oral Law; cf. Hill, *Matthew, ad loc*.

63. Cf. the thirteenth of the Eighteen Benedictions—a document frequently used in the dating of Matthew (though this part of the text may be later)—which includes 'the remnant of the *sôferîm*' in 'the righteous, the pious and the elders of Israel'. Apparently a *few* eminent persons retained something of the authority of the classical Soferim.

64. Cook declines to address this text, in which (alongside 13.52), he says, 'it is not clear that we are dealing with Jewish groups' (p. 25 n. 47).

65. In addition to the alterations by Matthew noted here, he makes the following changes: Instead of Jesus taking the initiative in the second exchange (in Luke the 'other' man responds defensively to Jesus' challenge) the disciple first makes the request and is given the challenge to follow as his answer. This may simply be part of Matthew's attempt to abbreviate the pericope and conform it to a question-answer format. Matthew also omits Lk. 9.60b and the third encounter in vv. 61f. Either Matthew is again abbreviating, or Luke has access to a fuller version than Matthew. Since we are not attempting an exhaustive exegesis of these verses, for our purposes these changes are not significant.

66. The same thing occurs at Mt. 9.3-6 (also in the Mark/Luke parallels). Indeed the Pharisees alone (without the scribes) are spoken to concerning the Son of Man only twice in Matthew (12.8 and 12.32) and in both of these son of man probably means 'anyone'. By far the majority of son of man utterances are made strictly to the disciples alone (15 times). In 13.51f. the

disciples' comprehension of Son of Man teaching (13.37, 41) is again associated with the scribe epithet. Mt 8.20 is the first mention of the Son of Man in Matthew, and as Patte (*The Gospel According to Matthew, ad loc.*) points out, it should be regarded as a new idea in the context of the Gospel.

67. Usually positive in Matthew (but see 22.16). For Légasse ('Scribes et disciples de Jésus', p. 343), this scribe is part of the wider crowd of 'disciples' that followed Jesus about; hence he argues for the originality of Matthew's γραμματεύς against Luke's τις.

68. Bultmann argued (*History of the Synoptic Tradition* [ET, rev. edn, Oxford, 1968], pp. 53f.) that Matthew's introduction of γραμματεύς (Luke's τις being original) is due to his belief that the person was rejected by Jesus (since Matthew, in his view, sees scribes consistently in a negative light). I suspect that the introduction was for precisely the opposite reason.

69. Cf. also 'Matthew's' response to the same challenge ('Follow me') in Mt. 9.9.

70. It is likely that Matthew considered that Jesus *accepted* these persons and that they became committed disciples. However, Matthew, as we have observed, may himself have been aware that his tradition (perhaps intentionally) left the question open; and his sympathy with the scribes and disciples does not necessarily rule out the possibility that these two did *not* finally commit themselves.

71. Rivkin's view, propounded in various forms ('Defining the Pharisees: The Tannaitic Sources', *HUCA* 40 [1969-70], pp. 205-49; *A Hidden Revolution* [Nashville, 1978]; 'Scribes, Pharisees, Lawyers, Hypocrites. A Study in Synonymity', *HUCA* 49 [1978], pp. 135-42), should be regarded with caution. It is flawed in several respects, including the uncritical acceptance of the historical value of the rabbinic mentions of the Pharisees, the unsupported premise that rabbinic Judaism is simply a continuation of Pharisaism, and some questionable logic in asserting syllogistically that if A = B in one text and situation, and B = C in another, then A is identical to C in all cases. Non-rabbinic data are not adequately considered. On general grounds it is unlikely that complete synonymity is the case. This is evident in the oddness of some of Rivkin's conclusions: all Pharisees, being *ḥakhāmîm*, were scholars and creators of halakhah, for example; the Pharisees are not the *ḥabērîm*; all anonymous halakhah comes from the Pharisees; and Pharisees, *ḥakhāmîm* and *sôferîm* are identical. The usage in the rabbinic literature is much more nuanced and diverse than can be accounted for in this way. Cf. esp. J. Neusner, '"Pharisaic-Rabbinic" Judaism. A Clarification', *History of Religions* 12 (1973), pp. 250-70.

Notes to Chapter 2

1. Goulder, *Midrash and Lection in Matthew*, p. 15.

2. Jeremias's brief article 'γραμματεύς' (*TDNT*, I, pp. 740-42) is usually cited as the standard reference work for the background to the NT concepts of the scribe, along with the fuller discussion in his *Jerusalem in the Time of Jesus*. A résumé of the use of the term is given in N. Hillyer, 'Scribe', *NIDNTT*, III, pp. 477-82. Reference may also be made to E. Schürer, *The History of the Jewish People in the Age of Jesus Christ (175 B.C.-A.D. 135)* (note 40 below), and the recent volume II.1 in the Compendia Rerum Iudaicarum series, M.J. Mulder (ed.), *Mikra. Text, Translation, Reading and Interpretation of the Hebrew Bible in Ancient Judaism and Early Christianity* (Assen, 1988), pp. 21ff.

3. A few brief comments on these references will be in order at this point. Seraiah, David's 'secretary' (RSV; MT: סופר) is in 2 Sam. 8.17 ranked with priests and others of David's leaders (cf. 2 Sam. 20.25; 1 Chron. 18.16). According to 1 Chron. 27.32, David's uncle Jonathan was a counsellor, 'a man of understanding and a scribe' (מבין וסופר). Another סופר was secretary of the commander of the army (2 Kgs 25.19). Shaphan the scribe (2 Kgs 22.3ff.; 2 Chron. 34.15, 18) is highly ranked in Josiah's court. He is associated with the discovery of the Book of the Law (2 Kgs 22.8); he reads it before the king, and is sent with the high priest and other eminent persons to inquire of the Lord via Huldah the prophetess. The implicit association of this scribe with the deuteronomistic concerns (true prophecy, custody and administration of the law), is particularly interesting: Shaphan's work is associated with Levitical (scribal) responsibilities in the temple. Ahikam, Shaphan's colleague here (his son, if the dual reference is to a single Shaphan in 2 Kgs 22.11), is responsible for saving Jeremiah (Jer. 26.24—clearly of interest to deuteronomistic scribes who may finally have edited the book), while the prompting of Josiah's reform rests squarely with Shaphan. The book of Jeremiah appears also to champion the 'true' scribalism against the false (see on Jeremiah, below). Compare the opposition between Baruch the scribe and Elishama the scribe (Jer. 36.12); the implicit opposition between Shaphan and his son and grandson (36.10ff.). It is worth recalling that elsewhere the Deuteronomist stresses the scribal authority of the Levites too (e.g. Deut. 17.18; cf. 17.9ff.; 33.8-10), as, later, does the Chronicler (e.g. specifying the Levitical pedigree of the 'keepers of the threshold' [2 Chron. 34.9; cf. 2 Kgs 22.14] and the scribal pedigree of some of the Levites [2 Chron. 34.13]).

4. Cf. the blinkered look in the rabbinic direction for parallels to Matthew's literary forms and style by von Dobschütz, Goulder and others (see Chapters 1 and 7).

5. This is Clines's phrase (D.J.A. Clines, *Ezra, Nehemiah, Esther* [NCB; London and Grand Rapids, 1984], *ad loc.*).

6. The term has, however, been appropriately revived for the apocalyptic Enoch (see Chapter 4).

7. But how, then, did the Chronicler see his own role? If as a *Schriftgelehrter*, may he not also, by the same token, have seen himself as an author, for example? Of course, the term *Schriftgelehrter* may *include* the idea of literary composition, as it may include the idea of *teaching*; but these aspects of the scribe's role need to be spelled out if the term is going to be accepted as adequate.

8. For a survey of scribal offices in the ancient Near East, see H. Duesberg and I. Fransen, *Les Scribes inspirés* (rev. edn; Maredsous, 1965), pp. 22-41.

9. The Chronicler is clearly aware of this—cf. the way he understands the office of Shimshai the scribe in Ezra 4.8ff. Many ancient Near Eastern inscriptions list scribes in similar company (cf. *ANET*, 3rd edn, pp. 431-34). Jeremiah associates with such eminent scribes (see below). Cf. also Sir. 39.4.

10. Some of the relevant material is cited in J.Z. Smith, 'Wisdom and Apocalyptic', in P.D. Hanson (ed.), *Visionaries and their Apocalypses* (Issues in Religion and Theology, 4; London, 1983), pp. 101-20; further material is cited by J.R. Lundbom, 'Baruch, Seraiah, and Expanded Colophons in the Book of Jeremiah', *JSOT* 36 (1986), pp. 89-114. The divinatory art belongs to the function of the scribe from the earliest recorded times. The Assurbanipal inscription, quoted in part in another context in ch. 6 n. 41, presupposes a much more ancient tradition of divinatory scribism. (I am grateful to my friend Dr Lawson Younger for guiding me in this literature.)

11. So, W. Rudolph, *Chronikbücher* (Tübingen, 1955); but cf. H.G.M. Williamson, *I and II Chronicles* (NCB; Grand Rapids and London, 1982), p. 283.

12. I do not, however, subscribe to the view (now rejected also by most scholars) that the Chronicler is to be identified with Ezra himself. But I do consider Ezra–Nehemiah and the books of Chronicles to be closely enough related to make it meaningful to treat all four books as deriving from a common origin, their author(s) being loosely called the Chronicler.

13. According to Williamson (*I and II Chronicles*, p. 15), 'the Chronicler's own thought comes most clearly to expression in a form of preaching that was probably used by teaching Levites'. C.C. Torrey (*Ezra Studies* [The Library of Biblical Studies; New York, 1970], p. 211) is one of several scholars who have suggested that the Chronicler was one of the Levitical temple singers, whose connections with *maśkîlîm* and *sôferîm* we have noted (see on Psalms below). The Chronicler's style occasionally makes use of

typical wisdom terminology; an example is the wisdom teacher's address 'my sons' to the Levites in 2 Chron. 29.11.

14. Cf. G. von Rad, 'The Levitical Sermon in I and II Chronicles', in *The Problem of the Hexateuch and Other Essays* (ET Edinburgh, 1966), pp. 267-80. For a discussion of this in relation to Matthew, see Goulder, *Midrash and Lection in Matthew*, p. 8.

15. Cf. J. Blenkinsopp, *Prophecy and Canon* (Notre Dame, 1977), esp. p. 131. This may be associated with the inclusion of the books of Chronicles in the prophetic corpus of the Hebrew canon. He urges: 'It is no longer surprising that the Chronicler, who rewrote the history of Israel from his own Jerusalemite and anti-Samaritan perspective, names prophets and seers among his historical sources with such frequency as to leave little doubt that he regarded the writing of history as a prophetic activity'.

16. Echoes of Jeremiah abound in Matthew (especially in view of the typology Matthew exploits betweeen the prophecies regarding the two destructions of Jerusalem; cf. e.g. Jer. 19.4; 7.25; 22.5f. with Mt. 23.34ff.—see Chapter 6), as well as explicit quotations (Jer. 3 1.15 in Mt. 2.18) and introduced mentions of Jeremiah by name (Mt. 16.14 [an apocalyptic expectation, cf. *4 Ezra* 2.18]; 27.9). Matthew 27 clearly has the text of Jeremiah very much in mind (hence the strictly inaccurate ascription of Zech. 11.13 to Jeremiah in 27.9), actually *conflating* the ideas of the potter and the field of blood in Jer. 18.1-6; 19.1ff.; 32.6ff. in Mt. 27.3-10. In this creative freedom he is a *direct* successor of the scribes who put Jeremiah's prophecies into their canonical form!

17. Cf. also Isa. 8.1; 30.8; Hab. 2.2; Ezek. 43.11.

18. Cf. G.W. Buchanan, 'The Word of God and the Apocalyptic Vision', *SBL 1978 Seminar Papers* (Missoula, 1978), II, pp. 183-92, who provides evidence that Jeremiah is using the OT midrashically in his prophecy. Jeremiah may then have been the head of a scribal school, Baruch and Seraiah being among his disciples (so Gevaryahu, 'Limmudim: Scribal Disciples in the Book of Isaiah' [Heb.], *Beth Mikra* 47 [1971], pp. 438-56, who also—as the title suggests—thinks Isaiah had a similar background; cited with approval by Lundbom, 'Baruch, Seraiah, and Expanded Colophons in the Book of Jeremiah', p. 108 and n. 61). So too R.J. Anderson, 'Was Isaiah a Scribe?', *JBL* 79 (1960), pp. 57-58. The same might also be said of Ezekiel, who is first shown a written prophecy and is told 'eat this scroll' (ספר) before divulging its contents (the work of a סופר). Lundbom suggests, further, that the 'messenger' role of the scribe in the ancient Near East is also reflected in Jeremiah's appellation (Jer. 1.7-9).

19. If only because he performs a similar role to Baruch's in 51.59ff. (where he is called the 'Quartermaster'). But it is very likely that Neriah's was a scribal family (including Baruch of course). So, Lundbom, 'Baruch, Seraiah', p. 102.

20. On Baruch as Jeremiah's biographer, see especially O. Eissfeldt, *The Old Testament: An Introduction* (ET Oxford, 1965), pp. 354f. The dual authorship is supported by Lundbom, 'Baruch, Seraiah', pp. 108f.

21. 'Baruch, Seraiah', pp. 96ff. Lundbom claims these *expanded* colophons follow in principle the standard colophon form found in scribal works throughout the ancient Near East (another Jewish scribal example of this form being Sir. 50.27-29). Lundbom's criteria for classification are taken from E. Leichty, 'The Colophon', *Studies Presented to A. Leo Oppenheim* (Chicago, 1964), pp. 147-54.

22. H.W. Wolff, *Joel and Amos* (ET Hermeneia; Philadelphia: 1977), pp. 11f.

23. On the 'prophetic' consciousness of scribes see on Ben Sira (whom Duesberg and Fransen [*Les Scribes inspirés*, p. 733] call 'le prophète du passé'), Targums, Josephus (relevant sections below) and on the Chronicler (above). Cf. Blenkinsopp, *Prophecy and Canon*, *passim*. Baruch and Ezra, of course, later *become* 'prophets' (see Chapter 4).

24. Cf. e.g. W.H. Bellinger, Jr, *Psalmody and Prophecy* (JSOTS, 27; Sheffield, 1984), who talks of the 'prophetic experience' which prompted some features of the Psalms, such as the 'certainty of a hearing', found in many of the psalms of lament. Bellinger is thereby responding to a common view which sees a more institutional 'cult prophecy' as responsible for much Psalm composition.

25. Psalm 119, for example, with its theme of the law, its wisdom features and its acrostic form, is clearly a literary composition of a scribal sort. See section C below.

26. In addition to the commentaries, see, for example, E.W. Heaton, *Solomon's New Men. The Emergence of Ancient Israel as a National State* (London, 1974); R.B.Y. Scott, *The Way of Wisdom in the Old Testament* (New York and London, 1971)—cf. esp. ch. 5, 'Prophecy and Wisdom' (pp. 101-35); D.F. Morgan, *Wisdom in the Old Testament Traditions* (Atlanta, 1981).

27. The terms overlap over a long period, at least from Ahikar (7th-6th cent. BCE; cf. *Ahik.* 1.1, 15, etc.) onwards (cf. e.g. Sir. 38.24ff.; 11QPs^{a}DavComp; 1 Cor. 1.20; Mt. 23.34).

28. J.Z. Smith, 'Wisdom and Apocalyptic', p. 103. The Egyptian Douaf (see Chapter 3 note 6) and Ben Sira are typical examples.

29. Mowinckel observes: 'More plainly than in 45,1 it cannot upon the whole be indicated who is the author of the book' (S. Mowinckel, *Prophecy and Tradition* [Oslo, 1946], p. 62).

30. Cf. e.g. Smith, 'Wisdom and Apocalyptic', p. 106: 'wisdom and apocalyptic are related in that they are both essentially scribal phenomena. It is the paradigmatic thought of the scribe—a way of thinking that is both paradigmatic and speculative—which has given rise to both.'

192 *The Understanding Scribe*

31. See now especially J.D. Martin, 'Ben Sira—A Child of His Time', *A Word in Season* (JSOTS; Sheffield, 1986), pp. 141-61. Cf. Chapter 3 and A 2 below.

32. Ben Sira was evidently acquainted with Qoheleth (for a balanced view of the parallels see R. Gordis, *Koheleth—The Man and His World. A Study of Ecclesiastes* [3rd edn; New York, 1968], pp. 46ff.) as well as Proverbs and Job. They have a great deal in common. For example, they share an interest in the wisdom of Solomon, a scribal concern (compare Sir. 47.14-17 with the picture of the scribe in 38.24-39.11) which is reflected in the (broadly contemporary) compilation of Proverbs, the Song of Songs and Qoheleth (cf. M. Hengel, *Judaism and Hellenism* [ET London, 1974], I, pp. 129f.).

33. It is misleading of them, however, to imply that only these wisdom writers belong in this category. They draw also perhaps too fine a distinction between the scribes of the royal pre-exilic courts and the post-exilic Torah-scribes (the *scribes du roi* and the *scribes de la loi*). The book of Proverbs, which for the most part does not show the later scribal expertise in the law nor the depth of Job, Qoheleth and Ben Sira, derives from the former 'scribes', whereas the latter, emerging in the more critical and profound post-exilic situation, represents a fundamental qualification of that early scribalism. Relying on Schaeder's interpretation of the merging of scribal roles in Ezra as the pivotal point in the change of the scribe's role, Duesberg–Fransen (pp. 405ff.) regard the gulf between the pre-exilic scribes and the post-exilic scribes as unbridged: 'Assurément les gens des rois de Juda ne sont plus; Esdras n'est pas de leur lignée; il n'hérite pas d'eux. La distance est trop grande pour imaginer raisonnablement une descendance spirituelle de Saphan à Néhémie' (p. 406). But Duesberg–Fransen, though recognizing Jeremiah's (and Baruch's) connections with the pro-prophetic scribal family of Shaphan (pp. 174ff.), make no mention of the ensuing creative role of the scribes who collated, redacted and composed Jeremiah and the late prophetic books and thus overlook a major strand in the scribal tradition that leads to Ezra and the so-called Torah-scribes.

34. Naturally enough, some of the redactions by later disciples do not share quite the same creative drive (cf. e.g. the redactor of Qoheleth [Qoh. 12.12]).

35. Cf. e.g. Goulder, *Midrash and Lection in Matthew*, ch. 1.

36. On the classical Soferim, the reader is referred also to the discussion of Mt. 17.10ff. in Chapter 1 above.

37. Cf. e.g. J. Neusner, *The Rabbinic Traditions about the Pharisees before 70* (3 vols.; Leiden, 1971); 'Evidence for the Study of First-Century Pharisaism', in W.S. Green (ed.), *Approaches to Ancient Judaism: Theory and Practice* (Missoula, 1978), pp. 215-28.

38. See section 2 C below.

39. *Dibrê hasôferîm* carry great (and ancient) authority by the time of the Mishnah. See on Mt. 17.10ff. in Chapter 1, and ch. 1 n. 55 above; further examples are found in *m. Orl.* 3.9; *m. Yeb.* 2.4; 9.3 (*m. Sot.* 9.15); *m. Par.* 11.4-6; *m. Tohor.* 4.7, 11; *m. Yad.* 3.2. By implication, however, Talmud sometimes apparently equates the *sôferîm* of the *dibrê sôferîm* with later scholars (compare e.g. *b. Yeb.* 2.4; *b. Kid.* 38a with *m. Orl.* 3.9). From the enigmatic mention of 'the rest of the Soferim' (פליתת סופרים) in the thirteenth of the Eighteen Benedictions (common text) it seems that some, into the Tannaitic period and beyond, could still lay claim to the authority of the eminent scribal tradition (though another tradition surfacing in *Meg. Ta'an.* 12 applies the term to a group in the time of Alexander Jannaeus—cf. ch. 1 n. 55).

40. Cf. E. Schürer, *The History of the Jewish People in the Age of Jesus Christ (175 B.C.-A.D. 135)* (rev. and ed. by G. Vermes, F. Millar and M. Black; Edinburgh, 1979), II, pp. 358f., and works cited there.

41. Simon, incidentally, is something of a hero to Ben Sira, though the latter does not portray Simon *himself* as a scribe (Sir. 50.1-21).

42. It may, however, be an indication of the governmental authority of the Soferim that at this time γραμματεύς and סופר/ספרא become equivalent to מחוקק (see section E 3 below). Cf. G. Vermes, *Scripture and Tradition in Judaism. Haggadic Studies* (Studia Post-Biblica, 4; Leiden, 1961), p. 55.

43. We recall that the Chronicler gives pride of place to סופרים (followed by שטרים [officials] and שוערים [gatekeepers]) as comprising the Levites in 2 Chron. 34.13. However, their status was evidently more mundane than that of Shaphan the Scribe in the same chapter.

44. Cf. e.g. *b. Baba Bathra* 15a.

45. References in Schürer, *History of the Jewish People*, II, p. 359 n. 5.

46. *Judaism and Hellenism*, I, pp. 176ff., cf. pp. 80f.

47. The *Letter of Aristeas*, on which Josephus's account is based, calls them 'elders' (46), translators (318), and their work διασάφεσις, 'explication' (305). They were 'men of the highest merit and of excellent education due to the distinction of their parentage; they had not only mastered the Jewish literature, but had made a serious study of that of the Greeks as well . . . they had a tremendous natural facility for the negotiation and questions arising from the law . . .' (*Aristeas* 121-122, trans. by R.S.H. Shutt in J.H. Charlesworth, *Old Testament Pseudepigrapha* [2 vols.; London 1983, 1985], II, p. 21). Certainly Ben Sira would have called them scribes (in the prologue to Sirach, his grandson compares his work of translation—also done in Egypt—to theirs).

48. The LXX translates מחוקק in Judg. 5.14 as 'searchers' (ἐξερευνῶντες); any link here with γραμματεύς is obscure, as is the LXX translation itself, but it may be that there is a similar sense to דורש and סופר here. The מחוקק is the Interpreter of the Law in CD 6.2-11.

49. *Scripture and Tradition*, p. 54.

50. Cf. e.g. B.D. Chilton, *The Glory of Israel. The Theology and Provenience of the Isaiah Targum* (Sheffield, 1982); *idem, A Galilean Rabbi and his Bible. Jesus' Use of the Interpreted Scripture of his Time* (Wilmington, 1984).

51. On this, see Vermes, *Scripture and Tradition*, pp. 49-55. The only exception is at Judg. 5.14. See note 48 above.

52. Vermes, pp. 52, 55. But the word already lends itself to interpretation in this way, especially if its root meaning of 'inscribe, engrave' (BDB, p. 349), is borne in mind. The association between 'ruler' and one who makes or interprets 'rules' could be made in English too.

53. מחוקק in Gen. 49.10 is related to 'scribes, teachers of the Torah' in general; Tg to Pss. 60.7ff. and 108.8f. reads for 'Judah is my sceptre': 'from the house of Judah are the scribes of my house of teaching'.

54. Frg, Onk. and Ps.-Jon. Targums to Deut. 33.21 relate מחוקק to 'Moses the Prophet, the Scribe of Israel'; for Num. 21.18 the chiefs of the people who 'dug the well' are 'Moses and Aaron, the scribes of Israel'.

55. The midrashim interpret מחוקק similarly to the Targums. Generally it is referred to Moses; cf. *Sifre Deut.* 355; *Gen. R.* 98.8 (on Gen. 49.10); *Deut. R.* 2.9; *Yalq.* 1.962.

56. See below, Chapter 4, on Enoch as scribe of righteousness.

57. For the meturgeman, teaching is clearly an important facet of the scribe's role. Compare e.g. Tg. Isa. 30.10 (where 'teachers' are similarly associated with prophets and are credited with instruction and interpretation of the law) with 29.10. In fact the word 'teacher' is also used to replace MT's מחוקק (cf. Tg. Isa. 33.22: MT מחוקק becomes Tg מללפנא (our teacher)—though here it refers to Yahweh).

58. Cf. similar replacements at Isa. 3.2b; Jer. 8.10b; 26.7a, 8b, 11a, 16a; Ezek. 7.26b.

59. However, there is some consistency to the targum's replacement of divination, be it prophetic or otherwise, by the instruction of the scribes: a similar equation is made (seer = teacher) within Tg. Isaiah (30.10), while 'vision' (חזון) is replaced by 'instruction' (אלפן) at Tg. Ezek. 7.26b and 12.27a and the 'seeing' of visions becomes 'teaching' (Tg. Ezek. 12.27a; 13.8a); similarly false diviners become false teachers (Tg. Ezek. 13.6ff.; Tg. Mic. 3.6f., 11) (cf. L. Smolar and M. Aberbach, *Studies in Targum Jonathan to the Prophets* [New York, 1983], p. 101).

60. Cf. the dual title of Moses as Prophet and Scribe in the Targums to Gen. 49.10.

61. 'Till now [the time of Alexander the Great] the prophets prophesied through the medium of the Holy Spirit; from now on incline your ear and hearken to the words of the Sages' (*Seder 'Olam Rabba*, 6; cf. *t. Sota* 13.2; *b. Sanh.* 11a; *b. Yoma* 9b; *b. Sota* 48b). Cf. *t. Baba Bathra* 12a: 'Since the

destruction of the Temple, prophecy was taken away from the Prophets and given to the Sages'.

62. See both Mishnah and Talmud, *passim.* The targums of course have quite a different history from these works, extending probably over a long period and not necessarily being 'rabbinic' in the mishnaic sense; thus the targumists themselves may have been regarded as 'different' from the usual sages. *B. Meg.* 3a (concerning the authorship of the Prophets Targum) certainly supports this impression.

63. On the latter, see W. Bacher, *Tradition und Tradenten in den Schulen Palästinas und Babyloniens* (repr. Berlin, 1966), pp. 160ff.

64. These are the eighteen largely euphemistic adjustments of the MT listed in *Midrash Tanhumah* and *Midrash Rabbah,* with the explanation: 'the men of the Great Synagogue altered these verses. And that is why they were called *sôferîm,* because they counted [Heb. ספר] all the letters of the Bible and expounded them' (*Midr. Tanh.* 1.1). Cf. also the *'ittûr sôferîm* (scribal embellishment, *b. Ned.* 37b) and the *dikdûkê sôferîm* (details of the scribes, *b. Suk.* 28a).

65. Cf. *b. Sota* 15a, where R. Gamaliel addresses the *hakhāmîm* as *'sôferîm'.* See also note 39 above. Cf. J. Bowker, *The Targums and Rabbinic Literature* (Cambridge, 1969), pp. 54f. and *Jesus and the Pharisees* (Cambridge, 1973), p. 22; cf. Rivkin, 'Defining the Pharisees', p. 231. Pharisees are called *sôferîm* in *t. T. Yom* 2.14 (in the context of making authoritative rulings).

66. Like *Midrash Tanhuma,* cited in note 64 above, *b. Kid.* 30a takes the etymology from ספר, to count (the letters of Torah). Cf. also *j. Shek.* 5.1; *b. Hag.* 15b; *b. Sanh.* 106b.

67. *M. Pes.* 3.1.

68. Cf. e.g. *m. Shab.* 12.5; *m. Ned.* 9.2; *m. Git.* 3.1; 7.2; 8.8; 9.8; *m. B.M.* 5.11; *m. Sanh.* 4.3; 5.5.

69. Y.F. Baer suggests that 'The Sages of the Mishnah who lived after the destruction of the Temple were . . . weak types in comparison with the Sages and the Hasidim who preceded the Hasmonean state. The latter, although they remained mostly anonymous, acted historically as creative forces far stronger than the later Sages, who wished merely to walk in the footsteps of their predecessors' (cited in E.E. Urbach, *The Sages,* p. 13, from Baer's *Israel among the Nations* [Heb.] [Jerusalem, 1955]).

70. See the 2nd-cent. Jewish inscriptions published in H.J. Leon, *The Jews of Ancient Rome* (1960), pp. 265-331; cf. *ibid.,* pp. 183-86.

71. J. Neusner, '"Pharisaic-Rabbinic" Judaism. A Clarification', *History of Religions* 12 (1973), pp. 267ff.

72. Cf. J. Blenkinsopp, 'Prophecy and Priesthood in Josephus', *JJS* 25 (1974).

73. 'From Artaxerxes to our own time the complete history has been written, but has not been deemed worthy of equal credit with the earlier

records, because of the failure of the exact succession of the prophets . . . For, although such long ages have now passed, no one has ventured to add, or to remove, or to alter a syllable' (*Ag. Ap.* 1.41-42). In view of his assertion, was Josephus perhaps endeavouring to rectify matters?

Notes to Chapter 3

1. WUNT, 6; Tübingen, 1980.

2. In a whole range of matters, Sirach bears close comparison with the First Gospel. Space forbids a full treatment of the possible influence of the book on Matthew; but it is hoped that this study will establish at least the potential fruitfulness of such an investigation.

3. While it is clear that Sirach was used by some rabbinic sages, it is sometimes listed with the 'outside books' whose readers (or expositors?) have no place in the world to come. See the discussion by S.Z. Leiman in 'The Talmudic and Midrashic Evidence for the Canonization of Hebrew Scripture' (Dissertation, University of Pennsylvania, 1970).

4. It is debatable, however, whether Heaton (*Solomon's New Men*, pp. 101ff.) is justified in relying quite as heavily as he does on Ben Sira for the monarchic period!

5. On this see especially V. Tcherikover, *Hellenistic Civilization and the Jews* (Philadelphia, 1961), pp. 143-45, and Hengel, *Judaism and Hellenism*, I, pp. 131-53 (for a cautionary note see G.W.E. Nickelsburg, *Jewish Literature between the Bible and Mishnah* [London, 1981], p. 64; T. Middendorp, *Die Stellung Jesu Ben Siras zwischen Judentum und Hellenismus* [Leiden, 1973], pp. 7-34).

6. Or of the tradition associated with him. The original version of 'The Satire of the Trades' dates from at least the Middle Kingdom (2150-1750 BC). For the text and notes see *ANET*, pp. 432-34.

7. We have already seen (Chapter 2) that this elevated social position was typical of scribes of earlier generations and other cultures.

8. G. Maier, *Mensch und freier Wille nach den jüdischen Religionsparteien zwischen Ben Sira und Paulus* (Tübingen, 1972), pp. 37-42.

9. Some of the affinities between Ben Sira and Qumran are brought out in the discussion between Lehmann and Carmignac (M.R. Lehmann, 'Ben Sira and the Qumran Literature', *RQ* 3 [1961/62], pp. 103-16; J. Carmignac, 'Les Rapports entre l'Ecclésiastique et Qumrân', *RQ* 3 [1961/62], pp. 209-18).

10. In terms of Jewish religious writing the book is unusual in eschewing the conventions both of anonymity and of pseudonymity, confidently identifying the true author. It is, however, a scribal convention to identify oneself in a brief colophon (see on Jeremiah in Chapter 2, above).

11. Cf. also Hengel, *Judaism and Hellenism*, I, pp. 134ff.

12. W. Baumgartner, 'Die literarischen Gattungen in der Weisheit des Jesus Sirach', *ZAW* 34 (1914), pp. 186f.

13. Hengel considers the reading 'probable' (*Judaism and Hellenism*, II, p. 89 n. 199).

14. Cf. Hengel, *Judaism and Hellenism*, I, pp. 136, 138.

15. *Judaism and Hellenism*, I, p. 136, citing R. Meyer, *TDNT*, VI, pp. 812ff.

Notes to Chapter 4

1. Remarkable as this may be, the apocalyptic literature has not previously been drawn upon as a source for elucidating scribal concepts. It is little short of astonishing to discover that no work dealing specifically with scribes, including the standard dictionary articles of Jeremias, Black and Hillyer, evaluates, nor yet mentions, this material. Even the most recent article on the scribes by M. Bar Ilan, 'Scribes and Books in the Late Second Commonwealth and Rabbinic Period', in M.J. Mulder (ed.), *Mikra. Text, Translation, Reading and Interpretation of the Hebrew Bible in Ancient Judaism and Early Christianity* (Compendia Rerum Iudaicarum ad Novum Testamentum, II.1; Assen and Philadelphia, 1988), pp. 21-37, completely ignores the apocalyptic scribes.

2. Cf. D.W. Suter, 'Fallen Angel, Fallen Priest: The Problem of Family Purity in 1 Enoch 6-16', *HUCA* 50 (1979), p. 134; P.D. Hanson, 'Jewish Apocalyptic against its Near Eastern Environment', *RB* 78 (1971), pp. 31-58, esp. 51-58; *idem*, *The Diversity of Scripture* (Philadelphia, 1982), esp. ch. 3; and the discussions by P. Vielhauer in E. Hennecke, *New Testament Apocalyptic* (London, 1965), vol. II, pp. 595ff.; J.D. Thomas, 'Jewish Apocalyptic and the Comparative Method', in *Scripture in Context. Essays on the Comparative Method*, ed. C.D. Evans *et al.* (Pittsburgh, 1980), pp. 245-62. O. Plöger, quoted by Vielhauer (*op. cit.*, p. 595), conveniently states the prevailing view that the origins of apocalyptic lie in 'eschatologically-stimulated circles in the post-exilic community (c. 400–200 B.C.), who stood in a certain opposition to the non-eschatological theocracy and who were therefore more and more forced into the role of sectarians, who were the "soft spots" on which the foreign ideas had influence'. For a brief discussion of the sociological setting underlying parts of 1 Enoch see S.B. Reid, '1 Enoch: The Rising Elite of the Apocalyptic Movement', *SBL 1983 Seminar Papers* (Chico, 1983), pp. 147-56.

3. It is, again, remarkable that this major aspect of the figure of Enoch has not yet been the subject of a full study. Indeed, the still standard

examination of the figure of Enoch by H.L. Jansen, *Die Henochgestalt* (Oslo, 1939), which compares the non-Jewish novelty of the Enoch-figure against the established individual concepts of 'prophet' and 'wise man', almost totally neglects the 'scribe' title. P. Grelot, 'La légende d'Hénoch dans les apocryphes et dans la Bible: Origine et signification', *Recherches de Science Religieuse* 46 (1958), pp. 5-26, 181-210, deals (pp. 18ff.) with the title scribe only in so far as it is involved in a comparison of Enoch with the Mesopotamian Enmeduranki and Xisouthros. Jansen and Grelot of course did not have the benefit of the Qumran fragments; but the otherwise excellent update of this field by J.C. VanderKam, *Enoch and the Growth of an Apocalyptic Tradition* (Washington, 1984), actually chooses to ignore the Qumran fragments and thus gives only a limited treatment of Enoch as scribe (pp. 104f., 132f.). H. Odeberg, in his *TDNT* article on Enoch (II, pp. 556ff.), does not mention the title 'scribe'. C.P. van Andel's 1955 dissertation, *De Structuur van de Henoch-Traditie en het Nieuwe Testament*, devotes only a few pages ostensibly to Enoch specifically as 'scribe of righteousness' (pp. 19ff.), and even there the title is barely discussed. F. Dexinger's useful study of the Apocalypse of Weeks, *Henochs Zehnwochenapokalypse und offene Probleme der Apokalyptikforschung* (Leiden, 1977), does recognize the importance of the title 'Schreiber' for Enoch, but his main concerns lie elsewhere.

4. The earliest parts of the Enoch literature are now commonly dated to the third century or the early second century BCE. Some scholars (cf. e.g. U. Cassuto, *A Commentary on the Book of Genesis* [Jerusalem, 1961], *ad loc.*) have suggested that the kind of speculation about Enoch that is represented in apocalyptic literature is ancient enough to have influenced the biblical (P) data itself in Gen. 5.21-24: the outstandingly brief life-span, coinciding suspiciously with the days of the solar year, maintained in the Enoch literature (cf. *1 Enoch* 75; 84); his place as seventh in line from Adam; his close standing with God and his rapture to heaven. Cf. esp. P. Grelot, 'La légende d'Hénoch'; but see the reservations of VanderKam, *Enoch*, p. 117.

5. Since considerable debate has focused on whether particular epithets applied to eminent persons are titular or merely descriptive (most notably in relation to the 'Son of Man' debate and the Similitudes of Enoch) we should perhaps explain that no part of our argument depends on a titular usage of 'scribe'. However, in some cases it is very likely that the term 'scribe' *is* used in a strictly titular way, especially in the case of the 'Great Scribe' (Tg. Ps.-Jon. to Gen. 5.24), and in 'scribe of righteousness' as found in later epigraphs (cf. J.T. Milik, *The Books of Enoch. Aramaic Fragments of Qumran Cave 4* [Oxford, 1976], pp. 100-106). The same would be true of Ezra the Scribe— apparently a title already in Ezra 7.12 and certainly a fixed title in later usage (cf. e.g. *m. Aboth* 1.1; *3 Enoch* 48d.10; *4 Ezra* 14.50f.). Since *1 Enoch* gives the first extant attestation to the epithet in relation to Enoch we cannot be

sure that it was already a title; it is fairly safe to assume, however, that from the moment God addresses Enoch as 'thou scribe of righteousness' (*1 Enoch* 12.4), this effectively becomes his title.

6. In *1 Enoch*, Enoch is otherwise referred to only as a 'righteous man' (1.2), and at 71.14 as 'that Son of Man'. In a Manichaean fragment of the Book of Giants (cf. Milik, *The Books of Enoch*, p. 307), Enoch is called 'apostle'.

7. Milik, *The Books of Enoch*, esp. pp. 106, 236f., 260, 305.

8. The Targum Pseudo-Jonathan to the Pentateuch (= the 'Jerusalem' Targum) achieved final form only about the ninth century CE (since it mentions Mohammed's wives) but it does include very early (pre-Christian) material and was probably subject to constant revisions (cf. J. Bowker, *The Targums and Rabbinic Literature*, pp. 26f.). It is not possible to date accurately its version of Gen. 5.24. Odeberg suggests its dependence on *3 Enoch* (5th or 6th century), but this is very uncertain since both *3 Enoch* and the Targum evolved over a very long period. It could equally well date back to pre-Christian times, whence ultimately it certainly derives.

9. But, as we shall see, there are indications that this may not be the primary meaning. In the contexts of *1 Enoch* at any rate, his scribe title does not relate to heavenly record-keeping.

10. Cited by J. Bowker, *The Targums and Rabbinic Literature*, p. 87.

11. The majority of scholars now date *Jubilees* to the mid-second century BCE (see e.g. G.W.E. Nickelsburg, *Jewish Literature between the Bible and the Mishnah* [London, 1981], pp. 78ff.; J.C. VanderKam, *Textual and Historical Studies in the Book of Jubilees* [Harvard Semitic Monographs, 14; Missoula, 1977], pp. 207-85). It certainly draws on early Enochic traditions, to which it refers, and is probably directly dependent on the early sections of *1 Enoch* (so e.g. Odeberg, art. Ἐνώχ, *TDNT*, II, p. 558). According to VanderKam, *Jub.* 4.16-25 also depends on Enochic sources other than *1 Enoch* ('Enoch Traditions in Jubilees and Other Second-Century Sources', *SBL 1978 Seminar Papers* [Missoula, 1978], I, pp. 229-51, esp. 231ff.; see also his *Enoch*, pp. 179ff.).

12. Cf. *Jub.* 10.17: 'Enoch's office was ordained for a testimony to the generations of the world so that he should recount all the deeds of generation unto generation, till the day of judgment'.

13. The prime example is, of course, Ezra 'the priest, the scribe' (Ezra 7.11, etc.), and at least until around the time of Ben Sira (broadly contemporary with *Jubilees*), when the Jewish 'school' was opened to the laity, it was probably true that most scribes were also priests or Levites, as indeed Ben Sira himself may have been (so, Stadelmann, p. 25 [full discussion on pp. 4-26]; cf. M. Hengel, *Judaism and Hellenism*, I, pp. 78ff., 133). The third-century Babylonian author, Berossus, source for the

Enmeduranki traditions, was himself a priestly scribe. On Enoch as priest, see VanderKam, *Enoch*, pp. 185f.

14. Cf. VanderKam, 'Enoch Traditions', pp. 235f.

15. 'Enoch Traditions', p. 240.

16. It also corresponds to the task of the *maśkîl* in Daniel and at Qumran (see section on the Teacher of Righteousness, below), which is to 'turn many to righteousness' (Dan. 12.3). Noah, incidentally, shares other 'scribal' characteristics: like Enoch before him he receives special instruction in mysteries and writes down what has been revealed to him. Abraham has a comparable role in *Jub.* 12.27.

17. The date of the final redaction of the present *1 Enoch* is still in dispute and depends on the hotly contested dating of chs. 37–71, the Similitudes or 'Parables' of Enoch. However (unlike the Similitudes) the other sections are all represented in the Qumran manuscripts, along with the related Book of Giants, and most if not all almost certainly pre-date the composition of *Jubilees*, the book of Daniel and the formation of the Qumran sect. See C.C. Rowland, *The Open Heaven* (London, 1982), pp. 248-67, on 'dating the apocalypses'. The Book of Watchers (BW, chs. 1–36), in which all the 'scribe' epithets occur (with the exception of 92.1—in the Apocalypse of Weeks) is often thought to be the oldest part of the Enochic collection.

18. It might reasonably be objected that the complex compository process involved in the work makes it unnecessary to assume that statements appearing relatively late in the text are to be explained only by reference to information given in earlier sections; and that Enoch's writing is mentioned after 12.3 (cf. 13.6), which may have determined the choice of title at 12.3. VanderKam (cf. *Enoch*, pp. 132f.) indeed thinks that the content of the title is contextually determined (and refers primarily to the writing of the petition for the Watchers). However, the text reads as if the writing is subsequent to the choice of Enoch who is *already* a 'scribe' and is chosen for that reason. It is certain, moreover, that chs. 1–19 (?1–36) belonged together in their present order at a very early stage in the composition of *1 Enoch* as a whole (cf. Nickelsburg, *Jewish Literature*, pp. 48f.). This makes it at least likely that the 'scribe' title belongs with the very earliest traditions about Enoch represented in *1 Enoch*.

19. The statement in fact corresponds closely to the divine commission in *2 Enoch* 36.3 (A), that Enoch 'will be scribe for my servants ...' (see relevant section below).

20. An early part of the Enoch tradition, dated by Milik (*The Books of Enoch*, p. 6) to the second century BCE.

21. Note, for example, the corresponding references to Numbers given above with the citations from *Jubilees* (p. 81). Cf. L. Hartman, *Prophecy Interpreted* (Lund, 1966), pp. 112f.; and especially VanderKam, *Enoch*, pp. 115-18. Compare also the 'parables' of Enoch (chs. 37–71).

22. Balaam's role as 'seer of the gods', privileged to witness the council of the gods according to the 5th cent. Deir 'Alla tablet, is very similar to that of Enoch in respects other than simply the formal stylization (see VanderKam, *ibid.*).

23. Bowker (*The Targums and Rabbinic Literature*, p. 149 n. a), taking his evidence from *Chron. Jer.* 26.20, claims that 'Enoch was described as a scribe because he was believed to have been "the author of many writings"'. In respect of the earlier Enoch literature this is a far more likely derivation than from ideas of heavenly administration. But other factors are involved, too: the *inspired*, revelatory character of the writings seems also to be implicit in the honorific description, as well as the basic association with interpretation and mediation of knowledge founded on special understanding.

24. This is not the only appropriate Jewish term for an 'apocalypticist'. Others would include 'prophet' (cf. e.g. Rev. 1.3; *5 Ezra* 1.1), 'wise man' (cf. H.P. Müller, 'Mantische Weisheit und Apokalyptik', *SVT* 22 [1972], and Hengel, *Judaism and Hellenism*, I, pp. 206ff.), or even 'apostle' (see note 6 above).

25. Dexinger uses 'Schreiber' rather than 'Schriftgelehrter' without explanation. Presumably he sees the latter, with its associations with biblical exposition, as less appropriate than the more general 'Schreiber'. But the content of the term in this literature, as we hope to show, makes the term 'Schreiber', 'writer', seem rather narrow.

26. Cf. E. Janssen, *Das Gottesvolk und seine Geschichte* (Neukirchen-Vluyn, 1971), p. 97. See the quotation from J.Z. Smith on p. 48 above.

27. Cf. Milik, *The Books of Enoch*, pp. 189f.

28. E. Isaac, in R.H. Charlesworth, *Old Testament Pseudepigrapha*, I, *ad loc.*, following his preferred Lake Tana manuscript rather than the Princeton manuscript or Charles's text.

29. *Ethiopic Enoch*, II, p. 92.

30. *Ethiopic Enoch*, II, p. 222.

31. Cf. Milik, *The Books of Enoch*, p. 261.

32. In the case of Ezra 7.11 there is a duplication of the word ספר, translated both times as 'scribe' in the AV ('Ezra the priest, the scribe, [even] a scribe of the words of the commandments of the Lord, and of his statutes to Israel'); in this respect it is quite similar to *1 Enoch* 12.3f. (simple title 'scribe' followed by expanded title 'scribe of . . . '); the second part of the verse bears some resemblance to 92.1.

33. וקרא שמיה מיטטרון ספרא רבא.

34. An original mention of Enoch as scribe could have invited such an intrusion, particularly in the rabbinic period when speculation about Metatron flourished while the earlier Enoch literature was regarded with suspicion. Enoch is of course already portrayed as scribe in literature

(*Jubilees*, *1 Enoch*) that is considerably earlier than the Talmudic mentions of Metatron (cf. *b. Hag. 15a*; *b. Sanh.* 38b; *b. AZ* 3b); Metatron in any case tends to intrude at various points in the literature and to assume the roles of other figures (e.g. Jahoel, Michael; cf. *Enc. Jud.*, XI, art. 'Metatron'); the Targum Ps.-Jonathan, interestingly enough, which identifies Enoch with Metatron, does not identify Michael with Metatron at Exod. 24.1 as the other targumists do. This appears to indicate that for this meturgeman Enoch was already a scribe figure, secondarily identified with Metatron because of the latter's 'scribal' functions.

35. In any case, Metatron is *not* called 'scribe' in the main Metatron literature (*Hekhalot Rabbati*, *3 Enoch*) nor in Talmud, though he is portrayed as heavenly recorder in *b. Hag.* 15a. The archaeological evidence (see Milik, *The Books of Enoch*, pp. 102-106, 128-30), points to quite separate traditions concerning on the one hand Enoch the scribe and on the other Metatron the exalted heavenly prince. However, contra Milik, this is not conclusive proof that the Enoch-Metatron identification was never made, in any circles, before the Middle Ages.

36. Cf. Dexinger, *Zehnwochenapokalypse*, p. 148.

37. On the (limited) relevance of ancient Near Eastern parallels for the study of Jewish apocalyptic, cf. J.D. Thomas, 'Jewish Apocalyptic and the Comparative Method', in C.D. Evans *et al.* (eds.), *Scripture in Context* (Pittsburgh, 1980), pp. 256ff. Cf. D.S. Russell, *The Method and Message of Jewish Apocalyptic* (London, 1964), e.g. pp. 112ff., 257-62, 346ff., and P.D. Hanson, 'Jewish Apocalyptic against its Near Eastern Environment', *RB* 78 (1971), pp. 31-58.

38. This understanding *may* be specifically alluded to in *1 Enoch* 92.1 (so, Charles and VanderKam, *ad loc.*); but see Knibb's translation, II, p. 222.

39. Cf. Hengel, *Judaism and Hellenism*, I, p. 215.

40. Cf. H. Gunkel, 'Der Schreiberengel Nabu im A.T. und im Judentum', *ARW* 1 (1898), pp. 294-300; H. Zimmern, 'Urkönige und Offenbarung', in E. Schrader, *Die Keilinschriften und das AT* (2 vols.; 3rd edn; ed. H. Zimmern and H. Winckler [Berlin, 1902-1903]), II, pp. 520-43; discussed briefly and not entirely satisfactorily by VanderKam, pp. 132f. Cf. Charles, *Enoch*, p. 28, who, following Gunkel and Zimmern, it seems, further identifies the figure with the man clad in linen with a scribe's inkhorn at his side (Ezek. 9.2ff.).

41. As recorded in cuneiform inscriptions, but especially in the writings of Berossus.

42. Though not in all of them; see VanderKam, *Enoch*, p. 34 (cf. his chart on pp. 36f.).

43. Cf. Russell, *Method and Message*, p. 112 and bibliographical note 3; also H.L. Jansen, *Die Henochgestalt*, p. 2; VanderKam, 'Enoch Traditions', p. 229; and the reservations of E. Dhorme, cited in Grelot, 'La légende

d'Hénoch', p. 78, and Grelot's own discussion, pp. 6-26. VanderKam has published an important defence of the derivation of aspects of the figure of Enmeduranki and his counterpart in the 'Sumerian' list of sages, Utu'abzu, which between them may account for the position of Enoch in the genealogy, his 365 years, his association with the heavenly realm, his divinatory powers and even his ascension to heaven. See VanderKam, *Enoch*, esp. pp. 43-51.

44. Zimmern (*op. cit.*, p. 405 n. 1), suggests that Enoch's title of 'scribe' may itself derive from Enmeduranki, Enoch's prototype in other respects, since he receives the heavenly tablets from Šamaš; the *heavenly* scribe idea, however, he derives from Nabu (who records the deeds and fates of humans).

45. Our knowledge of Berossus in fact derives largely from quotation of quotations (the work is not extant) from his *Babyloniaca* (which was dedicated to Antiochus I Soter and can thus be dated to c. 280 BCE), in Josephus, Eusebius and George Syncellus. Clearly, Berossus' work was of some international standing.

46. See VanderKam, *Enoch*, pp. 132ff.

47. *Enoch*, p. 201.

48. The figure of the angelic intermediary or 'scribe' through whom the earthly seer receives his revelations is given various names (cf. Rowland, *Open Heaven*, pp. 88f.) and is often anonymous. In *Hek. Rab.* 20, it is Gabriel who is given the title of heavenly 'scribe'.

49. *Enoch*, p. 51; cf. p. 184.

50. See Bowker, *The Targums and Rabbinic Literature*, pp. 147f.

51. There may be other additional reasons for the selection of Baruch and Ezra for veneration as heroes by the apocalyptic writers—since both biblical figures were involved in rebuilding the community after a national disaster they were clearly appropriate models for the rebuilding of the Jewish community after 70 CE—but their *scribal* role is the more significant factor in the choice of these figures (after all, there were other important non-scribal figures involved in the reconstruction of post-exilic Israel). Rowland recognizes that 'such an authoritative group [the scribes] would be eminently qualified to receive and pass on further revelations, which would not conflict with the heart of Jewish religion and which their scribal activities enabled them to understand so well' (*Open Heaven*, p. 64).

52. Just as there was probably an 'Enoch school' responsible for the transmission of traditions circulating under his name and indulging in speculations and distinctive exegesis (and perhaps halakhoth), we may also suspect a similar sociological phenomenon constituting the *Sitz im Leben* for the Baruch material. The biblical Baruch himself may (as we mentioned in Chapter 2) have been part of a 'school' that looked on Jeremiah as its founder. It is generally accepted that this is the case with the Isaianic school, the Ezekiel school, and probably that of Zechariah. See for example P.D.

Hanson, 'Jewish Apocalyptic against its Near Eastern Environment', *RB* 78 (1971), pp. 49ff.; cf. note 2 above and the discussion of Jeremiah in Chapter 2.

53. This is not contradicted by the description of Ezra's scribal role as eternal (cf. *4 Ezra* 14.49f. cited above), nor by such passages as 14.9, which seem to cater for a christianizing interest, where the emphasis is on the immutable, once-for-all authority of the honorific title.

54. Gunkel (p. 299) rightly points out the *heavenly* qualities given to both Enoch and Ezra—taken up to heaven, shown the divine mysteries, privileged to read or write heavenly books; but these privileges do not make Enoch and Ezra themselves heavenly figures—they remain solidly on earth as far as their 'scribal' eminence is concerned.

55. VanderKam, *Enoch*, p. 133.

56. Cf. S.B. Reid, '1 Enoch: The Rising Elite of the Apocalyptic Movement', *SBL 1983 Seminar Papers* (Chico, 1983), p. 150.

57. Cf. Milik, *The Books of Enoch*, p. 260.

58. Cf. BDB *ad loc.*; Levy, II, p. 301b.

59. In Ezra 4.18 it is presumably Artaxerxes' court scribes who interpret Shimshai's letter to him. In Neh. 8.7 it is strictly speaking the Levites rather than Ezra the scribe who do the interpreting. However, the Levites themselves share in Ezra's commission to 'teach' on the basis of their skill and insight (Ezra 7.25; cf. 8.18; 2 Chron. 30.32; see our discussion in Chapter 2 above).

60. This would in any case presumably require פרישׁא; cf. Levy, *ad loc.*

61. Milik (*The Books of Enoch*, pp. 261ff.), working back to the reconstructed Aramaic from the awkward Ethiopic, posits an intermediate version in Greek, reading γραμματεὺς τῶν σαφεστάτων ἔργων (mistranslated into Ethiopic). However, it has been shown (cf. e.g. Knibb, *Enoch*, II, pp. 37-46) that there is no need to assume a Greek translation between the Aramaic and the Ethiopic at all points. In any case, Aramaic פרשׁא itself can mean 'wonders' (Levy, II, p. 303bf.) and could thus, on its own, account for the Ethiopic translation, which, as we have just noted, might still contain the idea of interpretation.

62. For a similar instance of the explanation of records of 'wondrous deeds' in the context of Enoch the scribe, cf. *2 Enoch* 54.1 (J): 'To all who wish, recite them [the books], so that they may know about the extremely marvelous works of the LORD'; (A) 'For you will *explain* them to all who wish it, so that you [*sic*] will learn the works of the LORD'.

63. Cf. Milik, *The Books of Enoch*, pp. 173f.

64. VanderKam also approves Milik's claim (*The Books of Enoch*, p. 263) that *Jub.* 4.23 gives Enoch a judicial role. But, as we have pointed out, the recording of human deeds as they are done is not properly the work of a judge but of a heavenly clerk or notary (albeit a magnificent one).

65. Cf. J. Theisohn, *Der auserwählte Richter* (Göttingen, 1975), chs. 3–5. Theisohn regards ch. 71 as a secondary addition (p. 216 n. 4; cf. also J.J. Collins, 'The Son of Man who has Righteousness', in *SBL 1979 Seminar Papers*, II, p. 7), so that the apparent identification of the Son of Man with Enoch there does not lead him to discuss the possibility that Enoch the Scribe was given the title 'judge of all the earth'.

66. This is too easily assumed also by VanderKam (see below). E. Isaac in fact translates the phrase as 'noble in all the earth', applying it to Enoch rather than the 'songs of wisdom', of which he is the 'writer' rather than the 'scribe'.

67. 'Enoch Traditions', p. 236; cf. p. 241.

68. Cf. Charles, *Enoch*, p. 28. Charles does not mention the fact (indeed, neither do VanderKam and the other writers on Enoch) that both heavenly and earthly 'scribal' roles are also attributed to Elijah. Indeed in rabbinic literature Elijah is the principal figure in the heavenly administration of human records: translated to heaven before dying, he becomes an angelic figure; with the Messiah, he writes down the good deeds of humans (references in Ginzberg, *Legends of the Jews*, V, p. 139). The similarities with Enoch are obvious; indeed Elijah and Enoch frequently appear together in later literature (e.g. *Apoc. Elijah*), in one case as 'brothers' (*'Emek ha-Melek*, 175c). But the heavenly 'scribal' role of Elijah stands late in the development of the speculations, probably witnesses to an anti-Enoch reaction, and has little bearing on our discussion.

The rabbinic expectation that Elijah will return to give rulings on halakhic matters (*Sifre Deut.* 175; cf. *b. Menahot* 45a) and the claim that Elijah 'will produce the Book of Jashar of which the whole of this Torah is but one line' may also witness to a conception of Elijah as scribe, though in a quite different (non-heavenly) sense that recalls the apocalyptic mentions of the works of Enoch, Ezra and Baruch. The expected teacher of righteousness in CD 19.35 may also be Elijah. In 2 Chron. 21.12-15 Elijah is credited with the authorship of a letter containing a prophetic message; it is possible that the Chronicler's own scribal interest may be responsible for the beginnings of this idea. In this case, we may have an instructive analogy to Enoch for understanding the development from earthly scribe-seer concepts to the eventual heavenly scribe idea. In this context we can do no more than suggest this as a possibility, recognizing the complexity of the process.

69. Even in the judgment scene (cf. *2 Enoch* 40.13 [J]), Enoch writes down the names, deeds and judgments of those *already* condemned by the judge. According to *T. Abraham* 121 (B) Abel is the judge, and Enoch's task is merely to write down sins that have been atoned for (sins not atoned for are already recorded); against Gunkel, p. 299.

70. Hence the reassurance on this point given in *T. Abraham* 11.

71. The scribe-deity Nabu, however, has a similar position with respect to Marduk; cf. Gunkel, p. 298.

72. In addition to the passages in *1 Enoch* (in various versions) and the Qumran fragments discussed below, it occurs in *T. Abraham* and a number of later inscriptions also; cf. Milik, *The Books of Enoch*, pp. 102-106.

73. *The Books of Enoch*, p. 262.

74. Cf. Milik, *The Books of Enoch*, pp. 102-106.

75. Cf. the discussion of a similar phrase by Dexinger, pp. 151f.

76. On the Teacher of Righteousness as a scribe, see Chapter 5 below.

77. The title מורה צדק has been translated in various ways. A number of French scholars (e.g. Dupont-Sommer; Carmignac has 'docteur de justice') prefer the title 'maître de justice', but this leaves uncertainty as to how to take 'justice', while 'maître' obscures the clear emphasis on the teaching role of the figure (cf. for example the word-play [apparently based on Hos. 10.13] on the one who will 'rain'/teach [ירה] righteousness at the end of days; CD 6.11; cf. 1QM 19.2; 12.10). 'Right(eous) Teacher', preferred by W.H. Brownlee and others, while grammatically possible, seems weak as a title (which is how it almost certainly functions in most of its occurrences in the Scrolls), since it would surely be an automatic prerequisite for an acknowledged teacher's respect that he be considered personally 'righteous'. Nor can we accept Weingreen's overly pedantic claim (cf. 'The Title Moreh Sedek', *JJS* 6 [1961], pp. 162-74) that מורה does not mean 'teacher', nor צדק 'righteousness' and that the epithet approximates in meaning to 'true authoritative judge' and should best be left untranslated. It is likely that the title both implicitly witnesses to the personal righteousness of the Teacher (cf. e.g. 1QpHab 1.13), in contradistinction to the Wicked Priest and his company, and to his role in instructing his flock in righteousness (cf. e.g. CD 6.10f.). Righteousness is apparently seen as an entity that can be imparted (cf. esp. Isa. 45.8). In CD 1.14-15 the sect's opponent is called 'preacher/dripper of lies': the contrast is much more potent if the sect's leader is the 'teacher/rainer of righteousness'. In this understanding of the title we agree with G. Jeremias and the majority of English-speaking scholars, including Vermes and Rowley.

78. This view is accepted by VanderKam, *Enoch*, p. 133: 'The fact that Enoch is a scribe of righteousness also reflects the context of chaps. 12-16: he is a righteous man (15.1), and he records the legitimate sentence that awaits the sinful angels and giants'. The term 'scribe' itself is context-bound, claims VanderKam, and in BW relates to composition of the copy of the angel's petition and the reply to it (13.4-6; 14.1-16.4) (p. 132). However, VanderKam can still say that 'his ability with the pen is simply presupposed' (p. 132); and the fact remains that in the context of 12-16 the titles 'scribe' and 'scribe of righteousness' are used in the call of Enoch that precedes his specific activity in this section, so that VanderKam is surely wrong to assume that the

content of the terms can only be explained with reference to the following text. (This also means he is too quick to dismiss the possibility of a borrowing from the Mesopotamian Nabu, the heavenly scribe [pp. 132f.].)

79. *Enoch*, p. 28.

80. Cf. the 'secrets of righteousness' that are revealed to him in 71.3. Righteousness itself is 'revealed' according to CD 20.20; cf. 1QH 9.24 (as supplied by Vermes).

81. One is reminded of the reference to the '*inspired* scriptures' in 2 Tim. 3.16, which are given to be used 'for teaching, for reproof, for correction, and for training in righteousness'. This is precisely the function of the 'scribe of righteousness' in *1 Enoch*; and Enochites could equally have thus regarded the books of Enoch. Though the question whether any of the books of Enoch were included among these 'inspired scriptures' by the author of 2 Timothy is still a matter of debate, they were certainly treated as such by the author of Jude.

82. *Henochtraditie*, pp. 20f.; cf. p. 116.

83. A. Jaubert ('Le Pays de Damas', *RB* 65 [1958], p. 238), who also compares the Teacher of Righteousness with Enoch as scribe of righteousness, claims that 'la fonction de "scribe de justice" pour Hénoch consiste à enseigner; c'est d'ailleurs l'attribution normale du scribe à l'époque tardive'. For other parallels to the teaching of righteousness, Jaubert also refers to the מצדיקים and משכילים of Daniel 11 and 12, Noah as δικαιοσύνης κῆρυξ in 2 Pet. 2.5 and Paul as one who taught righteousness (δικαιοσύνην δίδαξας) in *1 Clement* 5.7.

84. It is possible that this is in response to an already current notion which the author sees as a false understanding of Enoch. However, the tone is consonant with an effort to nip such a misconception in the bud.

85. Had the two titles been transposed into 'Teacher of Righteousness and the Scribe of Heaven and Earth' we should hardly have had grounds for surprise. It may justifiably be asked if there is not some closer connection between this interpretation of Enoch and the perhaps stylized figure of the Essene leader than has hitherto been supposed (see Chapter 5).

86. Although the title 'teacher of heaven and earth' is drawn from *T. Abraham*, we have seen that it accurately reflects the characterization of Enoch's work according to *1 Enoch*. Van Andel's rendering of Enoch's title in *1 Enoch* as 'author-bookkeeper of righteousness' (*Henochtraditie*, pp. 17f.; cf. p. 115) neglects this important aspect of the scribe's role as well as the revelatory character of his work.

87. This is very much in keeping with the role of the anonymous angelic figure (probably Michael) who records the deeds of the shepherds in *1 Enoch* 89.16-17, 70f., 76f.; cf. 90.14, 22.

88. It is instructive to compare Enoch's role as 'scribe of righteousness' with the role of the priestly prophet in Ezekiel 3. Having 'eaten the scroll'

(2.8–3.3), a written prophecy, he is sent as a 'watchman' (3.16) for Israel, inspired (3.17) to give 'warning' to both wicked and righteous alike to keep them from iniquity. Here both the negative and positive aspects of the admonition and exhortation to righteousness are also clear. Ezekiel's scribal features have been frequently noted; see esp. W. Zimmerli, *A Commentary on the Book of the Prophet Ezekiel*, I (Philadelphia, 1979), pp. 70f. J. Blenkinsopp (*Prophecy and Canon*, pp. 71f.) speaks of the 'scribalization of prophecy' at this point in Israel's history, drawing attention to Ezekiel's reputation as a 'parable-monger' (Ezek. 20.49 = MT 21.5; cf. 33.32f.—as an example see 17.2ff.), skilled in the literary craft (12.21-25; 15.1-8; 16.1ff., etc.) and an exponent of halakhah. Ezekiel is the 'first to exhibit clearly in his work the collapse of prophetism into priestly and scribal forms', and Ezekiel constitutes 'the bridge between prophecy under the monarchy and ecclesiastical scribalism such as is found in P'. That characteristic feature of apocalyptic scribalism, the vision of the angelic scribe, is also present in Ezekiel (9.2ff.), and of course the striking affinities of other parts of the book with apocalyptic forms and ideas have often been noted.

89. On these Soferim, see Chapter 2 above. A number of rulings in Talmud (three in Mishnah: *Pe'ah* 2.6; *Eduy.* 8.7; *Yad.* 4.3) are described as 'a halakhah given to Moses on Sinai', while the 'words of the scribes' on some halakhic matters are superior even to the written law of Moses (cf. e.g. *b. RH* 19a). See Chapter 2.

90. It is noteworthy that Noah, the author of some halakhoth, was, like Enoch, a 'righteous man' who walked (הלך) with God, whence perhaps the thrust of the word halakhah itself.

91. See VanderKam, 'Enoch Traditions', pp. 239f.

92. Talmud, in any case, astonishingly makes no mention at all of Enoch.

93. A correlation between the title Sofer and legal rulings is apparent also in Sir. 38.33.

94. G.H. Dix, 'The Enochic Pentateuch', *JTS* 27 (1926), pp. 29-42, posits an Enochic Pentateuch composed in competition with the Mosaic law by a sectarian group of Enochites; the implication is that Enoch is superior to Moses (and thus the Enochite halakhoth superior to the Pharisaic) by virtue of his superior antiquity. But see J.C. Greenfield and M.E. Stone, 'The Enochic Pentateuch and the Date of the Similitudes', *HTR* 70 (1977), pp. 51-65.

95. Though evidently not written by Christian authors, contra Milik; cf. Nickelsburg, *Jewish Literature*, p. 192 nn. 86, 88; see below.

96. Conveniently available in a new translation by F.I. Andersen in vol. I of J.H. Charlesworth (ed.), *The Old Testament Pseudepigrapha. 2 Enoch* is very difficult to date, and suggestions vary widely (Charles: first century BCE, Milik: ninth century CE!). The likelihood is that the book has a long and

complex history, and that some of it at least dates back to an early Jewish setting (cf. Andersen [pp. 94-97], who dates it to the late first century CE). On quite other grounds than the specifically 'scribal' interest, which Andersen does not directly address, he notes the great affinities of the work with the First Gospel: 'Apart from similarities to Jude and 2 Pet, which are a distinct problem, 2En comes closer in language and ideas to Mt than to any other part of the NT ... It is more likely that Mt and 2En have a similar milieu than that a later Christian author of 2En was influenced by only one book of the NT' (p. 95 n. 13).

97. The titles of Enoch in the introductions to the various manuscripts employ a 'galaxy of epithets'; cf. Andersen, p. 102.

98. Andersen also mentions the title 'great scribe' as being represented amongst the titles in the various manuscripts (p. 102). Unfortunately he does not specify in which of the twenty manuscripts that he uses it occurs, so that I have not been able to identify the reference.

99. Andersen, p. 93.

100. This is already evident in Sir. 44.16, where Enoch is 'a miracle of knowledge *for all generations*'; cf. *Jub.* 4.19, 'he saw ... and understood ... and wrote ... and placed [his testimony] on earth *for all the children of men and for their generations*'. Cf. on *1 Enoch* 1.2, above.

101. Here there may be an implied Jewish ascription of halakhah to Enoch.

102. Much of the ethical instruction is very similar to elements of the Matthean Sermon on the Mount. Some of the more obvious correspondences (e.g. on oaths [49.1f.; cf. Mt. 5.34f.]) are almost certainly secondary and dependent on Matthew. But even in the purely Jewish 'halakhic' sections there are clear reminiscences of Jesus' teaching of 'righteousness'. It is noteworthy that the ethical instruction proper begins immediately after Enoch's characterization as 'scribe' and 'witness' (36.3), so that in function if not title, Enoch is here still the 'scribe of righteousness'.

103. Cf. Mt. 13.11, 17; 1 Pet. 1.12.

104. Now dated with some confidence (e.g. by P. Alexander; cf. Charlesworth [ed.], *Old Testament Pseudepigrapha*, I, p. 229) to the 5th to 6th cent. CE in its present form, with a stong likelihood that some traditions are maintained in it that stem from tannaitic times and earlier.

105. The figure here portrayed is principally a heavenly one, and the identification with Enoch in ch. 4 is thus of a fundamentally different order from the identification of Enoch with 'that Son of Man' in *1 Enoch* 71—in fact the revelation is the converse of this, with the heavenly figure being identified as the elevated *earthly* one. Correspondingly, we are dealing principally with the heavenly figure Metatron rather than with the earthly scribe-seer Enoch.

106. Cf. Odeberg, *3 Enoch*, II, p. 62.

107. Odeberg, *3 Enoch*, I, p. 111.

108. *3 Enoch*, I, p. 80; cf. p. 95.

109. Odeberg may be right to suggest a dependence of the Tg. Ps.-Jonathan to Gen. 5.24 on Enoch-Metatron traditions, since it is unlikely that this meturgeman himself should have been the first to make the identification between Enoch and Metatron. That the targum should be directly dependent on *3 Enoch* (cf. Odeberg, *3 Enoch*, I, p. 95), however, is less likely, both on grounds of probable date and since neither Metatron nor Enoch is called 'scribe' in *3 Enoch*. Possibly the title was deduced from Metatron's acknowledged role as heavenly recorder, and his other activities that might be called 'scribal'; or the title may have been associated with him early on as a result of the influences from the heavenly scribal figures in Mesopotamia and Egyptian mythology, and may just happen not to have been specifically mentioned elsewhere in rabbinic literature. A third, and we think more convincing explanation relies on the fact that Enoch, independently of Metatron, was already known (from the earlier Enochic literature) to have the title 'scribe' (or *great scribe*—this certainly is the force of the title in the divine address in the much earlier passages in *1 Enoch* [12.3f.; 15.1]), so that: (1) Enoch is already the Great Scribe; (2) Enoch and Metatron are already identified in some tradition, possibly because of similar heavenly scribal roles; (3) the meturgeman simply assumes (1) and gives his approval to (2) (as the Fragment and Onkelos Targums do not, in an apparent endeavour to 'correct' the dangerous esteem paid to Enoch). Cf. P.S. Alexander, 'The Historical Setting of the Hebrew Book of Enoch', *JJS* 28 (1977), p. 164.

110. This is at some variance with *b. Hag.* 15a, where Metatron is recorder of human deeds (though even here he is not called 'scribe').

111. Cf. our discussion of *sôfēr* in Chapter 2, especially with regard to Josephus.

112. Although Metatron-Enoch speaks in the first person within the book, the book itself is presented as being the writing of R. Ishmael, so that *3 Enoch* is not a 'book of Enoch' in the same sense as *1* and *2 Enoch*, which are directly attributed to that eminent scribe, in particular by the use of the first person singular.

113. He also holds classes in Torah for those children who have died before completing their Torah-studies (48c.12, quoting Isa. 28.9).

114. Indeed the primary aspect of the traditional 'scribal' role, namely the transmission of mysteries in writing, is now attributed (by implication) to a rabbi, R. Ishmael (died c. 132 CE), who is associated, interestingly enough, with a number of traditions that would together qualify him as a 'scribe like Enoch' (cf. P.S. Alexander, in Charlesworth [ed.], *The Old Testament Pseudepigrapha*, I, p. 255). In rabbinic lore he is characterized as a visionary (*b. Ber.* 7a), a priest (e.g. *b. Ket.* 105b) and a learner of divine secrets (*b. Ber.* 51a); his name is also associated with a school of (esoteric) exegesis (*b. Yoma*

67b). One suspects that this 'school' was responsible for at least the early stages of the history of *3 Enoch*.

115. When preparing this study, I was not aware of any previous suggestion that Daniel might be best classed in this way. I have since found that E. Bickerman, *From Ezra to the Last of the Maccabees—Foundations of Postbiblical Judaism* (New York, 1962), pp. 70f., observes: 'Daniel, who explains the secret meaning of royal dreams at the Babylonian court, is the ideal scribe as visualized by Ben Sira'.

116. Nor indeed in rabbinic Judaism; cf. *b. Meg.* 3a. He is, however, so described at Qumran and in Josephus (e.g. *Ant.* 10.266).

117. On the literary level, the book of Daniel can be seen to apply *pesher* exegesis; but it is also a facet of the figure of Daniel that he is involved in *pesher*-type interpretation of Nebuchadnezzar's dreams and the writing on Belshazzar's wall. (Von Rad suggests that the second part of the book might be appropriately described as a *pesher* of Isaiah [*Theology of the Old Testament*, I, p. 314 n. 29].)

118. משכלים בכל־חכמה וידעי דעת ומביני מדע

119. וללמדם ספר ולשון כשדים

120. נתן להם האלהים מדע והשכל בכל־ספר וחכמה

121. This is of course not the exclusive privilege of scribes as such but of seers in general. But the point is that it is precisely typical of the eminent, mantic *scribes* we find in the other, closely related, apocalyptic literature.

122. נהירו ושכלתנו וחכמה. These qualities are compared to the 'wisdom of the gods'; perhaps, particularly in view of the mention of Nebuchadnezzar in the same verse (5.11), the principal god in mind is Nabu (= Nebu), the divine scribe!

123. רוח יתירה ומנדע ושכלתנו מפשר חלמין ואחוית אחידן ומשרא קטרין

124. Collins in fact translates משׂכילים in Daniel as 'wise instructors': they guide the people by 'making them understand'. He suggests that in precise terms this means on the one hand the explanation of scripture and on the other hand *pesher* interpretation of visions and prophecy (J.J. Collins, *The Apocalyptic Vision of the Book of Daniel* [Missoula, 1977], pp. 168-70).

125. See Chapter 3 section 2 above.

126 Cf. Collins, *The Apocalyptic Vision*, p. 210.

127. This is not to dispute the parallels Collins sees in the Wisdom of Solomon (pp. 210-12).

128. It is worth recalling here the similar role of Ahikar, 'wise man and scribe', the high-ranking official in the court of Sennacherib. It is quite possible that the biblical figure of Daniel is itself largely coloured by influence from this internationally venerated and very ancient document (witness the 5th cent. BCE Aramaic MS found at Elephantine), if we make the reasonable assumption that the kind of wisdom education exemplified in contemporary Sirach was also common to the hasidic circles responsible for the book of Daniel.

129. *The Book of Daniel* (London, 1979), p. 27, cf. n. 15.

130. On its own, this is certainly no guarantee that Daniel is to be seen as 'scribe'; but most, if not all, of the eminent scribes have priestly connections: Ezra in particular, but also Ben Sira and the apocalyptic Enoch (cf. also Ezekiel and Jeremiah [if indeed they are scribes], Baruch and the Teacher of Righteousness, and the Babylonian Berossus). Daniel's role in the Babylonian court, moreover, bears comparison with Ezra's, who indeed holds the high imperial office of ספרא as well as priest (Ezra 7.12). It is commonly held that the emergence of the scribes in the post-exilic period derives very largely from the shift of focus in priestly activity from cultic activity to occupation with the study of Torah during the exile.

131. On the different types of visionary experience, cf. Rowland, *Open Heaven*, pp. 52ff.

132. Cf. N. Porteous, *Daniel* (London, 1979), p. 17. According to Lacocque (*The Book of Daniel*, p. 3 n. 10), this association would support von Rad's derivation of apocalyptic from wisdom. It hardly does this convincingly, but it does point to an association of *scribal* wisdom with apocalyptic, which we have noticed on other grounds.

133. Ben Sira mixes the two terms freely in his picture of the scribe (see Chapter 3). See also the mixture in e.g. Ahikar and 11QPs^{a}DavComp, discussed in Chapter 5.

134. Cf. Chapter 1 note 71.

135. There is a great deal more to be said on the relationship between Daniel and scribal wisdom, but it lies mainly outside the scope of this study (see, however, below, on the apocalyptic authors as scribes). It is interesting to note that there are movements in this direction from a number of scholars. See in particular Collins, *Apocalyptic Vision*, p. 169, who credits *maśkîlîm* with the visionary material as well as the court tales; Müller, 'Mantische Weisheit und Apokalyptik'; Blenkinsopp, *Prophecy and Canon*, pp. 130-32; Smith, 'Wisdom and Apocalyptic'; cf. E.W. Heaton, *Daniel*, pp. 19-24. Von Rad's derivation of apocalyptic from wisdom recognizes the scribal contacts, though his argument is vitiated by a one-sided view of wisdom as scholastic, in opposition to prophecy (i.e. not acknowledging the discrete role of mantic wisdom) (cf. *Theology of the Old Testament*, II, esp. pp. 306f.). Von Rad there cites with approval Eissfeldt's statement that Daniel contains an 'almost overwhelming admixture of erudition'.

136. In company with most scholars, we take *4 Ezra* as broadly contemporary with Matthew's Gospel, perhaps a little later (i.e. 90–100 CE) in its final redaction, but with a good proportion of its ideas deriving from earlier traditions and sources, and to have a Palestinian or near-Palestinian provenance. This makes it, on *a priori* considerations alone, a useful document to compare with Matthew. It is all the more significant a comparison for the fact that the pseudepigraphic Ezra material was closely

associated with the Gospel of Matthew in the second century, as recent work has confirmed (see, for example, G.N. Stanton, '5 Ezra and Matthean Christianity in the Second Century', *JTS* 28 [1977], pp. 67-83; cf. Nickelsburg, *Jewish Literature*, p. 294). It is by no means beyond the bounds of possibility that some of the 'Mattheanisms' in *4 Ezra* and even *5 Ezra* are contemporary with or actually antedate Matthew's Gospel, with a common dependency on earlier materials. To some extent this is probably true of *2 Baruch* also (see below).

To my knowledge, no study of the apocalyptic Ezra as scribe has ever been carried out, and studies of the person of the central figure *per se* are also lacking.

137. See on Enoch's simple title, above, p. 83.

138. 1 Esdras moves away from using γραμματεύς also: except in 1 Esdr. 8.3, Ezra is called 'reader (of the law)', ἀναγνώστης (τοῦ νόμου); 1 Esdr. 8.9, 19; 9.39, 49. It is not easy to see exactly why this shift takes place. There may be an implicit reaction here against certain contemporaries who insist on calling themselves 'scribes'. Its omission of reference to Nehemiah may possibly reflect opposition to such scribal schools as that of the probably contemporary Ben Sira, who—as we mentioned in Chapter 3—lauds Nehemiah while omitting to mention Ezra (Sir. 49.13; cf. also *2 Macc.* 1.18-2.3). Alternatively, this may belong to the totally non-apocalyptic orientation of the work. But the notorious difficulties involved in assigning a date, provenance and *Sitz im Leben* to the book preclude certainty on this point (cf. R.J. Coggins, *The First and Second Books of Esdras* [London, 1979], pp. 4-6).

139. Probably, this ending was omitted when the new ending to the book (chs. 15f.) was added to form the document now known as 2 Esdras. Cf. e.g. M.A. Knibb, *The First and Second Books of Esdras* (London, 1979), p. 283; J.M. Myers, *I and II Esdras* (Garden City, 1974), p. 329. However, G.H. Box, *IV Ezra* (Oxford, 1913), ascribed this ending to the redactor of the work (which he dated to ca 120 CE).

140. The apocalyptic Ezra, who in other respects takes on many of the attributes and functions of Enoch his predecessor, may also be expected to show some traces of the parallels drawn between that figure and Balaam; see on the introduction to *1 Enoch*, above.

141. The identification of Ezra with Shealtiel, Zerubbabel's father, apparently inferred from 1 Chron. 3.17 (cf. Oesterley, p. xiv; cf. Ezra 3.2; 5.2; Neh. 12.1), is probably incidental and certainly has no real bearing on the rest of the narrative. M.R. James's attempt ('Ego Salathiel qui et Ezras', *JTS* 18 [1917], pp. 167-69 and 'Salathiel qui et Esdras', *JTS* 19 [1918], pp. 347-49) to follow some mediaeval authors in distinguishing between two Ezras is fundamentally flawed. He distinguishes the historical Ezra the scribe from the fictitious hero of *4 Ezra*, Ezra the prophet (= Salathiel/

Assir), whose only feature held in common with Ezra the scribe is his having been credited with the historical Ezra's restoration of the scriptures: 'I think it correct to say that the seer and the scribe have absolutely nothing else in common' (*JTS* 18, p. 168). In fact, however, what they *do* have in common (assuming for the moment that such a distinction is to be made at all) is precisely the title 'scribe': the historical Ezra with the classical scribe title, the apocalyptic Ezra with the mantic scribal role of special understanding, visionary experience and the writing of inspired instruction.

The central figure of *4 Ezra* is indeed only very loosely based on the biblical Ezra, since the outlook of the former is thoroughly apocalyptic in character, in particular owing much to the Danielic and the Enochic models; but the *unifying factor* between the two, and the justification for identifying them, seems to be the fact that each is an eminent, authoritative *scribe*. The historical discrepancies between the biblical and the apocalyptic Ezra are in all likelihood due on one hand to the confusion inherent in the biblical accounts themselves and on the other to the need to place the figure in the '30th year' of the destruction of Jerusalem by Nebuchadnezzar to match the time of writing (up to 30 years after the destruction of Jerusalem by the Romans). Compare the suitable choice for a similar situation of Baruch the central figure in *2 Baruch*; cf. P.M. Bogaert, 'Le nom de Baruch dans la littérature pseudépigraphique: L'apocalypse syriaque et le livre deutéro-canonique', in W.C. van Unnik (ed.), *La Littérature Juive entre Tenach et Mischna* (Leiden, 1974), pp. 56-72.

142.   Knibb, *The First and Second Books of Esdras*, p. 80.

143.   One may compare the stylization of John as the author of written 'prophecy' in Rev. 1.3; 22.9, etc. D. Hill (*New Testament Prophecy* [London, 1979], pp. 70-76 [= *NTS* 18 (1972), pp. 401-16], cf. p. 73), sees this as a 'feature which marks it [Revelation] as distinct from the writings of apocalyptic' (p. 71). Unfortunately, he does not refer to the similar claim in 2 Esdras. The claim to the 'prophetic' nature of writings does not in itself prove that the author is or was seen as a true 'prophet' (cf. Sir. 24.33; on Josephus's similar prophetic self-understanding see J. Blenkinsopp, 'Prophecy and Priesthood in Josephus', *JJS* 25 [1974], pp. 239-62), but is primarily a legitimation of the writing as 'inspired'. (For a discussion of Hill's argument see E. Schüssler Fiorenza, 'Apokalypsis and Propheteia', in J. Lambrecht, *L'Apocalypse johannique et l'Apocalyptique dans le Nouveau Testament* [Gembloux, 1980], pp. 107-28, esp. 107ff.)

144.   Cf. *5 Ezra* 1.32, which, though 'based directly on Matt. 23:34-6, and the parallel, Luke 11:49-51' (Knibb, *Second Esdras*, p. 86), refers exclusively to 'prophets', not mentioning Matthew's 'wise men and scribes' nor Luke's 'apostles'.

145.   Myers, *I and II Esdras*, p. 298.

146.   We noted this already in the case of the targums and Ben Sira, and it

is true also of David the scribe in 11QPs[a], whose compositions are 'spoken in prophecy', and of Josephus, the priestly scribe whose 'prophetic' aspirations have been well documented (cf. n. 143 above). See the relevant sections of this study.

147. There has been a considerable measure of scholarly disagreement as to the reason for the author's choice of Ezra as pseudonym and the degree to which the author's own views are to be read in Ezra's words over against Uriel's. This is not a matter that can be addressed at length in the present context. However, it is important to acknowledge the weight of the following points: the evident inconsistencies in the viewpoints expressed individually by Ezra and the angel effectively rule out the view of Harnisch (W. Harnisch, *Verhängnis und Verheissung der Geschichte. Untersuchungen zum Zeit- und Geschichtsverständnis im 4. Buch Esra und in der syrischen Baruchapokalypse* [Göttingen, 1969]) that the author's views are represented by Uriel, who is refuting the questioning of his opponents voiced by Ezra (cf. A.P. Hayman, 'The Problem of Pseudonymity in the Ezra Apocalypse', esp. pp. 50ff.). In fact it is most likely that the revered, eminent scribe is chosen as a platform for the author's own views, even if they do lack some consistency (cf. *ibid.*, p. 50). In Hayman's view, which is very close to that of Gunkel (in Kautzsch's *Die Apokryphen und Pseudepigraphen des Alten Testaments*, vol. II [Tübingen, 1900], pp. 331-52), the author's questionings and optimism are both facets of his inner faith struggle, reflected in the alternative viewpoints of Ezra and the angel. We would accept this view of the literary thrust of the book, adding only this: the 'faith'-struggle is largely one of *insight*. The scribe questions because he does not understand. He has intellectual problems, particularly in working out an acceptable theodicy, which are not exactly answered in rational terms, but which are *transcended* by insight into the mysteries revealed to him, leaving him in the end 'filled with understanding'. His is a pilgrimage of spiritual insight. No wonder the author selected Ezra the scribe for this—this is precisely the experience of the eminent, insightful *scribe* in all the pseudepigraphal literature we have considered, as well as in Ben Sira.

148. Cf. the fraternal relationship between John the scribe-prophet and his 'brothers' the prophets in Rev. 22.9 (see section 2 A).

149. Cf. the superiority attributed to the Teacher of Righteousness, who understands what the the prophets wrote of but did not understand (e.g. 1QpHab 7.4f.).

150. Cf. Mt. 13.51f., discussed in Chapter 6 below.

151. Possibly, but by no means certainly, a reference to drugs (cf. Hengel, *Judaism and Hellenism*, II, p. 137 n. 632).

152. This hardly needs demonstration; compare, for example, *4 Ezra* 3.1 with Dan. 7.1, 15; *4 Ezra* 6.13 with Dan. 10.11 (and context), *4 Ezra* 9.24 with Dan. 1.5, 8-16, *4 Ezra* 11 with Dan. 7, etc.: the Danielic influence permeates the whole work.

153. *2 Baruch* is brought into the discussion not only because in Baruch we have another scribal figure; but because of its proximity to *4 Ezra* and the Gospel of Matthew in provenance and date, though its date may be slightly posterior to *4 Ezra* in its final redaction (Bogaert, *Apocalypse de Baruch*, I, pp. 294-95, dates it to 96 CE, i.e. about ten years after Matthew; A.F.J. Klijn, *2 Baruch* [in Charlesworth, *The Old Testament Pseudepigrapha*, vol. I] to 100-120 CE: accuracy is not possible in this question); also because of the close proximity of ideas between the books (for some time it was thought that *4 Ezra* and *2 Baruch* shared the same author—see Charles, *Apocrypha and Pseudepigrapha*, II, pp. 476f.) and the probable dependency of late redactions of *4 Ezra* and especially *2 Baruch* on Matthew (for parallels, see Charles, *ibid.*, pp. 479f.).

154. Cited by C.A. Moore, *Daniel, Esther and Jeremiah: The Additions* (Anchor Bible; Garden City, 1977), p. 261.

155. Their proximity in this respect even gave rise to the anachronistic speculation that Baruch was the teacher of Ezra the Scribe in Babylon (cf. *b. Meg.* 16b).

156. See on Ezra, above, and Chapters 2 and 3 above.

157. Cf. Sir. 24.30ff., discussed in Chapter 3. For prophecy mediated by a scribe's letter, compare Jeremiah 29, Enoch's 'epistle' (= *1 Enoch* 92-105; cf. 100.6), and John's letters to the seven churches (Rev. 1.11-3.22).

158. We may note at this point that the commission (*2 Bar.* 76.5) bears more than a passing resemblance to Mt. 28.19f. (See Chapter 6.)

159. Compare Mt. 23.2, especially taken together with Mt. 11.25.

160. As it is in general in 'wisdom' literature (cf. e.g., from a whole host of possible examples, Prov. 8 and *passim*; Hos. 14.9; Sirach and Wis. Sol., *passim*) and 'apocalyptic' literature (cf. e.g. Dan. 12.3).

161. The dating of the Onkelos targum (the 'official', 'Babylonian' targum of the Pentateuch) is debated; the most usual date for the basic work (some of its readings are much later), assuming 'Onkelos' to be an alternative form of 'Aquila', is the early second century CE; but the likelihood is that it fixes traditions that had long been in circulation in synagogue use (see e.g. M. McNamara, *Targum and Testament* [Shannon, 1972], pp. 82ff., whose comments to this effect on the 'Palestinian' Targum also apply to Onkelos, which he also considers to be of Palestinian provenance). The notion is in any case common to other targums: Tg. Onkelos to Deut. 33.21 and Tg. to Songs 1.2; 2.4; 3.3 and Ps. 62.12 use a similar title in reference to Moses.

162. On the latter text, see above in the first section of this chapter.

163. —Written in half a day! (Ginzberg, *Legends of the Jews*, III, pp. 439f.). According to Maimonides, 'Moses was like a scribe writing down from dictation' (*Commentary on the Mishnati*, San. 10.7).

164. For references, see Ginzberg, *Legends of the Jews*.

165. Dated by Priest (Charlesworth, *Old Testament Pseudepigrapha* I, pp. 920f.) to the first century CE.

166. Clearly the prophecies in mind are *written* ones found in, or identical with, the Law, or possibly again the written Song of Moses (Deut. 32).

167. Of course, already in Deuteronomy the expounded Law is presented as a revelation to Moses, as is the Deuteronomic Song of Moses in particular (cf. 31.19). One wonders indeed whether the 'origins' of Jewish 'apocalyptic' might not reasonably be sought in this early sphere of revelatory scribal exegesis.

168. *T. Moses* also has a heavenly counterpart for Moses in the enigmatic person of Taxo, who is not, however, portrayed as a scribe, though he is in a sense a mediator.

169. See Ginzberg, *Legends*, III, pp. 419, 438. Cf. Philo's description cited below, and the references in the following note.

170. Cf. Dan. 12.3; and esp. 11QPs^{a}DavComp 1ff.; cf. also *1 Enoch* 58.3; 104.2, etc.; *2 Enoch* 22.10; 66.7f.; *T. Abr.* 2; *T. Levi* 4.2ff., etc.; Mt. 13.42 (see Chapter 6 below).

171. *De Vita Mosis* 6; note again that their 'prophecy' is given via the medium of writing. 'Hierophancy' is an appropriate equivalent for the revelatory function of the inspired scribe.

172. Philo apparently saw his own role in similar terms. In his own allegorical interpretations of scripture he appears to consider he has perceived its true meaning, which is hidden from most men. The 'divine and secret ordinances' are only for 'initiated persons who are worthy of the knowledge of the most holy mysteries. . . . The Sacred Revelation is not for those who are afflicted with the uncurable disease of pride of language' (*On the Cherubim*, 12). And in *On the Special Laws* 3 he describes an ostensibly apocalyptic, certainly mystical, experience of his own: 'I appeared to be raised on high and borne aloft by a certain inspiration of the soul, and to dwell in the regions of the sun and the moon. . . . Implanted in my soul from early youth, I have a desire for instruction. . . . I open the eyes of my soul . . . and I am irradiated with the light of wisdom.' It is in keeping with this that he asks of Moses: 'O Sacred Guide, even if we close the eye of our soul and take no care to understand such mysteries . . ., be you our prompter . . . and introduce those who are duly initiated to the hidden light of the sacred Scriptures . . . which is invisible to those who are uninitiated' (*On Dreams*, 26).

173. Perhaps there is an Egyptian connection here with the LXX version of the exodus narrative: in Exod. 5.6, 10, 14, 15, 19, the overseers, both Egyptian and Hebrew (MT: שטרים), are called γραμματεῖς, the latter being closely associated with Moses and Aaron (v. 20).

174. In this respect it is quite natural and appropriate that Ezra the Scribe should recreate this scene as a type of Moses, himself teaching 'the book of the law of Moses which the Lord had given to Israel' (Neh. 8.1ff.; cf. Ezra 7.6, 10, 11) in the presence of 'all the people' who had 'gathered as one man'

(Neh. 8.1; cf. 'all the assembly of Israel', Deut. 31.30). Note also how the testament concerning Levi (Deut. 33.8-11, esp. v. 10) is fulfilled in Neh. 8.7ff.

In describing a similar stage of redactional work in the book of Amos, Coote notes (R.B. Coote, *Amos among the Prophets. Composition and Theology* [Philadelphia, 1981], p. 64) that the conjunction of 'wisdom' and the deuteronomistic tradition there 'occasions no surprise given that both "wisdom" and the deuteronomistic tradition derive in their present forms from the scribal circles of the urban ruling elite in Jerusalem near the end of the monarchic period where the arts of writing and literature were practiced and controlled'. Cf. D.F. Morgan, *Wisdom in the Old Testament Traditions* (Atlanta, 1981), ch. 5 (pp. 94-106), 'Wisdom and the Deuteronomic Movement'.

175. Cf. *T. Moses* 1.14; also 3.12, where the 'witness' against the people idea (Deut. 31.19, 28) is reiterated. For the work of another scribe as 'witness', cf. Enoch, in *Jubilees* and *2 Enoch*; see on Enoch, above.

176. Cf. e.g. Philo, *De Vita Mosis* 1.5, 6. For examples of the products and influence of the Egyptian scribal schools which flourished in this period see e.g. Heaton, *Solomon's New Men*, pp. 103ff., 132ff.

177. Cf. M.E. Stone, 'Enoch and Apocalyptic Origins', in P.D. Hanson (ed.), *Visionaries and their Apocalypses* (Philadelphia and London, 1983), p. 97.

178. Cf. e.g. Hengel, *Judaism and Hellenism*, I, pp. 175-218, esp. pp. 180ff.

179. For a discussion of the tenuous nature of the widely accepted identification of the Hasidim as a distinctive party see P.R. Davies, 'Hasidim in the Maccabean Period', *JJS* 28 (1977), pp. 127-40. These 'pious', the 'doers of the law', far from being sectarian, may be simply the 'orthodox' or 'committed' Jews of the period.

180. Some even see them as Pharisaic works. P. Bogaert, *Apocalypse de Baruch. Introduction, traduction du syriaque et commentaire*, 2 vols. (Sources Chrétiennes, 144, 145; Paris, 1969), ascribes *2 Baruch* to Eliezer ben Hyrcanus. Opponents of this view include J. Hadot, *Semitica* 20 (1970), pp. 59-76; cf. C. Thoma, 'Jüdische Apokalyptik am Ende des ersten nachchristlichen Jahrhunderts', *Kairos* 11 (1969), pp. 134-44.

181. It is not our purpose to pursue such reconstructions. For an interesting attempt to isolate an albeit vague historical *Sitz im Leben* for the early Enoch material see D.W. Suter, 'Fallen Angel, Fallen Priest: The Problem of Family Purity in 1 Enoch 6-16', *HUCA* 50 (1979), pp. 115-35. Suter states (*ibid.*, p. 134, and with reference to Tcherikover): 'The use of Enoch, the heavenly scribe, as the vehicle for the revelations in the Book of the Watchers suggests that the myth reflects scribal opinion of some sort, and one is reminded that in the third century BCE the scribes are in the process of taking over the interpretation of the Torah from the priests.' Sociological and

political struggles may well be associated with the development of these works (cf. the socio-historical reconstructions of O. Plöger, *Theologie und Eschatologie* [Neukirchen-Vluyn, 1968] and P.D. Hanson, *The Dawn of Apocalyptic* [Philadelphia, 1975]—but see the criticisms of J.D. Thomas, 'Jewish Apocalyptic and the Comparative Method', in C.D. Evans [ed.], *Scripture in Context* [Pittsburgh, 1980], esp. pp. 255ff.) and though it is hazardous to be specific in identifying groups for whom very little evidence is available, it is in any case clear that scribal circles are involved in the production of the literature (see below).

182. Even to the point of introducing probable anachronisms—cf. e.g. E.L. Curtis, *Chronicles* (ICC; Edinburgh, 1910; repr. 1965), on 2 Chron. 17.7-9.

183. Heaton (*Daniel*, p. 248), notes that 'THE WISE [maskilim] indicates the members of the loyal scribal circles in which this book was produced . . . ' That is, (a) the authors are themselves the *maśkîlîm* mentioned in the text, and (b) the *maśkîlîm*-authors are scribes. We would add that the inheritors of this material also fall within both categories.

184. Cf. Collins, *Apocalyptic Vision*, p. 169.

185. Cf. F.F. Bruce, 'The Book of Daniel and the Qumran Community', in E.E. Ellis and M. Wilcox (eds.), *Neotestamentica et Semitica. Studies in Honour of Matthew Black* (Edinburgh, 1969), pp. 221-35. The 'Many' of Dan. 11.33f., 39; 12.2ff., 10 also find their use in the designation of social categories at Qumran.

186. 'The Book of Daniel and the Qumran Community', p. 228.

187. These are van Andel's terms (*Henoch-Traditie*, pp. 17f., cf. p. 115).

188. D.S. Russell, *The Method and Message of Jewish Apocalyptic* (London, 1964), p. 137.

189. *Ibid.*, p. 138.

190. Robinson's influential article, 'The Hebrew Conception of Corporate Personality', *ZAW* 66 (1946), pp. 49-62 (also in G.M. Tucker [ed.], *Corporate Personality in Ancient Israel* [rev. edn; Philadelphia, 1980], which contains a bibliography on the subject) has been seriously criticized by J.W. Rogerson, 'The Hebrew Conception of Corporate Personality: A Re-examination', *JTS* 21 (1970), pp. 1ff. D. Patte, in explaining pseudonymity in this way (*Early Jewish Hermeneutic in Palestine* [Missoula, 1975], pp. 177-80), overlooks the difficulty with this concept and with the concept of contemporaneity. However, there are good grounds for the recognition of *some* such concept (as long as the question of the philosophical presuppositions involved is satisfactorily resolved); cf. e.g., in another context, T.G. Allen, 'Exaltation and Solidarity with Christ. Ephesians 1.20 and 2.6', *JSNT* 28 (1986), p. 119 n. 33. The phenomenon of pseudonymity with integrity and authority is best explained along these lines. For a critique of 'contemporaneity', cf. J. Barr, *The Semantics of Biblical Language* (London, 1961), pp. 78ff.

191. Rowland, *The Open Heaven*, pp. 243ff., with reference to J. Lindblom, *Prophecy in Ancient Israel* (Oxford, 1962), pp. 17, 44 and *Gesichte und Offenbarungen* (Lund, 1968), p. 45 n. 19.

192. Rowland, *Open Heaven*, p. 245. His comments come in an illuminating chapter entitled 'An Attempt to Elucidate the Origins of Apocalyptic Visions' (pp. 214-47), within an excursus on visionary experience and pseudonymity (pp. 240-47).

193. Even apocalyptic literature without an expressly scribal central figure is of a scribal sort. The Testaments in particular would stand investigation in this regard. In the case of *T. Levi*, for example, the scribal sympathies and concerns are evident in such passages as 13.2, 9, and probably in the positive mention of scribes in 8.17. We have already observed a similar interest in *T. Abraham*.

194. The English translation has 'book-wisdom' (P. Vielhauer, in Hennecke [ed.], *New Testament Apocalyptic*, II, p. 58).

195. E. Janssen, *Das Gottesvolk und seine Geschichte* (Neukirchen-Vluyn, 1971), p. 98 n. 40.

196. *Das Gottesvolk*, pp. 96-104 (quotation from p. 97).

197. E.g. F. Dexinger; see above on *1 Enoch* 92.1.

198. *Das Gottesvolk*, p. 97.

199. Some of these factors are actually closely paralleled in the explicitly scribal work of Ben Sira. Cf. J.D. Martin, 'Ben Sira—A Child of His Time', in P.R. Davies and J.D. Martin (eds.), *A Word in Season. Essays in Honour of William McKane* (Sheffield, 1986), pp. 141-61.

200. Cf. also the characterization of Ben Sira's scribal product as 'prophecy'. In Revelation, 'testimony' is practically synonymous with 'prophecy' (cf. 1.2f.; 22.16, 18ff.).

201. It even has a (superior) counterpart to the heavenly scribe figure prevalent in that literature, in the form of the Lamb, who is responsible for the Book of Life.

202. A. Farrer, *The Revelation of St. John the Divine* (Oxford, 1964), pp. 23ff. Rowland (*Open Heaven*, p. 483 n. 61) finds his view particularly illuminating.

203. *The Revelation*, p. 26.

204. Cf. Buchanan, 'The Word of God and the Apocalyptic Vision', *SBL 1978 Seminar Papers* (Missoula, 1978), II, pp. 183-92.

205. J. Massyngberde-Ford's commentary (*Revelation* [Anchor Bible; Garden City, 1975]) regards the major part of the book (chs. 4–22) as non-Christian Jewish apocalyptic literature, and similar viewpoints have been repeatedly expressed since Marcion. Bultmann, for example, saw it as a 'weakly Christianized Judaism'. Cf. the discussion by G.R. Beasley-Murray, 'How Christian is the Book of Revelation?', in R. Banks (ed.), *Reconciliation and Hope. New Testament Essays on Atonement and Eschatology Presented to*

L.L. Morris on his 60th Birthday (Grand Rapids, 1974), pp. 275-84.

206. L. Cerfaux-J. Cambier, *L'Apocalypse de S. Jean lue aux chrétiens* (Paris, 1955), p. 89, cited in Cothenet, *art. cit.*, p. 81; cf. A. Feuillet, 'L'Apocalypse. Etat de la question', *DBS* (1963), p. 65. A. Schlatter, *Das Alte Testament in der johanneischen Apokalypse* (Beiträge zur Förderung christlicher Theologie, 16,6; Gütersloh, 1912), pp. 104ff., draws out the 'typisch schriftgelehrten Elemente' of the book. See also R.H. Charles, *A Critical and Exegetical Commentary on the Revelation of St. John*, I (ICC; Edinburgh, 1920), pp. lxv-lxxxvi; Charles lists (pp. lxviii-lxxxii) some 15 pages of agreements indicating Revelation's dependence on or influence from the Old Testament. See also the more recent F. Jenkins, *The Old Testament in the Book of Revelation* (Grand Rapids, 1976), who points out the creative use of the OT in the book. According to H. Kraft, 'Zur Offenbarung des Johannes', *TR* n.s. 38 (1973), p. 85, the book is concerned only to be an exposition of the OT. The author was certainly well acquainted with Jewish apocalyptic ideas and literature (cf. the parallels and similarities listed in Charles, *op. cit.*, pp. lxxxiif.; P.M. Bogaert [*Les apocalypses contemporaines de Baruch, d'Esdras et de Jean*] argues for the special dependence of the book on *2 Baruch*), and possibly with Targumic material (cf. M. McNamara, *The New Testament and the Palestinian Targum to the Pentateuch* [AB, 28; Rome, 1966], pp. 97-125). All this strongly suggests the author had received some kind of scribal education. For a study of the 'midrashic' composition of some other New Testament and Jewish apocalyptic texts see L. Hartman, *Prophecy Interpreted. The Formation of Some Jewish Apocalyptic Texts and of the Eschatological Discourse Mark 13 par.* (Lund, 1966).

207. The term was apparently introduced by L. Gaston (*No Stone on Another. Studies in the Significance of the Fall of Jerusalem in the Synoptic Gospels* [NovTSupp, 23; Leiden, 1970], p. 56) with reference to the mode of composition of Mark 13; he recognizes this as an apocalyptic line of tradition represented by post-exilic prophecy and here by Christian prophets, who indulge in 'prophetic midrash of the OT' (*ibid.*). It is a concept adopted by: E. Cothenet, 'Les prophètes chrétiens comme exégètes charismatiques de l'écriture', in J. Panagopoulos (ed.), *Prophetic Vocation in the New Testament and Today* (NovTSupp, 45; Leiden, 1977), pp. 77-107; and by D.E. Aune, *Prophecy in Early Christianity and the Ancient Mediterranean World* (Grand Rapids, 1983), esp. pp. 339-46.

208. On this, see esp. J.W. Doeve, *Jewish Hermeneutics in the Synoptic Gospels and Acts* (Assen, 1954); D. Patte, *Early Jewish Hermeneutic in Palestine* (Missoula, 1975); E.E. Ellis, *Prophecy and Hermeneutic in Early Christianity* (WUNT, 18; Tübingen and Grand Rapids, 1978); W.H. Brownlee, 'The Background of Biblical Interpretation at Qumran', in M. Delcor (ed.), *Qumrân. Sa piété, sa théologie et son milieu* (Leuven, 1978), pp. 183-93; F.F. Bruce, *Biblical Exegesis in the Qumran Texts* (Grand Rapids,

1959); O. Betz, *Offenbarung und Schriftforschung in der Qumransekte* (Tübingen, 1960); and more recently G.J. Brooke, *Exegesis at Qumran. 4QFlorilegium in its Jewish Context* (Sheffield, 1985); M. Fishbane, *Biblical Interpretation in Ancient Israel* (Oxford, 1985).

209. 'The Apocalypse as Christian Prophecy: A Discussion of the Issues Raised by the Book of Revelation for the Study of Early Christian Prophecy', *SBL 1974 Seminar Papers*, II, pp. 43-62. The quotation is from p. 55.

210. Cf. also Buchanan, 'The Word of God and the Apocalyptic Vision'. We have already mentioned Daniel in this respect. It is even conceivable that it represents a midrashic (*pesher*) literary type; cf. e.g. A. Szörényi, 'Das Buch Daniel ein kanonisierter *pescher*?', *Volume du Congrès* (Geneva, 1965; VTS 15; Leiden, 1966, pp. 278-94). Ellis (*Prophecy and Hermeneutic in Early Christianity*) lists a number of exegetical passages in the later prophets; see p. 56 and n. 46, p. 133 and n. 19. (See also R.J. Anderson, 'Was Isaiah a Scribe?', *JBL* 79 [1960], pp. 57-58.) Ellis sees a similar principle at work in the pneumatic NT communities as well as at Qumran. The NT specifies 'prophets and teachers' as the authoritative Christian instructors and exegetes; Ellis points out the fluidity of the distinction here, noting also the similarity of the Danielic and Qumranian notions of the *maśkîl*. But he appears not to recognize the *scribal* background to this dual function.

211. D.E. Aune, *Prophecy in Early Christianity and the Ancient Mediterranean World* (Grand Rapids, 1983), p. 342. Russell (*Method and Message*, pp. 172f.) suggests: 'in apocalyptic inspiration we have a link between the original inspiration of the prophets and the more modern inspiration of a literary kind. Again and again the apocalyptist showed that he believed himself to be writing under the direct influence of the spirit of God in a manner akin to that of the prophets, and even when he accepted the conventional literary framework, as he often did, he still believed himself to be divinely inspired'. This is simply to describe what we have recognized as the inspiration of the *scribe*.

212. It should be evident, in passing (we shall return to this issue in Chapter 7), that the recognition of the scribal nature of charismatic exegesis (even when practised by prophets and apocalypticists) goes a long way to resolving the scholarly debate concerning the derivation of some NT material from Christian prophets. The dilemma of choosing between *teachers* and *prophets* in this respect largely dissolves if the alternative is recognized, namely the group of charismatic, specialist writers and exegetes traditionally called 'scribes'.

Notes to Chapter 5

1. Cf. e.g. R. de Vaux, *Archaeology and the Dead Sea Scrolls. The*

Schweich Lectures 1959 (ET rev. edn, Oxford, 1972), pp. 29-33. For a reconstructed arrangement of the tables see his Plate XXIb. Typically, Rudolf Meyer (*Tradition und Neuschöpfung* [Berlin, 1965], p. 40) sees this as 'a most graphic picture' of the activity of scribes. Not all scholars interpret the evidence in this way, however. Cf. Dupont-Sommer, pp. 76ff.: 'The assertion that the Essenes wrote or even copied their library by themselves in the so-called 'Scriptorium' of Qumran is really quite absurd'. See also note 6. For a different view again, see K.H. Rengstorf, 'Ḥirbet Qumrân und die Bibliothek vom Toten Meer', in *Studia Delitzschiana* 5 (Stuttgart, 1960).

2. Though J.T. Milik reminds us (*Ten Years of Discovery*, p. 32 n. 2) that 'we should, however, be careful not to assume Essene authorship for any non-biblical work merely from the circumstance of its being found at Qumrân'.

3. Cf. the thesis of K. Stendahl, *The School of St. Matthew and its Use of the Old Testament* (ASNU, 20; Uppsala, 1954; = 2nd edn, 1968).

4. J.H. Dampier, 'The Scrolls and the Scribes of the New Testament', *BEvThS* 1/3 (1958), pp. 8-19. Dampier argues that 'the scribes' in the New Testament, placed alongside the Pharisees, are to be identified with their rivals, the Essenes. This flies in the face of the fact that the Gospels give uniform witness to the fundamental collusion between the 'scribes' and the 'Pharisees'. There is, furthermore, nothing distinctively Essenic to be discerned in their doctrines or charges against Jesus. Nor can the theory explain why Matthew equates the scribes and the Pharisees by hendiadys ('scribes and Pharisees, hypocrites'—ch. 23, *passim*) and by his replacement of 'scribes' by 'Pharisees' in a number of adaptations of Mark (see above, Chapter 1). But is should be noted that the theory is only at all conceivable on the recognition of the supposedly broadly 'scribal' nature of the Essene community at Qumran.

5. We refer in particular to the (largely negative) discussion of Milik's view (see his *The Books of Enoch*), who posits an Enochic Pentateuch at Qumran that included the 'Book of Giants'—replaced at a very much later date by the Similitudes of Enoch.

6. H. del Medico, *The Riddle of the Scrolls* (ET London, 1958) rejects the whole notion of a 'library' at Qumran; instead we have a *genizah* of defective and heretical manuscripts of a variety of sorts.

7. Since other Sirach passages are present, it would be odd if this central passage, so essential to Ben Sira's self-justification and presentation, should have been unknown. A few verses of the section, 38.24-27, incidentally, are preserved (though in a somewhat different version) in the Cairo Genizah Hebrew text, though here again the following verses up to 39.14 inclusive are missing. Curiously, Hillyer (art. 'Scribe', *NIDNTT*, III, p. 479) states that 'part of this hymn [viz. Sir. 38.24–39.11] appears in an earlier form in 11QPsDav; *Discoveries in the Judaean Desert* IV, 1965, 77ff.'. Hillyer is

either making a completely unsubstantiated claim for the relation between this passage in Sirach and 11QPs[a]DavComp (which appears on pp. 91ff. in *DJD*, IV), or is thinking of the probable relation of 11QPs[a]Sirach (*DJD*, IV, pp. 79ff.) to Sir. 51.13ff. But he may simply have misunderstood the notes by Hengel (*Judaism and Hellenism*, II, p. 54 n. 166, or p. 89 n. 188), on whom he is otherwise dependent. On the relationship between Sirach and Qumran in general see the discussion between Carmignac (J. Carmignac, 'Les rapports entre l'Ecclésiastique et Qumrân', *RQ* 3 [1961], pp. 209-18), and Lehmann (M.R. Lehmann, 'Ben Sira and the Qumran Literature', *RQ* 3 [1961], pp. 103-16). Specifically on some literary connections, in some respects 'verblüffend ähnlich', between the two passages under discussion, see Stadelmann, *Ben Sira als Schriftgelehrter*, p. 242 and literature cited there.

8. This link is intriguing. This version of Sirach 51, if the passage is correctly identified as such, may have had an existence independent of Sirach and even be more original than our present Sirach 51 (cf. Sanders, *DJD*, IV, *ad loc.*). Be that as it may, it is striking that the passage is included with Psalms and psalmic works expressly associated with scribal inspiration, exactly as Ben Sira understood his own work (cf. e.g. 24.32ff.; 50.27; 51.17, 20; see on the 'spirit of understanding' in Chapter 3 above).

9. It should, furthermore, be already clear from our examination of Ben Sira and the apocalyptic scribes (above) that the *sôfēr* has considerably more authority and prestige in the respective communities than would be due simply to an educated person.

10. H. Stadelmann, *Ben Sira als Schriftgelehrter*, p. 228 n. 1. The long dominant view that Ben Sira and apocalyptic are quite incompatible has recently been seriously questioned by a number of studies, particularly those of H.-P. Müller ('Mantische Weisheit und Apokalyptik', *SVT* 22 [1972], pp. 268-93; cf. his 'Magisch-mantische Weisheit und die Gestalt Daniels', *UF* 1 [1969], pp. 79-94); J.Z. Smith, 'Wisdom and Apocalyptic', in P.D. Hanson (ed.), *Visionaries and their Apocalypses*, pp. 102-20; J.C. VanderKam, *Enoch and the Growth of an Apocalyptic Tradition* (CBQMS, 16; Washington, 1984)—see his conclusion, p. 190. M. Hengel (*Judaism and Hellenism*, I, pp. 206f.) notes that the old dichotomy is a false one (cf. pp. 202-20). See also the contribution of J.C. VanderKam, 'The Prophetic-Sapiential Origins of Apocalyptic Thought' and J.D. Martin, 'Ben Sira—A Child of His Time', in P.R. Davies and J.D. Martin (eds.), *A Word in Season. Essays in Honour of William McKane* (JSOTS, 42; Sheffield, 1986), pp. 163-76 and 141-61 respectively. Martin points out a whole range of features that Sirach shares with contemporary, apocalyptic literature; the texts he deals with do not in fact include the central passage in Sirach (38.24–39.11) with which we have been concerned.

11. Other points of contact with apocalyptic concerns include the astronomical (solar calendar) interest implied in the number of David's

compositions (cf. the similar interest found in *1 Enoch, Jubilees and Qumran*), the emphasis on the 'solar' brilliance of the wise (cf. e.g. Dan. 12.3; *T. Levi* 4.3; 18.4; *2 Enoch* 19.1; 22.10; 66.7ff.; *1 Enoch* 39.7; 58.3, 5; 104.2; 106; 108.12; etc.; cf. 4QTestAmram; 4Q184; Mt. 13.43) and the use of the divine name 'Most High' (favoured in Daniel, *4 Ezra, 2 Baruch* and *T. Levi*, etc.); also, interestingly enough, in Sirach: Sir. 39.5, in our parallel passage, even contains the exact phrase 'before the Most High'. On the possible apocalyptic significance of 'all these things', see on Mt. 13.51f. in Chapter 6.

12. See on Ezra, above.

13. Cf. of Daniel in Dan. 5.11f., 14, where, indeed, there is also in other respects a striking coincidence of language with our text.

14. Levi of course also has scribal associations.

15. Here perhaps נבא should be read for נבע; see Hengel, *Judaism and Hellenism*, II, p. 89 n. 199, and our discussion in Chapter 3 above.

16. It is instructive in connection with this text to compare the additional Psalm 154, also preserved with Qumran's Cave 11 psalmic material. In many respects it bears comparison with others of the canonical Psalms (to which it was apparently considered, or designed, to belong); but it has very close affinities with other works found at Qumran, not least 11QPs^aDavComp, and may reflect early Essene ideas of community (יחד [11QPs^a 154.4]; 'good ones', 'innocent ones' [v. 3]; 'simple ones' [vv. 4, 7]; 'righteous ones' [vv. 11, 12]; 'congregation of the pious ones' [v. 12]; cf. their eating and drinking in fellowship [בחבר; v. 13]); indeed, P.W. Skehan ('Qumran and Old Testament Criticism', *Qumrân, sa piété, sa théologie et son milieu*, p. 169) calls this psalm 'a reflex of the Essene religious assemblies and communal meals'. As Charlesworth and Sanders point out (*Old Testament Pseudepigrapha*, II, p. 618), however, these features, though characteristic, are not distinctively Essene. But there is a very strong correspondence between the tone of this Psalm and that of the Hodayoth, particularly the author's emphasis on his 'announcing the glory of the Lord' through divinely imparted wisdom (v. 5), the 'recounting of his many deeds' (v. 6; cf. 1QH 4.27; 6.9ff.; 2.18ff.; 11.25; 12.22f.). Moreover, concerning the 'congregation of the pious ones', 'when they eat . . . and drink in fellowship together' (vv. 12f.): 'Their meditation is on the Law of the Most High; their words to announce his power' (v. 13). This is highly reminiscent of the Qumran study-groups, which are also associated with the communal meals (e.g. 1QS 6.3-8; cf. 8.15ff.). All this, the emphasis on study of the Law (of the Most High), explanation to those of limited understanding, and proclamation of God's glory in inspired poetic song, points once more to the *scribal* associations of the author of the work and his community. Cf. esp. Sir. 39.1, where the ideal *scribe* is depicted as one who 'devotes himself to the study of the Law of the Most High'; and Sir. 39.5-9 very neatly matches the evident abilities and concerns of the psalmist here.

17.　Whether or not this is actually a personage distinct from the founding Teacher of Righteousness; cf. G. Jeremias, *Der Lehrer der Gerechtigkeit* (Göttingen, 1963), p. 272.

18.　It may be that there was only ever one person to whom this title was given; but several scholars have argued that the epithet designates an office rather than a personal title (cf. e.g. G.W. Buchanan, 'The Priestly Teacher of Righteousness', *RQ* 6 [1967-69], pp. 553-58). The point is immaterial for our present purposes, however, since our concern is not with the history of individual figures but with the perceived *role* of the (incumbent) Teacher in relation to the vitality of the community. And this is above all a matter of the authoritative and revelatory exegetical instruction provided by the Teacher.

19.　The latter passage, incidentally, is very much in the style of prophetic wisdom-instruction, and is at the same time very reminiscent of the Danielic concept of the *maśkîl*. Cf. Isa. 52.13, 15b; 55.1; cf. also 1QH 1.35ff. The opening sections of CD are also, of course, similar to non-prophetic wisdom addresses such as we find in Proverbs 1-9, where the declared purpose is also 'that men may know wisdom and instruction, understand words of insight, receive instruction in wise dealing, righteousness, justice and equity' (Prov. 1.2f.); late prophecy and wisdom are in any case by no means unrelated. Wisdom-insight and interpretation necessarily always belong together. In form, in CD we have something of a stereotyped wisdom address; but in relation to its underlying *subject*, the new revelatory teaching and guidance of the Teacher, we have to do with a different mode of wisdom, bordering on the mantic and of a kind with the anointing of the 'spirit of understanding' that has graced the eminent scribes we have examined.

20.　Cf. G. Jeremias, *Der Lehrer der Gerechtigkeit*, pp. 165f. The reception of revelation, though ascribed first to the eminent Teacher of Righteousness, devolves on the community which follows his revelations. See below on the Essene authors.

21.　Cf. 1QH 11.34f.: 'Thou hast set [hymns of praise (Vermes)] within the mouth of Thy servant and hast established for me a response of the tongue'; 1QH 17.16 'because of the spirits which Thou hast given to me I [will bring forth] a reply of the tongue to recount Thy righteous deeds'. Many similar passages leave no doubt that the Teacher regarded his hymns, as well as his teaching, as inspired.

22.　E.g. 1QpHab 2.1-10; cf. CD 20.32f., where following 'the precepts of righteousness' is equated with 'listening to the voice of the Teacher of Righteousness'. The parallel with the apocalyptic scribes, Enoch, Ezra and Baruch, in this regard is close in that there too the scribe himself is the author of inspired material that is to be venerated by his posterity (cf. also Daniel).

23.　This has led many scholars to identify him in fact as a rival to the High Priest in Jerusalem, typically seen as ousted or persecuted by his rival, the

'Wicked Priest' (frequently identified as Jonathan Maccabaeus).

24. CD 6.11 has frequently been understood to refer to the founding 'Teacher of Righteousness'. But its unequivocally future reference makes this unlikely (cf. P.R. Davies, *The Damascus Covenant* [Sheffield, 1982], pp. 123f.).

25. The 'best representative' of this view, according to Jeremias (G. Jeremias, *Der Lehrer der Gerechtigkeit*, p. 154), is A. Jaubert, in 'Le Pays de Damas', *RB* 65 (1958), pp. 214-48, esp. 236f. Cf. also T.H. Gaster, *The Scriptures of the Dead Sea Sect* (London, 1957), p. 108; N. Walker, 'Concerning the 390 Years and the 20 Years of the Damascus Document', *JBL* 76 (1957), p. 58; discussion in Jeremias, *Der Lehrer der Gerechtigkeit*, pp. 153ff. The concern in these studies has been for the most part with historical reconstruction possibilities, whereas our present interest lies simply with the comparative roles of Ezra and the Teacher of Righteousness.

26. R. Leivestad, 'Das Dogma von der prophetenlosen Zeit', *NTS* 19 (1972), pp. 288-99.

27. *Ibid.*, p. 298. Here, Leivestad follows J. Roloff, 'Der johanneische "Lieblingsjünger"', who explains the role of the latter by analogy with the Teacher of Righteousness as *meliṣ*, or pesher-exegete (pp. 144f.). Roloff however discounts, without discussion, the suitability of the epithet 'Schriftgelehrter' for the Teacher. We hope to have already demonstrated that the eminent scribe figure found in Daniel, Sirach and Jewish Apocalyptic is quite compatible with the role of 'secondary revelation' (Roloff, p. 145) or inspired interpretation. But Roloff, in company with the majority of scholars, has too easily drawn his understanding of the scribe exclusively from later rabbinic usage (he implicitly equates the 'Schriftgelehrter' with rabbinic 'Schulhäupter' [p. 144]).

28. If the roles are not identical, and if they are in fact performed by more than one person, still this does not detract from our recognition that they are essentially scribal roles. Each too was eminent at least in the eyes of the community of his own day.

29. Indeed, as is indicated by its earlier title in the history of Qumran studies (Manual of Discipline), 1QS has the marks of a manual, and presumably it was intended for the Maskil himself.

30. Vermes (*The Dead Sea Scrolls in English* [2nd edn, Harmondsworth, 1975], pp. 18-25) argues that the Maskil/Interpreter of the Law was a Levite (while the Teacher, of course, was a priest). A.R.C. Leaney (*The Rule of Qumran and its Meaning* [London, 1966], p. 115) calls the suggestion that the author of 1QS 10-11, at any rate, is the same as the author of 1QH (namely the Teacher of Righteousness) 'a most reasonable conjecture'. Such identifications are, of course, always doubtful. If the Teacher of Righteousness was the Maskil *par excellence* in the eyes of the Qumran community, and

thus the model for each incumbent Maskil of the community, there is clearly at the least a close relationship betweeen them underlying 1QS itself. The Maskil in 1QS may no longer carry quite the same air of authority as the *founding* Teacher of Righteousness, since founders tend to be in a class by themselves, but a *teacher*, of *righteousness*, he still is. From the point of view of their role and function in the community, we need not, therefore, insist on a rigid distinction between Teacher of Righteousness and Maskil.

31. Thus it is appropriate that his alternative appellation, 'Interpreter of the Law', should be given titular capitalization in translation. The latter title, as we have noted, is scribal through and through; it extends from the characterization of Ezra the 'scribe skilled in the Law of Moses' (Ezra 7.6) and 'learned in matters of the commandments of the Lord and of his statutes for Israel' (7.11) as one devoted to 'studying the Law' (דרש התורה) and to 'teaching his statutes and ordinances in Israel', to at least as far as Luke's equivalent use of νομοδιδάσκαλος for γραμματεύς (Lk. 5.17; cf. Acts 5.34).

32. This is not to say that *as a historical social group* the *maśkîlîm* of Daniel are the same as, or even necessarily directly related to, the Qumran Essenes. We are not concerned here to make any such socio-historical connections. Thus we do not here align ourselves with any of the suggested historical identifications of the Teacher of Righteousness, the Interpreter of the Law, the Wicked Priest, Man of the Lie, etc., with which several scholars continue to be perhaps disproportionately occupied. We do, however, note that on the *literary* level there are real connections between the book of Daniel and the self-portrayal of the Essenes in the scrolls; the book is a treasure-store of imagery and associations emerging frequently in various scrolls; in particular the 'revelation of mysteries' (רזים) theme, central to the scrolls' view of the Teacher and the Maskil, is almost certainly borrowed from the book of Daniel, and the Essenes' self-application of the terms *maśkîlîm* and *rabbîm* is a clear indication of a considerable preoccupation with Daniel 11 and 12. And it seems equally clear that Daniel is a type of the Teacher of Righteousness; indeed, in effect, in one sense the Teacher is a New Daniel, who instead of finally *not* understanding (cf. Dan. 12.8) *does* understand, as the eschatological Maskil *par excellence* of the prophecy (Dan. 12.10). See further on Mt. 13.51 in Chapter 6.

33. A. Jaubert has drawn attention to the close affinities ('d'étonnantes affinités') between the role of the Teacher of Righteousness in 1QH 8 ('raining' [ירה] of righteousness [1QH 8.16, etc.] that characterizes, by definition, the role of the Teacher [מורה] of Righteousness), and the description of the teaching of the inspired scribe in Sirach (cf. esp. Sir. 24.23f.: 'I will pour out instruction like prophecy').

34. In 11QPs^a the attributes of Maskil (שכל) and scribe (בין, חכם) are quite naturally combined, as we have seen.

35. See esp. the 'manual'-like character of 1QS in which the Maskil figures so prominently. It is very unlikely that the title Maskil was only given to one eminent person (cf. Leaney, *Rule of Qumran*, p. 230). In CD 6.7 the reference to the 'staves' apparently relates to successive 'interpreters of the law', since the term is also used in the singular of the 'Interpreter of the Law' (CD 6.7; 7.18); it may be that other members of the community would be called thus (in 1QS 6.6, cf. 8.12, one in each group of ten members is required to be 'studying the Law' [דרש התורה] at any one time—perhaps the man who 'enquires' and receives revelation of 'all the matters that were hidden from Israel' [1QS 8.12]).

36. In view of the text-critical interest in the biblical scrolls preserved at Qumran it was perhaps inevitable that the Qumran community, who certainly preserved the scrolls, should have been associated, almost to the point of identity, with the copyists responsible for the transmission of the documents. However, there is such a wide range of scripts and thus of relative dating of manuscripts on palaeographical grounds, that it is clear that at least a good proportion of the scrolls were copied outside Qumran and certainly outside Qumran's flourishing periods.

37. The rather romantic picture of a monastic community typically seated at a large communal table engaged primarily in copying manuscripts in a scriptorium is probably a false one; at least the discovery in the remains at Qumran of two separate inkwells and a table, now on display in the Shrine of the Book in the Israel Museum in Jerusalem is no evidence of this (see n. 1, above).

38. Cf. Brooke, *Exegesis at Qumran*, pp. 8-17.

39. Cf. e.g. Hengel, *Judaism and Hellenism*, I, pp. 175ff.

40. We have seen, too, that Sirach itself does not escape this influence.

41. D. Patte, *Early Jewish Hermeneutic in Palestine*, p. 299.

42. Noting the similarities between pesher in Daniel and Qumran, W.H. Brownlee ('The Background of Biblical Interpretation at Qumran', in M. Delcor [ed.], *Qumrân* [Gembloux, 1978], p. 185) observes: 'When the people of Qumran reapply the prophecies of the Old Testament to their own day and to the imminent future, they are standing precisely in this prophetic-apocalyptic tradition of post-exilic Judaism'.

43. Cf. Brownlee ('The Background of Biblical Interpretation at Qumran', pp. 188f.), who equates their emendations for interpretative purposes with the *tiqqûnê-hassôferîm* of rabbinic tradition (who would be broadly contemporary with the Essenes). It is in this context that Brownlee uses the phrase 'scribes of Qumran'.

44. 1QS 6.7; cf. 8.11f. In the light of 1QS 6.3f. and 8.1f., the interpreters here may be identified with one of the priests present. However, this in no way detracts from the *scribal* nature of the role of interpretation, with which it is entirely consonant. See above on the Teacher of Righteousness as priest.

In any case, the whole community membership is responsible for such intensive round-the-clock searching of the scriptures (1QS 6.8).

45. Such as targums, of which 11QTgJob is an example; though the Hebrew pesharim belong to a different genre, a similar, exegetical goal is evident (cf. the interpretations into the vernacular of the Levites associated with Ezra [Neh. 8.7ff.]). These are all expert, scribal interpretations, as, indeed, are the 'typological rewritings' of biblical narratives (such as the Genesis Apocryphon and the earlier book of *Jubilees*; cf. Brownlee, 'The Background of Biblical Interpretation at Qumran', p. 184). It is interesting that Brooke refers to the authors of scrolls as 'scribes', suggesting, for example, that '1QS was written by the same scribe as 4QTest' (G.J. Brooke, *Exegesis at Qumran*, p. 349 n. 190) on the basis of their similar *content* in a couple of respects. 4QTest, an eschatological midrash, would, as it happens, be entirely in keeping with what might be the expected output of an 'understanding scribe'.

Notes to Chapter 6

1. This is a reflection of the difficulty of the passage. After his own attempt to exegete it, P.J. Becker ('Erwägungen zu Fragen der neutestament-lichen Exegese', *BZ* 13 [1969], pp. 99-102) wistfully observes: 'Man kann nicht behaupten, daß das Gleichnis durch den Eingriff des Evangelisten an Verständlichkeit gewonnen hat. Die Exegese mag es wie bisher auch weiterhin umrätseln'. Variously nuanced interpretations are offered by all the commentators. For a list, by no means comprehensive, of differing interpretations of 'the new and the old' in 13.52 see O. Betz, 'Neues und Altes im Geschichtshandeln Gottes. Bemerkungen zu Mattäus 13,51f.', in H. Feld & J. Nolte (eds.), *Wort Gottes in der Zeit. FS Schelke* (Düsseldorf, 1973), pp. 71ff.

2. Occasionally to a mixture of both—with Matthew reworking a parable he found in his own sources (cf. e.g. Becker, 'Erwägungen'). Hoh ('Der christliche γραμματεύς [Mt 13,52]', *BZ* 19 [1926], p. 259) regrets that no parallel can be adduced to help explain the verse. In Chapter 7 we suggest such a parallel, though our exposition here is not dependent on its recognition. Betz offers no basis at all, suggesting that Matthew more or less simply 'made it up' ('Neues und Altes im Geschichtshandeln Gottes', p. 70).

3. The statistical evidence is overwhelming:

	Mt.	Mk	Lk.	Jn
διὰ τοῦτο	10	3	4	16
γραμματεύς	22	21	14	(1)

μαθητεύω	3	0	0	0 (Acts: 1)
βασιλεία τῶν οὐρανῶν	33	0	0	0
ἄνθρωπος + noun	7	0	1	0
οἰκοδεσπότης	7	1	4	0
θησαῦρος	9	1	4	0
ἐκβάλλω	28	18	20	6

4. A theory associated with B.W. Bacon, *Studies in Matthew* (London, 1930). It is now generally accepted that the Gospel is structured around five main discourse sections. But the similarity to the Pentateuch ends there—Matthew's apparent interest in presenting Jesus with overtones of the Mosaic giving of the Law is evidently not carried through to the extent of making Jesus a New Moses and his teaching the New Law.

5. I.H. Jones (forthcoming, I believe, from Leiden: Brill).

6. Cf. e.g. B. Gerhardsson, 'The Seven Parables in Matthew XIII', *NTS* 19 (1972-73), pp. 16-37, who argues that the author of 13.52 (not to be identified with the final redactor of ch. 13) was responsible for the 'Tract of 7 Parables'; 13.52 itself is not part of this collection. According to Jülicher (*Die Gleichnisreden Jesu* [repr. Darmstadt, 1976], part II, p. 128), the verse 'steht auf der Grenze zwischen Gleichnis und einfacher Vergleichung'.

7. Cf. e.g. R. Bultmann, *Geschichte der synoptischen Tradition*, p. 79; Becker, 'Erwägungen'; D. Zeller, 'Zu einer jüdischen Vorlage von Mt 13,52', *BZ* 20 (1976), pp. 223-26. Bultmann reconstructs the original *mashal* thus:

> Wie ein Hausvater, der aus seinem Schatz Neues und Altes hervorholt,
> So ist ein Schriftgelehrter, der für das Himmelreich gelehrt ist.

8. Cf. D. Wenham, 'The Structure of Matthew XIII', *NTS* 25 (1979), pp. 516-22.

9. The difficulty of translation is due to two main uncertainties: (1) whether to take μαθητευθείς transitively (as in 28.19) in the passive mood (i.e. 'made a disciple') or as a middle ('become a disciple'), and (2) whether the dative τῇ βασιλείᾳ indicates a relationship between the disciple and the personified object of his discipleship (cf. 27.57, where Joseph is 'discipled' to Jesus) or simply indicates the field in which the training or discipleship is pursued. Along with most scholars (e.g. Kremer, Hoh) we take μαθητευθείς transitively—as Dalman (*Worte*, p. 87) points out, the middle form would have no exact Semitic equivalent—but we depart slightly from the majority in taking the dative in the more general sense of 'with respect to'.

10. The majority of commentators in fact do this. An extreme expression of this is Dupont's (J. Dupont, 'Nova et Vetera [Matthieu 13:52]', in *L'Evangile hier et aujourd'hui* [Geneva, 1968], p. 61). Going a step further than Légasse ('Scribes et disciples de Jésus') in seeing the central figure as the converted Jewish scribe, he suggests that in fact the verse introduces a

completely new, specifically Christian type of scribe (cf. also J. Gnilka, *Verstockung*, p. 96). An exception to this common view is R. Walker, *Die Heilsgeschichte im ersten Evangelium* (Göttingen, 1967), who rejects the notion of the existence of 'Christian scribes' in Matthew's community in line with his salvation-historical reading of Matthew. 23.34 then belongs to the period of ταῦτα γενέα which is the past epoch and has no abiding, current significance. 8.19f. involves a rejection of the 'scribe' by Jesus, contrasted with the accepted 'disciple' in 8.21f. Similarly, the 'scribe' of 13.52 is only a positive category by virtue of the conversion that is referred to in μαθητευθείς, and the point of the parable is the challenge of 'Reservelosigkeit'—i.e. preparedness to relinquish all, including the 'old things'—which is the mark of true discipleship. The term 'scribe' as such has no weight or special significance and cannot be held to apply to the first evangelist nor to Christian scribes; the ταῦτα πάντα understood by the disciples in v. 51 refers to the basic message of the kingdom parables, which is the kerygmatic challenge to discipleship. We are bound to disagree with every one of these claims, as will be clear from our exegesis of the passage. We do consider that Matthew is not simply referring to specifically Christian scribes in his own 'Gentile' community; however, this is not because of a 'salvation-historical' programme but because Matthew uses only Jewish categories. Cf. esp. J. Freudenberg, 'Die synoptische Weherede' (Diss. Münster, 1972), pp. 38, 64, and the whole thrust of O. Steck, *Israel und das gewaltsame Geschick der Propheten* (Neukirchen, 1967).

11. Cf. the discussions of G. Barth, 'Matthew's Understanding of the Law', in G. Bornkamm, G. Barth & H.J. Held (eds.), *Tradition and Interpretation in Matthew* (ET 2nd edn; London, 1982), pp. 105-24, and especially U. Luz, 'Die Jünger im Matthäusevangelium', *ZNW* 62 (1971), pp. 141-71 [for ET see bibliography]; also R.A. Edwards, 'Uncertain Faith: Matthew's Portrait of the Disciples', in F. Segovia (ed.), *Discipleship in the New Testament* (Philadelphia, 1985), pp. 47-61.

12. Cf. Hoh ('Der christliche γραμματεύς', p. 257): 'Ce διὰ τοῦτο donne bien du tracas aux commentateurs qui cherchent un enchaînement rigoureusement logique'. J. Wellhausen (*Das Evangelium Matthaei*, p. 73) already missed the point here: 'Der Spruch ist trotz διὰ τοῦτο in Wahrheit isoliert und wird durch 13,51 nur sehr notdürftig mit den Gleichnissen verbunden'. Hoh's exegesis does not deal with this question at all. Cf. also J. Kremer, '"Neues und Altes". Jesu Wort über den christlichen "Schriftgelehrten" (Mt 13,52)', in J. Kremer *et al.*, *Neues und Altes. Zur Orientierung in der augenblicklichen Situation der Kirche* (Freiburg, 1974), p. 12: 'V.52 kann ... nicht als Fortsetzung von V.51 entstanden sein'; Zeller ('Zu einer jüdischen Vorlage', p. 225) speaks of an 'ungeschickte Anknüpfung mit διὰ τοῦτο'.

13. Cf. e.g. Dupont, 'Nova et Vetera', p. 60.

14. Cf. Jülicher, *Die Gleichnisreden*, p. 133. This is also the case with 23.34, according to some commentators.

15. See discussion of this verse below.

16. Partial exceptions are M.D. Goulder, *Midrash and Lection in Matthew*, who (p. 13) notes the relevance of the heritage of Sirach for Matthew's self-understanding; and Zeller, 'Zu einer jüdischen Vorlage', who (p. 225) briefly notes the parallels. Betz ('Neues und Altes im Geschichtshandeln Gottes', p. 82) notes the proximity of Matthew's art to that of the Qumran exegetes (though within limits; cf. p. 83). But to my knowledge no scholar draws expressly on the vast amount of relevant apocalyptic material to inform the interpretation of this passage.

17. It is astonishing to find, for example, that such an eminent Matthean scholar as Eduard Schweizer does not consider 'understanding' of sufficient interest to warrant special discussion in his commentary, nor even a mention in his index of subjects. R.H. Gundry's recent commentary, by contrast, is surely correct to give the subject considerable prominence.

18. See Barth, 'Matthew's Understanding of the Law', pp. 105-25; Luz points out that the disciples' lack of understanding in Mark is the only unflattering aspect of the Markan picture of the disciples that Matthew has consistently 'improved' ('Die Jünger im Matthäusevangelium', p. 148 [ET p. 102]).

19. Compare the relative frequency of the verb also in Sirach. See below.

20. Cf. Ps. 94.8, where the verb is משכיל!

21. Matthew omits Jesus' mention of 'not understanding' in Mk 8.17. He does, however, retain the 'not yet perceive' (οὔπω νοεῖτε). This does not, however, contradict the picture. See note 23.

22. 'Matthew's Understanding of the Law', pp. 105-12.

23. The disciples, like Ezra, do need further instruction later, but as Luz rightly notes ('Disciples' [ET], p. 103), this is for the fine tuning of the ability to understand; in 15.16 and 16.9 the 'not' becomes 'not yet'. The matter of deficiency in faith is a quite separate issue for Matthew, as both Barth and Luz have shown.

24. J.D. Kingsbury, *The Parables of Matthew 13*, pp. 130ff.

25. Though even there there may be an implication that Peter is presented as a scribe. See below.

26. Cf. Jn 6.6; 1QS 5.20ff.; 6.13ff.; 9.1f.; 1QH 2.13f.; 12, etc.; Sir. 39.4. Numerous examples also in rabbinic literature.

27. 'Matthew's Understanding of the Law', p. 118.

28. 'Matthew's Understanding of the Law', p. 109.

29. J. Lambrecht, *Die Redaktion der Markus-Apokalypse* (Rome, 1967), pp. 85-88, 283-84.

30. Compare also E. Brandenburger, *Markus 13 und die Apokalyptik*

(Göttingen, 1984), who suggests (p. 50) that this is a clear notice to the reader to see events in terms of the Danielic prophecy. He refers to the similar allusive method in Rev. 13.18; 17.9. 'Es liegt eine typische Deuteanweisung konkreter apokalyptischer Hermeneutik vor.'

31. This is the garb of a heavenly scribe in Ezek. 9.2.

32. Not just in the eschatological-apocalyptic sense, but in the sense of revealed mysteries in general (cf. the thesis of C. Rowland, *The Open Heaven*).

33. We find it easier to see a purpose in the triple mention of 'all these things' in 6.32f. than to charge Matthew (or Q) simply with bad style (Luke, however, omits the second 'all'). There may well be a real connection with our passage. In 6.33 the context, after all, is the 'seeking' of the *kingdom* and its righteousness—exactly what the disciples are doing in Matthew 13 when 'all these things' become theirs (13.51). Their understanding is 'given' (cf. 13.11) just as 'all these things' are 'added' to them (6.33). 'Seeking', moreover, often associated with understanding and sometimes with the understanding of righteousness (cf. e.g. ζητεῖν in Prov. 2.4, 9) is the main task of the scribe (cf. ἐκζητεῖν in Sir. 39.1, 3); cf. the use of דרש at Qumran. Righteousness is again closely associated with the kingdom in 13.43.

34. What Brandenburger (pp. 50ff.) says about Mk 13.14b applies equally to this passage: What is meant by this understanding is 'nicht einfach die Vernunft, die ratio, vielmehr der durch himmlische Weisheit und damit auch durch die theologische Tradition der Apokalyptik eingeweihte Verstand'. It is expected that the readers will make the connection in identifying themselves with the biblical group in the similar situation (cf. e.g. 2 Thess. 2; *Didache* 16; *4 Ezra* 12.10ff.

35. S. Freyne, 'The Disciples in Mark and the Maskilim in Daniel', *JSNT* 16 (1983), pp. 7-23.

36. Matthew has 'righteous' for Daniel's 'wise'. But like Daniel, Matthew uses righteous and wise in parallel (as do the Dead Sea Scrolls, the Wisdom of Solomon and Sirach; cf. also *1 Enoch* 91.10; 99.10—how precisely this echoes Matthew's concerns!; *2 Bar.* 46.4f.; 51.3f. amongst many similar passages). The shining of the righteous is a feature of some of the eminent scribes and the disciples of apocalyptic literature also (cf. e.g. *1 Enoch* 38.4; 39.76; 50.1; 58.3; 104.2; 108.12; *2 Enoch* 65.11; 66.7; *4 Ezra* 7.97), and, strikingly, of the 'understanding', 'wise man' and 'scribe' of 11QPs^{a}Dav Comp.

37. Perhaps there is a common factor in the Levitical allegiance of these figures at Qumran. As we noted in Chapter 2, where the priesthood lacks total authority Levitic heredity seems to go hand in hand with scribalism over a long period: witness Ezra's Levites (Neh. 8), the Chronicler, the authors of the *Testament of Levi* and other testaments. The scribes of Qumran, who are specified as Levites as well as Maskilim, are no exception.

Cf. also Joshua b. Hananiah and Eleazar b. Jacob, Levitical scribes mentioned in Talmud (references in J. Jeremias, *Jerusalem in the Time of Jesus*, p. 234), and the Levite teacher associated with Antioch, Barnabas (Acts 13.1). Perhaps the apparent alias of Mark's Levi as Matthew in the First Gospel is an indication of Matthew's levitical family line.

38. Cf. e.g. 1QH 8.16ff.; 18.21ff.; 1QpHab 2.

39. *The Setting of the Sermon on the Mount*, p. 108; cf. p. 96: 'Christians always remain for him [Matthew] disciples of a teacher of righteousness'.

40. This does not rule out the possibility of an additional, allegorical level of interpretation in which the οἰκοδεσπότης (as has been suggested from Origen to Doyle) represents Jesus himself, in accordance with other uses of the term in the Gospel. (Cf. the underlying sense of Beelzebul—'master of the house'—which Matthew may in his characteristic style be reversing with some irony. 10.25 in fact strongly suggests this identification.)

41. The association of the scribe with the bringing to light of the hidden treasures of mysteries is found throughout the ancient Near East. Compare, for example, from the Assurbanipal apology (cf. D.D. Luckenbill, *Ancient Records of Assyria and Babylon* [Chicago, 1927], II, pp. 378f.): 'Nabû, the universal scribe, made me a present of his wisdom . . . The art of the Master Adapa I learned—the hidden treasure of all scribal knowledge, the [signs] of heaven and earth . . . I have studied the heavens with the learned masters of oil divination . . . I have read the artistic script of Sumer (and) the dark (obscure) Akkadian . . . ' See also n. 57 below.

42. For this, see especially M.J. Suggs, *Wisdom Christology and Law in Matthew's Gospel* (Cambridge, Mass., 1970); see also Celia Deutsch, *The Hidden Wisdom and the Easy Yoke. Wisdom, Torah and Discipleship in Matthew 11.25-30* (JSNTS; Sheffield, 1987).

43. So e.g. E. Haenchen, 'Matthäus 23', *ZThK* 48 (1951), pp. 52f.; S. Schulz, *Q. Die Spruchquelle der Evangelisten* (Zürich, 1972), pp. 336-45; Sand, 'Propheten, Weise und Schriftkundige in der Gemeinde des Matthäus-evangeliums', p. 173 (but cf. p. 174 n. 17). Tilborg (pp. 68, 140) regards the verse as a quotation which cannot have been constructed by the editor in view of its Jewishness. On the other hand he regards the closely related 13.52 as redactional. I would regard both as Jewish, and both as largely redactional compositions.

44. Hill (*Gospel of Matthew, ad loc.*), calls this usage 'apocalyptic'.

45. This is but one aspect of a series of striking parallels with Jeremiah 7–9 in this whole section, including also the mention of סופרים and חכמים (8.8f.); the context—the impending destruction of Jerusalem—is of course itself exactly paralleled. It was already suggested in Chapter 1 that Matthew makes heavy use of Jeremiah, with whom he has much in common.

46. Cf. e.g. 10.41f., in a similar context, and 23.28f., 35, in the same context; for the emphasis on the 'wise' cf. 2.1ff.; 7.24; 10.16; 24.45; 25.2, 8f.

47. Sand ('Propheten, Weise und Schriftkundige', pp. 180f.) may be too hastily dismissive of his own evidence when he acknowledges this possibility but argues for identifiable groups within Matthew's community.

48. *T. Levi* 6.17 has a similarly positive trio in the announced 'priests, judges and scribes'.

49. The disciples are portrayed as figuring in the eschatological fulfilment of prophecy at various points in Matthew's Gospel. We have argued strongly for this in Matthew 13. In Mt. 5.11 also, for example, where the subject is identical to that of our verse (namely the vindicated righteous suffering of the disciples) there is probably the idea that the disciples are fulfilling the prophecies. Cf. E. Lohmeyer, *Das Evangelium nach Matthäus, ad loc.*

50. D.R.A. Hare (*The Theme of the Jewish Persecution of Christians in the Gospel according to St. Matthew* [Cambridge, 1967]) argues that an early intra-mural but fairly mild initial Jewish persecution lies behind these references. The *birkhat ha-mînim* was only 'formulated' at the Jamnian conference, and may well have already been practised for some time (cf. G. Stemberger, 'Die sogenannte "Synode von Jabne" und das frühe Christentum', *Kairos* 19 [1977], p. 16). According to Stemberger the *birkhat* reflects 'internal Jewish conflict' (p. 18) and thus did not particularly affect the Jewish-Christians; and the Christians in any case had effectively already seceded because of the numbers of Gentiles among them. However, the Matthean community may have suffered from such exclusions throughout its history; it is unlikely to have been a completely new experience which suddenly prompted the fervour of protest we see evidenced in the First Gospel.

51. 'From house to house' (Acts 8.3) and in the synagogues (9.2). Note the further connection between 'stoning those who are sent to you' (Mt. 23.37) and the martyrdom of Stephen (Acts 7.54ff.). Compare also Acts 7.51ff. with Mt. 23.29-37.

52. On the mixed fortunes of Sirach in rabbinic Judaism see Leiman, 'Talmudic Evidence', pp. 177-216.

53. Possibly including Matthew's own work. See the discussion in K.G. Kuhn, 'Gilyonim und sifre minim', *ZNW* 26 (1964), esp. pp. 31-35. The term עון גליון, evidently a Hebraization of Greek εὐαγγέλιον, is actually associated with the (mis)quotation from Mt. 5.17 in *b. Shab.* 116a. It is easy to see how the literature of the First Evangelist, especially with its Essene and apocalyptic affinities, would have been readily classed as a *sefer mînim*. Moreover, it would have been objectionable on other grounds: 'Mt 5,17 ist also hier [*b. Shab.* 116] verstanden, und konnte von den Rabbinen nur so verstanden werden, daß das Evangelium das christliche Gesetzbuch ist, so wie die Tora das jüdische ist' (Kuhn, p. 54 n. 110). Kuhn (p. 38) provides evidence of a veritable 'Vernichtungskampf der Rabbinen gegen jüdisch-häretische Bibeltexte'. According to S.Z. Leiman ('The Talmudic and

Midrashic Evidence for the Canonization of Hebrew Scripture' [Ph.D. Dissertation; Ann Arbor: University Microfilms, 1970], p. 192), R. Akiba's ban of the 'outside books' 'was intended against all literature with biblical pretensions'. This might include Matthew's literature as it might Ben Sira's. Such developments were possibly already implicit in the deliberations about canon at Jamnia. But on the latter the sources leave us very much in the dark. Some recent studies have queried the whole notion of the Jamnian conference decisions (cf. e.g. J.P. Lewis, 'What do we mean by Jabneh?', in S.Z. Leiman [ed.], *The Canon and Masorah of the Bible. An Introductory Reader* [New York, 1974], pp. 254-61). However, the talmudic evidence, such as it is, may be sufficiently coherent to provide some indication of the kind of activity that went on in the pre-70 'persecutions' by the Pharisees. They may not have been as innocuous as Hare maintains.

54. Cf. in particular M.J. Wilkins, *The Concept of Disciple in Matthew's Gospel as Reflected in the Use of the Term* Μαθητής (Leiden, 1988) (published after this manuscript was completed).

55. Cf. Hoh, 'Der christliche γραμματεύς', who cites approvingly (p. 266) Wellhausen's recognition of the 'Christian scribe' in 5.19. (I would prefer the omission of the adjective.)

56. G. Bornkamm ('The Authority to "Bind" and "Loose" in the Church in Matthew's Gospel' [ET in G.N. Stanton (ed.), *The Interpretation of Matthew*], p. 94) cites with approval Streeter's classification of Peter, on this basis, as 'a kind of "supreme Rabbi"' (cf. B.H. Streeter, *The Four Gospels. A Study of Origins* [London, 1924], p. 515). As Sand correctly recognizes, however ('Propheten, Weise und Schriftkundige', p. 176) the epithet 'rabbi' is quite antithetical to the anti-rabbinic emphasis of Matthew (cf. 23.8-10). The traditional Jewish title 'scribe', however, is very appropriate. Moreover, in view of the exclusions in 23.8-10 it is difficult to think of any other appropriate label! The title scribe is in fact applied to Peter by J. Kahmann, 'Die Verheissungen an Petrus. Mt. XVI, 18-19 im Zusammenhang des Matthäusevangeliums', in M. Didier (ed.), *L'Evangile selon Matthieu. Rédaction et théologie* (Gembloux, 1972), pp. 274ff. He regards Peter as being the acknowledged source of halakhah for the Matthean community (represented in the Gospel itself).

57. Cf. e.g. *3 Enoch* 48 (c)K and Lm (3): 'He committed to Metatron—that is Enoch, the son of Jared—all treasuries (אוצרות). And I appointed him over all the stores that I have in every heaven. And I committed into his hands the keys of each heavenly store'; 48 (d): Metatron is called Sagnesakiel 'Because all the treasuries of wisdom are committed in his hand'. Odeberg (*3 Enoch*, I, p. 188) dates these passages not later than the first century CE. Cf. also *3 Enoch* 10.6; 48 d (10); *Hekhalot Rabbati* 29; *1 Enoch* 46.7 ('the Son of man reveals all the treasures of that which is hidden'); 51.3 (from the mouth of the Elect One 'shall pour forth all the secrets of wisdom and counsel'); *2 Bar.* 44.14, etc.

58. Essenes feature frequently in Josephus as predictors of events and interpreters of dreams (cf. e.g. Jos. *Ant.* 7.13.3). See M. McNamara, 'Were the Magi Essenes?', *IrEcclRev* 110 (1968), pp. 305-28.

Notes to Chapter 7

1. P.J. Becker, 'Erwägungen zu Fragen der neutestamentlichen Exegese', *BZ* 13 (1969), pp. 99-102; J. Dupont, 'Nova et Vetera [Matthieu 13:52]', in *L'Evangile hier et aujourd'hui. Mélanges offerts au Professeur Franz-J. Leenhardt* (Geneva, 1968), pp. 55-63 (60-62); M.D. Goulder, *Midrash and Lection in Matthew*, ch. 1. Cf. J. Kremer, '"Neues und Altes", Jesu Wort über den christlichen "Schriftgelehrten" (Mt 13,52)', in J. Kremer *et al.*, *Neues und Altes. Zur Orientierung in der augenblicklichen Situation der Kirche* (Kirche im Gespräch; Freiburg, Basel, Wien, 1974), p. 21. The perception is very common.

2. R.H. Gundry, *Matthew. A Commentary on his Literary and Theological Art* (Grand Rapids, 1982); M.D. Goulder, *Midrash and Lection in Matthew* (London, 1974); O. Lamar Cope, *Matthew. A Scribe Discipled to the Kingdom of Heaven* (CBQMS, 5; Washington, 1976). Cf. also the work by Minear, cited in note 5.

3. Goulder correctly queries Hummel's view (*Die Auseinandersetzung zwischen Kirche und Judentum im Matthäusevangelium*, p. 17) that 'scribe' is a neutral term for Matthew.

4. Contra E. von Dobschütz ('Matthäus als Rabbi und Kathechet'), K. Stendahl (*The School of St. Matthew*, p. 30), W.D. Davies ('Matthew as Christian Rabbinism', in *Apocalyptic and Christianity*, p. 30), and many others.

5. In his unusual study-book, *Matthew. The Teacher's Gospel* (London, 1982) P.S. Minear recognizes the importance of this passage for our understanding of the Gospel as a whole: 'the entire Gospel of Matthew was designed to train scribes for the kingdom of heaven. This purpose is central to chapter 13' (p. 86). For the association between authoritative instructional material and the notion of inspiration, compare Sir. 24.33f. and 2 Tim. 3.16.

6. By virtue of the emphatic position of the word καινά.

7. Sir. 21.15; 39.6; cf. 18.29. See Chapter 3.

8. See for example the essays in R.T. France and D. Wenham (eds.), *Gospel Perspectives III. Studies in Midrash and Historiography* (Sheffield, 1983).

9. It was in this sense that, a generation ago, J.W. Doeve applied it to the 'new things' of 13.52 (*Jewish Hermeneutics in the Synoptic Gospels and Acts*

[Assen, 1954]). Jesus' teaching in the chapter is 'new Christian midrash'; sharing Jesus' new understanding of scripture because of their relationship to the kingdom of heaven, the disciples will themselves expound scripture in a new way. We consider that the passage presents a principle of understanding and instruction, rather than a literary method; and it can apply to more than just the OT scriptures.

10. In P. Stuhlmacher (ed.), *Das Evangelium und die Evangelien. Vorträge vom Tübinger Symposium 1982* (WUNT, 28; Tübingen, 1983), pp. 273-87.

11. *The Passion Narrative according to Matthew* (Leuven, 1975), pp. 335f.

12. 'Matthew as Interpreter of the Miracle Stories', in G. Bornkamm, G. Barth & H.J. Held, *Tradition and Interpretation in Matthew* (ET 2nd edn; London, 1982), p. 298.

13. Cf. e.g. Gundry, *Matthew*, p. 71.

14. Compare, for example, the relationship between 21.16, 21.13 and Mk 11.17: 21.16 is suggested by 21.13, following Mk 11.17.

15. Cf. Gundry, *Matthew*, ad loc.

16. Cf. Stanton, 'Matthew as a Creative Interpreter', p. 277.

17. *The Use of the Old Testament in St. Matthew's Gospel* (Leiden, 1967); the quotations are from p. 3 and n. 8.

18. We relate this to Matthew contra Boring, *Sayings*, p. 95, who, correctly distinguishing two main hermeneutical stances within Early Judaism and Early Christianity, which he unfortunately labels the 'scribal-rabbinic' and the 'pneumatic-apocalyptic', places Matthew incongruously in the former category. According to Boring, 'This approach distinguishes clearly between the word of Scripture and the word of the interpreter'. Though Matthew does make such a distinction in the formula quotations, his reformulation of dominical sayings and the allusive character of the eschatological discourse and the parables discourse show that he cannot be firmly contained within rabbinic categories. Scribal, yes; rabbinic, no.

19. Gundry's citation is from C. Taylor, *The Gospel in the Law* (Cambridge, 1869), p. xxi.

20. *Commentary on Luke*, ad loc.

21. Compare Chapter 6 note 40 above.

22. This is in fact one of Stanton's examples of Matthean expansion; cf. 'Matthew as a Creative Interpreter', p. 280.

23. Cf. S. Sandmel, 'Parallelomania', *JBL* 81 (1962), pp. 1-13.

24. We hope this study will encourage further attempts at making sense of the Matthew–apocalyptic connection, such as the varying approaches of J. Theisohn, *Der auserwählte Richter* (Göttingen, 1975), D.R. Catchpole, 'The Poor on Earth and the Son of Man in Heaven. A Re-appraisal of Matthew XXV.31-46', *BJRL* 61 (1979), pp. 355-97, and G.N. Stanton, '5 Ezra and Matthean Christianity in the Second Century', *JTS* 28 (1977), pp. 67-83. Since this study was completed there are indications of considerably

increased scholarly interest in these connections. It is not possible to deal fully with the most recent literature here, but reference should at least be made to Margaret Barker's *The Older Testament. The Survival of Themes from the Ancient Royal Cult in Sectarian Judaism and Early Christianity* (London, 1987), who offers formidable evidence of the influence of apocalyptic literature, particularly that relating to Enoch, on the New Testament writers. See also *Apocalyptic and the New Testament. Essays in Honor of J. Louis Martyn*, ed. J. Marcus and M. Soards (JSNTS, 24; Sheffield, 1989), particularly the articles by S.H. Brooks, 'Apocalyptic Parenesis in Matthew 6.19-34' (pp. 95-112) and O. Lamar Cope, '"To the Close of the Age": The Role of Apocalyptic Thought in the Gospel of Matthew' (pp. 113-24).

25. Especially where the working definition of 'prophecy' limits it specifically to the oral realm. (A case in point is the recent unnecessarily apologetic article by G.F. Hawthorne, 'The Role of Christian Prophets in the Gospel Tradition', in *Tradition and Interpretation in the New Testament. Essays in Honor of E. Earle Ellis*, ed. G.F. Hawthorne with O. Betz [Grand Rapids and Tübingen, 1988].) This is in fact unappreciative of the nature of prophetic inspiration in the latter part of the Old Testament, and throughout the whole of the intertestamental period, in which, as we have seen, 'prophecy' emerges largely in a situation of study and writing. There is no doubt that we owe the New Testament to scribes who enjoyed the liberty of a sense of prophetic inspiration.

BIBLIOGRAPHY

General works, such as introductions, background and historical studies, are not listed except if specifically cited in the text.

Texts, Translations and Reference Works

Bauer, W., *A Greek-English Lexicon of the New Testament and Other Early Christian Literature*, ET W.F. Arndt & F.W. Gingrich; 2nd rev. edn by W.F. Gingrich & E.W. Danker (Chicago and London, 1979).

Black, M., *Apocalypsis Henochi Graece* (Pseudepigrapha Veteris Testamenti Graece, 3; Leiden, 1970).

—(in consultation with James C. VanderKam), *The Book of Enoch or I Enoch. A New English Edition with Commentary and Textual Notes* (Leiden, 1985).

Blass, F. & A. Debrunner, *A Greek Grammar of the New Testament and Other Early Christian Literature* (ET R.W. Funk; Chicago, 1961).

Brown, C. (ed.), *The New International Dictionary of New Testament Theology* (5 vols.; Exeter and Grand Rapids, 1975-1978).

Brown, F., S.R. Driver & C.A. Briggs (eds.), *A Hebrew and English Lexicon of the Old Testament* (Oxford, 1907).

Charlesworth, J.H. (ed.), *The Old Testament Pseudepigrapha* (2 vols.; London, 1983, 1985).

Computer-Konkordanz zum Novum Testamentum Graece (Berlin and New York, 1980).

Danby, H., *The Mishnah. Translated from the Hebrew with Introduction and Brief Explanatory Notes* (Oxford, 1933).

Delling, G., *Bibliographie zur jüdisch-hellenistischen und intertestamentarischen Literatur 1900-1970* (Berlin, 1975).

Encyclopaedia Judaica Jerusalem (16 vols.; New York, 1972).

Epstein, I. (ed.), *Hebrew-English Edition of the Babylonian Talmud* (London, 1965-).

Fitzmyer, J.A., *The Dead Sea Scrolls and Major Publications and Tools for Study* (SBL Sources for Biblical Study, 8; Missoula, 1977).

Freedman, H. & M. Simon (eds.), *Midrash Rabbah* (10 vols.; London, 1939-).

Gaster, T., *The Scriptures of the Dead Sea Sect* (London, 1957).

Huck, A., *A Synopsis of the First Three Gospels* (9th edn; Eng. edn ed. F.L. Cross, Oxford, 1948).

Jastrow, M., *A Dictionary of the Targumim, the Talmud Babli and Yerushalmi, and the Midrashic Literature* (2 vols.; New York, 1950).

Josephus. Loeb Classical Library (8 vols.; London, 1926-).

Kittel, G. (ed.), *Theological Dictionary of the New Testament* (ET 10 vols.; Grand Rapids, 1964-76).

Kuhn, K.G., *Konkordanz zu den Qumran-Texten* (Göttingen, 1960).

—'Nachträge zum Konkordanz zu den Qumran-Texten', *RQ* 4 (1963-64), pp. 163-234.

Lévi, I. (ed.), *The Hebrew Text of the Book of Ecclesiasticus* (Leiden, 1951).
Levy, J., *Chaldäisches Wörterbuch über die Targumim und einen großen Theil des rabbinischen Schrifttums* (repr. of 3rd edn; Köln, 1959).
Liddell, H.G. & R. Scott, *A Greek-English Lexicon* (Oxford, 1925-1940).
Philo. Loeb Classical Library (10 vols.; London, 1929-).
Pritchard, J.B. (ed.), *Ancient Near Eastern Texts Relating to the Old Testament* (Princeton, 1950).
Rahlfs, A. (ed.), *Septuaginta* (2 vols.; 3rd edn; Stuttgart, 1949).
Sanders, J.A., *The Psalms Scroll of Qumrân Cave 11 (11QPs^a)* (Discoveries in the Judean Desert of Jordan, IV; Oxford, 1965).
Soden, W. von, *Akkadisches Handwörterbuch* (Wiesbaden, 1976).
Sparks, H.F.D., *A Synopsis of the Gospels* (2 vols. in 1; London, 1977).
—(ed.), *The Apocryphal Old Testament* (Oxford, 1984).
Sperber, A., *The Bible in Aramaic* (4 vols.; London, 1959-).
Wagner, G. (ed.), *Bibliographical Aids. An Exegetical Bibliography on the Gospel of Matthew* (Rüschlikon/Zürich, 1974).
Yadin Y., *The Ben Sira Scroll from Masada, with introduction, emendations and commentary* (ET Jerusalem, 1965).

Secondary Literature

Abel, E.L., 'Who Wrote Matthew?', *NTS* 17 (1970-71), pp. 138-52.
Adler, W., 'Enoch in Early Christian Literature', *SBL 1978 Seminar Papers* (Missoula, 1978), I, pp. 271-75.
Albertz, M., *Die synoptischen Streitgespräche* (Berlin, 1921).
Alexander, P.S., 'The Historical Setting of the Hebrew Book of Enoch', *JJS* 28 (1977), pp. 156-80.
—'Rabbinic Judaism and the New Testament', *ZNW* 74 (1983), pp. 237-46.
Alon, G., *Jews, Judaism and the Classical World* (ET I. Abrahams; Jerusalem, 1977).
Andel, C.P. van, 'De structuur van de Henoch-Traditie en het Nieuwe Testament. Een onderzoek naar het milieu van apocalyptische en sectarische tradities binnen het jodendom in zijn relatie tot het milieu van het oer-christelijk kerugma' (Diss. Utrecht, 1955).
Aune, D.E., 'Christian Prophecy and the Sayings of Jesus. An Index to Synoptic Pericopae Ostensibly Influenced by Early Christian Prophets', *SBL 1975 Seminar Papers* (Missoula, 1975), pp. 131-42.
—*Prophecy in Early Christianity and the Ancient Mediterranean World* (Grand Rapids, 1983).
Bacher, W., *Tradition und Tradenten in den Schulen Palästinas und Babyloniens. Studien und Materialien zur Entstehungsgeschichte des Talmuds* (repr. Berlin, 1966 [1st edn: Leipzig, 1914]).
Bacon, B.W., *Studies in Matthew* (London, 1930).
Baeck, L., *The Pharisees and Other Essays* (New York, 1947).
Baer, Y.F., *Israel among the Nations* [Hebr.] (Jerusalem, 1955).
Baird, J.A., *Audience Criticism and the Historical Jesus* (Philadelphia, 1969).
Bammel, E., 'Sadduzäer und Sadokiden', *ETL* 55 (1979), pp. 107-115.
—and C.F.D. Moule (eds.), *Jesus and the Politics of his Day* (Cambridge, 1983).
Bampfylde, G., 'The Similitudes of Enoch. Historical Allusions', *JSJ* 15 (1984), pp. 9-31.

Barker, M., 'Slippery Words III. Apocalyptic', *ExpT* 89 (1977-78), pp. 324-29.

Baron, S.W., *A Social and Religious History of the Jews* (2nd edn; New York, 1952).

Barr, J., 'Jewish Apocalyptic in Recent Scholarly Study', *BJRL* 58 (1975), pp. 9-35.

—*The Semantics of Biblical Language* (London, 1961).

Barth, G., 'Matthew's Understanding of the Law', in G. Bornkamm, G. Barth & H.J. Held (eds.), *Tradition and Interpretation in Matthew* (ET 2nd edn; London, 1982), pp. 58-164.

Bauckham, R.J., 'The Rise of Apocalyptic', *Themelios* 3 (1978), pp. 10-23.

Bauer, W., *Orthodoxy and Heresy in Earliest Christianity* (ET of 2nd German edn; Philadelphia, 1971).

Baumbach, G., *Jesus von Nazareth im Lichte der jüdischen Gruppenbildung* (Berlin, 1971).

—'"Volk Gottes" im Frühjudentum. Eine Untersuchung des "ekklesiologischen" Typen des Frühjudentums', *Kairos* 21 (1979), pp. 30-47.

Baumgarten, A.I., 'The Name of the Pharisees', *JBL* 102 (1983), pp. 411-28.

Baumgarten, J.M., 'Qumran Studies', *JBL* 77 (1958), pp. 249-57.

Beale, G.K., *The Use of Daniel in Jewish Apocalyptic Literature and in the Revelation of St. John* (Lanham, New York, London, 1984).

Beare, F.W., *The Gospel according to Matthew: A Commentary* (Oxford, 1981).

Beasley-Murray, G.R., 'How Christian is the Book of Revelation?', in R. Banks, *Reconciliation and Hope. New Testament Essays on Atonement and Eschatology* (Grand Rapids, 1974), pp. 275-84.

—'Jesus and Apocalyptic, with Special Reference to Mark 14.62', in J. Lambrecht, *L'Apocalypse johannique et l'Apocalyptique dans le Nouveau Testament* (BETL, 53; Leuven, 1980), pp. 415-29.

Becker, Jürgen, *Untersuchungen zur Entstehungsgeschichte der Testamente der zwölf Patriarchen* (Leiden, 1970).

Becker, P. Joachim, 'Erwägungen zu Fragen der neutestamentlichen Exegese', *BZ* 13 (1969), pp. 99-102.

Beilner, W., *Christus und die Pharisäer: Exegetische Untersuchung über Grund und Verlauf der Auseinandersetzung* (Vienna, 1959).

—'Der Ursprung des Pharisäismus', *BZ* 3 (1959), pp. 235-51.

Berger, K., *Die Amen-Worte Jesu. Eine Untersuchung zum Problem der Legitimation apokalyptischer Rede* (BZNW, 39; Berlin, 1970).

Betz, O., 'Neues und Altes im Geschichtshandeln Gottes. Bemerkungen zu Matthäus 13.51f', in H. Feld *et al.* (eds.), *Wort Gottes in der Zeit* (Festschrift K.H. Schelke; Düsseldorf, 1973), pp. 69-84.

—*Offenbarung und Schriftforschung in der Qumransekte* (Tübingen, 1960).

Bickerman, E., 'La chaîne de la tradition pharisienne', *RB* 59 (1952), pp. 44-54.

—*From Ezra to the Last of the Maccabees—Foundations of Postbiblical Judaism* (New York, 1962).

Billerbeck, P. & H.L. Strack, *Kommentar zum Neuen Testament aus Talmud und Midrasch* (6 vols.; München, 1922-61).

Black, M., 'Scribe', *Interpreter's Dictionary of the Bible*, IV (New York and Nashville, 1962), pp. 246-48.

—*The Scrolls and Christianity. Historical and Theological Significance* (London, 1969).

Blenkinsopp, J., *Prophecy and Canon. A Contribution to the Study of Jewish Origins* (Notre Dame and London, 1977).

—'Prophecy and Priesthood in Josephus', *JJS* 25 (1974), pp. 239-62.

244 *The Understanding Scribe*

Bloch, J., *On the Apocalyptic in Judaism* (JQR Monograph Series, 2; Philadelphia, 1952).

Bogaert, P., *Apocalypse de Baruch. Introduction, traduction du syriaque et commentaire* (Sources chrétiennes, 144, 145; 2 vols.; Paris, 1969).

—'Le nom de Baruch dans la littérature pseudépigraphique: L'apocalypse syriaque et le livre deutérocanonique', in W.C. van Unnik (ed.), *La Littérature Juive entre Tenach et Mischna* (Leiden, 1974), pp. 56-72.

Bonnard, P., *L'Evangile selon Saint Matthieu* (2nd edn; Neuchâtel, 1970).

—'Matthieu, éducateur du peuple chrétien', in *Mélanges bibliques en hommage au R.P. Béda Rigaux* (Gembloux, 1970), pp. 1-7.

Boring, M.E., 'The Apocalypse as Christian Prophecy: A Discussion of the Issues Raised by the Book of Revelation for the Study of Early Christian Prophecy', *SBL 1974 Seminar Papers*, II (Cambridge, Mass., 1974), pp. 43-62.

—'Christian Prophecy and Matt. 10:23: A Test Exegesis', *SBL 1976 Seminar Papers* (Missoula, 1976), pp. 127-33.

—'Christian Prophecy and the Sayings of Jesus: The State of the Question', *NTS* 29 (1983), pp. 104-12.

—*Sayings of the Risen Jesus. Christian Prophecy in the Synoptic Tradition* (SNTSMS, 46; Cambridge, 1982).

Bornkamm, G., 'Die Binde- und Lösegewalt in der Kirche des Matthäus', in *Geschichte und Glaube, 2. Teil* (Gesammelte Aufsätze, IV, 1971), pp. 37-50; ET in G.N. Stanton (ed.), *The Interpretation of Matthew*, pp. 85-97.

—'Matthäus als Interpret der Herrenworte', *TLZ* 73 (1954), cols. 341-46.

—G. Barth & H.J. Held, *Tradition and Interpretation in Matthew* (ET 2nd edn; London, 1982).

Boston, J.R., 'The Wisdom Influence upon the Song of Moses', *JBL* 78 (1968), pp. 198-202.

Boucher, M., *The Mysterious Parable. A Literary Study* (CBQMS, 6; Washington, 1977).

Bousset, W., *Volksfrömmigkeit und Schriftgelehrtentum* (Berlin, 1903).

Bowker, J., *Jesus and the Pharisees* (Cambridge, 1973).

—*The Targums and Rabbinic Literature* (Cambridge, 1969).

Box, G.H., *4 Ezra*, in R.H. Charles (ed.), *The Apocrypha and Pseudepigrapha of the Old Testament*, II (Oxford, 1913), pp. 542-624.

—'Scribes and Sadducees in the New Testament', *Expositor* series 8, 15 (1918), pp. 401-11; 16 (1918), pp. 55-69.

Brandenburger, E., *Markus 13 und die Apokalyptik* (FRLANT, 134; Göttingen, 1984).

Braun, H., *Qumran und das Neue Testament* (2 vols.; Tübingen, 1966).

—*Spätjüdisch-häretischer und frühchristlicher Radikalismus* (2 vols.; Tübingen, 1957).

Bronner, L., *Sects and Separatism during the Second Jewish Commonwealth* (New York, 1967).

Brooke, G.J., *Exegesis at Qumran. 4QFlorilegium in its Jewish Context* (JSOTS, 29; Sheffield, 1985).

Brown, J.P., 'The Form of "Q" Known to Matthew', *NTS* 8 (1961), pp. 27-42.

Brownlee, W.H., 'The Background of Biblical Interpretation at Qumran', in M. Delcor (ed.), *Qumrân. Sa piété, sa théologie et son milieu* (Gembloux and Leuven, 1978), pp. 183-93.

—'Biblical Interpretation among the Sectaries of the Dead Sea Scrolls', *BA* 14 (1951), pp. 54-76.

—*The Midrash Pesher of Habakkuk* (SBLMS Series; 1979).

Bruce, F.F., 'The Book of Daniel and the Qumran Community', in E.E. Ellis and M. Wilcox (eds.), *Neotestamentica et Semitica. Studies in Honour of Matthew Black* (Edinburgh, 1969), pp. 221-35.

Buchanan, G.W., 'The Word of God and the Apocalyptic Vision', *SBL 1978 Seminar Papers* (Missoula, 1978), II, pp. 183-92.

Buck, E., 'Anti-Judaic Sentiments in the Passion Narrative according to Matthew', in P. Richardson & D. Granskou (eds.), *Anti-Judaism in Early Christianity*, I: *Paul and the Gospels* (Studies in Christianity and Judaism, 2; Waterloo, 1986), pp. 165-80.

Budesheim, T.L., 'Jesus and the Disciples in Conflict with Judaism', *ZNW* 62 (1971), pp. 190-209.

Büchler, A., *Types of Jewish-Palestinian Piety from 70 BCE to 70 CE. The Ancient Pious Men* (London, 1922).

Bultmann, R., *Die Geschichte der synoptischen Tradition* (6th edn; Göttingen, 1964; ET *The History of the Synoptic Tradition* [rev. edn; Oxford, 1968]).

Burrows, M., J.C. Trever & W.H. Brownlee, *The Dead Sea Scrolls of St. Mark's Monastery* (2 vols.; ASOR; New Haven, 1950, 1951).

Carlston, C.E., *The Parables of the Triple Tradition* (Philadelphia, 1975).

Carmignac, J., 'Qu'est-ce que l'Apocalyptique? Son emploi à Qumrân', *RQ* 10 (1979), pp. 3-33.

—'Les rapports entre l'Ecclésiastique et Qumrân', *RQ* 3 (1961), pp. 209-18.

Carson, D.A., 'The Jewish Leaders in Matthew's Gospel: A Reappraisal', *JETS* 25/2 (1982), pp. 161-74.

Catchpole, D.R., 'The Poor on Earth and the Son of Man in Heaven. A Re-appraisal of Matthew XXV.31-46', *BJRL* 61 (1979), pp. 355-97.

Charles, R.H., *The Apocrypha and Pseudepigrapha of the Old Testament in English* (2 vols.; Oxford, 1913; repr. 1978).

—*The Book of Enoch or 1 Enoch* (Oxford, 1912).

—*A Critical and Exegetical Commentary on the Revelation of St. John* (ICC; Edinburgh, 1920).

—*Religious Development between the Old and New Testaments* (repr. London, 1977 [1919]).

Charlesworth, J.H. (ed.), *The Old Testament Pseudepigrapha* (2 vols.; London, 1983, 1985).

—*The Pseudepigrapha and Modern Research, with a Supplement* (SBL Septuagint and Cognate Studies Series, 75; Chico, 1981).

Chernus, I., *Mysticism in Rabbinic Judaism. Studies in the History of Midrash* (Studia Judaica. Forschungen zur Wissenschaft des Judentums, 11; Berlin and New York, 1982).

Christ, F., *Jesus Sophia. Die Sophia-Christologie bei den Synoptikern* (ATANT, 57; Zürich, 1970).

Chwolson, D., *Das letzte Passamahl Christi und der Tag seines Todes, nach den in Übereinstimmung gebrachten Berichten der Synoptiker und des Evangelium Johannis, nebst Schlußwort und Anhang* (2nd edn; Leipzig, 1908).

Clark, K.W., 'The Gentile Bias in Matthew', *JBL* 66 (1947), pp. 165-72.

Coggins, R.J., *1 Esdras. Part I of The First and Second Books of Esdras* (CBC; London, New York, Melbourne, 1979).

Cohn, L., *Einteilung und Chronologie der Schriften Philos* (Leipzig, 1899).

Collins, J.J., 'The Son of Man Who Has Righteousness', *SBL 1979 Seminar Papers* (Missoula, 1979), II, pp. 1-13 (= 'The Heavenly Representative. The "Son of Man" in the Similitudes of Enoch', in G.W.E. Nickelsburg & H. Orlinsky [eds.], *Ideal Figures in Ancient Judaism. Profiles and Paradigms* [Septuagint and Cognate Studies, 12; Chico, 1980], pp. 111-33)

—*The Apocalyptic Vision of the Book of Daniel* (Missoula, 1977).

Cook, M.J., 'Jesus and the Pharisees: The Problem as it Stands Today', *JES* 15 (1978), pp. 441-60.

—*Mark's Treatment of the Jewish Leaders* (Leiden, 1978).

Coote, R.B., *Amos among the Prophets. Composition and Theology* (Philadelphia, 1981).

Cope, O. Lamar, *Matthew. A Scribe Trained for the Kingdom of Heaven* (CBQMS, 5; Washington, 1976).

Cothenet, E., 'Les prophètes chrétiens dans l'Evangile selon Saint Matthieu', in M. Didier (ed.), *L'Evangile selon Matthieu*, pp. 281-308.

Cowley, A., *Aramaic Papyri of the 5th Century B.C.* (Oxford, 1923).

Curtis, E.L., *Chronicles* (ICC; Edinburgh, 1920, repr. 1965).

Dampier, J.H., 'The Scrolls and the Scribes of the New Testament', *BEvThS* 1 (1958), pp. 8-19.

Daniel, C., '"Faux Prophètes": Surnom des Esséniens dans le Sermon sur la Montagne', *RQ* 7 (1969), pp. 45-80.

Daube, D., 'ἐξουσία in Mark 1.22 and 27', *JTS* 39 (1938), pp. 45-59.

—*The New Testament and Rabbinic Judaism* (London, 1956).

Davies, P.R., *The Damascus Covenant* (JSOTS; Sheffield, 1982).

—'Hasidim in the Maccabean Period', *JJS* 28 (1977), pp. 127-40.

Davies, W.D., 'Apocalypticism and Pharisaism', *ExpT* 59 (1948), pp. 233-37.

—*Christian Origins and Judaism* (London, 1962).

—*Introduction to Pharisaism* (Philadelphia, 1967).

—*Paul and Rabbinic Judaism* (2nd edn; London, 1955).

—*The Setting of the Sermon on the Mount* (Cambridge, 1964).

Delcor, M., *Le Testament d'Abraham* (Studia in Veteris Testamenti Pseduepigrapha, 2; Leiden, 1973).

Delobel, J. (ed.), *Logia. Les Paroles de Jésus—The Sayings of Jesus. Mémorial Joseph Coppens* (BETL, 59; Leuven, 1982).

Denis, A.M., 'Les paraboles du royaume, révélation de mystéres (Matt. 13)', *Communio* 1 (1968), pp. 327-46.

Dequeker, L., 'The "Saints of the Most High" in Qumran and Daniel', *OTS* 18 (1973), pp. 108-87.

Dewey, J., *Markan Public Debate. Literary Technique, Concentric Structure, and Theology in Mark 2:1-3:6* (SBLDS; Chico, 1980).

Dexinger, F., *Henochs Zehnwochenapokalypse und offene Probleme der Apokalyptik-forschung* (Studia Post-Biblica, 29; Leiden, 1977).

—'Die Sektenproblematik im Judentum', *Kairos* 21 (1979), pp. 273-87.

Didier, M., *L'Evangile selon Matthieu. Rédaction et théologie* (BETL, 29; Gembloux, 1972).

Dix, G.H., 'The Enochic Pentateuch', *JTS* 27 (1926), pp. 29-42.

Dobschütz, E. von, 'Matthäus als Rabbi und Katechet', *ZNW* 27 (1928), pp. 338-48 (ET in G.N. Stanton [ed.], *The Interpretation of Matthew* [Issues in Religion and Theology, 3; London and Philadelphia, 1983], pp. 19-29).

Doeve, J.W., *Jewish Hermeneutics in the Synoptic Gospels and Acts* (Assen, 1954).

Doyle, R., 'Disciples as Sages and Scribes in Matthew's Gospel', *Word in Life* [North Sydney, NSW] 32 (1984), pp. 4-9.

Duesberg, H. and I. Fransen, *Les Scribes Inspirés* (rev. edn; Maredsous, 1966 [1937]).

Dunn, J.D.G., 'The Prophetic "I"-Sayings in the Jesus Tradition. The Importance of Testing Prophetic Utterances in Early Christianity', *NTS* 24 (1978), pp. 175-98.

—*Unity and Diversity in the New Testament. An Inquiry into the Character of Earliest Christianity* (London, 1977).

Dupont, Jacques, 'Le chapitre des paraboles', *Nouvelle Revue Théologique* 89 (1967), pp. 800-20.

—'Nova et Vetera (Matthieu 13:52)', in *L'Evangile hier et aujourd'hui. Mélanges offerts au Professeur Franz-J. Leenhardt* (Genève, 1968), pp. 55-63.

Dupont-Sommer, A., *The Essene Writings from Qumran* (ET Oxford, 1961).

Edwards, R.A., 'Christian Prophecy and the Q Tradition' *SBL 1976 Seminar Papers* (Missoula, 1976), pp. 119-26.

—'Uncertain Faith. Matthew's Portrait of the Disciples', in F. Segovia (ed.), *Discipleship in the New Testament* (Philadelphia, 1985), pp. 47-61.

Eerdmans, B.D., 'Pharisees and Sadducees', *The Expositor* Series 8, 8 (1914), pp. 299-315.

Ellis, E.E., 'Luke xi.49-51: An Oracle of a Christian Prophet?', *ExpT* 74 (1963), pp. 157-58.

—*Prophecy and Hermeneutic in Early Christianity* (WUNT, 18; Tübingen and Grand Rapids, 1978).

Evans, C.D. *et al.* (eds.), *Scripture in Context. Essays on the Comparative Method* (Pittsburgh, 1980).

Farbstein, D., 'Waren die Pharisäer und die Schriftgelehrten Heuchler?', *Judaica* 8 (1952), pp. 193-207.

Farmer, W.R., 'The Post-Sectarian Character of Matthew and its Post-War Setting in Antioch of Syria', *Perspectives in Religious Studies* 3 (1976), pp. 235-47.

Farrar, A., *The Revelation of St. John the Divine* (Oxford, 1964).

Fenton, J.C., *St. Matthew* (London, 1963).

Finkel, A., 'The Prayer of Jesus in Matthew', in A. Finkel (ed.), *Standing before God. Studies on Prayer in Scripture and in Tradition with Essays in Honor of John M. Oesterreicher* (New York, 1981), pp. 131-70.

—*The Pharisees and the Teacher of Nazareth. A study of their background, their halakhic and midrashic teachings, the similarities and differences* (Leiden, 1964).

Finkelstein, L., *Pharisaism in the Making. Selected essays* (New York, 1974).

Fiorenza, E. Schüssler, 'Apokalypsis and Propheteia', in J. Lambrecht (ed.), *L'Apocalypse et l'Apocalyptique dans le Nouveau Testament* (Gembloux, 1980), pp. 107-28.

Fishbane, M., *Biblical Interpretation in Ancient Israel* (Oxford, 1985).

Fleddermann, H., 'A Warning about the Scribes (Mark 12:37b-40)', *CBQ* 44 (1982), pp. 52-67.

Flusser, D., 'Two Anti-Jewish Montages in Matthew', *Immanuel* 5 (1975), pp. 37-45.

Förster, W., *Palestinian Judaism in New Testament Times* (ET London, 1964 [of 3rd rev. German edn, Hamburg, 1959]).

France, R.T. & D. Wenham (eds.), *Gospel Perspectives III. Studies in Midrash and Historiography* (Sheffield, 1983).
Frankemölle, H., *Jahwebund und Kirche Christi. Studien zur Form- und Traditionsgeschichte des Evangeliums nach Matthäus* (Münster, 1974).
Franzmann, M.H., *Follow Me: Discipleship according to Saint Matthew* (St Louis, 1961).
Frend, W.H.C., *Martyrdom and Persecution in the Early Church* (Oxford, 1965).
—'The Persecutions: Some Links between Judaism and the Early Church', *JEH* 9 (1958), pp. 141-58.
Freudenberg, J., 'Die synoptische Weherede. Tradition und Redaktion in Mt 23 par.' (Diss. Münster, 1972).
Freyne, S., 'The Charismatic', in G.W.E. Nickelsburg & J.J. Collins (eds.), *Ideal Figures in Ancient Judaism* (Chico, 1980), pp. 223-58.
—'The Disciples in Mark and the Maskilim in Daniel. A Comparison', *JSNT* 16 (1983), pp. 7-23.
Funk, R.W. (ed.), *Apocalypticism* (*Journal of Theology and the Church*, 6; New York, 1967).
Gaechter, P., *Das Matthäus Evangelium* (Innsbruck, Wien, München, 1962).
Garland, D.E., *The Intention of Matthew 23* (Leiden, 1979).
Gaston, L., *No Stone on Another. Studies in the Significance of the Fall of Jerusalem in the Synoptic Gospels* (NovT Supp, 23; Leiden 1970).
Gerhardsson, B., 'The Seven Parables in Matthew XIII', *NTS* 19 (1972-73), pp. 16-37.
Gevaryahu, 'Biblical Colophons: A Source for the "Biography" of Authors, Texts and Books', *VTS 28* (1974), pp. 42-59.
—'Limmudim: Scribal Disciples in the Book of Isaiah' [Heb.], *Beth Mikra* 47 (1971), pp. 438-56.
Gilat, Y.D., 'Soferim', *Encyclopaedia Judaica*, XV, pp. 79-81.
Ginzberg, L., *The Legends of the Jews* (7 vols.; Philadelphia, 1946-1947).
—'Some Observations on the Attitude of the Synagogue towards the Apocalyptic-Eschatological Writings', *JBL* 41 (1922), pp. 115-36.
Glasson, T.F., 'Anti-Pharisaism in St. Matthew', *JQR* 51 (1960-61), pp. 316-20.
Glatzer, N.N., *Anfänge des Judentums* (Gütersloh, 1966).
Gnilka, J., 'Die Kirche des Matthäus und die Gemeinde von Qumrân', *BZ* 7 (1963), pp. 43-63.
—*Die Verstockung Israels. Isaias 6,9-10 in der Theologie der Synoptiker* (München, 1961).
Gordis, R., *Poets, Prophets, and Sages* (Bloomington, Indiana, 1971).
Goulder, M.D., *Midrash and Lection in Matthew* (London, 1974).
Green, H.B., *The Gospel according to Matthew* (New Clarendon Bible Commentary; Oxford, 1975).
Greenfield, J.C. & M.E. Stone, 'The Enochic Pentateuch and the Date of the Similitudes', *HTR* 70 (1977), pp. 51-65.
Grelot, P., 'Hénoch et ses Ecritures', *RB* 82 (1975), pp. 481-500.
—'La légende d'Hénoch dans les apocryphes et dans la Bible: Origine et signification', *Recherches de Science Religieuse* 46 (1958), pp. 5-26, 181-210.
Gruenwald, I., 'Jewish Apocalyptic Literature', in H. Temporini and W. Haase (eds.), *Aufstieg und Niedergang der römischen Welt. Geschichte und Kultur Roms im Spiegel der neueren Forschung* II, 19.1 (Berlin and New York, 1979), pp. 89-118.

—'The Jewish Esoteric Literature in the Time of the Mishnah and Talmud', *Immanuel* 4 (1974), pp. 37-46.

Grundmann, W., *Das Evangelium nach Matthäus* (Theologischer Handkommentar zum Neuen Testament, 1; Berlin, 1968).

—& J. Leipoldt, *Umwelt des Urchristentums* (3 vols.), esp. 'Die Pharisäer' (I, pp. 269-86).

Guelich, R.A., *The Sermon on the Mount. A Foundation for Understanding* (Waco, Texas, 1982).

Guignebert, C., *The Jewish World in the Time of Jesus* (ET London, 1939).

Gundry, R.H., *Matthew. A Commentary on his Literary and Theological Art* (Grand Rapids, 1982).

—Review of Tilborg, *The Jewish Leaders in Matthew*, *JBL* 92 (1973), pp. 138-40.

—*The Use of the Old Testament in St. Matthew's Gospel with special reference to the messianic hope* (NovT Supp. 18; Leiden, 1967).

Gunkel, H., 'Der Schreiberengel Nabû im Alten Testament und im Judentum', *Archiv für Religionswissenschaft* 1 (1898), pp. 294-300.

Guttmann, A., *Rabbinic Judaism in the Making. A chapter in the history of the halakhah from Ezra to Judah I* (Detroit, 1970).

Hadfield, P., 'Matthew the Apocalyptic Editor', *London Quarterly and Holborn Review* 28 (1959), pp. 128-32.

Hadot, J., 'Contestation socio-religieuse et apocalyptique dans le judéo-christianisme', *Archives de Sociologie des Religions* 12 (1967), pp. 35-47.

—'La datation de l'apocalypse syriaque de Baruch', *Semitica* 15 (1965), pp. 79-95.

—'Le problème de l'apocalypse syriaque de Baruch d'après un ouvrage récent', *Semitica* 20 (1970), pp. 59-76 [critical review of P. Bogaert's commentary].

Haenchen, E., 'Matthäus 23', *ZThK* 48 (1951), pp. 38-63.

Hainz, J. (ed.), *Kirche im Werden. Studien zum Thema Amt und Gemeinde im Neuen Testament* (München, Paderborn, Wien, 1976).

Hanson, P.D., *The Dawn of Apocalyptic* (Philadelphia, 1975).

—*The Diversity of Scripture. A Theological Interpretation* (Overtures to Biblical Theology, 11; Philadelphia, 1982).

—'Jewish Apocalyptic against its Near Eastern Environment', *RB* 78 (1971), pp. 31-58.

—(ed.), *Visionaries and their Apocalypses* (Issues in Religion and Theology, 2; London and Philadelphia, 1983).

Hare, D.R.A., *The Theme of Jewish Persecution of Christians in the Gospel according to St Matthew* (SNTSMS, 6; Cambridge, 1967).

Harnisch, W., *Verhängnis und Verheißung der Geschichte. Untersuchungen zum Zeit- und Geschichtsverständnis im 4. Buch Esra und in der syrischen Baruchapokalypse* (Göttingen, 1969).

Harrington, D.J., 'Research on the Jewish Pseudepigrapha during the 1970s', *CBQ* 42 (1980), pp. 147-59.

—'The Wisdom of the Scribe according to Ben Sira', in G.W.E. Nickelsburg and J.J. Collins (eds.), *Ideal Figures in Ancient Judaism* (Chico, 1980), pp. 181-88.

Hartman, L., *Prophecy Interpreted. The Formation of Some Jewish Apocalyptic Texts and of the Eschatological Discourse Mark 13 Par.* (Lund, 1966).

Hayman, A.P., 'The Problem of Pseudonymity in the Ezra Apocalypse', *JJS* 6 (1975), pp. 47ff.

Heaton, E.W., *The Book of Daniel. Introduction and Commentary* (Torch Bible; London, 1956).

—*Solomon's New Men. The Emergence of Ancient Israel as a National State* (London and New York, 1974).

Hengel, M., *Judaism and Hellenism. Studies in their Encounter in Palestine during the Early Hellenistic Period* (ET 2 vols.; London, 1973).

Hennecke, E., *New Testament Apocrypha*, ed. W. Schneemelcher (ET ed. R. McL. Wilson; 2 vols.; London, 1965).

Herford, R.T., *The Pharisees* (3rd edn; London, 1962).

—*Talmud and Apocrypha. A Comparative Study of the Jewish Ethical Teaching in the Rabbinical and Non-Rabbinical Sources in the Early Centuries* (London, 1933).

Hill, D., 'ΔΙΚΑΙΟΙ as a Quasi-Technical Term', *NTS* 11 (1964-65), pp. 296-302.

—*The Gospel of Matthew* (New Century Bible, London, 1972).

—*New Testament Prophecy* (London, 1979).

Hillyer, N., 'Scribe', *NIDNTT* (ed. C. Brown; Exeter, 1978), III, pp. 477-82.

Himmelfarb, M., 'A Report on Enoch in Rabbinic Literature', *SBL Seminar Papers, 1978* (Missoula, 1978), I, pp. 259-69.

Hoffmann, P. (ed.), *Orientierung an Jesus. Zur Theologie der Synoptiker. Festschrift Josef Schmid* (Freiburg, Basel, Wien, 1973).

—*Studien zur Theologie der Logienquelle* (Münster, 1972).

Hoh, J., 'Der christliche γραμματεύς (Mt 13,52)', *BZ* 17 (1926), pp. 256-69.

Holm-Nielsen, S., *Hodayot. Psalms from Qumran* (Aarhus, 1960).

Hultgren, A.J., 'Paul's Pre-Christian Persecutions of the Church. Their Purpose, Locale, and Nature', *JBL* 95 (1976), pp. 97-111.

Hummel, R., *Die Auseinandersetzung zwischen Kirche und Judentum in Matthäusevangelium* (Beiträge zur evangelischen Theologie, 33; 2nd edn; München, 1966).

Huppenbauer, H.W., 'Enderwartung und Lehrer der Gerechtigkeit im Habakuk-Kommentar', *TZ* 20 (1964), pp. 81-86.

James, M.R., 'Ego Salathiel qui et Ezras', *JTS* 18 (1917), pp. 167-69.

—'Salathiel qui et Esdras', *JTS* 19 (1918), pp. 347-79.

Jansen, H.L., *Die Henochgestalt. Eine vergleichende religionsgeschichtliche Untersuchung* (Skrifter utgitt av det Norske Videnskaps-Akademi i Oslo; II. Hist.-Filos. Klasse, 1; 1939).

Janssen, E., *Das Gottesvolk und seine Geschichte. Geschichtsbild und Selbstverständnis im palästinensischen Schrifttum von Jesus Sirach bis Jehuda ha-Nasi* (Neukirchen-Vluyn, 1971).

Jaubert, A., 'Le pays de Damas', *RB* 65 (1958), pp. 214-48.

Jeremias, G., *Der Lehrer der Gerechtigkeit* (SUNT, 2; Göttingen 1963).

Jeremias, J., γραμματεύς, *TDNT*, I, pp. 740-43.

—*Jerusalem in the Time of Jesus* (ET London, 1969).

—*New Testament Theology*, vol. I: *The Proclamation of Jesus* (ET London, 1971).

—*The Parables of Jesus* (ET 3rd edn; London, 1972).

—'Zur Hypothese einer schriftlichen Logienquelle Q', *ZNW* 29 (1930), pp. 147-49.

Jonge, M. de, 'Christian Influence in the Testaments of the Twelve Patriarchs, *NovT* 4 (1960-61), pp. 182-235.

—'Once More: Christian Influence in the Testaments of the Twelve Patriarchs', *NovT* 5 (1962), pp. 311-19.

—*The Testaments of the Twelve Patriarchs. A Critical Edition of the Greek Text* (Leiden, 1978).

Joüon, P., 'ὑποκριτής dans l'Evangile et hébreu hánéf', *Recherches de Science Religieuse* 20 (1930), pp. 312-16.

Jülicher, A., *Die Gleichnisreden Jesu* I (2nd edn; Tübingen, 1910; repr. Darmstadt, 1976).

Kahmann, J., 'Die Verheissung an Petrus. *Mt.* XVI, 18-19 im Zusammenhang des Matthäusevangeliums', in M. Didier (ed.), *L'Evangile selon Matthieu. Rédaction et théologie* (BETL, 29; Gembloux, 1972), pp. 261-80.

Käsemann, E., 'The Beginnings of Christian Theology', in Funk, R.W. (ed.), *Apocalypticism* (*JThCh* 6; New York, 1969), pp. 17-46.

—'On the Topic of Primitive Christian Apocalyptic', *ibid.*, pp. 99-133.

Kelly, M., 'The Woes against the Scribes and Pharisees', *Service International de Documentation Judéo-Chrétienne* (*SIDIC*) 10 (1977), 17-22.

Kilpatrick, G.D., *The Origins of the Gospel according to St. Matthew* (2nd edn; Oxford, 1950).

Kingsbury, J.D., *Matthew. A Commentary for Preachers and Others* (London, 1978).

—*Matthew as Story* (2nd edn, Philadelphia, 1988).

—*The Parables of Jesus in Matthew 13. A Study in Redaction Criticism* (Richmond, Virginia, 1969).

Klausner, J., *Jesus of Nazareth. His Life, Times, and Teaching* (ET London, 1925; repr. 1947).

Klijn, A.F.J., 'Scribes, Pharisees, High-priests and Elders in the New Testament', *NovT* 3 (1959), pp. 259-67.

Klíma, J., 'L'apport des scribes mésopotamiens à la formation de la jurisprudence', *Folia Orientalia* 21 (1980), pp. 211-20.

Klostermann, E., *Das Matthäusevangelium* (Handbuch zum Neuen Testament, 4; 4th edn; Tübingen, 1927; repr. 1971).

Knibb, M.A., 'The Date of the Parables of Enoch: A Critical Review', *NTS* 25 (1978-79), pp. 345-59.

—*2 Esdras.* Part II of *The First and Second Books of Esdras* (CBC; London, New York, Melbourne, 1979).

—(in consultation with E. Ullendorf) *The Ethiopic Book of Enoch. A New Edition in the Light of the Aramaic Dead Sea Fragments* (2 vols.; Oxford, 1978).

Koch, K., *The Rediscovery of Apocalyptic. A polemical work on a neglected area of biblical studies and its damaging effects on theology and philosophy* (ET Studies in Biblical Theology, 2nd series, 22; London, 1972).

Kocis, E., 'Apokalyptik und politisches Interesse im Spätjudentum', *Judaica* 27/28 (1971-72), pp. 71-89.

Kosmala, H., *Hebräer-Essener-Christen: Studien zur Vorgeschichte der frühchristlichen Verkündigung* (Leiden, 1959).

Kraft, R.A., 'Philo (Josephus, Sirach and Wisdom of Solomon) on Enoch', *SBL Seminar Papers 1978* (Missoula, 1978), I, pp. 253-57.

Kremer, J., '"Neues und Altes". Jesu Wort über den christlichen "Schriftgelehrten" (Mt 13,52)', in J. Kremer *et al.*, *Neues und Altes. Zur Orientierung in der augenblicklichen Situation der Kirche* (Kirche im Gespräch; Freiburg, Basel, Wien, 1974), pp. 11-33.

Kuhn, K.G., *Konkordanz zu den Qumran-Texten* (Göttingen, 1960).

—'Gilyonim und sifre minim', in W. Eltester (ed.), *Judentum, Urchristentum, Kirche. Festschrift für J. Jeremias* (BZNW, 26; 2nd edn; Berlin, 1964), pp. 24-61.

—'Nachträge zum Konkordanz zu den Qumran-Texten', *RQ* 4 (1963-64), pp. 163-234.

Kümmel, W.G., *Introduction to the New Testament* (ET London, 1975).

—'Die Weherufe über die Schriftgelehrten und Pharisäer (Matthäus 23,13-36)', in
W.P. Eckert, *et al.*, *Antijudäismus im Neuen Testament?* (München, 1967),
pp. 135-47.

Künzel, G., *Studien zum Gemeindeverständnis des Matthäus-Evangeliums* (Calwer
Theologische Monographien: A, Bibelwissenschaft, 10; Stuttgart, 1978).

Lachs, S.T., 'Studies in the Semitic Background to the Gospel of Matthew', *JQR* 67
(1977), pp. 195-217.

Lacocque, A., *The Book of Daniel* (ET London, 1979).

Ladd, G.E., 'Why not Prophetic-Apocalyptic?', *JBL* 76 (1957), pp. 192-200.

Lagrange, M.J., *Evangile selon Saint Matthieu* (7th edn; Paris, 1948).

Lambrecht, J. (ed.), *L'Apocalypse johannique et l'Apocalyptique dans le Nouveau
Testament* (Gembloux, 1980).

—*Die Redaktion der Markus-Apokalypse. Literarische Analyse und Strukturunter-
suchung* (Analecta Biblica, 28; Rome, 1967).

LaSor, W.S., *The Dead Sea Scrolls and the Christian Faith* (rev. edn; Chicago,
1962).

Lategan, B.C., 'Die Botsing tussen Jesus en die Fariseërs volgens Matt. 23' [The
Conflict between Jesus and the Pharisees according to Mt. 23], *NedGerefTeolTyd*
10 (1969), pp. 217-30.

Lauterbach, J.Z., *Rabbinic Essays* (Cincinnati, 1951).

Leaney, A.R.C., *The Rule of Qumran and its Meaning* (London, 1966).

Légasse, S., 'L'oracle contre "cette génération" (Mt 23,34-36 par. Lc 11,49-51) et la
polémique judéo-chrétienne dans la source des Logia', in J. Delobel (ed.), *Logia.
Les Paroles de Jésus—The Sayings of Jesus. Mémorial Joseph Coppens* (Leuven,
1982), pp. 237-56.

—'Scribes et disciples de Jésus', *RB* 68 (1961), pp. 321-45, 481-505.

Lehmann, M.R., 'Ben Sira and the Qumran Literature', *RQ* 3 (1961-62), pp. 103-
16.

Leiman, S.Z. (ed.), *The Canon and Masorah of the Hebrew Bible. An Introductory
Reader* (New York, 1974).

—'The Talmudic and Midrashic Evidence for the Canonization of Hebrew Scripture'
(Dissertation, University of Pennsylvania; Ann Arbor, 1970).

Leivestad, R., 'Das Dogma von der prophetenlosen Zeit', *NTS* 19 (1972-73), pp. 288-
99.

Le Moyne, J., *Les Sadducéens* (Paris, 1972).

Liebermann, S., 'The Discipline in the So-called Dead Sea Manual of Discipline', *JBL*
71 (1952), pp. 199-206.

Limbeck, M., 'Apokalyptik oder Pharisäismus? Zu einigen Neuerscheinungen',
Theologische Quartalschrift 152 (1972), pp. 145-56.

Lindars, B., 'Jesus and the Pharisees', in E. Bammel *et al.* (eds.), *Donum Gentilicium.
New Testament Studies in Honour of David Daube* (Oxford, 1978), pp. 51-63.

—*New Testament Apologetic. The Doctrinal Significance of the Old Testament
Quotations* (London, 1961).

Lindblom, J., *Gesichte und Offenbarungen* (Lund, 1968).

—*Prophecy in Ancient Israel* (Oxford, 1962).

Lindsey, R.L., 'A Modified Two-Document Theory of the Synoptic Dependence and
Interdependence', *NovT* 6 (1963), pp. 239-63.

Lohmeyer E. & W. Schmauch, *Das Evangelium des Matthäus* (Sonderband, Kritisch-
exegetischer Kommentar über das Neue Testament; Göttingen, 1967).

Löhr, M., 'Bildung aus dem Glauben. Beiträge zum Verständnis der Lehrreden des Buches Jesus Sirach' (Dissertation; Bonn, 1975).

Lohse, E., *The New Testament Environment* (ET London, 1976).

Longenecker, R.N., *The Christology of Early Jewish Christianity* (Studies in Biblical Theology, 2nd series, 17; London, 1970).

—*New Testament Social Ethics for Today* (Grand Rapids, 1984) (ch. 2).

Lührmann, D., *Das Offenbarungsverständnis bei Paulus und in den paulinischen Gemeinden* (WMANT, 16; Neukirchen-Vluyn, 1965).

—*Die Redaktion der Logienquelle* (WMANT, 33; Neukirchen-Vluyn, 1969).

Lundbom, J.R., 'Baruch, Seraiah, and Expanded Colophons in the Book of Jeremiah', *JSOT* 36 (1986), pp. 89-114.

Luz, U., 'Die Jünger im Matthäusevangelium', *ZNW* 62 (1971), pp. 141-71.

Maier, Johann & J. Schreiner (eds.), *Literatur und Religion des Frühjudentums. Eine Einführung* (Würzburg and Gütersloh, 1973).

Malina, B.J., 'Jewish Christianity or Christian Judaism: Toward a Hypothetical Definition', *JSJ* 7 (1976), pp. 46-57.

Manson, T.W., *The Sayings of Jesus* (London, 1949; repr. 1977).

—'Some Reflections on Apocalyptic', in *Aux sources de la tradition chrétienne. FS M. Goguel* (Neuchâtel, 1950), pp. 139-45.

Marböck, J., *Weisheit im Wandel. Untersuchungen zur Weisheitstheologie bei Ben Sira* (Bonn, 1971).

Marcus, R., 'Pharisees, Essenes, and Gnostics', *JBL* 73 (1954), pp. 157-61.

—'The Pharisees in the Light of Modern Scholarship', *JR* 32 (1952), pp. 153-64.

Marshall, I.H., *The Gospel of Luke. A Commentary on the Greek Text* (Exeter, 1978).

Martin, Konrad, *Letzte Strafrede Jesu nach Matthäus Cap. XXIII. Mit besonderer Hinsicht auf den wahren Geist des Pharisäismus, exegetisch bearbeitet* (Köln, 1835).

Massyngberde-Ford, J., *Revelation* (AB; Garden City, 1975).

McKane, W., *Prophets and Wise Men* (SBT; London, 1965).

McNamara, M., *The New Testament and the Palestinian Targum to the Pentateuch* (Analecta Biblica, 28; Rome, 1966).

—'Were the Magi Essenes?', *IrEcclRev* 110 (1968), pp. 305-28.

McNeile, A.H., *The Gospel according to St. Matthew* (London, 1915).

Mearns, C.L., 'Dating the Similitudes of Enoch', *NTS* 25 (1978-79), pp. 360-69.

Medico, H.E. del, *The Riddle of the Scrolls* (ET London, 1958).

Meeks, W., *The First Urban Christians* (New Haven, 1983), pp. 171-80.

—'"Since then you would need to go out of the world": Group Boundaries in Pauline Christianity', in T.J. Ryan (ed.). *Critical History and Biblical Faith: New Testament Perspectives* (Villanova, 1979), pp. 4-29.

—'Social Functions of Apocalyptic Language in Pauline Christianity', in D. Hellholm (ed.), *Apocalypticism in the Mediterranean World and the Near East* (Tübingen, 1983), pp. 687-705.

Meier, J.P., *The Vision of Matthew: Christ, Church and Morality in the First Gospel* (New York, 1979).

Merkel, H., 'Jesus und die Pharisäer', *NTS* 14 (1967-68), pp. 194-208.

Mertens, A., *Das Buch Daniel im Lichte der Texte vom Toten Meer* (Würzburg, 1971).

Meyer, Ed., *Ursprung und Anfänge des Christentums*, vol. II: *Die Entwicklung des Judentums und Jesus von Nazaret* (Stuttgart and Berlin, 1921).

Meyer, Rudolf, *Tradition und Neuschöpfung im antiken Judentum. Dargestellt an der Geschichte des Pharisäismus* (Sitzungsberichte der sächsischen Akademie der Wissenschaften zu Leipzig, 110; Berlin, 1965).

Meyers, E.M & J.F. Strange, *Archaeology, the Rabbis and Early Christianity* (London, 1981).

Michaelis, W., *Die Gleichnisse Jesu. Eine Einführung* (3rd edn; Hamburg, 1956).

Michel, A. & Le Moyne, J., 'Pharisiens', *Supplément au Dictionnaire de la Bible* , vol. VII (Paris, 1966), pp. 1022-1115.

Middendorp, T., *Die Stellung Jesus Ben Siras zwischen Judentum und Hellenismus* (Leiden, 1973).

Milik, J.T., *The Books of Enoch. Aramaic Fragments of Qumrân Cave 4* (Oxford, 1976).

—*Ten Years of Discovery in the Wilderness of Judaea* (Studies in Biblical Theology, 26; London, 1959).

Minear, P.S., *Matthew. The Teacher's Gospel* (New York, 1982).

—*New Testament Apocalyptic* (Interpreting Biblical Texts; Nashville, 1981).

Mitton, C.L., 'Matthew's Disservice to Jesus', *Epworth Review* 6 (1979), pp. 47-54.

Mohrlang, R., *Matthew and Paul. A Comparison of Ethical Perspectives* (Cambridge, 1984).

Molin, G., 'Qumran-Apokalyptik-Essenismus', *Saeculum* 6 (1955), pp. 244-81.

Moore, C.A., *Daniel, Esther and Jeremiah: The Additions. A New Translation with Introduction and Commentary* (Anchor Bible; Garden City, 1977).

Moore, G.F., *Judaism in the First Centuries of the Christian Era: The Age of the Tannaim* (3 vols.; Cambridge, Mass., 1927-30).

Morgan, D.F., *Wisdom in the Old Testament Traditions* (Atlanta, 1981).

Mottu, H., & F. Vouga, 'La Passion de la Parole. Jésus, prophète invectivant et souffrant', *Bulletin du Centre Protestant d'Etudes* 30 (1978), pp. 38-46.

Moule, C.F.D., *The Birth of the New Testament* (3rd edn; London, 1981).

Mowry, L., *The Dead Sea Scrolls and the Early Church* (Chicago, 1962).

Müller, H-P., 'Magisch-mantische Weisheit und die Gestalt Daniels', *Ugarit-Forschungen* 1 (1969), pp. 79-94.

—'Mantische Weisheit und Apokalyptik', *SVT* 22 (1972), pp. 268-93.

—'Märchen, Legende und Enderwartung—Zum Verständnis des Buches Daniel', *VT* 26 (1976), pp. 338-50.

Munck, J., *Paul and the Salvation of Mankind* (ET London, 1959).

Myers, J.M., *I and II Esdras*. Introduction, Translation and Commentary (Anchor Bible; Garden City, 1974).

Nepper-Christensen, P., *Das Matthäusevangelium—ein judenchristliches Evangelium?* (Acta Theologica Danica, 1; Aarhus, 1958).

Neusner, J., *First Century Judaism in Crisis. Yohanan ben Zakkai and the Renaissance of Torah* (New York, 1975).

—*Judaism in the Beginning of Christianity* (Philadelphia, 1984).

—*Judaism. The Evidence of the Mishnah* (Chicago and London, 1981)

—'"Pharisaic-Rabbinic" Judaism: A Clarification', *History of Religions* 12 (1973), pp. 250-70.

—*The Rabbinic Traditions about the Pharisees before 70* (3 vols.; Leiden, 1971).

—'The Use of Later Rabbinic Evidence for the Study of First-Century Pharisaism', in W.S. Green (ed.), *Approaches to Ancient Judaism: Theory and Practice* (Missoula, 1978), pp. 215-28.

—*A Life of Rabban Yohanan Ben Zakkai. Ca. 1-80 C.E.* (Leiden, 1962).

Nickelsburg, G.W.E., 'Enoch, Levi, and Peter: Recipients of Revelation in Upper Galilee', *JBL* 100 (1981), pp. 575-600.
—*Jewish Literature between the Bible and the Mishnah. A Historical and Literary Introduction* (Philadelphia, 1981).
—*Resurrection, Immortality and Eternal Life in Intertestamental Judaism* (Cambridge, Mass., 1972).
—'Social Aspects of Palestinian Jewish Apocalypticism', in D. Hellholm (ed.), *Apocalypticism in the Mediterranean World and the Near East* (Tübingen, 1983).
North, R., 'Prophecy to Apocalyptic via Zechariah', *Congress Volume, Uppsala, 1971* (Leiden, 1971), pp. 47-71.
Odeberg, H., Ἐνώχ, *TDNT*, II, pp. 556ff.
—*3 Enoch or The Hebrew Book of Enoch* (Cambridge, 1928).
—*Pharisaism and Christianity* (ET St. Louis, 1964).
Oepke, ἀποκαλύπτω, *TDNT*, III, pp. 563-92.
Oesterley, W.O.E., *II Esdras (The Ezra Apocalypse)* (Westminster Commentaries; London, 1933).
—*Judaism and Christianity* (1937).
Osten-Sacken, P. von der, *Die Apokalyptik in ihrem Verhältnis zu Prophetie und Weisheit* (= *Theologische Existenz heute*, 157; München, 1969).
Otto, R., *Reich Gottes und Menschensohn* (München, 1934).
Patte, D., *Early Jewish Hermeneutic in Palestine* (SBLDS, 22; Missoula, 1975).
—*The Gospel According to Matthew. A Structural Commentary on Matthew's Faith* (Philadelphia, 1987).
Pearson, B.A., 'The Pierpont Morgan Fragments of a Coptic Enoch Apocryphon', in G.W.E. Nickelsburg (ed.), *Studies on the Testament of Abraham* (Septuagint and Cognate Studies, 6; Missoula, 1976), pp. 227-83.
Perrin, N., 'Apocalyptic Christianity', in P.D. Hanson (ed.), *Visionaries and their Apocalypses* (Issues in Religion and Theology, 2; London, 1983), pp. 121-45; repr. of *The New Testament: An Introduction* (New York, 1974), pp. 65-85.
Pesch, R., 'Levi-Mattäus (Mc 2,14/Mt 9,9; 10,3). Ein Beitrag zur Lösung eines alten Problems', *ZNW* 59 (1968), pp. 40-56.
Pesch, W., 'Theologische Aussagen der Redaktion von Matthäus 23', in P. Hoffmann (ed.), *Orientierung an Jesus. Zur Theologie der Synoptiker* (Freiburg, Basel, Wien, 1973), pp. 286-99.
Philonenko, M., 'La littérature intertestamentaire et le Nouveau Testament', in J.E. Ménard (ed.), *Exégèse Biblique et Judaïsme* (Strasbourg, 1973), pp. 116-25.
Plöger, O., 'Prophetisches Erbe in den Sekten des frühen Judentums', *TLZ* 79 (1954), pp. 291-95.
—*Theokratie und Eschatologie* (WMANT, 2; 3rd edn; Neukirchen-Vluyn, 1968).
Plummer, A., *An Exegetical Commentary on the Gospel according to S. Matthew* (New York, 1910).
Polag, A., *Die Christologie der Logienquelle* (WMANT, 45; Neukirchen-Vluyn, 1977).
Porteous, N.W., *Daniel* (OTL; 2nd edn; London, 1979).
Prince, D., 'Scribes and Pharisees', in *Encyclopaedia Biblica*, IV (London, 1903), cols. 4321-29.
Przybylski, B., *Righteousness in Matthew and his World of Thought* (SNTSMS, 41; Cambridge, 1980).
—'The Setting of Matthean Anti-Judaism', in P. Richardson & D. Granskou (eds.),

Anti-Judaism in Early Christianity, vol. I: *Paul and the Gospels* (Waterloo, 1986), pp. 181-200.

Rabin, C., *Qumran Studies* (Oxford, 1957).

Rad, G. von, 'The Levitical Sermon in I and II Chronicles', *The Problem of the Hexateuch and Other Essays* (ET Edinburgh, 1966), pp. 267-80.

Rasp, H., 'Flavius Josephus und die jüdischen Religionsparteien', *ZNW* 23 (1924), pp. 27-47.

Reicke, B., *The New Testament Era. The World of the Bible from 500 BC to AD 100* (ET London, 1969).

Reid, S.B., '1 Enoch: The Rising Elite of the Apocalyptic Movement', *SBL 1983 Seminar Papers* (Chico, 1983), pp. 147-56.

Rengstorf, K.H., ἀποστέλλω, *TDNT*, I (Grand Rapids, 1964), pp. 398-447.

—*Ḥirbet Qumran und die Bibliothek vom Toten Meer* (Studia Delitzschiana, 5; Stuttgart, 1960) (ET [abbreviated] *Ḥirbet Qumrân and the Problem of the Dead Sea Caves* [Leiden, 1963]).

Renov, I., 'The Seat of Moses', *IEJ* 5 (1955), pp. 262-67.

Riesner, R., *Jesus als Lehrer. Eine Untersuchung zum Ursprung der Evangelien-Überlieferung* (WUNT, 2; Tübingen, 1981).

Rigaux, B., *The Testimony of St. Matthew* (ET Chicago, 1968).

Rivkin, E., 'Defining the Pharisees: The Tannaitic Sources', *HUCA* 40 (1969-70), pp. 205-49.

—*A Hidden Revolution* (Nashville, 1978).

—'Scribes, Pharisees, Lawyers, Hypocrites. A Study in Synonymity', *HUCA* 49 (1978), pp. 135-42.

Robinson, J.A.T., *Redating the New Testament* (London, 1976).

Robinson, J.M., 'ΛΟΓΟΙ ΣΟΦΩΝ: On the Gattung of Q', in *The Future of Our Religious Past. Essays in Honour of Rudolf Bultmann* (London, 1971), pp. 84-130.

Rohde, J., *Rediscovering the Teaching of the Evangelists* (ET London, 1968).

Rollins, W.G., 'The New Testament Apocalyptic', *NTS* 17 (1971), pp. 454-76.

Rolloff, J., 'Der johanneische "Lieblingsjünger" und der Lehrer der Gerechtigkeit', *NTS* 15 (1968-69), pp. 129-51.

Rössler, D., *Gesetz und Geschichte. Untersuchungen zur Theologie der jüdischen Apokalyptik und der pharisäischen Orthodoxie* (Neukirchen, 1960).

Rost, L., *Einleitung in die alttestamentlichen Apokryphen und Pseudepigraphen einschließlich der großen Qumran-Handschriften* (Heidelberg, 1971).

Rowland, C., *The Open Heaven. A Study of Apocalyptic in Judaism and Early Christianity* (London, 1982).

Rowley, H.H., *Jewish Apocalyptic and the Dead Sea Scrolls* (The Ethel M. Wood Lecture, 12th March, 1957; London, 1957).

Rubenstein, R.L., 'Scribes, Pharisees, and Hypocrites. A Study in Rabbinic Psychology', *Judaism* 12 (1963), pp. 456-68.

Russell, D.S., *The Method and Message of Jewish Apocalyptic* (London, 1964).

Sabourin, L., 'Traits apocalyptiques dans l'Evangile de Matthieu', *Science et Esprit* 33 (1981), pp. 357-72.

Safrai, S. & M. Stern (eds.), *The Jewish People in the First Century. Compendia Rerum Iudaicarum ad Novum Testamentum* (2 vols.; Amsterdam, 1976).

Saldarini, A.J., 'Apocalyptic and Rabbinic Literature', *CBQ* 37 (1975), pp. 348-58.

Sand, A., 'Propheten, Weise und Schriftkundige in der Gemeinde des Matthäus-evangeliums', in J. Hainz (ed.), *Kirche und Werden. Studien zum Thema Amt und*

Gemeinde im Neuen Testament (München, Paderborn, Wien, 1976), pp. 167-84.

Sandmel, S., *The First Century in Judaism and Christianity: Certainties and Uncertainties* (New York, 1969).

—'Parallelomania', *JBL* 81 (1962), pp. 1-13.

Schaeder, H.H., *Esra der Schreiber* (Beiträge zur historischen Theologie, 5; Tübingen, 1930).

Schäfer, P., 'Die sogenannte Synode von Jabne. Zur Trennung von Juden und Christen im ersten/zweiten Jahrhundert n. Chr.', *Judaica* 31 (1975), pp. 54-64, 116-24.

Schechter, S., *Documents of Jewish Sectaries* (Prolegomena by J.A. Fitzmyer; New York, 1970; repr. of 1910 edn).

Schiffman, L.H., *The Halakhah at Qumran* (Leiden, 1975).

Schlatter, A., *Der Evangelist Matthäus. Seine Sprache, sein Ziel, seine Selbständigkeit* (Stuttgart, 1957).

—*Das Alte Testament in der johanneischen Apokalypse* (Beiträge zur Förderung christlicher Theologie, 16/6; Gütersloh, 1912), esp. pp. 104ff.

Schlesinger, K., *Die Gesetzeslehrer* (Berlin, 1936).

Schmidt, J.M., *Die jüdische Apokalyptik. Die Geschichte ihrer Erforschung von den Anfängen bis zu den Textfunden von Qumran* (Neukirchen-Vluyn, 1969).

Schmithals, W., *The Apocalyptic Movement: Introduction and Interpretation* (ET Nashville and New York, 1975).

—'Jesus und die Apokalyptik', in G. Strecker (ed.), *Jesus Christus in Historie und Theologie. Neutestamentliche Festschrift für H. Conzelmann* (Tübingen, 1975).

Schniewind, J., *Das Evangelium nach Matthäus* (Göttingen, 1968).

Schoeps, H.-J., *Jewish Christianity: Factional Disputes in the Early Church* (ET Philadelphia, 1969).

Scholem, G.G., *Die jüdische Mystik in ihren Hauptströmungen* (Zürich, 1957).

Schoonheim, P.L., 'Probleme und Impulse der neutestamentlichen Apokalyptika', *Miscellanea Neotestamentica* (VTS, 47; Leiden, 1978), pp. 129-45.

Schreiner, J., 'Die apokalyptische Bewegung', ch. 13 in J. Maier & J. Schreiner (eds.), *Literatur und Religion des Frühjudentums. Eine Einführung* (Würzburg and Gütersloh, 1973), pp. 214-53.

Schubert, K., 'Jewish Religious Parties and Sects', in A. Toynbee (ed.), *The Crucible of Christianity* (London, 1969), pp. 87ff.

—*Die jüdischen Religionsparteien in neutestamentlicher Zeit* (Stuttgart, 1970).

—'Das Zeitalter der Apokalyptik', in K. Schubert (ed.), *Bibel und zeitgemäßer Glaube* I (Klosterneuburg, 1965), pp. 263-85.

Schulz, S., 'Der historische Jesus. Bilanz der Fragen und Lösungen', in G. Strecker (ed.), *Jesus Christus in Historie und Theologie. Neutestamentliche Festschrift für H. Conzelmann* (Tübingen, 1975), pp. 3-25.

—*Q. Die Spruchquelle der Evangelisten* (Zürich, 1972).

Schürer, E., *The History of the Jewish People in the Age of Jesus Christ (175 B.C.—A.D. 135)* (rev. edn by G. Vermes, F. Millar & M. Black; 2 vols. Edinburgh, 1973, 1979).

Schürmann, H., *Traditionsgeschichtliche Untersuchungen zu den synoptischen Evangelien* (Düsseldorf, 1968).

Schweizer, E., *Das Evangelium nach Matthäus* (NTD, 2; Göttingen, 1973); ET *The Good News according to Matthew* (Atlanta, 1975).

—*Matthäus und seine Gemeinde* (Stuttgarter Bibelstudien, 71; Stuttgart, 1974).

Scott, E.F., 'The Place of Apocalyptical Conceptions in the Mind of Jesus', *JBL* 41 (1922), pp. 137-42.

Seitz, O.J.F., 'The Commission of Prophets and "Apostles": A Reexamination of Matthew 23:34 with Luke 11:49', *Studia Evangelica IV*, ed. F.L. Cross (Texte und Untersuchungen, 102; Berlin, 1968), pp. 236-40.

Senior, D.P., *The Passion Narrative according to Matthew* (Leuven, 1975).

Sheppard, G.T., *Wisdom as a Hermeneutical Construct* (BZAW, 151; Berlin, New York, 1980).

Siegel, J.P., 'The Scribes of Qumran. Studies in the Early History of Jewish Scribal Customs, with special reference to the Qumran Biblical Scrolls and to the Tannaitic Traditions of Massekheth Soferim' (Dissertation: Brandeis University, 1972).

Sigal, P., *The Emergence of Contemporary Judaism*, Vol. I: *The Foundations of Judaism from Biblical Origins to the Sixth Century AD*, Part I: *From the Origins to the Separation of Christianity* (Pennsylvania, 1980).

—'The Halakhah of Jesus of Nazareth according to the Gospel of Matthew' (Dissertation, University of Pittsburgh, 1979; Ann Arbor).

Silva, M., 'The Pharisees in Modern Scholarship', *WTJ* 42 (1979), pp. 395-405 [review of E. Rivkin, *A Hidden Revolution*].

Simon, M., *Jewish Sects at the Time of Jesus* (ET Philadelphia, 1967).

Smallwood, E.M., *The Jews under Roman Rule* (Leiden, 1976).

Smith, C.W.F., 'The Mixed State of the Church in Matthew's Gospel', *JBL* 82 (1963), pp. 149-68.

Smith, J.Z., 'Wisdom and Apocalyptic', in B.A. Pearson (ed.), *Religious Syncretism in Antiquity* (Missoula, Montana, 1975), pp. 131-56; and in P.D. Hanson (ed.), *Visionaries and their Apocalypses* (Issues in Religion and Theology, 2; London, 1983), pp. 101-20.

Smith, Morton, 'Palestinian Judaism in the First Century', in M. David (ed.), *Israel: Its Role in Civilisation* (New York, 1956), pp. 67-81.

—*Palestinian Parties and Politics that Shaped the Old Testament* (New York, 1971).

—'The Pharisees in the Gospels', in his *Jesus the Magician* (London, 1978), pp. 153-57.

Snaith, J.G., *Ecclesiasticus* (CB; Cambridge, 1974).

Sparks, H.F.D. (ed.), *The Apocryphal Old Testament* (Oxford, 1984).

Stadelmann, H., *Ben Sira als Schriftgelehrter: Eine Untersuchung zum Berufsbild des vormakkabäischen Sofer unter Berücksichtigung seines Verhältnisses zu Priester-, Propheten- und Weisheitslehrertum* (WUNT, 2; Tübingen, 1980).

Stanton, G.N., 'On the Christology of Q', in B. Lindars & S. Smalley (eds.), *Christ and Spirit in the New Testament* (Cambridge, 1973), pp. 27-42.

—'5 Ezra and Matthean Christianity in the Second Century', *JTS* 28 (1977), pp. 67-83.

—(ed.), *The Interpretation of Matthew* (Issues in Religion and Theology, 3; London and Philadelphia, 1983).

—'The Gospel of Matthew and Judaism', *BJRL* 66 (1984), pp. 264-84.

—'Matthew as a Creative Interpreter of the Sayings of Jesus', in P. Stuhlmacher (ed.), *Das Evangelium und die Evangelien. Vorträge vom Tübinger Symposium, 1982* (WUNT, 28; Tübingen, 1983), pp. 273-87.

—'The Origin and Purpose of Matthew's Gospel: Matthean Scholarship from 1945-1980', in H. Temporini & W. Haase (eds.), *Aufstieg und Niedergang der Römischen Welt* II, 25.3 (Berlin, 1983), pp. 1889-1951.

Steck, O.H., *Israel und das gewaltsame Geschick der Propheten. Untersuchungen zur Überlieferung des deuteronomistischen Geschichtsbildes im Alten Testament*,

Spätjudentum und Urchristentum (WMANT, 23; Neukirchen-Vluyn, 1967).

Stemberger, G., 'Die sogenannte "Synode von Jabne" und das frühe Christentum', *Kairos* 19 (1977), pp. 14-21.

Stendahl, K., *The School of St. Matthew* (2nd edn; Philadelphia, 1968).

Stone, M.E., 'The Book of Enoch and Judaism in the Third Century BCE', *CBQ* 40 (1978), pp. 479-92.

—'Lists of Revealed Things in the Apocalyptic Literature', in F.M. Cross (ed.), *Magnalia Dei. The Mighty Acts of God: Essays on the Bible and Archaeology in Memory of G. Ernest Wright* (New York, 1976), pp. 414-52.

Strack, H.L. & P. Billerbeck, *Kommentar zum Neuen Testament aus Talmud und Midrasch* (München, 1924-61).

Strecker, G. (ed.), *Jesus Christus in Historie und Theologie. Neutestamentliche Festschrift für Hans Conzelmann zum 60. Geburtstag* (Tübingen, 1975).

—*Der Weg der Gerechtigkeit. Untersuchung zur Theologie des Matthäus* (FRLANT, 82; 2nd edn; Göttingen, 1962).

Suggs, M.J., *Wisdom Christology and Law in Matthew's Gospel* (Cambridge, Mass., 1970).

Suter, D., 'Fallen Angel, Fallen Priest: The Problem of Family Purity in 1 Enoch 6-16', *HUCA* 50 (1979), pp. 115-35.

—*Tradition and Composition in the Parables of Enoch* (SBLDS, 47; Missoula, 1979).

Szörényi, A., 'Das Buch Daniel, ein kanonisierter Pescher?', in *VTS 15* (1966), pp. 278-94.

Tcherikover, V., *Hellenistic Civilization and the Jews* (Philadelphia, 1961).

Telford, W.R., Review of M.J. Cook, *Mark's Treatment of the Jewish Leaders* (Leiden, 1978), *JTS* 31 (1980), pp. 154-62.

Temporini, H. & W. Haase (eds.), *Aufstieg und Niedergang der römischen Welt. Geschichte und Kultur Roms im Spiegel der neueren Forschung*, II, 19.1: *Religion (Judentum: Allgemeines; Palästinisches Judentum)* (Berlin and New York, 1979).

Theisohn, J., *Der auserwählte Richter. Untersuchungen zum traditionsgeschichtlichen Ort der Menschensohngestalt der Bilderreden des Äthiopischen Henoch* (SUNT, 12; Göttingen, 1975).

Theissen, G., *The First Followers of Jesus. A Sociological Analysis of the Earliest Christianity* (ET London, 1978).

Thieme, K., 'Matthäus, der schriftgelehrte Evangelist', *Judaica* 5 (1949), pp. 130-52, 161-82.

Thoma, C., 'Jüdische Apokalyptik am Ende des ersten nachchristlichen Jahrhunderts', *Kairos* 11 (1969), pp. 134-44.

—'Der Pharisäismus', in J. Maier & J. Schreiner (eds.), *Literatur und Religion des Frühjudentums. Eine Einführung* (Würzburg and Gütersloh, 1973), pp. 254ff.

Thomas, J.D., 'Jewish Apocalyptic and the Comparative Method', in C.D. Evans *et al.*, *Scripture in Context. Essays on the Comparative Method* (Pittsburgh Theological Monograph Series, 34; Pittsburgh, 1980), pp. 245-62.

Tigay, J.H., 'An Early Technique of Aggadic Exegesis', in H. Tadmor and M. Weinfeld (eds.), *History, Historiography and Interpretation. Studies in Biblical and Cuneiform Literatures* (Jerusalem, 1983), pp. 169-89.

Tilborg, S. van, *The Jewish Leaders in Matthew* (Leiden: Brill, 1972).

Toussaint, S.D., 'The Introductory and Concluding Parables of Matthew Thirteen', *BibSac* 121 (1964), pp. 351-55.

Trilling, W., 'Amt und Amtsverständnis bei Matthäus', in *Mélanges bibliques en hommage au R.P. Béda Rigaux* (Gembloux, 1970), pp. 29-44.

—*Das wahre Israel. Studien zur Theologie des Matthäus-Evangeliums* (München, 1964).

Tuckett, C.M., *The Revival of the Griesbach Hypothesis. An Analysis and Appraisal* (Cambridge, 1983).

Urbach, E.E., 'Class-Status and Leadership in the World of the Palestinian Sages', *Proceedings of the Israel Academy of Science and Humanities* 2 (1968), pp. 38-74.

—'Derasha as a Basis of Halakhah and the Problem of the Soferim', *Tarbiz* 27 (1958), pp. 166-82.

—*The Sages. Their Concepts and Beliefs* (2 vols.; ET Jerusalem, 1975).

VanderKam, J.C., *Enoch and the Growth of an Apocalyptic Tradition* (CBQMS, 16; Washington, 1984).

—'Enoch Traditions in Jubilees and other Second-Century Sources', *SBL Seminar Papers 1978* (Missoula, 1978), I, pp. 229-51.

Vaux, R.de, *Archaeology and the Dead Sea Scrolls* (The Schweich Lectures, 1959; ET rev. edn; Oxford, 1972).

Vermes, G., *The Dead Sea Scrolls in English* (2nd edn, Harmondsworth, 1975; 3rd edn, Sheffield, 1988).

—'The Impact of the Dead Sea Scrolls on Jewish Studies During the Last Twenty-Five Years', in W.S. Green (ed.), *Approaches to Ancient Judaism: Theory and Practice* (Missoula, 1978), pp. 201-14.

—*Jesus and the World of Judaism* (London, 1983).

—*Jesus the Jew. A Historian's Reading of the Gospels* (London, 1973).

Vielhauer, P., 'Apocalypses and Related Subjects: Introduction', in E. Hennecke, *New Testament Apocrypha*, II, pp. 581-607.

—'Apocalyptic in Early Christianity: Introduction', in *ibid.*, II, pp. 608-42.

Volz, P., *Die Eschatologie der jüdischen Gemeinde im neutestamentlichen Zeitalter. Nach den Quellen der rabbinischen, apokalyptischen und apokryphen Literatur* (Hildesheim, 1966; repr. of Tübingen, 1934 edn).

Walker, R., *Die Heilsgeschichte im ersten Evangelium* (Göttingen, 1967).

Weber, J.C., Jr, 'Jesus' Opponents in the Gospel of Mark', *Journal of Bible and Religion* 34 (1966), pp. 214-22.

Weingreen, J., 'The Title Moreh Sedek', *JSS* 6 (1961), pp. 162-74.

Weiss, H.F., 'Der Pharisäismus im Lichte der Überlieferung des Neuen Testaments', in R. Meyer, *Tradition und Neuschöpfung im antiken Judentum* (Berlin, 1965).

Welch, A., 'The Scribes and Pharisees in Moses' Seat (Matt 23.2,3)', *ExpT* 7 (1896), pp. 522-26.

Wellhausen, J., *Das Evangelium Matthaei übersetzt und erklärt* (Berlin, 1904).

—*Die Pharisäer und die Sadducäer* (3rd edn; Göttingen, 1967).

Wenham, D., 'The Structure of Matthew XIII', *NTS* 25 (1979), pp. 516-22.

Wernberg-Møller, P., *The Manual of Discipline* (Leiden, 1957).

Westerholm, S., *Jesus and Scribal Authority* (Coniectanea Biblica, New Testament Series, 10; Lund, 1978).

Willi-Plein, I., 'Das Geheimnis der Apokalyptik', *VT* 27 (1977), pp. 62-81.

Wilckens, W., 'Die Redaktion des Gleichniskapitels Mark. 4 durch Matth.', *TZ* 20 (1964), pp. 305-27.

Winter, P., *On the Trial of Jesus* (Studia Judaica, 1; rev. edn; Berlin and New York, 1974).

—'Sadoqite Fragments IV 20,21 and the Exegesis of Genesis 1.27 in Late Judaism', *ZAW* 68 (1956), pp. 71-84.

Wolf, C.U., 'The Gospel to the Essenes', *Biblical Research* 3 (1958), pp. 28-43.

Woude, A.S. van der, *Die messianischen Vorstellungen der Gemeinde von Qumran* (Assen, 1957).

Zeitlin, S., 'Jewish Apocryphal Literature', *JQR* 40 (1950), pp. 223-50.

Zeller, D., 'Zu einer jüdischen Vorlage von Mt 13,52', *BZ* 20 (1976), pp. 223-26.

Zimmerli, W., *Ezekiel. A Commentary on the Book of the Prophet Ezekiel* (ET 2 vols.; Philadelphia, 1979, 1983).

Zimmern, H., 'Nabû', in E. Schrader, *Die Keilinschriften und das Alte Testament*, ed. H. Zimmern & H. Winckler (3rd edn; Berlin, 1903), II, pp. 399-408.

—'Urkönige und Uroffenbarung', in *ibid.*, II, pp. 530-43.

INDEXES

INDEX OF BIBLICAL & OTHER REFERENCES

OLD TESTAMENT

NEW TESTAMENT

APOCRYPHA

PSEUDEPIGRAPHA

QUMRAN LITERATURE

EARLY CHRISTIAN LITERATURE

INDEX OF AUTHORS

DATE DUE